Robert Browning

His Poetry and His Audiences

Robert Browning

His Poetry and His Audiences

LEE ERICKSON

Cornell University Press

ITHACA AND LONDON

Copyright © 1984 by Cornell University Press

All rights reserved. Except for brief quotations in a review, this book, or parts thereof, must not be reproduced in any form without permission in writing from the publisher. For information, address Cornell University Press, 124 Roberts Place, Ithaca, New York 14850.

First published 1984 by Cornell University Press.
Published in the United Kingdom by
Cornell University Press Ltd., London.

International Standard Book Number 0-8014-1618-3
Library of Congress Catalog Card Number 83-45934
Printed in the United States of America
*Librarians: Library of Congress cataloging information
appears on the last page of the book.*

*The paper in this book is acid-free and meets the guidelines
for performance and durability of the Committee on Production
Guidelines for Book Longevity of the Council on Library Resources.*

For my mother and father

Contents

	Acknowledgments	9
	Abbreviations	11
	Introduction	15
1	*Pauline, Paracelsus, Strafford,* and *Sordello*	22
2	*Bells and Pomegranates*	65
3	Elizabeth Barrett and Robert Browning	104
4	*Men and Women:* Background and Audiences	132
5	*Men and Women:* The Self and Others	155
6	*Dramatis Personae*	191
7	*The Ring and the Book*	221
8	The Later Poetry	239
	Selected Bibliography	273
	Index	279

Acknowledgments

My work on Browning had its beginning in an essay on "'Childe Roland to the Dark Tower Came'" written for an undergraduate seminar given by Leslie Brisman at Yale University. At Yale I also attended the lectures on Victorian poetry of J. Hillis Miller, who later graciously read a draft of this book, and profited from seminars given by Michael Seidel, Bruce Stovel, and the late Thomas Weiskel. Later, at UCLA, Alan Roper supervised my studies of Browning, taught me what historical criticism should be, and was generous with his time, even though the duties of editing Dryden and teaching pressed upon him. My great debt to him can be repaid only by trying to be as helpful to others. My critical method owes much to Stanley Fish, whose faithful reader I still am, and to Angus Fletcher, whose passion for critical balance I share. I have also learned much from the advice and comments of Alexander Welsh, Robert Wohl, and Joseph Riddel. The helpful suggestions and constructive criticism of Herbert F. Tucker, Jr., and David G. Riede gave direction to the evolution from manuscript to book. My editors at Cornell University Press have been patient and have saved me from many an error. To all go my thanks.

A portion of chapter 5 appeared in *Victorian Poetry* 21 (1983) under the title of "The Self and Others in Browning's *Men and Women*." I am grateful to the editor of the journal for permission to reprint it in revised form.

I could not have written in an inquiring spirit without my conversations with James Gilles. And without my parents' assistance I would never have had the time. My love goes to Ellen Martin, who listened

Acknowledgments

to much of this before it was written, and read and commented on it afterward. Her devotion to literature and her love and support have been my true liberal education.

LEE ERICKSON

New York City

Abbreviations

Bibliography	*Robert Browning: A Bibliography, 1830–1950.* Comp. Leslie Nathan Broughton, Clark Sutherland Northup, and Robert Pearsall. Cornell Studies in English, vol. 39. Ithaca: Cornell University Press, 1953.
Complete Works	*The Complete Works of Robert Browning.* Ed. Roma A. King, Jr. 5 vols. of a projected 13. Athens: Ohio University Press, 1969–81.
Handbook	William Clyde DeVane. *A Browning Handbook,* 2d ed. New York: Appleton-Century-Crofts, 1955.
JEGP	*Journal of English and Germanic Philology.*
Letters	*Letters of Robert Browning and Elizabeth Barrett Barrett, 1845–1846.* Ed. Elvan Kintner. 2 vols. Cambridge, Mass.: Harvard University Press, 1969.
Letters, ed. Hood	*Letters of Robert Browning Collected by Thomas J. Wise.* Ed. Thurman L. Hood. New Haven: Yale University Press, 1933.
Major Victorian Poets	*The Major Victorian Poets: Reconsiderations.* Ed. Isobel Armstrong. London: Routledge & Kegan Paul, 1969.
MLN	*Modern Language Notes.*
MLR	*Modern Language Review.*
MP	*Modern Philology.*
New Letters	*New Letters of Robert Browning.* Ed. William Clyde DeVane and Kenneth Leslie Knickerbocker. New Haven: Yale University Press, 1950.
New Poems	*New Poems by Robert Browning and Elizabeth Barrett Browning.* Ed. Frederic G. Kenyon. London: Smith, Elder, 1914.

Abbreviations

PQ	*Philological Quarterly.*
SEL	*Studies in English Literature.*
SP	*Studies in Philology.*
TSLL	*Texas Studies in Language and Literature.*
UTQ	*University of Toronto Quarterly.*
VP	*Victorian Poetry.*
VS	*Victorian Studies.*
Works	*The Works of Robert Browning.* Ed. F. G. Kenyon. 10 vols. London: Smith, Elder, 1912. "The Centenary Edition."

Unless otherwise attributed, all quotations of Browning's poetry are from the Centenary Edition of his works (*Works*).

Robert Browning

His Poetry and His Audiences

Introduction

Browning was once invited, sometime in the 1880s, to read his poetry to the young ladies of the Newnham College Browning Society, and, after having had tea and buttered muffins, and having been ceremoniously crowned with a laurel of roses, he began to read "A Serenade at the Villa" to his admiring audience. But catching sight of himself in a mirror, he laughed and asked, "My dear young ladies, shall I not read the 'Patriot' instead? 'It was roses, roses all the way.'"[1] This charming anecdote is not without its quiet irony, for "The Patriot" tells the story of a man who is first feted and then forgotten by the public. Browning obviously relished the adulation of the young ladies. But after his long neglect by the public, his success seems always to have tasted bittersweet; and, when he saw himself in the mirror, one imagines he had a mixed feeling of déjà vu as he remembered the cautionary tale of the patriot. The suspicions concealed by his show of urbanity toward the ardent readership he acquired late in his career were at least partially justified in 1885, when, to the great consternation of the *Academy*'s Browning lovers and the amusement of the press, the girls of Girton disbanded their Browning Society and voted to spend the treasury's remaining funds on chocolates, which they then ate.[2]

---

[1] E[dward] F[rederick] Benson, *As We Were: A Victorian Peep Show* (London: Longmans, Green, 1930), p. 124. This anecdote may well be secondhand, since Benson, as a man, could not have been a student at Newnham College.

[2] William S. Peterson, *Interpreting the Oracle: A History of the London Browning Society* (Athens: Ohio University Press, 1969), pp. 174–77.

Introduction

There are countless other stories of fervent admiration for and exasperated disgust with Browning. When Swinburne was a student at Oxford, for example, instead of reading Euclid for his examinations he memorized *Sordello* and was "ploughed for smalls."[3] In contrast, Douglas Jerrold, a minor playwright and a journalist best known for his contributions to *Punch* in its early years, tried to read the same poem when he was recovering from an illness and, unable to understand a single sentence, thought he had lost his mind.[4] The ambiguity and ambivalence of Browning's relationship with his audiences and of theirs with him have never been mere historical footnotes but have, instead, always seemed close to the heart of his poetry. The three major modern interpretations of Browning—E. D. H. Johnson's chapter on him in *The Alien Vision of Victorian Poetry*, Robert Langbaum's discussion of his use of the dramatic monologue in *The Poetry of Experience*, and J. Hillis Miller's chapter on him in *The Disappearance of God*—have all dealt more or less explicitly with Browning's relations with his audiences. Johnson has shown how Browning dramatized his alienation from his audiences in his poetry; Langbaum has demonstrated how Browning's monologues require that the reader's response be divided between sympathy for and judgment of the speakers; and Miller, more abstractly, has pointed to the split between Browning's universal sympathy with all that is in the world and his uncertainty about his ultimate audience—God.

These modern interpretations mark a radical departure from the late-Victorian view of Browning as a healthy, vigorous, optimistic

[3]Swinburne to Browning, February 25, 1875: "I believe I am not exaggerating when I say that at nineteen I knew Sordello by heart from end to end—nay, I believe my blood is on your head and his, for I got 'ploughed for smalls' owing to confining my study for the month previous to *that* in lieu of Euclid—and the hard hearts of the examiners would not have accepted a declamation of Salinguerra's soliloquy as compensation for a sum in rule-of-three" (*The Swinburne Letters*, ed. Cecil Y. Lang, 6 vols. [New Haven: Yale University Press, 1959–62], III, 20).

[4]"In the progress of his convalescence a parcel arrived from London, which contained, among other things, this new volume of Sordello; the medical attendant had forbidden Mr. Jerrold the luxury of reading, but, owing to the absence of his conjugal 'life guards' he indulged in the illicit enjoyment. A few lines put Jerrold in a state of alarm. Sentence after sentence brought no consecutive thought to his brain. At last the idea crossed his mind that in his illness his mental faculties had been wrecked. The perspiration rolled from his forehead, and smiting his head, he sat down in his sofa, crying, 'O, God, I *am* an idiot!' When his wife and her sister came, they were amused by his pushing the volume into their hands, and demanding what they thought of it. He watched them intently while they read—at last his wife said: I don't understand what the man means; it is gibberish. The delighted humorist sank in his seat again: 'thank God I am *not* an idiot'" (Thomas Powell, *The Living Authors of England* [New York: D. Appleton, 1849], p. 73).

Christian poet whose difficulties were clear to the elect and whose chief accomplishment was his vindication of the intellectual and religious adequacy of Victorian middle-class life. Since Browning himself was loath to discourage this view late in life, was certainly a believer in the existence of the soul, and was "very sure of God,"[5] the interpretation of his career and his poetry has been immensely complicated. Had Browning clearly manifested early in his career the defiant stance of, say, George Sand, Flaubert, or Matthew Arnold in opposition to bourgeois culture, instead of appearing on the one hand to defy and on the other to court a popular audience, Henry James would never have been frustrated in his attempts to reconcile the old literary lion with his early poetry;[6] Betty Miller might not have been tempted to psychoanalyze Browning's relations with the women in his life;[7] nor would Morse Peckham have iconoclastically proclaimed Browning's happiness with Elizabeth a myth of Browning's own creation.[8] But despite his refusal to compromise with his public in his poetry, Browning succumbed to the temptations of eminent Victorianism in his life. The difficulty of interpreting Browning's career and poetry, then, lies in some sense within the larger problem of interpreting the institutionalization of radical and evangelical sentiment in the Victorian period. Browning saw how one's spiritual aspirations could easily be betrayed by this institutionalization and dramatized the problem as early as *Sordello*, but he was not himself exempt from it.

Browning changed from the defiant author of *Sordello* to the inspired ventriloquist of *Men and Women*, to the bereaved poet of *Dramatis Personae* and *The Ring and the Book*, to the confused and troubled poet of *La Saisiaz*, and, finally, to the complacent versifier of *Asolando*. To see how and why he changed as a poet and to understand his poetry, one does best to examine Browning's relationships with his audiences and to see how his poems dramatize the relationship between speakers and their audiences.

Contrary to his reader's expectations, Browning's poems do not begin with a self-sufficient ego that through its perception and expression orders and shapes experience, but instead with a speaker who is seeking form and a sense of self in the world. The drama of self-

---

[5] *La Saisiaz*, l. 604.
[6] Browning served as the model for the hidden side of Clare Vawdry in James's tale "The Private Life."
[7] Betty Miller, *Robert Browning: A Portrait* (London: John Murray, 1952).
[8] Morse Peckham, *Victorian Revolutionaries* (New York: George Braziller, 1970), pp. 95–96.

Introduction

development, not the expression of an assured perspective, is the subject of his poetry. Moreover, this process of self-realization requires the active participation of others, for the speakers gain their self-consciousness by being recognized by their audiences. This poetic developed gradually during Browning's career and was grounded in Browning's own search for an audience and a form that would allow him to express himself fully as a poet and as a man.

The search for recognition by others implicitly involves one's recognition of others and also a discrimination among audiences that will grant one a hearing and are worthy of being heard. For Browning, this means first that the quest for recognition is to be differentiated morally from the desire for power over others. One should not, like the Duke of Ferrara, establish one's own sense of self at the expense of others, for, finally, to demean or destroy another is to undermine the foundation of one's self. This naturally leads to the realization that if recognition is to engender spiritual growth, the audience which grants it must be equal to or above one. The ideal audience, then, will be one that both loves and is loved—Elizabeth Barrett Browning in "One Word More" or Jesus Christ in "Saul." Conversely, in the absence of one's beloved or God, one will be unable to find or express oneself fully, like the speaker of "Never the Time and the Place," who laments that he is not together with his love in May. If one supposes that one can sacrifice one's private self-realization for the sake of the public's enlightenment and so as a prophet address the multitude instead of one's lover, one risks abandoning the ground of one's self in love and giving in to one's satanic desires to be raised above others and to become their tyrant. Djabal, for example, is torn between his love for Anael and his desire to become the Druses' Hakeem. Or, by misunderstanding spiritual greatness in terms of material monuments, as Childe Roland does in "'Childe Roland to the Dark Tower Came,'" one may seek to establish oneself in history and attempt to join the company of the ghosts of the past. I distinguish, then, between audiences in terms of the poles of present or absent, and of single or multitudinous, thus giving rise to four types of audience that are most fully discussed in chapter 4. Browning also thinks of audiences both within and for his poetry in terms of whether they are free or controlled and, since he despises tyranny in any form, seeks to let his readers arrive at the truth of his poetry on their own. In some sense, he feels that the greatest love he can show his readers is to stimulate their poetic and interpretive faculties so that they willingly give him their full attention in order to arrive at the truth and to see within their limits the love of God that transcends them. But focusing upon this heuristic identification of possible audiences risks overlooking the dramatic development of a speaker's self in terms of others. Given a choice among one's lover, an absent beloved, the public multitude, and the ghosts of the past, Browning thinks one should see that love is best because it grounds one's self through the mutual recognition of spirit in God.

My purpose throughout is to offer readings of Browning's poetry that analyze his characters' relationships with their audiences. To help to account for the development of Browning's poetic practice and for the changes in his attitude toward his audiences, these readings are placed within the context of his biography, and especially of his love for Elizabeth—how Browning sought an audience for his poetry, found one in Elizabeth Barrett, and lost one when she died. Since Browning's poetry develops from *Pauline* through *Bells and Pomegranates*, culminates in *Men and Women*, and falls off gradually in *Dramatis Personae* and *The Ring and the Book* and rapidly thereafter, I have tried to let the issues related to Browning's and his speakers' search for an audience emerge as naturally as possible from readings of his early work, then to see how because of his love for Elizabeth and hers for him *Men and Women* dramatizes his thinking about audiences in the fullest and most satisfying way, and finally to examine the poetic consequences of his losing his audience when Elizabeth died. I have concentrated particularly on the figure of the audience within Browning's poems, and, with an eye toward explicating the poems and toward understanding Browning's view of the poet's private and public position in the world, have examined the speakers' attitudes toward their audiences in relationship with Browning's toward his. By speaking of "audiences" instead of a single, unified and unifying "audience" for and within Browning's poetry, I point to the great conflict between his and his speakers' desires for an ideal unity and their observation of a disturbing multiplicity. In particular, I discuss how Browning's desire for a great family of sympathetic and understanding readers is deeply disappointed, how he is reconciled to being read with love by Elizabeth and by God, and how he understands writing poetry in terms of their love for him. I have preferred "audience" to "auditor" or "interlocutor" throughout because the word not only means "listener or listeners" but also implies the possibility of response and rec-

Introduction

ognition that the other words do not. For Browning, it is the dramatic recognition of others, especially in the form of love, that gives his speakers their sense of self. I have also chosen the word because its flexibility readily lends itself not only to rhetorical but also to figural, thematic, and biographical criticism—all of which may have to be in operation at any given moment while reading Browning's poetry. My approach to the question of Browning's audiences, then, is not narrowly rhetorical but largely psychological and philosophical. Insofar as my method presupposes a philosophical and theoretical perspective, it is for the most part a Hegelian one stemming from Hegel's account of self-conscious intersubjectivity in *The Phenomenology of Mind* and of romantic art in his *Aesthetics*. This point of view receives its fullest exposition in chapter 5.

I have attempted to provide a coherent framework within which to view Browning's career and oeuvre that shows how his need for his audiences' recognition affected his poetic strategies and that ties his treatment of relationships between speakers and their audiences not only to his development of the dramatic monologue but also to his later movement away from that form. The anticipated and actual critical reception of his work is also discussed as an influence upon his poetics.[9] Browning turns from seeking the applause of a general audience (abandoning explicitly political poetry in the process) and turns toward Elizabeth and the spiritual sustenance of love. He comes to believe that man's only true audience is God and that one comes to know God only through the love of another, a belief which began in the 1880s to strike a sympathetic chord in the British public.

Browning does not speak to us today in the way that he spoke to late-Victorian and Edwardian readers. The aesthetic and metaphysical implications of his forms, the modernity of his language and poetic rhythms, and the energy of his thinking count for much more today than his religious faith. His celebration of human love still touches us, though. There may indeed be extraordinary pressures upon society to rationalize its reproduction along the lines of industrial production that will soon make Browning's belief in love and its importance seem as much of a delusion and as outmoded and casuistic as his faith. But

---

[9]In this respect my procedure somewhat resembles Hans Robert Jauss's examination of "the horizon of expectations of the first [historical] reading" in the light of the poet's aesthetic distance from them; see *Toward an Aesthetic of Reception*, trans. Timothy Bahti, Theory and History of Literature, no. 2 (Minneapolis: University of Minnesota Press, 1982), pp. 25–28, 139–85.

Introduction

for the moment Browning's coming to terms with himself as a poet and as a man through his love for Elizabeth and the expression of this self-realization in his poetry still remain contributions to the progress of the human spirit. Reading Browning gives us both pleasure and a better understanding of who we are.

I

Pauline, Paracelsus, Strafford, and *Sordello*

And still more labyrinthine buds the rose.
—*Sordello*, I, 476

Robert Browning's poetry plunges one immediately into labyrinthine complexities. No matter where one starts, one is soon isolated in the middle of things. To be read with care, his poetry requires from the reader not only a well-developed flexibility of mind and strong powers of comprehension but also a certain security.[1] One must try to bring order out of chaos even while recognizing that one cannot. The involution of his poetry is a sign of someone unaccustomed to any but the most sympathetic of readers and, together with the rapidity of his thought, reflects someone who really expects no one else to understand. Especially in the early narratives, one catches something of the suburban isolation of Browning's family life in Camberwell, of the intensity and idiosyncrasy of his private education, and of the uncomprehending indulgence of Browning's father, a senior clerk in the Bank of England who had collected a library of six thousand volumes, dabbled in drawing and antiquarian researches, and happily supported Robert's poetic ambitions until Robert married Elizabeth in 1846.[2] And, in the compulsion both Browning and his speakers have to explain themselves, despite their feeling that no one

---

[1]Swinburne said of reading Browning that "the proper mood in which to study for the first time a book of Mr. Browning's is the freshest, clearest, most active mood of the mind in its brightest and keenest hours of work" (*The Complete Works of Algernon Charles Swinburne*, ed. Edmund Gosse and Thomas James Wise, 20 vols. [London: William Heinemann, 1925–27], XII, 146).

[2]For the family background, see John Maynard, *Browning's Youth* (Cambridge, Mass.: Harvard University Press, 1977).

will comprehend what they say, one senses that they are incomplete without an understanding audience and that there can be no development of their souls without recognition from others.

The formlessness of the early narratives and the search of consciousness for a sense of self in them reflect Browning's dependence upon an external order (finally God) to provide meaning to his work. This reliance upon a shaping force external to the poetry allows an astonishing combination of confidence and insecurity in his speakers and also makes possible Browning's critique of their pride. His heroes' proud self-absorption is portrayed as a blindness which prevents them from seeing their need for God.[3] But their morbid introspection also precludes their looking toward others and so finding themselves.[4] As readers beginning with J. S. Mill have felt, this excessive inwardness indicates Browning's having insufficiently objectified his own quest for recognition and self-realization.[5] The *Pauline*-poet, Paracelsus, Strafford, and Sordello all seem versions of himself.[6] Further, the social vacuum in which his speakers live creates a stylistic and rhetorical drive to anticipate life's eventual revelations in the absence of dramatic experience.[7] Because Browning moves too easily from introspection to self-renunciation,[8] the drama becomes subordinated to doctrine.[9] Both Browning and his speakers never realize how much they depend upon their audiences for their sense of self, and so the readers of these early works are often asked for more than they can humanly give,[10]

---

[3]J. Hillis Miller discusses this problem in *The Disappearance of God: Five Nineteenth-Century Writers* (Cambridge, Mass.: Harvard University Press, 1963), pp. 81–156.

[4]For the Romantic background of this phenomenon, see Robert Preyer, "Robert Browning: A Reading of the Early Narratives," *ELH* 26 (1959):531–48.

[5]Mill said of *Pauline* that "the writer seems to me possessed with a more intense and morbid self-consciousness than I ever knew in any sane human being" (in *Robert Browning: A Collection of Critical Essays*, ed. Philip Drew [London: Methuen, 1966], p. 176). See also Walter Samuel Swisher, "A Psychoanalysis of Browning's *Pauline*," *Psychoanalytic Review* 7 (1920):115–23.

[6]On *Pauline*, see Betty Miller, *Robert Browning*, pp. 21–22; also see Thomas J. Collins, "Shelley and God in Browning's *Pauline*: Unresolved Problems," *VP* 3 (1965): 151–60. On *Paracelsus* and *Sordello*, see Betty Miller, *Robert Browning*, pp. 3–5, 21–26.

[7]See Herbert F. Tucker's discussion of this rhetoric of anticipation in *Browning's Beginnings: The Art of Disclosure* (Minneapolis: University of Minnesota Press, 1980), p. 10.

[8]Preyer sees this self-renunciation as a product of a general social repression, "Robert Browning," pp. 534–39, 547–48.

[9]W. David Shaw is right to see a general analogue for this abstract drama in the movements between Kierkegaard's aesthetic, ethical, and religious stages, in *The Dialectical Temper: The Rhetorical Art of Robert Browning* (Ithaca: Cornell University Press, 1968).

[10]See the account of Thomas R. Lounsbury in *The Early Literary Career of Robert Browning* (New York: Charles Scribner's Sons, 1911), pp. 62–94.

while the human drama and the audiences necessary for it are never fully developed.

I

In his *Essay on Chatterton* (1842), Browning outlines three stages in a poet's development:

> Genius almost invariably begins to develop itself by imitation. It has, in the short-sightedness of infancy, faith in the world: and its object is to compete with, or prove superior to, the world's already recognized idols, at their own performances and by their own methods. This done, there grows up a faith in itself: and, no longer taking the performance or method of another for granted, it supersedes these by processes of its own. It creates, and imitates no longer. Seeing cause for faith in something external and better, and having attained to a moral end and aim, it next discovers in itself the only remaining antagonist worthy of its ambition, and in the subduing of what at first had seemed its most enviable powers, arrives at the more or less complete fulfilment of its earthly mission.[11]

Poetic genius begins by imitating great poets; then, by acquiring faith in itself, it gives up imitation for original creation; and, finally, by struggling against itself and its pride, it submits its poetry to an exterior ideal. The first two stages in this dialectic of poetic development correspond to a Romantic conception of poetic genius. But the view of the Wordsworthian and the Byronic ego which holds that the self's pride needs to be subjugated to morality is a Victorian one. The argument's weakness lies in its implicit assumption that poets have no other audience than themselves. Indeed, Browning labors throughout the essay to show that Chatterton's suicide was not a sign of his despair of ever acquiring an audience for his poetry but a moral renunciation of his pride:[12] "No sooner is the intellectual effort made than the moral one succeeds and destroying these poems he determines to kill himself."[13]

---

[11]*Browning's "Essay on Chatterton,"* ed. Donald Smalley (Cambridge, Mass.: Harvard University Press, 1948), p. 111.

[12]Ibid., p. 39.

[13]Ibid., p. 129. Chatterton's Rowley poems, his life, and his suicide are the harbingers of the artist's isolation, created by industrialization and the mass market. Arnold's *Empedocles on Etna* is still perhaps the best portrait of the modern artist's predicament—his isolation from society and his despair over its decay. See Frank Kermode's discussion of the artist in isolation in his *Romantic Image* (London: Routledge & Kegan Paul, 1957), pp. 1–29.

Pauline, Paracelsus, Strafford, and Sordello

Pauline (1833), *Paracelsus* (1835), and *Sordello* (1840) all dramatize this self-destructive poetic, which would allow only the poet's self to be its antagonist and which repudiates the struggle for earthly fame by embracing God. This poetic answered to Browning's passion for a protective chameleon coloring that would conceal him from the public's critical eye and to his difficulty in finding a form that would allow him to depict this great passion objectively. By adopting a poetic which held that self-expression for its own sake was morally dangerous, Browning could give voice to his fears of inadequacy and rejection and could also write poetry that would gain the approval of others. He planned a poetic career around a series of anonymous publications that would follow the pattern of and include *Pauline*: "The world was never to guess that 'Brown, Smith, Jones and Robinson' (as the spelling books have it) the respective authors of this poem, the other novel, such an opera, such a speech etc. etc. were no other than one and the same individual."[14]

Before *Pauline*, he had written a number of poems at the age of twelve or thirteen, which he later called *Incondita* (disordered pieces), and had destroyed them when his parents had failed to find a publisher for them.[15] The destruction of these poems and the great reluctance Browning displayed in republishing *Pauline* in the 1868 edition of his works point to his sensitivity to any embarrassing self-revelation. The 1868 preface defensively asserts, quoting from his preface to *Dramatic Lyrics*, that like his other work *Pauline* is to be considered wholly imaginary: "The thing was my earliest attempt at 'poetry always dramatic in principle, and so many utterances of so many imaginary persons, not mine.'"[16] His fear of his audience's prying into his

---

[14]Browning's remarks in the copy of *Pauline* annotated by J. S. Mill, now in the Forster and Dyce Collection of the Victoria and Albert Museum, quoted in *Handbook*, p. 41. Michael A. Burr suggests that these remarks were a self-critical reply to Mill's comments; see "Browning's Note to Forster," *VP* 12 (1974):343–49. The traditional interpretation of Browning's response to Mill's criticism of his "morbid self-consciousness" is that it "changed the course of Browning's career" (*Handbook*, p. 107). Masao Miyoshi argues that Browning was aware of *Pauline*'s deficiencies from the beginning; see "Mill and *Pauline*: The Myth and Some Facts," *VS* 9 (1965), 154–63. Still O. P. Govil is right to suggest in his reply to Miyoshi that Browning was stung by Mill's criticism; see "A Note on Mill and Browning's *Pauline*," *VP* 4 (1966), 287–91. But however thin the autobiographical veil, *Pauline* is a dramatic poem. Mill's remarks did not materially affect Browning's poetic development but instead confirmed him in his initial dramatic impulse.

[15]*Handbook*, p. 554. "The First-Born of Egypt" and "The Dance of Death" survive in the transcription made by Eliza Flower in a letter to W. J. Fox and are published in *New Poems*, pp. 3–12.

[16]*Works*, I, xxi.

life (no doubt aggravated by the badgering of his late wife's would-be biographers) has prompted readers to wonder if Browning was hiding anything, to speculate about the poem's meaning, and to see in it a thinly disguised allegory of a youthful passion.[17] But it seems more likely that Browning's anonymous publication of *Pauline* was designed to limit the audience of his first efforts to his closest friends and relatives and to minimize the effect of any harsh criticism.[18] Above all, he seems to have wanted to establish himself as a poet in his family's eyes and so merit his father's patronage of further publications. As Browning later said in his *Essay on Chatterton*, "in nine cases out of ten his [the young poet's] first assumption of the license will be made in a borrowed name. The first communication, to even the family circle or the trusted associate, is sure to be 'the work of a friend'; if not, 'something extracted from a magazine,' or 'Englished from the German.' So is the way gracefully facilitated for Reader and Hearer finding themselves in a new position with respect to each other."[19] Browning arranged with his aunt, Mrs. Silverthorne, to publish *Pauline* without his parents' knowing about it.[20] When the review by W. J. Fox in the *Monthly Review* was favorable,[21] he revealed his success to them, having created the circumstances which would put the reader and hearer "in a new position with respect to each other." In this way he established himself as a poet in his father's eyes and, having made the antiquarian bank clerk proud of his literary son, never had to look elsewhere for financial assistance in publishing his poetry.[22]

The search for a sympathetic relationship between the poet and his audiences is at the heart of *Pauline: A Fragment of a Confession*. The poem's poet confesses that he is no longer what he has been (as he hints in the first epigraph from Marot) and asks for the sympathy of Pauline, Shelley, God, and the reader for his imaginative predicament. He also warns his potential audiences away, both in the second epi-

---

[17]See, for example, Mrs. Sutherland Orr, *Life and Letters of Robert Browning*, 2d. ed. (London: Smith, Elder, 1891), p. 37; also see Betty Miller, *Robert Browning*, pp. 31–34.

[18]Browning wrote about *Pauline* in the postscript to a letter to W. J. Fox in 1833: "I have forgotten the main thing—which is to beg you not spoil a loophole I have kept for backing out of the thing if necessary, 'sympathy of dear friends,' etc., etc., none of whom know anything about it" (quoted in Orr, *Life and Letters*, p. 55).

[19]*Browning's "Essay on Chatterton,"* p. 116.

[20]Orr, *Life and Letters*, p. 54.

[21][W. J. Fox], review of *Pauline, Monthly Repository*, n.s. 7 (1833):252–62.

[22]There was little or no market for poetry in the 1830s. Poets had to agree to cover the costs of publication. See Harold G. Merriam, *Edward Moxon: Publisher of Poets*, Columbia University Studies in English and Comparative Literature, no. 137 (New York: Columbia University Press, 1939), p. 56.

graph taken from Cornelius Agrippa's *Of Occult Philosophy* and in the opening address, because he fears that his imaginative sympathy is a dangerous magic. But although he warns his readers away, he pleads with them, as he does with Pauline, Shelley, and God, to provide him with an audience in order to prevent his spirit from dissipating itself in the world through the action of his sympathetic imagination. He wants his audiences to act as a kind of metaphysical enclosure protecting him from himself.

We can divide *Pauline* into the following sections: lines 1 through 259 appeal first to Pauline and then to Shelley; lines 260 through 728 relate the poet's psychological autobiography; lines 729 through 810 propose to Pauline a retreat into the woods; and lines 811 through 1031 are a combination of prayer and peroration oscillating wildly between visions of future happiness and intimations of the poet's death. This last confusion makes the poem an irretrievable failure, for, as Mrs. Orr says, "We are left in complete doubt as to whether the crisis is that of approaching death or incipient convalescence, or which character it bears in the sufferer's mind; and the language used in the closing pages is such as to suggest, without the slightest break in poetic continuity, alternately the one conclusion and the other."[23] She suggests this confusion was designed "to assist his anonymity."[24] But Browning's anonymity would have been preserved more effectively if the poet had died and if Pauline had been editing his poetical remains, a possibility which apparently had crossed Browning's mind, as Pauline's note to line 811 suggests. Browning seems instead to have intended to leave his poet at death's door and so to arouse interest in the sequels he had planned.[25]

Paralleling Browning's uncertainty about his anonymity in the poem and how it would affect his readers both near and far is the *Pauline*-poet's uncertainty about whether Pauline, Shelley, God, or a strange phantom crowd is his true audience, an uncertainty that reflects an ambivalence about the poet's decided preference for private loves over public fame. The poem describes two types of audience: an enclosed, private audience for which the central image is the act of

---

[23] Orr, *Life and Letters*, p. 59.
[24] Ibid.
[25] Clyde de L. Ryals considers the poem as a fictional edition, in "Browning's *Pauline*: The Question of Genre," *Genre* 9 (1976):231–45. According to Browning's unpublished letter of August 9, 1837, to Amédée de Ripert-Monclar, he had finished a second work, "Pauline, Part 2" (Maynard, *Browning's Youth*, pp. 222, 436 n. 71). This work seems likely to have been an early version of *Sordello*.

reading; and a universal crowd of admirers for which the central image is slavery. The implicit contradiction between the desire for universal sympathy and the vision of a universal slavery is never fully confronted in the poem; instead, there is a retreat into the imagery of enclosure and personal audience, as well as an attempt to resolve problems of poetic pride by moralizing.

The poem's opening address is a kind of exorcism. The invocation's adjuration, addressed to Pauline, serves as the pattern for the exorcism of the poet's past sins in the remainder of the poem: he thinks of each audience he addresses as protecting him from the demonic fancies which he casts out as he calls them up. By ridding himself of these poetic demons, the speaker hopes to win a universal sympathy from others and to establish a correspondence between his inner self and the outer world: he wants to sing as "one entering bright halls where all / Will rise and shout for him" (ll. 78–79) and hopes that his desire to "be all, have, see, know, taste, feel, all" will be mirrored by the world's intimacy with him (l. 278).[26]

The poet feels that his return to writing poetry is possible only because of the praise given Shelley posthumously—"His award" (l. 142). But there is an extraordinary irony in his view of the posthumous praise accorded to Shelley. Although it inspires him, it does so because it reveals the foul and dark motivations of the vile curiosity seeker, whose image is the startled spider (ll. 146–49). Moreover, the *Pauline*-poet's strained melancholy here indicates his (and Browning's) ambivalent desire for fame: both he and Browning want to be famous and despise those who might praise them. So for the poet the famous Shelley of "the foolish crowd of rushers-in upon genius" is less than the Shelley of his private reading.[27] He prefers the time when Shel-

[26] Compare Browning's comment on his letter writing in a letter to Elizabeth of May 3, 1846: "But this is very foolish, all the same, I need not be told—and is part & parcel of an older—indeed primitive folly of mine, which I shall never wholly get rid of, of desiring to do nothing when I cannot do all; seeing nothing, getting, enjoying nothing, where there is no seeing & getting & enjoying *wholly*" (*Letters*, I, 53–54). This desire has a Byronic analogue in *Childe Harold's Pilgrimage*, canto 3, st. 72: "I live not in myself, but I become / Portion of that around me" (*Poetical Works*, ed. Frederick Page and John Jump [London: Oxford University Press, 1970], p. 219).

[27] The phrase is from Robert's letter to Elizabeth, November 16, 1845, *Letters*, I, 271. Compare his lack of interest in poets who received the public's approval in their lifetime, voiced in another letter to Elizabeth of August 22, 1846: "Heaven knows that I could not get up enthusiasm enough to cross the room if at the other end of it all Wordsworth, Coleridge & Southey were condensed into a little China bottle yonder, after the Rosicrucian fashion . . they seem to 'have their reward' and want nobody's love or faith" (*Letters*, II, 986) (his ellipsis). Browning first read his neglected Shelley in the editions traced by Frederick A. Pottle in *Shelley and Browning: A Myth and Some Facts* (Chicago: Pembroke Press, 1923).

ley's works were a spell to him alone because he was unaware that Shelley was known to others, and he feels that he was then worshipping at "a sacred spring / Scarce worth a moth's flitting" (ll. 172–73), which "one small tree embowers droopingly" (l. 174), and "joying to see some wandering insect won / To live in its few rushes" (ll. 175–76). To his dismay he lost his sense of private communion with his favorite author when he dsicovered this spring to be "the fountain-head, / Long lost, of some great river" (ll. 179–80). The womblike private pleasure of his early reading is lost in his contemplation of the public's possession of Shelley's work.

The subsequent self-analysis that constitutes the bulk of the poem is a medley of ideas, not a consistent, coherent account of his past. His governing self is a "principle of restlessness" (l. 277) that "would be all, have, see, know, taste, feel all" (l. 278). This is really a declaration that he has an independent will to which his imagination is subject. For what the poet means by poetic power is more closely defined as the selective repression of imagination. It is able to "quell" the past "regally" (l. 290), though his "mind / Forgets not, not a shred of life forgets" (ll. 287–88). The process of imaginative composition outlined here is parallel to the process of exorcism the entire poem displays: the poet exercises his will in an effort to remember the past in order to repress it. He connects this remembering with his evil pride, which revels in its mastery over a troop of imaginary shades that kneel to him and shout, "Thyself, thou art our king!" (l. 487). His pride, then, is a projection of his hopes for fame and of his desire to enslave his audiences by writing poetry. At the same time, this mastery paradoxically stems from his creative impulse to surrender himself to the world and dissipate himself in it. This dissipation prevents him from capturing the fair forms of Shelley and allows him to be imprisoned by the "foul forms" that fasten on him (l. 213). To write beautiful poetry he must discipline his sympathetic imagination by directing it toward a selected audience that will, he hopes, give it a spiritual home.

While Shelley is the emblem of his happy past and particularly of his private reading, Pauline seems to promise the sense of enclosure he once had and now so desperately desires. He asks her to come with him to a

> new retreat
> Walled in with a sloped mound of matted shrubs,
> Dark, tangled, old and green, still sloping down
> To a small pool whose waters lie asleep

> Amid the trailing boughs turned water-plants:
> And tall trees overarch to keep us in.
>
> [ll. 749–54]

Like the private pool to which he compared his experience of reading Shelley, this small space is formed by a stream that has broken off from its parent river (ll. 768–77). This womblike setting allows him to let his imagination wander among the intertwined beauties of nature and enter into the intimate intricacies of private communion with them. But this secret pool is clearly an image of psychological regression, imaginatively substituting for the love he desires but does not feel sure he has from others and from Pauline in particular. The picture of natural confinement does give him a sense of self but does not bring complete spiritual satisfaction:

> Hedgerows for me—those living hedgerows where
> The bushes close and clasp above and keep
> Thought in—I am concentrated—I feel;
> But my soul saddens when it looks beyond:
> I cannot be immortal, taste all joy.
>
> [ll. 806–10]

He can find natural spaces in which his ego can be concentrated and so imaginatively feel its powers. But his self-contained ego is only an imaginative fiction, because, as he knows from the simple fact of his mortality, he cannot be the ground of his own being and soul. He is not a god, and so is destined to die.

His insight goes no further, though. And so while there is much of the Ghost of Old Hamlet's "Remember me" at the poem's end, it is little more than wild raving. God is urged to remember him (ll. 822–30), Pauline is implored to love him (ll. 860–985), and Shelley is asked to be with him always, especially when he dies (ll. 1020–31). But the egocentric voice can only call for attention without giving much of a reason for granting it. This reminds the reader that *Pauline* is, above all, a poet's appeal for his audiences to sympathize with him in his maudlin, self-conscious sorrow and to forgive his sinful pride in feeling he deserves their love and attention.

II

In *Paracelsus* Browning further develops the inner struggles of his protagonist and makes them more coherent. The poem clarifies the conflict he perceives between love, fame, and God and fashions this conflict into a kind of developmental dialectic that is argued out in terms of Paracelsus's various audiences.

Browning's composition of *Paracelsus* began with a dare. According to Mrs. Orr, Amédée de Ripert-Monclar, to whom the poem is dedicated, was discussing with Browning likely subjects for a poem about love. In the course of this conversation, the alchemist Paracelsus was mentioned and then quickly dismissed by Monclar because the Renaissance scholar had been castrated and therefore could not provide a suitable subject for a young man's theories about love. Browning immediately, and somewhat perversely, saw a challenge in the subject of Paracelsus and conceived of making him a man who eventually discovers the power and the meaning of love.[28] But prior to any composition, there had to be a deliberate forgetting of Paracelsus's physical incapacity for love. A sign of the hidden conflict at the heart of the poem and its genesis lies in the notes Browning appended from the *Biographie universelle*. Browning translates the French notice of Paracelsus's life into English, but at the crucial point where the story of Paracelsus's castration is told, Browning not only represses the passage by relegating it to a footnote but also disguises Renauldin's remarks by translating the French into Latin.

To indicate the nature of Browning's Victorian reserve here, it is worth looking briefly at Balzac's *Sarrasine* (1831), which also considers a castrato in connection with the theme of love. The narrator of Balzac's novella attends a party given by a wealthy Parisian family, meets there a beautiful young singer with whom he desires a rendezvous, and procures one by promising to reveal to her the story of a repulsive old man who had been fascinated by her voice and who was evidently connected to the Parisian family. The next day the narrator tells her that the old man at the party, on whose fortune that of the family is founded, was originally the famous castrato, La Zambinella. The narrator tells her how a sculptor, Jean Sarrasine, fell in love with La Zambinella, thinking he was a woman, and how Sarrasine, discovering his

---

[28]Orr, *Life and Letters*, pp. 71–72. On the poem's background and for a discussion Renaissance, Victorian, and modern views of Paracelsus, see Frederick S. Boas, "Browning's *Paracelsus*, 1835–1935," *Quarterly Review* 265 (1935):280–95. For a discussion of the poem's Shelleyan and Platonic ideas of love, see William O. Raymond, *The Infinite Moment and Other Essays on Robert Browning*, 2d ed. (Toronto: University of Toronto Press, 1965), pp. 156–75. On the poem's dramatic and structural irony, see F. E. L. Priestley, "The Ironic Pattern of Browning's *Paracelsus*," *UTQ* 34 (1964):68–81. For a discussion of Browning's notions of temporality in the poem, see Tucker, *Browning's Beginnings*, pp. 53–83.

disguise, attempted to murder the castrato singer but was killed instead by La Zambinella's confederates. The story disgusts the young woman so that the narrator, ironically, is denied the favors he had expected in return for telling the story. The castration of La Zambinella, as Roland Barthes has brilliantly argued, becomes both a symbol and, because of the story's arrangement, the structural principle of unrequited love.[29]

Although Browning may have read *Sarrasine* in the winter of 1834–35, when he looked into Balzac at Monclar's urging,[30] there is nothing to suggest that Balzac's story furnishes anything more than an interesting contrast to *Paracelsus*, highlighting Browning's reasons for selecting a castrato as the hero of a poem about love. Balzac focuses upon the image of the castrato by having his narrator create an air of mystery about the old man who was La Zambinella and having him hide the old man's secret until he is forced to reveal it to the woman at the story's climax in order to have any hope of closing his bargain with her. Browning, in contrast, represses the fact that Paracelsus had been castrated and mystifies his hero's alienation from, and inability to understand, human love. While in Balzac castration intensifies sexual interest and passion, in Browning it provides private justification for a rarefied, Neoplatonic disquisition on love.

With an abstract, almost allegorical argument in mind, Browning felt it necessary to develop the story of Paracelsus (Phillipus Aureolus Theophrastus Bombastus ab Hohenheim) in discrete stages in order to make clear the dialectical progression of love. Interested in recording the development of a particular passion, and not the events surrounding it, he relegates the historical background to his explanatory notes and divides Paracelsus's career into five scenes. The first contains a friendly discussion of Paracelsus's worldly aspirations among Paracelsus, Festus, and Festus's wife, Michal, at Würzburg. The second depicts a meeting between the wandering Paracelsus and Aprile, a young poet, at Constantinople in 1521. In the third scene Paracelsus describes to Festus his professorial triumph at Basel in 1526 and also predicts his future failure. In the fourth scene, set two years later at Colmar, Paracelsus tells Festus of his dismissal from the university at Basel. The last scene records Paracelsus's dying vision of God's divine order as told to Festus at Salzburg in 1541. The separation of the scenes

---

[29]See Roland Barthes's intriguing analysis of Balzac's novella in *S/Z*, trans. Richard Miller (New York: Hill & Wang, 1974).
[30]See Maynard, *Browning's Youth*, pp. 303, 446 n. 35.

compels the reader to supply the continuity between them and to see each scene as a stage in Paracelsus's quest for the meaning of life and love.

In this light, *Paracelsus* is not so much a drama or a dramatic monologue as it is a monodrama, which A. Dwight Culler persuasively defines as being about the rise and fall of a particular passion.[31] As Browning puts it in his preface to the poem,

> I therefore anticipate his [the reader's] discovery, that it is an attempt, probably more novel than happy, to reverse the method usually adopted by writers whose aim it is to set forth any phenomenon of the mind or the passions, by the operation of persons and events; and that, instead of having recourse to an external machinery of incidents to create and evolve the crisis I desire to produce, I have ventured to display somewhat minutely the mood itself in its rise and progress, and have suffered the agency by which it is influenced and determined, to be generally discernible in its effects alone, and subordinate throughout, if not altogether excluded.[32]

Browning believes that the poet should reflect the progress of an emotion in its various moods and that the reader must reverse this minute impressionism and mold the observations into a whole: "It is certain, however, that a work like mine depends more immediately on the intelligence and sympathy of the reader for its success—indeed were my scenes stars, it must be his co-operating fancy, which supplying all chasms, shall collect the scattered lights into one constellation—a Lyre or a Crown."[33] Readers must be willing to part with their narrative expectations and their desire for a historical biography so that they can attend to the stages of Paracelsus's quest for knowledge and love. And the ultimate goal of this quest, for both Paracelsus and the reader, is an understanding of God's love and how it alone allows one to reunite the fragmented world:

---

[31]A. Dwight Culler, "Monodrama and the Dramatic Monologue," *PMLA* 90 (1975):366–85.

[32]*Complete Works*, I, 65. Compare the following passage from Robert's letter to Elizabeth of June 14, 1845: "One should study the mechanical part of the art, or nearly all that there is to be studied—for the more one sits and thinks over the creative process, the more it confirms itself as 'inspiration,' nothing more nor less. Or, at worst, you write down old inspirations, what you remember of them—but with *that* it begins: 'Reflection' is exactly what it names itself—a *re*-presentation, in scattered rays from every angle of incidence, of what first of all became present in a great light, a whole one" (*Letters*, I, 95).

[33]*Complete Works*, I, 65.

> And God renews
> His ancient rapture. Thus he dwells in all,
> From life's minute beginnings, up at last
> To man—the consummation of this scheme
> Of being, the completion of this sphere
> Of life: whose attributes had here and there
> Been scattered o'er the visible world before,
> Asking to be combined, dim fragments meant
> To be united in some wondrous whole,
> Imperfect qualities throughout creation,
> Suggesting some one creature yet to make,
> Some point where all those scattered rays should meet
> Convergent in the faculties of man.
>   [v, 680–92]

Our investigation, like Paracelsus's, leads back to man's faculties. We discover man's vision to be the evidence of God's vision, and in particular man's "blind, oft-failing, yet believing love" to be a "supplementary reflux of light" (v, 704, 714), which "illustrates all the inferior grades, explains / Each back step in the circle" (v, 715–16). The love brought to the text by the reader in search of its meaning and the love displayed by Paracelsus in his quest for an understanding of the world are finally the poem's twin revelations. They both allow the apprehension of, and also provide the evidence for, God's love for the world.

At the poem's opening, Paracelsus announces to Festus and Michal that he is leaving the peaceful, provincial backwater of Würzburg to seek universal knowledge. But Paracelsus's quest will only indirectly benefit mankind, as his dream concerning his fate reveals:

> I seemed to long
> At once to trample on, yet save mankind,
> To make some unexampled sacrifice
> In their behalf, to wring some wondrous good
> From heaven or earth for them, to perish, winning
> Eternal weal in the act.
>   [I, 460–65]

There is a strange Byronic or Promethean ambivalence here concerning mankind. Paracelsus wants to help man but wants to be a kind of Nietzschean *Übermensch*, so that he will not have to accept praise for his work. He says, "I never will be served by those I serve" (I, 613). Paracelsus bases his romantic disdain of men's applause upon a kind of subjective Neoplatonism in which seeking truth necessitates a turning to the truths in the self in order to know onself, instead of to an empirical observation of the world. In one of the most Blakean passages in Browning, Paracelsus claims that this turning toward inner truth requires that the purely human be sloughed off:

> But, friends,
> Truth is within ourselves; it takes no rise
> From outward things, whate'er you may believe.
> There is an inmost centre in us all,
> Where truth abides in fulness; and around,
> Wall upon wall, the gross flesh hems it in,
> This perfect, clear perception—which is truth.
> A baffling and perverting carnal mesh
> Binds it, and makes all error: and to KNOW
> Rather consists in opening out a way
> Whence the imprisoned splendour may escape,
> Than in effecting entry for a light
> Supposed to be without.
>
> [I, 725–37]

This mystical individualism accords with his spurning of the purely human audiences for his actions. Like the poet of *Pauline* who felt the divinely infinite was outside his private retreat in the woods, Paracelsus feels he must leave Michal's garden and the circle of his friends at Würzburg to effect an entry into the infinite within himself. But while the imagery focuses on pictures of escaping radiance (reminding us of Browning's lighthouse image of his poetry),[34] Paracelsus's action reflects more his dissatisfaction with the intellectual confinement of his circumstances than his resolve for rigorous self-examination. And while he talks of contemplation, his wandering through the world in pursuit of neglected arcana resembles more the ambitious scholar's pursuit of fame.

This contradiction points to the illusory nature of Paracelsus's inner conflict. According to the alchemist himself, he is putting knowledge above love, reason above passion. But the underlying struggle seems

---

[34]"These scenes and song-scraps *are* such mere and very escapes of my inner power, which lives in me like the light in those crazy Mediterranean phares I have watched at sea, wherein the light is ever revolving in a dark gallery, bright and alive, and only after a weary interval leaps out, for a moment, from one narrow chink, and then goes on with the blind wall between it and you" (Robert to Elizabeth, February 11, 1845, *Letters*, I, 17).

instead to pit pride and the desire for fame against love. In pursuing knowledge Paracelsus is in fact seeking to establish himself in history. The contradiction between the surface and the essential opposition is revealed in Paracelsus's meeting with Aprile in the second scene and in his struggle with the students and professors of Basel in the fourth scene.

At the beginning of the second scene, Paracelsus is suffering from the scholar's melancholy and recites this lovely poem, reminiscent of Landor at his best, which he finds in the margin of a dusty manuscript:

> "Time fleets, youth fades, life is an empty dream,"
> It is the echo of time; and he whose heart
> Beat first beneath a human heart, whose speech
> Was copied from a human tongue, can never
> Recall when he was living yet knew not this.
> Nevertheless long seasons pass o'er him
> Till some one hour's experience shows what nothing,
> It seemed, could clearer show; and ever after,
> An altered brow and eye and gait and speech
> Attest that now he knows the adage true
> "Time fleets, youth fades, life is an empty dream."
> [II, 43–53]

The poem expresses Paracelsus's lament for his youth lost in pursuit of scholarly knowledge and fame. At this point, Aprile, the poet of love and youth, enters. His appearance and death are designed to underscore the dichotomy between the quest for love and the quest for knowledge and to suggest that Paracelsus should be looking for a combination of knowledge and love and that Aprile and Paracelsus are two "halves of one dissevered world" (II, 634). But this artificial resolution is insufficient: Aprile dies, and Paracelsus is left alone.

Moreover, behind both the quest to know and the quest to love is the desire for fame. The song of the lost poets which Aprile sings makes this clear (II, 297–339). Like the anonymous poet of the dusty manuscript, these abandoned poets have no audience other than themselves. Theirs is a despairing cry for sympathy. So, too, is Aprile's. He believes his poetic genius will appear when he has a listener: "All will flash forth at last, with thee to hear!" (II, 382). Like the *Pauline*-poet, he dissipates himself in his imaginative sympathy with his surroundings, tries to make poetry from fragments of the world, and "would

LOVE infinitely, and be loved!" (II, 385). Above all, Aprile wants to be famous:

> I would live
> For ever in the thoughts I thus explored,
> As a discoverer's memory is attached
> To all he finds; they should be mine henceforth,
> Imbued with me, though free to all before:
> For clay, once cast into my soul's rich mine,
> Should come up crusted o'er with gems.
> [II, 560–66]

Aprile thinks of the world as his soul's "mine," in the equivocal sense of the word; he loves the world (and not so much the world as himself) for what he can get from it.

Paracelsus superficially attains his goal of uniting love with wisdom as he grieves over the dying Aprile. But his solitariness after Aprile's death suggests that Paracelsus has not learned to love anyone other than himself. As Philarète Chasles said in the *Revue des deux Mondes* in 1840, "C'est Faust réduit à la réalité, n'écoutant d'autre Méphistophélès que ses passions et son amour-propre, entouré d'ennemis, d'envieux et d'admirateurs, plein de mépris pour l'espèce humaine, qui est si facile à tromper, irrité jusqu'au délire de notre impuissance à pénétrer les secrets de la vie."[35] Browning's Paracelsus is in some sense Goethe's Faust "reduced to reality," because Paracelsus's self-love and passions play the part of Mephistopheles. But Paracelsus is also Faust without Margarethe, and this makes Browning's poem an abstract version of Part II of *Faust* instead of Part I. *Paracelsus* is not a poem about the triumph of bourgeois love over reason, but a poem about the triumph of God's love over man's pride.

In the third scene Paracelsus deliberately, and perversely, pretends to be a quack. To Festus's protests that this failure is merely a pose, Paracelsus replies: "I toil, you listen; I explain, perhaps / You understand: there our communion ends" (III, 725–26). His burning of books, his contempt for authorities, his zany shows in the medical theater are calculatingly designed (Browning would have us believe) to

---

[35] Philarète Chasles, "De l'Art dramatique et du Théâtre actuel en Angleterre," *Revue des deux Mondes*, ser. 4, 22 (1840):127. ("This is Faust reduced to reality, listening to no Mephistopheles other than his passions and his self-love, surrounded by enemies, enviers, and admirers, full of contempt for the human race, which is so easy to fool, irritated until mad with our inability to penetrate the secrets of life"—my translation.)

make the audience think for themselves. In his despair of ever attaining complete knowledge, Paracelsus flamboyantly defies his audience to prove him a fraud, believing that once others show him to be a quack he will, paradoxically, have succeeded in teaching his students to go beyond him. By the fourth scene Paracelsus has achieved this goal and has lost his post at Basel. But he is still contemptuous of those for whom he feels he has sacrificed himself and worries in the fifth scene about his place in history and how his peers will receive him after his criticism of their work:

> Here stand my rivals; Latin, Arab, Jew,
> Greek, join dead hands against me: all I ask
> Is, that the world enrol my name with theirs,
> And even this poor privilege, it seems,
> They range themselves, prepared to disallow.
> Only observe! why, fiends may learn from them!
> How they talk calmly of my throes, my fierce
> Aspirings, terrible watchings, each one claiming
> Its price of blood and brain; how they dissect
> And sneeringly disparage the few truths
> Got at a life's cost; they too hanging the while
> About my neck, their lies misleading me
> And their dead names browbeating me! Grey crew,
> Yet steeped in fresh malevolence from hell,
> Is there reason for your hate?
>
> [v, 161–75]

Like the giants "ranged along the hill-sides" viewing the last of Childe Roland (l. 199), these ghosts from the past torment the dying Paracelsus because he fears they may not allow him to become famous. He imagines they will treat him like some cadaver, "each one claiming / Its price of blood and brain." The crowds of the living and the dead reinforce his suspicions of mankind's enmity toward him.

But after he realizes that God is all in all and "dwells in all, / From life's minute beginnings, up at last / To man" (v, 681–83), he finally begins to understand that his contempt for his audience was instrumental in his failure:

> In my own heart love had not been made wise
> To trace love's faint beginnings in mankind,
> To know even hate is but a mask of love's,
> To see a good in evil, and a hope
> In ill-success; to sympathize, be proud

Pauline, Paracelsus, Strafford, and Sordello

>   Of their half-reasons, faint aspirings, dim
>   Struggles for truth, their poorest fallacies,
>   Their prejudice and fears and cares and doubts.
>   [v, 872–79]

Only by coming to terms with God can Paracelsus finally reconcile his own desire to love and be loved by the multitude with his desire to know and please himself; only then can he see hate as "a mask of love's." Only by seeing in God a union of these disparate desires does he understand how he has failed and also realize how in recognizing his failure he has succeeded.

III

Although it was performed and printed before *Sordello* (1840) was completed and published, *Strafford* (1837) is usually discussed in the company of the plays of *Bells and Pomegranates* (1841–46). But to consider the first of Browning's plays in the order of its publication gives a better idea of the complexity of Browning's early career and, because the writing of *Strafford* interrupted *Sordello*'s composition, lends welcome direction to a stylistic and thematic analysis of *Sordello*.[36] Browning wrote *Strafford* as a vehicle for William Macready. The play's style reflects Macready's practice of speaking against the rhythm of blank verse, a kind of conversational counterpoint which Browning cultivated to excess in *Sordello* and which forms the basis of his style in his later monologues. The play also foreshadows his intense interest in creating the impression of historical density and psychological and political complexity, through its portrayal of the Earl of Strafford caught between his aristocratic loyalty to King Charles I and his sympathy for England's Parliament and people.

During the 1830s and 1840s Macready was the "eminent tragedian" of the London stage. He was active in reforming the theater, in restoring the full text of Shakespeare's plays to the stage, and in developing and encouraging new playwrights.[37] Browning met him at W. J.

---

[36]William C. DeVane has attempted to reconstruct the lengthy and troubled composition of *Sordello* in "*Sordello*'s Story Retold," *SP* 27 (1932):1–24; see also his summary in his *Handbook*, pp. 72–85. Laurence Poston, III, has suggested that "Browning's exploration of the period of the English Civil War was important to *Sordello* both stylistically and thematically" ("Browning's Political Skepticism: *Sordello* and the Plays," *PMLA* 88 [1973]:261).

[37]See Alan S. Downer, *The Eminent Tragedian: William Charles Macready* (Cambridge, Mass.: Harvard University Press, 1966), pp. 157–252.

Fox's house in November of 1835, three months after the publication of *Paracelsus*. Macready read Browning's poem within the next two weeks and recorded in his diary that, although he didn't think the poem was altogether successful, he did feel the author was "destined for very great things."[38] On December 31 Macready introduced Browning to John Forster, who had reviewed *Paracelsus* favorably in the *Examiner*.[39] Forster became friends with Browning and a little later asked him to assist him with the biography of Strafford he was writing for his *Lives of the British Statesmen*.[40] In return for this, one suspects, Forster wrote another review of *Paracelsus* for the *New Monthly Magazine*, finding in Browning, as the title suggests, "Evidences of a New Genius for Dramatic Poetry."[41] No doubt with this review in mind, Macready, after the dinner celebrating the opening night of Talfourd's *Ion*, said to him: "Write a play Browning, and keep me from going to America."[42] Browning eagerly responded to Macready's request in a letter, saying, "Should I succeed, my way of life will be very certain."[43] So it would have been, since a successful run of twenty nights at that time usually brought the author three hundred pounds, while, by comparison, Browning's father made only three hundred pounds a year as a senior clerk in the Bank of England when he retired. Although Browning's parents cheerfully supported his poetic ambitions, the financial independence of a successful playwright seems to have been a very attractive prospect to Browning and to some extent, at least, explains his feverish attempts to gain a footing on the stage in the early 1840s. Even the relatively unsuccessful five-night run of *Strafford* gained him sixty pounds, probably enabling him to pay for his trip to Italy in 1838, and the three-night run of *A Blot in the 'Scutcheon* presumably made him thirty-six pounds, probably making possible his second trip to Italy in 1844.[44]

Browning had actively attended the theater and had acted in private

[38]*The Diaries of William Charles Macready, 1833–1851*, ed. William Toynbee, 2 vols. (New York: G. P. Putnam's Sons, 1912), I, 265.

[39][John Forster], review of *Paracelsus*, *Examiner*, September 6, 1835, pp. 563–64.

[40]The extent of Browning's contribution is still a matter of scholarly dispute. For a review of the evidence, see William S. Peterson, "A Re-examination of Robert Browning's *Prose Life of Strafford*," *Browning Newsletter* 3 (1969):12–22.

[41][John Forster], "Evidences of a New Genius for Dramatic Poetry," *New Monthly Magazine* 46 (1836):289–308.

[42]Orr, *Life and Letters*, p. 88.

[43]Browning to Macready, May 28, 1836, *New Letters*, p. 12.

[44]Figures for *Strafford* from William Irvine and Park Honan, *The Book, the Ring, and the Poet* (New York: McGraw-Hill, 1974), p. 66. The rate of twelve pounds a night is assumed for *A Blot in the 'Scutcheon*.

theatricals before Macready asked him to write a play. He had, in fact, consciously decided to become a poet after seeing one of Edmund Kean's last performances in *Richard III* on October 22, 1832, the date recorded at the end of *Pauline*. What he would have heard and seen in Kean's and Macready's performances was a style of tragic acting which had been infected by melodramatic action and speech. Instead of declaiming in the classical, rhythmical style of John Philip Kemble, Kean and Macready spoke blank verse as if it were prose and melodramatically highlighted specific words and phrases by varying the volume and intensity of their voices. Coleridge said that to see Kean act was "like reading Shakespeare by flashes of lightning."[45] Macready improved upon Kean's nervous style by adding the "Macready pause," a technique of slowing his speech that made abrupt transitions of mood or thought more natural, gave in soliloquy the impression of a man thinking to himself, and elsewhere often created suspenseful uncertainty in the audience about his next word or action.[46] Macready believed that the goal of the actor was "to fathom the depths of character, to trace its latent motives, to feel its finest quiverings of emotion, to comprehend the thoughts that are hidden under words, and thus possess oneself of the actual mind of the individual man."[47] His style and its underlying motivation obviously have great affinities with the method and psychology of Browning's later monologues and, more immediately, closely resemble those evident in Browning's recitation of his poetry. D. G. Rossetti, in describing a reading that occurred in 1856, tells us that Browning "read with as much sprightly variation as there was in Tennyson sustained continuity."[48]

Macready's favorite vehicle throughout his career was Sheridan Knowles's *Virginius* (1822), which reflects better than any of Byron's classicizing plays the melodramatic sentiment and acting present in the tragic drama of the late Romantic stage. Its style also illustrates the kind of rhythm and excitement Macready's speech had. At the climax of the play, Virginius despairs of saving his daughter, betrothed to

---

[45]*Table Talk* (April 27, 1823), in *The Complete Works of Samuel Taylor Coleridge*, ed. [W. G. T.] Shedd, 7 vols. (New York: Harper & Brothers, 1853), VI, 265. Also see Alan S. Downer, "Players and Painted Stage: Nineteenth-Century Acting," *PMLA* 61 (1946):522–76; Downer, *Eminent Tragedian*, pp. 69–80; and George Rowell, *The Victorian Theatre: A Survey*, 2d ed. (Cambridge, England: Cambridge University Press, 1978).
[46]Downer, *Eminent Tragedian*, p. 71.
[47]Quoted by Downer, ibid., p. 80.
[48]*Dante Gabriel Rossetti: His Family Letters with a Memoir by W. M. Rossetti*, ed. W. M. Rossetti, 2 vols. (London: Ellis & Elvey, 1895), I, 95.

Icilius, from being declared a slave and then being seized by the lustful tyrant Appius. So he asks for one more moment with her:

> Another moment, pray you. Bear with me
> A little—'This my last embrace. 'Twont try
> Your patience beyond bearing, if you're a man!
> Lengthen it as I may, I cannot make it
> Long! My dear child! Virginia!
>   [*Kissing her.*
> There is only one way to save thine honour—
> 'Tis this!—
>   [*Stabs her and draws out the knife.*[49]

One may catch a very faint echo here of Lear bending over the dead Cordelia. But the domestic touch of the last embrace in *Virginius* is not directed toward any dramatic recognition, as it is in *King Lear*; instead, Virginius's emotional speech rises by fits and starts from the calm resignation of his request to broken exclamations and ends with a calculated, melodramatic surprise filled with tears and terror. The sudden movement of the prosy verse from relative calm to troubled exclamation is typical of the play, and not just of this scene where it is dramatically justified. There is a constant effort to create local excitement in otherwise desultory conversation so as to make each actor's speech end with the upward movement of an exclamation or a question and thus allow the actor's voice to rise over the noise of the three thousand unruly spectators seated in Covent Garden.

When he reviewed *Strafford* for the *Edinburgh Review* in 1837, Herman Merivale remarked that the style of Browning's play had suffered from the playwright's attempt to imitate the method of the modern actor, which Merivale described as "a fashion of breaking up his language into fragments; conveying a meaning, as it were, by starts and jerks; rarely finishing a sentence at all; and when he does, cutting it short with disagreeable abruptness."[50] Its style reminded Merivale of the emphatic, breathless fragments spoken by Alfred Jingle, Esq., the strolling player of Dickens's *Pickwick Papers* (1836).[51] The exaggerated

---

[49]*The Dramatic Works of James Sheridan Knowles*, 3 vols. (London: Edward Moxon, 1841–43), I, 141.

[50][Herman Merivale], review of *Strafford, Edinburgh Review* 65 (1837):143–44. R. H. Horne accused Browning of "turning tragedy into a spasmodic skeleton" (*A New Spirit of the Age*, 2 vols. [London: Smith Elder, 1844], II, 159).

[51][Merivale], pp. 144–45. Another reviewer later echoed both Merivale and Horne by saying that "the language was spasmodic, and tortured almost into the style of Alfred

abruptness of the style is well illustrated by Strafford's speech to King Charles I after having been accused of urging Archbishop Laud's war against the Scots:

> I! I! that was never spoken with
> Till it was entered on! That loathe the war!
> That say it is the maddest, wickedest . . .
> Do you know, sir, I think within my heart,
> That you would say I did advise the war;
> And if, through your own weakness, or what's worse,
> These Scots, with God to help them, drive me back,
> You will not step between the raging People
> And me, to say . . .
>   I knew it! from the first
> I knew it! Never was so cold a heart!
> Remember that I said it—that I never
> Believed you for a moment!
>   —And, you loved me?
>   [II, ii, 224–35]

The exclamations, the fragments, the anacoluthons, and the pauses implied by the ellipses, dashes, and breaks in the lines clearly display the mental agitation of Strafford, as Macready must have played him. But they also make for difficult reading. Because Browning has built so much rhetorical direction for the actor into the rhythm and punctuation, the rhythm of the blank verse is almost unrecognizable. The dialogue constantly shouts, and finishes always, as in *Virginius*, with the rising intonation of an exclamation or an excited question.

This writing for Macready's acting style differs greatly from the smooth Shelleyan style of *Pauline* and *Paracelsus* and foreshadows the contorted, compressed style of *Sordello*, as one can see by comparing the following two passages on giant killing from *Pauline* and *Strafford*:

> Sun-treader, I believe in God and truth
> And love; and as one just escaped from death
> Would bind himself in bands of friends to feel
> He lives indeed, so, I would lean on thee!
> Thou must be ever with me, most in gloom
> If such must come, but chiefly when I die,
> For I seem, dying, as one going in the dark

Jingle Esq." ("Robert Browning and the Poetry of the Age," *British Quarterly Review* 6 [1847]:496).

Robert Browning: His Poetry and His Audiences

> To fight a giant: but live thou for ever,
> And be to all what thou hast been to me!
> [*Pauline*, ll. 1020–28]

> Ah? you know?
> Well. I shall make a sorry soldier, Lucy!
> All knights begin their enterprise, we read,
> Under the best of auspices; 't is morn,
> The Lady girds his sword upon the Youth
> (He's always very young)—the trumpets sound,
> Cups pledge him, and, why, the King blesses him—
> You need not turn a page of the romance
> To learn the Dreadful Giant's fate. Indeed,
> We've the fair Lady here; but she apart,—
> A poor man, rarely having handled lance,
> And rather old, weary, and far from sure
> His Squires are not the Giant's friends. All's one:
> Let us go forth!
> [*Strafford*, II, ii, 282–95]

In *Pauline*, the poet addresses Shelley, the Sun-Treader, and excitedly asks him for his spiritual support in facing Death's giant. The enjambed blank verse, the sacrifice of exact scansion to the easy flow of thought, the pure, classical diction, and the argument by simile attest to Browning's Shelleyan inheritance. But in the moment of recapitulation and explanation provided by the parenthetical and rhythmically irregular "dying," there is early evidence of Browning's counterpointing the Shelleyan smoothness and turning the Shelleyan speed from the creation of mythic phantasmagoria to the reflection of psychological rumination. On the other hand, in *Strafford*'s finest poetic moment, where Strafford wearily addresses Lady Carlisle before going forth to do battle with Parliament and king, one can admire without apology Browning's careful cultivation of colloquial diction, phrasing, and rhythm. Strafford's quiet, conversational acknowledgment of his audience appears in the phrases "we read," "you need not turn the page," "We've the fair Lady here," and "Let us go forth." These, along with the confiding aside of "He's always very young" and the ironically regretful "why," underline at once Lady Carlisle's loyalty to and the king's distance from Strafford. In addition, the two passages differ greatly in tone: the storybook sentiments of *Pauline* are explicitly repudiated by Strafford as inadequate in the treacherous palace and parliamentary intrigue.

The play as a whole, however, does not display this exquisite rhetorical control, and in its confused scenes catches more the babble of voices in the struggle between king and Parliament than it does the predicament of a man of action caught in political turmoil. How Browning ever convinced Macready that the play was stageworthy is difficult to imagine, as the actor himself found when he coolly wrote about the play in his diary:

> In all the historical plays of Shakespeare, the great poet has only introduced such events as act on the individuals concerned, and of which they are themselves a part; the persons are all in direct relation to each other, and the facts are present to the audience. But in Browning's play we have a long scene of passion—upon what? A plan destroyed, by whom or for what we know not, and a parliament dissolved, which merely seems to inconvenience Strafford in his arrangements.[52]

The play lacked any comprehensible action and concentrated upon Browning's portrayal of Strafford's involuted psychology in such an operatic way as to make nonsense of the surrounding circumstances. Strafford interested Browning because the ill-fated lord seemed to be an ideal subject for portraying the great emotional stress anyone would have to undergo in struggling to maintain his sense of self while trying to reconcile the conflicting political demands made upon him by his audiences. The earl's attempt to make peace without allowing himself to compromise either his parliamentary sympathies or his loyalty to his king results not only in the self-effacing paralysis of his will but also in his becoming a scapegoat to be sacrificed in order to divert temporarily the social and political pressures undermining the established order.

Strangely enough, Browning supposes in the preface to *Strafford* that the "mere reader" will not require the historical detail he has provided for the spectator.[53] But this omission would inevitably have produced a play even less comprehensible and more static than the one we have; and Browning's refusal to supply the historical circumstances and events which bear upon Strafford's psychological struggle unquestionably led to the play's languishing upon the stage. William Bell Scott, who had gone to applaud the play after hearing from Leigh

---

[52] Macready's diary entry, April 28, 1837, *Diaries*, I, 390. For Browning's use of history, see Harold Orel, "Browning's Use of Historical Sources in *Strafford*," in *Six Studies in Nineteenth-Century English Literature and Thought*, ed. Harold Orel and George J. Worth, Humanistic Studies, no. 35 (Lawrence: University of Kansas, 1962), pp. 23–27.

[53] *Complete Works*, II, 9.

Hunt that it was to be performed recorded his disappointment in his *Autobiographic Notes*:

> My admiration for *Paracelsus* was so great I determined to go and to applaud, without rhyme or reason; and so I did, in the front of the pit. From the first scene it became plain that applause was not the order. The speakers had every one of them orations to deliver, and no action of any kind to perform. The scene changed, another door opened, and another half-dozen gentlemen entered as long-winded as the last. Still I kept applauding, with some few others, till the howling was too overpowering, and the disturbance so considerable that for a few minutes I lost my hat. The truth was that the talk was too much the same, and too much in quantity; it was no use continuing to hope something would turn up to surprise the house.[54]

The play failed, despite encouraging notices.[55]

In principle Strafford's story would seem to offer the materials for a great drama. He had returned from successfully administering Ireland as lord lieutenant and was created Earl of Strafford by Charles I. He was then sent, with insufficient funds, to conduct Archbishop Laud's war against the Scots, was forced to retreat in battle, and was recalled to London. Fearful of and furious with Strafford, Parliament put him on trial. But his defense was so impressive that the bill of attainder returned against him seemed an unconscionably weak and cowardly act on Parliament's part. Nevertheless, Strafford himself recommended that the king let him be executed in order to appease Parliament's fury, and he was. But the Strafford in Browning's play hardly seems an able administrator or a man of action. Instead, he despairs of the king's vacillating, proud, and vulnerable character and of his own ability to persuade the king to take the proper course of action. He dreams of reconciling the king and Parliament but cannot present his plan for doing so in a convincing or forceful manner. Moreover, in accordance with Browning's interest in "Action in Character rather than Character in Action,"[56] Strafford's defeat at the hands of the Scots takes place between the events of Acts II and III, and Strafford's defense occurs behind closed doors in Act III.

[54]William Bell Scott, *Autobiographic Notes of the Life of William Bell Scott*, ed. W. Minto, 2 vols. (London: James R. Osgood, 1892), I, 124–25.
[55]*Strafford*'s performances received sixteen notices, which was more than any work of Browning's was to receive again until *Men and Women*. See *Bibliography*, pp. 85–87, 96–99.
[56]*Complete Works*, II, 9.

Pauline, Paracelsus, Strafford, and Sordello

What one sees is Strafford's resolute blindness to his own potential political power, a blindness that he steadfastly maintains in order to shore up the existing hierarchy. And one also sees in Lady Carlisle's suppression of her love for Strafford how this psychology of determined self-effacement operates on a more intimate level. Strafford refuses to see himself as a king-maker:

> Did I make kings? set up, the first, a man
> To represent the multitude, receive
> All love in right of them—supplant them so,
> Until you love the man and not the king—
> The man with the mild voice and mournful eyes
> Which send me forth.
> [II, ii, 404–9]

The confusion of monarchical and representative government in this passage is emblematic of the country's in the period, and Strafford's concentration on his love for the man who is king points to his personal solution to England's political difficulties and to his sacrifice of himself to the ideal image of Charles I he has created. The general principle of this self-effacement in the love of another finds its most poetic expression in the complicated metaphor of "a flaw i' the diamond" that Lady Carlisle employs in at once denying herself the right to express her love for Strafford and in describing this act of self-suppression as it is taking place:

> Could you but know what 't is to bear, my friend,
> One image stamped within you, turning blank
> The else imperial brilliance of your mind,—
> A weakness, but most precious,—like a flaw
> I' the diamond, which should shape forth some sweet face
> Yet to create, and meanwhile treasured there
> Lest nature lose her gracious thought for ever!
> [II, ii, 347–53]

Her love for Strafford both prevents her from asserting her "imperial" self and declaring her affection and is also to be treasured as nature's "gracious thought."[57] So, in the intricate psychological economy of the play, she conceals her love for Strafford in hopes of preventing his

---

[57]See Herbert F. Tucker's analysis of the temporal implications of the "flaw i' the diamond" passage in *Browning's Beginnings*, pp. 140–41.

political bankruptcy by not complicating his personal accounting any further, while Strafford constantly sacrifices whatever popular capital he has with Parliament in order to prevent the king from losing face in his subjects' eyes. Another playwright might have treated the play's conflict in terms of class struggle or looked for contemporary political parallels,[58] but Browning consistently spiritualizes Strafford's struggle and sees it solely in terms of a conflict between loyalties to public and private audiences.

IV

Browning's *Sordello* was published by Edward Moxon in 1840. *Sordello* is a poem in six books, consisting of roughly six thousand lines written in highly enjambed and heavily caesuraed couplets. Browning had originally planned to write something like his earlier *Pauline*, which would portray the life and loves of a young poet coming into manhood and public notice. But in Venice, in 1838, against the contemporary background of rising Chartist agitation in England and nationalistic stirrings in a divided and occupied Italy, Browning decided to inscribe his version of the story of Sordello in the history of the medieval war between the Guelfs and Ghibellines. He did not depict Sordello as a poet-critic of tyranny, as Dante saw him in the *Purgatorio*,[59] but as an actor on the political stage—that is, as a figure caught between the forces of popular liberation headed by the pope, and the forces of oppression headed by the barons of the Austro-German empire. Indeed, insofar as it projected a modern, Victorian consciousness upon Sordello and his age, the poem adhered to an aesthetic which Arnold felt his own *Empedocles on Etna* had followed and which he repudiated in the preface to his *Poems* of 1853: "A true allegory of the state of one's mind in a representative history . . . is perhaps the highest thing that one can attempt in the way of poetry."[60] As he had already hinted at in *Strafford*, Browning sought to dramatize in his historical allegory how, despite its liberal republican senti-

---

[58]In 1837, Lower Canada attempted to secede from Upper Canada, and Lord Durham was sent out as military governor to deal with both the insurrection and parliamentary problems. One could see parallels between Strafford and Durham, especially since Durham resigned from his post in 1838. But *Strafford* was composed in advance of the events, for which see J. S. Mill, "Lord Durham's Return," *London and Westminster Review* 32 (1838):241–60.
[59]See C. M. Bowra, "Dante and Sordello," *Comparative Literature* 5 (1953):1–15.
[60]J. M. Ludlow, quoted by Arnold in *The Complete Prose Works of Matthew Arnold*, ed. R. H. Super, 11 vols. (Ann Arbor: University of Michigan Press, 1960–77), I, 8.

ments, the bourgeois class was at odds with its sympathies because of its political alliance with the aristocracy.[61] Sordello, a poet of republican sentiments, discovers to his horror that he is descended from the Ghibelline aristocracy,[62] and, after making this terrible discovery, dies of emotional strangulation. Further, although Browning sets *Sordello* in what he sees as a struggle between the oppressed and their tyrants, he tends to moralize and spiritualize class conflict by seeing Sordello's predicament not as the result of class struggle, but as the result of the inevitable contradictions between this world and the next and of his ambition to become a public, political leader who seeks to reconcile the various interests of a fragmented people.

[61]The political circumstances bearing upon this contradiction were the Reform Bill of 1832 on the one hand and on the other the rising Chartist agitation. Young men of the middle class like Browning, who had fathers that could vote and who were themselves likely to become voters, were still only heirs apparent to, rather than the possessors of, power. They tended to have republican and democratic sympathies, tempered by the implicit bourgeois assumption that individual liberties and property should be protected. Patrick Brantlinger astutely analyzes Elizabeth Barrett Browning's rejection of French socialism in her *Aurora Leigh* and Robert's thoroughgoing distrust of institutionalized power in his narrative poems and his plays as the product of what Brantlinger calls "liberal individualism," in *The Spirit of Reform: British Literature and Politics, 1832–1867* (Cambridge, Mass.: Harvard University Press, 1977), pp. 151–79. James McNally argues that "Browning appears to have held but four political ideas: the desirability of freedom, service to humanity, allegiance to England, the susceptibility of people to rule when their sense of awe is aroused. The last two beliefs tended to cancel out the first two in actual operation" ("Browning's Political Thought," *Queen's Quarterly* 77 [1970]:585). John Lucas seizes upon the central point of Browning's meditation on the poet's politics when he says that Browning was not so much interested in the "actual political content" of his poets' visions as in "whether they can and ought to be politically influential at all" ("Politics and the Poet's Role," in *Literature and Politics in the Nineteenth Century*, ed. John Lucas [London: Methuen, 1971], p. 29). And Trevor Lloyd provides a detailed political and parliamentary background for Browning's poems but leans too heavily on the sentiment of "The Lost Leader" and the betrayal felt by a leader's loyal followers as the touchstone of Browning's politics, in "Browning and Politics," in *Robert Browning: Writers and Their Background*, ed. Isobel Armstrong (London: G. Bell & Sons, 1974), pp. 142–67. But surprisingly enough none of these writers examines social class as either a central issue or a complicating factor in Browning's poetic politics. My analysis of *Sordello* and the plays depends in part on the class-consciousness implicit in them. For a detailed discrimination of classes in Browning's society, see Maisie Ward, *Robert Browning and His World* (London: Cassell, 1968–69).

[62]The importance of metaleptic discovery of one's origins in Victorian literature is discussed with reference to Daniel Deronda's discovery of his Jewishness in Cynthia Chase, "The Decomposition of Elephants: Double-Reading *Daniel Deronda*," *PMLA* 93 (1978):215–27. *Metalepsis* is the rhetorical substitution of effect for cause and of the present for the past, and affirms one's control of the past. Harold Bloom offers a less optimistic and more deterministic interpretation of metalepsis as the final maneuver of the poet seeking to evade a precursor's influence in *The Anxiety of Influence* (New York: Oxford University Press, 1973), chap. 6. Paul de Man sees metalepsis as crucial to what he calls the "textual allegory" and prophetic history, in his reading of Rousseau's *Social Contract* in *Allegories of Reading: Figural Language in Rousseau, Nietzsche, Rilke, and Proust* (New Haven: Yale University Press, 1979), pp. 274–77.

The critical events of Sordello's political campaign and disillusionment occur during three evenings. But Browning enormously complicates his narrative by introducing a motley showman in a booth, who tells the story of his diorama and of Sordello.[63] The showman's opening remarks to his audience (I, 1–73), his presentation of the historical background of the war between the Guelfs and Ghibellines informing an evening's street scene in Verona (I, 73–345), and his introduction of Sordello in conference with Palma that same night in Verona and invocation of Dante (I, 345–73) appear to promise the beginning of a conventional, if historically obscure, story. But this turns out to be just a preview. Instead of then telling us about Sordello's political career, the showman inserts the extensive story of Sordello's life as a young boy at Goito, his career as a poet in Mantua, his subsequent withdrawal from the world, and his resolve to return to it (I, 603–III, 221). This long flashback illuminates Sordello's character, telling us about his pride, idealism, and poetic nature, but it makes the confusing chronicle of late-medieval Italian politics all the less clear. After having wound his way back to Sordello's conversation with Palma in Verona and Sordello's decision to become the voice of the people (III, 221–607), Browning further obscures the narrative line by dropping both Sordello's story and his narrative mask to describe his personal decision to consider Sordello's political as well as poetical career (III, 607–1022). Following this extraordinary interruption, the last three books narrate Sordello's political career and its failure in a relatively straightforward manner—that is, if one allows for the clutter of historical detail, the picture of Ferrara ravaged by war, and the long, static explanatory monologues of Sordello, Palma, and Salinguerra, which are either delivered or paraphrased in this part of the poem.

If the complex narrative structure were the only difficulty presented to the reader, reading *Sordello* would be a relatively simple task. But in order to put us within Sordello's poetic consciousness, Browning presents the story as if it were taking place in a dream.[64] Historical details intrude oddly into the account of Sordello's youth at Goito; the difference between Browning's, the narrator's, and Sordello's consciousness is rarely clear; the subjective, cameralike changing of

---

[63]For a discussion of the relationship between *Sordello* and the invention and popularity of the diorama, see Daniel Stempel, "Browning's *Sordello*: The Art of the Makers-See," *PMLA* 80 (1965):554–61.

[64]For a discussion of *Sordello* as a kind of dioramic dream, see Stempel, "Browning's *Sordello*," pp. 555–56. Michael Mason examines Browning's "elusive oddness of manner" in "The Importance of *Sordello*," in *Major Victorian Poets*, pp. 134–42.

scenes without a controlling narrative voice—particularly evident in the surrealistic intrusion of Eglamor's funeral train upon Sordello's solitude at Goito (II, 169–295)—unsettle the reader; and the syntax and "para-grammar" of the poem often make it almost impossible to read for sense.[65]

Sordello is in a very self-conscious way a poem about itself and its poetics.[66] But Browning himself, in his 1863 preface to the poem, suggests that the "historical decoration was purposely of no more importance than a background requires; and my stress lay on the incidents in the development of a soul: little else is worth study."[67] There is some hint in this disclaimer and in some of his revisions to the text in 1863 that Browning was not only pointing to an aesthetic flaw in the work but also to the fact that his politics had subsequently become more conservative than those reflected in *Sordello*. Nevertheless, there is in the poem "a massive subordination of history to theme," which, Mason correctly suggests,[68] explains the narrative's imbalance in weighing thirty years at Goito against three days in the Italian political arena and underscores the division of the poem into two parts—the first three books, which consider Sordello as a poet, and the last three books, which consider him as a politician. This contrast of poetics and politics points to the poem's twofold argument: first, that the best, but least popular, poet makes audiences do the most work by making them poets and so leading them to God; and second, that the generous impulse of this poetic, which would make others see the world better than they do, will not produce a pragmatic politics.

The first part of *Sordello* makes a distinction between two types of poets, which are roughly equivalent to the first two types distinguished in the *Essay on Chatterton*—the first being the poet who, believing in the world and its aesthetic standards, imitates it in accord with its poetic conventions; and the second being the poet who, dissatisfied with merely imitating and pleasing the world, struggles to express the originality of his imagination. But prior to either of these conscious poetic states, there is, according to Browning's confused di-

---

[65]For a discussion of the problem of identifying the speaker, see Robert R. Columbus and Claudette Kemper, "Sordello and the Speaker: A Problem in Identity," *VP* 2 (1964):251–67. On Eglamor's funeral train, see Mason, "Importance of *Sordello*," p. 139. On the alteration of the reader's perspective through description, see Isobel Armstrong, "Browning and the 'Grotesque' Style," in *Major Victorian Poets*, pp. 99–105. *Paragrammar* is Mason's word, "Importance of *Sordello*," p. 135.

[66]See the analysis in Mason, "Importance of *Sordello*," pp. 125, 129–31.

[67]*Complete Works*, II, 123.

[68]Mason, "Importance of *Sordello*," p. 126.

alectic, a state of original, unconscious, prepoetic existence, which is really a condition of the youthful soul. Souls in their childish state do not distinguish between the conscious and the unconscious, and so invest the "lifeless thing with life from their own soul" (1, 491), acting as if the inanimate were alive and every living thing conscious. In the springtime of his life when he is in communion with nature, the young Sordello plays in his Edenic Goito:

> He o'er-festooning every interval,
> As the adventurous spider, making light
> Of distance, shoots her threads from depth to height,
> From barbican to battlement: so flung
> Fantasies forth and in their centre swung
> Our architect,—the breezy morning fresh
> Above, and merry,—all his waving mesh
> Laughing with lucid dew-drops rainbow-edged.
> [1, 664–71]

Sordello's youthful perception of the world is self-centered, at one with nature, and oblivious to any disjunction between his fantasies and reality. Moreover, this awakening consciousness, as in Wordsworth's "Immortality Ode," has a privileged vision of God:

> Up and down
> Runs arrowy fire, while earthly forms combine
> To throb the secret forth; a touch divine—
> And the scaled eyeball owns the mystic rod;
> Visibly through his garden walketh God.
> [1, 500–4]

The young Sordello has a clarity of vision that allows him to see God in the world around him.

Sordello's infancy has been unduly prolonged by his confinement at Goito, so that instead of learning about the mortal burden of time from others, he must learn from nature, from the "coarse brown rattling crane" of autumn, which was once summer's poppy (1, 708). Having been stripped of his glorious vision of the world, he becomes conscious of how his fantasies had given life to the world around him, and his self-conscious soul "proclaims each new revealment born a twin / With distinctest consciousness within" (1, 525–26). The self-conscious soul discovers poetry within itself and not in the world, and so it directs its homage not toward the world but toward itself: "So, homage, other souls direct / Without, turns inward" (I, 535–36). The imaginative instinct now becomes an object of consciousness itself; the beauty of its springtime perception of the world is revealed as the product of its dreaming. But even as this soul pays homage to itself, it also seeks the approval of others to feed its pride in itself; and, seeking to aggrandize himself, Sordello eventually seeks the plaudits of the crowd. He goes to Mantua, enters the poetry contest held by Palma's Court of Love, and wins it by singing one of Eglamor's songs. As Browning says in his *Essay on Chatterton*, "Genius almost invariably begins to develop itself by imitation. It has, in the short-sightedness of infancy, faith in the world: and its object is to compete with, or prove superior to, the world's already recognized idols, at their own performances and by their own methods."[69] His wishes dreamily fulfilled (compare Sordello's dream about Palma, I, 936–62), he withdraws to Goito.

There he meditates on his relationship to Eglamor, who is a different type of poet, and who, unlike Naddo, does not flatter his listeners and counsel other poets to build on the common "human heart" (II, 798). Eglamor instead loved art for its own sake and did not "care, take counsel for / Cold hearts, comfortless faces" (II, 221–22). As an example of the second type of poet, Eglamor ignored the crowd's demands and wrote to please himself. Following Eglamor's course and hoping to capitalize upon his superior poetic talent, Sordello rejects the conventional expectations of the crowd and seeks to work poetic language into a form suitable for expressing his private dreams:

> He left imagining, to try the stuff
> That held the imaged thing, and, let it writhe
> Never so fiercely, scarce allowed a tithe
> To reach the light—his Language.
> [II, 570–73]

But he fails to transmute pure perception into poetry:

> "Accomplished! Listen, Mantuans!" Fond essay!
> Piece after piece that armour broke away,
> Because perceptions whole, like that he sought
> To clothe, reject so pure a work of thought
> As language: thought may take perception's place

---
[69]*Browning's "Essay on Chatterton,"* ed. Smalley, p. 111.

> But hardly co-exist in any case,
> Being its mere presentment—of the whole
> By parts, the simultaneous and the sole
> By the successive and the many. Lacks
> The crowd perception? painfully it tacks
> Thought to thought, which Sordello, needing such,
> Has rent perception into: it's to clutch
> And reconstruct—his office to diffuse,
> Destroy: as hard, then, to obtain a Muse
> As to become Apollo.
>
> [II, 587–601]

This reminds one of Browning's preface to *Paracelsus* and his reliance upon the reader's "co-operating fancy, which supplying all chasms, shall collect the scattered lights into one constellation—a Lyre or a Crown."[70] To express his feelings and perceptions, Sordello must transform "the simultaneous and the sole" into "the successive and many" words of language; he must destroy the immediacy of experience in order to convey it to others. The audience, in turn, must "clutch / And reconstruct" from his words the original perception in all of its quicksilver essence. But since this view of poetry forces the audience to work as hard as the poet, Sordello's efforts go unappreciated. Sordello finds that being a poet who writes poetry for poetry's sake does not satisfy the demands of his egotistic pride, which needs the satisfaction of the Mantuans' recognition. Sordello has transformed himself, then, into the second type of poet Browning talks about in the *Essay on Chatterton* by seeking to create his own art and has discovered that he still must struggle with his pride and will in order to convert his poetry to a "moral end and aim."[71]

He becomes, then, the third type of poet, who, casting aside the world, addresses himself to an eternal ideal, a perfect audience which Palma calls the "out-soul" (III, 320). This poet seems to be the troubadour, who, seeking to eliminate all contaminating influence upon his art, imagines in the form of an ideal lady an ethereal audience, perfect and unapproachable, which he then assimilates within himself:

> The common sort, the crowd,
> Exist, perceive; with Being are endowed,
> However slight, distinct from what they See,

---

[70]*Complete Works*, I, 178.
[71]*Browning's "Essay on Chatterton,"* ed. Smalley, p. III.

> However bounded; Happiness must be
> To feed the first by gleanings from the last,
> Attain its qualities, and slow or fast
> Become what they behold; such peace-in-strife,
> By transmutation, is the Use of Life
> The Alien turning Native to the soul
> Or body—which instructs me; I am whole
> There and demand a Palma; had the world
> Been from my soul to a like distance hurled,
> 'T were Happiness to make it one with me:
> Whereas I must, ere I begin to Be,
> Include a world, in flesh, I comprehend
> In spirit now.
> [III, 159–74]

On a greater scale than the crowd that becomes what it beholds, the third type of poet, whom Browning calls the *Maker-see*, can both subordinate art to the comprehension of some supreme ideal and also incorporate that perfect other within, becoming in the process all but God.

Browning is advancing a theory of poetry that is tied to his thinking about our spiritual evolution. At present, he believes, we have no clear idea of our soul's offices and "simply experiment / Each on the other's power" (III, 837–38) in our efforts to discover our purpose here on earth:

> So occupied, then, are we: hitherto,
> At present, and a weary while to come,
> The office of ourselves,—nor blind nor dumb,
> And seeing somewhat of man's state,—has been,
> For the worst of us, to say they so have seen;
> For the better, what it was they saw; the best
> Impart the gift of seeing to the rest.
> [III, 862–68]

The least able of men describe what they have seen; the better able interpret this reality, saying what it is; and the best give the others the moral and spiritual framework to describe and interpret what they see. The best, the "Makers-see" (III, 928), are the true poets. One might, Browning suggests, erroneously believe that this task of making others see is equivalent to the creation of visionary escapism and impressionistic pictures of varying moods and so mistakenly praise, for example, the poet Plara, who grew up in a sunless, dirty town but hailed "in twice twelve sonnets, Tempe's dewy vale" (III, 900). In that way one would merely be subscribing to Naddo's view of the poet as the man who "tells his own joys and woes" (II, 796) and endorsing Lucio's poetry because it portrays "the mood itself" (III, 908).

Given this common view of poetry, it is no wonder that the crowd looks to men of action like Salinguerra instead of to poets like Sordello to govern their affairs:

> Not so unwisely does the crowd dispense
> On Salinguerras praise in preference
> To the Sordellos: men of action, these!
> Who, seeing just as little as you please,
> Yet turn that little to account,—engage
> With, do not gaze at,—carry on, a stage,
> The work o' the world, not merely make report
> The work existed ere their day! In short,
> When at some future no-time a brave band
> Sees, using what it sees, then shake my hand
> In heaven, my brother!
>
> [III, 917–27]

Browning seems to see himself as creating "a brave band" of revolutionary poets who would both see what to do and do it, in opposition to those poets who act as cultural historians by reporting the work of the past. One should note, however, that Browning supposes this brave band of poets will only exist "at some future no-time"; that is, when this group of poets appears, heaven will exist on earth. Consequently, he sees no early end to mankind's spiritual struggle. Nevertheless, he tells us that we should not yearn for a more conventional and easier poetry that would soothe our souls during the long trials ahead:

> Meanwhile where's the hurt
> Of keeping the Makers-see on the alert,
> At whose defection mortals stare aghast
> As though heaven's bounteous windows were slammed fast.
> Incontinent? Whereas all you, beneath,
> Should scowl at, bruise their lips and break their teeth
> Who ply the pullies, for neglecting you.
>
> [III, 927–33]

Browning suggests that those who deplore his poetry for slamming fast "heaven's bounteous windows" should instead be scowling at poetry that neglects the human condition and the lower classes, and he claims to be alerting poets to the necessity of writing about life instead of heavenly visions in order to reform the world.

Contained within the doctrine of the Makers-see, then, is a kind of Neoplatonic egalitarianism, which holds that the philosopher-poet should convey to those still in the cave what the world of light is like. And in the fifth book, when Sordello explains his political thinking to Salinguerra, Palma, and the people of Ferrara, he advances a view of poets and poetry which goes beyond Shelley's proposition in *A Defence of Poetry* that "poets are the unacknowledged legislators of the world."[72] He declares that, because of advances in poetry and because of the enlightened state of the people, he can give voice to their innermost thoughts, since he can rely upon their knowledge of history and so tap through language into the collective unconscious. At the heart of Sordello's argument is his belief that man's action is based upon thought and finally—if one can see it—upon God's will:[73]

> Thought is the soul of act, and, stage by stage,
> Soul is from body still to disengage
> As tending to a freedom which rejects
> Such help and incorporeally affects
> The world, producing deeds but not by deeds,
> Swaying, in others, frames itself exceeds,

---

[72]It is important to remember that Shelley's essay first appeared posthumously in *Essays, Letters from Abroad, Translations and Fragments*, ed. Mary Shelley, 2 vols. (London: Edward Moxon, 1840). While dated 1840, the essay actually appeared late in 1839 and could conceivably have influenced *Sordello*, though Browning was by then in the last phase of revision.

[73]Earl Hilton discusses Sordello's paralysis of will in terms of God's will and the poet's overly intellectual nature, in "Browning's *Sordello* as a Study of the Will," *PMLA* 69 (1954):1127–34. One does better, however, to see Sordello's problem as a struggle between a Christian and a Romantic sense of will. As Renato Poggioli says, "Within modern culture a romantic and Schopenhauerian concept is in the process of displacing the classical, Christian, Stoic, and humanistic concept of the will. In this newer concept the will is no longer a human faculty, but instead a vital energy and cosmic force; not a restraint or inhibition, but an impulse or an instinct. The hypothesis of will power as a conscious, rational, and autonomous faculty has thus yielded to the opposite hypothesis of an unconscious, irrational, and automatic will" (*The Theory of the Avant-Garde*, trans. Gerald Fitzgerald [Cambridge, Mass.: Harvard University Press, 1968], p. 189). From this perspective, one might say that Sordello hopes to make history's will act through his own but discovers he is not the man of action for his time and must instead seek to understand God's will outside his own.

> Assigning them the simpler tasks it used
> To patiently perform till Song produced
> Acts, by thoughts only, for the mind: divest
> Mind of e'en Thought, and, lo, God's unexpressed
> Will draws above us!
>
> [v, 567–77]

Neither Sordello nor Browning is at his best when speaking philosophically. But from this abstract argument one can extract the following: that just as the soul tends toward freedom from the body, so thought can now increasingly influence man's actions where only song could before. This general proposition leads to a historical corollary concerning the development of art. According to Browning's 1863 annotations to *Sordello*, first the epic poet appears, then the dramatist, and finally the "synthesist."[74] The epic poet, represented by Dante, teaches us the simplest of lessons about good and evil by making individual men and women into allegorical figures representing particular virtues and vices. The dramatist frees men and women from static allegory and shows them in action in the world, letting the audience judge the characters for itself. The synthesist plunges deeper into man's soul, at once giving "freer play" to man's "inmost life" and casting "external things away / And natures composite so decompose" (v, 617–19). And as Browning interpolates while revising the 1863 edition, "Why he writes *Sordello!*" (v, 620).

Sordello's argument, as Browning's interjection suggests, seems to have drifted into a self-conscious discussion of the author's poetic principles, instead of outlining the connections between the troubadour's poetics and his politics. Consequently Sordello's picture of a political praxis hidden within art seems not only strained but impossibly visionary. Just as Browning had claimed in his preface to *Strafford* that he could omit the historical details surrounding Strafford's predicament in his dramatic development because his audience would supply them, so Sordello argues that the poet will be able to get closer to the audience by adopting a practice of historical allusion that will allow him to get at the subtleties of soul:

> And how have you advanced! since evermore
> Yourselves effect what I was fain before
> Effect, what I supplied yourselves suggest,

---

[74]For the 1863 annotations, see *Browning: Poetical Works, 1833–1864*, ed. Ian Jack (London: Oxford University Press, 1970), pp. 270–77.

> What I leave bare yourselves can now invest.
> How we attain to talk as brothers talk,
> In half-words, call things by half-names, no balk
> From discontinuing old aids. To-day
> Takes in account the work of Yesterday:
> Has not the world a Past now, its adept
> Consults ere he dispense with or accept
> New aids? a single touch more may enhance,
> A touch less turn to insignificance
> Those structures' symmetry the past has strewed
> The world with, once so bare. Leave the mere rude
> Explicit details! 't is but brother's speech
> We need, speech where an accent's change gives each
> The other's soul—no speech to understand
> By former audience: need was then to expand,
> Expatiate—hardly were we brothers!
> [V, 621–39]

Sordello assumes that everyone now knows history and can follow complex historical analysis, so that he can talk "in half-words, call things by half-names" and have others understand his discourse because they share this common knowledge. Therefore, instead of being forced to reconstruct the past symmetrically, detail for detail and as a whole, one need only allude to it and by "an accent's change" convey one's understanding to the other. By speaking allusively, the poet can trace the development of the soul—both that of the people in general and his own in particular. As Tiburzio says, speaking to Luria, "A people is but the attempt of many / To rise to the completer life of one" (*Luria*, V, 299–300). So Sordello, as a Maker-see, hopes to be able to give through his life and discourse expression to the people's thoughts, to make them and Salinguerra see how the world should be divinely ordered, and to bring the Guelfs to power in Italy.

This poetics of historical revision also requires a transformed style. "An accent's change" refers not only to the stress placed upon certain aspects of the past but also to a change in the rhythm of the poet's speech. Browning's lines in *Sordello* are still enjambed as they were in *Pauline*, but the frequent early caesuras and the metrical inversions for emphasis—"Leave the," "speech where," "need was then to"—impede their easy movement. He intends his "accent's change" (on the level of meter, here his substitution of trochees for iambs) to indicate to his reader the natural intonation of the speaker's voice, as he had done for Macready in *Strafford*. By interjecting exclamations and by mixing high and colloquial diction, he tries to speak his "brother's speech." This is hardly an exhaustive analysis of either the redemptive strategy of historical allusion that Browning has in mind or the poem's stylistic difficulties, particularly those of syntax,[75] but it does point to the chief aim of Browning's new style in *Sordello*: the inversions, caesuras, the parenthetical exclamations, and the colloquial diction act as counterpoint to the restrictions of the meter and the couplet rhyme, and attempt to work the almost impossible feat of producing in couplets the effect of conversation or prose.

This revolutionary poetic and its accompanying poetic revolution are undercut not rhetorically but dramatically. Palma tells Sordello that he is not an orphan but the son of Ghibelline parents, Retrude and Salinguerra. Then Salinguerra offers him the leadership of the Ghibellines. In this way Sordello discovers that his personal and natural interests are in conflict with his liberal sentiment and his political poetics. His discovery paralyzes him. He does manage to throw away the Ghibelline badge Salinguerra has given him. But the effort costs him his life, because he cannot fully reconcile his political feelings with his newly discovered inheritance, nor the Ghibelline aristocracy with the merits of the Guelf cause. Sordello's naive faith in human understanding and his ignorance of mankind's selfish interests finally undo both him and his rhetoric; and, dying of emotional shock, he can only turn toward God like a spent swimmer who "spies / Help from above in his extreme despair" (VI, 616–17).[76] And here Sordello's story has been completed, Browning rounding out the poem's frame by returning to his showman, who asks his audience for their approval of what they have seen and heard.

V

In a deep way *Sordello*'s theory of art anticipates Victor Shklovsky's view of art's purpose in "Art as Technique": "The purpose of art is to

---

[75] On the syntax of *Sordello*, see Armstrong, "Browning and the 'Grotesque' Style," pp. 99–105; Isobel Armstrong, *Language as Living Form in Nineteenth-Century Poetry* (Sussex, England: Harvester Press; Totowa, N.J.: Barnes & Noble, 1982), pp. 141–71; and Park Honan, "Browning's Poetic Laboratory: The Uses of *Sordello*," *MP* 56 (1959):162–66. On the temporal implications of *Sordello*'s syntax, see Tucker, *Browning's Beginnings*, pp. 16–29, 84–119.

[76] In his letter to Elizabeth of December 21, 1845, Browning offers this translation and slight condensation of Dante's *Purgatorio*, V, 52–57, as being "just my Sordello's story": "And sinners were we to the extreme hour; / Then, light from heaven fell, making us aware, / So that, repenting us and pardoned, out / Of life we passed to God, at peace with Him / Who fills the heart with yearning Him to see" (*Letters*, I, 336).

impart the sensation of things as they are perceived and not as they are known. The technique of art is to make objects 'unfamiliar,' to make forms difficult, to increase the difficulty and length of perception because the process of perception is an aesthetic end in itself and must be prolonged."[77] And so, Shklovsky holds, "The language of poetry is, then, a difficult, roughened, impeded language."[78] To be sure, Browning's aesthetic has affective motivations, in its desire to make poets of his audience, that Shklovsky's modern, formalist poetics would reject as a subjugation of the play of the forms. Nevertheless, Browning overlays the past with both its own past and the compositional and narrative presents; he confuses voices; he puts great pressure on his method of decomposition by writing in couplets; and he relies on names as an allusive mechanism, even though events, objects, and costumes are much easier to grasp as archeological evidence. Indeed, Browning creates the closest thing in poetry to Abel Gance's "poly-vision," in his film *Bonaparte* (1925–71), superimposing image upon image, event upon event, voice upon voice, the creation and revision upon historical representation.[79] As Elizabeth later said, "The principle of association is too subtly in movement throughout it—so that *while* you are going straight forward you go at the same time round & round, until the progress involved in the motion is lost sight of by the lookers on."[80] *Sordello* was a problematic experiment that at once expected too much of its Victorian readers and delivered too little in poetic pleasure, but Browning painfully learned from the response of others to the poem that his poetry was not necessarily his "brother's speech." Only later, in *The Ring and the Book*, was he to find a form more appropriate for the superimposition of voices and for the exploration of the connections between past and present experience.

To measure the modernity of Browning's *Sordello* more exactly, one should look for a moment at another problematic poetic project, Ezra Pound's *Cantos*. When Pound found himself thinking that his imagist theory of poetry perhaps prevented him from writing an epic, as he wanted to do, he turned to *Sordello* as a model to react against.[81] The

[77]Victor Shklovsky, "Art as Technique," in *Russian Formalist Criticism: Four Essays*, trans. Lee T. Lemon and Marion J. Reis (Lincoln: University of Nebraska Press, 1965), p. 12.
[78]Ibid., p. 22.
[79]See Steven B. Kramer and James M. Welsh, *Abel Gance* (Boston: Twayne, 1978).
[80]Elizabeth to Robert, December 21, 1845, *Letters*, I, 342.
[81]See the discussion of the beginning of Pound's *Cantos* and Browning's *Sordello* in Ronald Bush, *The Genesis of Ezra Pound's "Cantos"* (Princeton: Princeton University Press, 1976), p. 75.

"Three Cantos," which he began to publish in *Poetry* in June 1917, demonstrates that Pound grounded *The Cantos* in a method and a style opposed to those of Browning's poem:

> Hang it all, there can be but one *Sordello*!
> But say I want to, say I take your whole bag of tricks,
> Let in your quirks and tweeks, and say the thing's an art-form,
> Your *Sordello*, and that the modern world
> Needs such a rag-bag to stuff all its thoughts in;
> Say that I dump my catch, shiny silvery
> As fresh sardines flapping and slipping on the marginal cobbles?
> (I stand before the booth, the speech; but the truth
> Is inside this discourse—this booth is full of the marrow of Wisdom.)
> Give up th' intaglio method.[82]

Poetry for Pound is the impression of history on the present; it is subjective, and cannot be "objective" poetry. He later points to Sordello's font at Goito (I, 410–42), "some two centuries outside the picture" (l. 29) as proof of his position. So he urges both Browning and himself to give up "th' intaglio method" of historical representation. Now an intaglio is a design created by cutting a figure into stone, so that the figure is embedded in its background; while, in contrast, a cameo is a design created by raising a figure from its background, by removing the stone so that the figure stands out. In opposition to Browning's objective, intaglio history of figures set in their backgrounds, Pound prefers a subjective, free-floating, cameo history of figures. Extending the shorthand, used in *Sordello*, of having Charlemagne personify the Ghibellines' strength, of having Hildebrand (Gregory VII), in contrast, stand for the Guelfs' knowledge (V, 130–205), and of having the passage from the poetical to the political world summed up in the line "Ferrara's reached, Goito's left behind," (V, 239), there is in *The Cantos*: "Then Actaeon: Vidal, / Vidal" (IV, 52–53) and "Between KUNG and ELEUSIS" (LII, 38), where names stand for entire stories and systems of belief.[83]

Pound also objects to Browning's narrative method, to his introduction of the motley showman in the booth to tell the story of Sordello.

---

[82] Ezra Pound, "Three Cantos" (ll. 1–10), *Poetry* 10 (1917):113. *The Cantos of Ezra Pound*. Copyright © 1934, 1962 by Ezra Pound. Reprinted by permission of New Directions Publishing Corporation and Faber & Faber Ltd. Jacob Korg takes Pound's homage too literally and finds Browning's view of history as modern as Pound's, in "The Music of Lost Dynasties: Browning, Pound, and History," *ELH* 39 (1972):420–40.

[83] Ezra Pound, *The Cantos* (New York: New Directions, 1972), pp. 14, 258.

Pauline, Paracelsus, Strafford, and *Sordello*

For Pound "the truth / Is inside the discourse," not in its being given to someone else to speak; and so he thinks that Browning, in his attempt to present his version of Sordello's story as objective history, has only succeeded in evading the full significance of his subjective experience of Sordello's life:

> You had your business
> To set out so much thought, so much emotion;
> To paint, more real than any dead Sordello,
> The half or third of your intensest life
> And call that third *Sordello*;
> And you'll say, "No, not your life,
> He never showed himself."
> Is't worth the evasion, what were the use
> Of setting figures up and breathing life upon them,
> Were't not *our* life, your life, my life extended?
> [1, 32–41][84]

By marvelously evoking the ambiguity and inconsistency of pronomial reference in *Sordello*, Pound questions Browning's attempt to hide himself behind a mask. He senses in Browning's adoption of another voice to narrate Sordello's story both a deep distrust of subjective expression and an implicit belief in objective truth. So, while he admires Browning's "new form, the meditative, / Semi-dramatic, semi-epic story" (1, 100–101),[85] Pound feels nevertheless that Browning's form answers to the needs of another age and subordinates individual experience to a perverse historical impersonality, instead of conveying directly Browning's experience in reading and writing about Sordello.

Unlike Pound, who saw the expression of his picture of *paideuma* as poetry's end, Browning tried to show in *Sordello* how every man's soul tends toward God. Without fully realizing what he was doing, he wrote an avante-garde poem, a poem, which, because it is both more and less thematic than he had intended, is at once his best and his worst, and so is a poem that is more important to the history of English poetry than has been acknowledged or recognized. But while one has to read *Sordello* as a modernist poem to begin to account for it adequately, Browning's own misreading of *Sordello*—his view that "the soul's development" is its sole significance—not only vitiates any modernist claims upon the poem (since its forms are intended to be

---

[84]Pound, "Three Cantos," pp. 114–15.
[85]Ibid., p. 117.

subordinate to their thematic motivations) but also guaranteed his making Sordello's inability to come to terms with his audiences his own failure as well. Nevertheless, one can see *Sordello* as a stage in Browning's development that is both fiendishly difficult to interpret and historically fascinating in itself, and yet one that sheds much light upon Browning's vision of his relationships with his audiences and explains, in part, the direction of his future career.

2

Bells and Pomegranates

> Or from Browning some "Pomegranate," which cut deep down the middle,
> Shows a heart within blood-tinctured, or a veined humanity.
> —Elizabeth Barrett, "Lady Geraldine's Courtship"

Mrs. Bridell-Fox, daughter of W. J. Fox, provides us with a glimpse of Browning before 1840 in this charming recollection:

> Mr. Browning entered the little drawing-room, with a quick light step; and on hearing from me that my father was out, and in fact that nobody was at home except myself, he said: "It's my birthday today; I'll wait till they come in," and sitting down to the piano, he added: "If it won't disturb you, I'll play till they do." And as he turned to the instrument, the bells of some neighbouring church suddenly burst out with a frantic merry peal. It seemed to my childish fancy, as if in response to the remark that it was his birthday. He was then slim and dark, and very handsome; and—may I hint it—just a trifle of a dandy, addicted to lemon-coloured kid gloves and such things: quite "the glass of fashion and the mould of form."[1]

The "quick light step," the "lemon-coloured kid gloves," and the youthful prepossession in saying "It's my birthday today; I'll wait till they come in"—all sketch a remarkably suggestive portrait. This young poet, full of himself and happy with the world, also appears in his swaggering letters to Macready and Fox, his pretentious prefaces to *Pauline* and *Paracelsus*, and his celebration of his birthday in *Sordello*: "My own month came; / 'T was a sunrise of blossoming and May" (II, 296–97). But nowhere else does one quite catch the loneli-

---

[1] Eliza F. Bridell-Fox, "Robert Browning," *Argosy* 19 (1890):112.

ness of Browning's cheerful self-admiration as here in a young girl's imagining the ringing church bells merrily observing his birthday.

Browning had good reason to be cheerful and confident in the late 1930s after the publication of *Paracelsus* and the appearance of *Strafford* upon the stage and in print. He was admitted by the cognoscenti to be a coming force in poetry and had been hailed by Forster as a new dramatic genius.[2] Macready, hearing of the imminence of *Sordello*'s publication and of Browning's high hopes for it, feared that the failure of *Strafford*, which he felt to be highly probable, would be his own undoing but would not affect Browning's reputation.[3] And though *Strafford* was not a success at the box office, it received good reviews, which were partially late acknowledgments of *Paracelsus* and partially expressions of hope that the theater had found a new playwright capable of writing plays that were both popular and also respectable as literature. Even the *Edinburgh Review*, the arbiter of conservative intellectual taste, noticed *Strafford* in a long article.[4]

But the *Edinburgh Review* did not feel compelled to notice his work again until 1864, when it reviewed the 1863 edition of his works together with *Dramatis Personae*.[5] The reason he remained so little read for so long was *Sordello*. As the repeated conversations, bewildered witticisms in private diaries, and remarks in letters show, the readers of modern, sophisticated poetry, who numbered a few hundred in early Victorian England and whose attention was necessary before any popular success of a serious poet was possible, simply couldn't understand the poem.[6] The value of his literary stock plunged overnight and was not to regain its former level for a quarter of a century. The desertion of his readership and Macready's understandable reluctance to stage either *King Victor and King Charles* or *The Return of the Druses* left Browning at a loss as to what to do. An early indication of

[2][John Forster], "Evidences of a New Genius for Dramatic Poetry," *New Monthly Magazine* 46 (1836):289–308.

[3]Macready's diary entry of April 28, 1837, *The Diaries of William Charles Macready, 1833–1851*, ed. William Toynbee, 2 vols. (New York: G. P. Putnam's Sons, 1912), I, 290.

[4][Herman Merivale], review of Browning's *Strafford*, *Edinburgh Review* 65 (1837):132–51.

[5][William Stigand], *Edinburgh Review* 120 (1864):537–65.

[6]The number of readers of new, modern poetry by unestablished poets may be estimated by the sale of Tennyson's *Poems* of 1833. Moxon printed eight hundred copies and had sold only three hundred by the spring of 1835 (Orr, *Life and Letters*, p. 69). On Moxon and the publishing of poetry in the period, see Harold G. Merriam, *Edward Maxon: Publisher of Poets*, Columbia University Studies in English and Comparative Literature, no. 137 (New York: Columbia University Press, 1939).

his trouble is found in his response to his closest friend, Alfred Domett, who had complained about the difficulty of *Sordello*:

> The one point that wants correcting is where you surmise that I am "difficult on system." No really—the fact is I live by myself, write with no better company, and forget that the "lovers" you mention are part and parcel of that self, and their choosing to comprehend *my* comprehensions are but indifferent testimony to their value.[7]

His "lovers"—his immediate family, relatives, and friends—give him little idea of the intellectual attainment of the Victorian common reader, much less the cultivated men of Oxford and Cambridge. As he said in a later letter to Domett, "At present, I don't know if I stand on head or heels: what men require, I don't know—and of what they are in possession know nearly as little."[8] The isolation of his upbringing, the eccentricity of his education, and the religious foundation of his pride set him apart from his readers both intellectually and socially and made the imaginative chasm between his poetry and his readers' expectations all the more difficult to bridge.

After *Sordello* failed to win him readers, Browning's publisher, Edward Moxon, persuaded him to issue his poetry in pamphlet publications to cut costs. The eight numbers of *Bells and Pomegranates* (1841–46) were printed on cheap paper in double columns; they cost sixpence at first but gradually rose in price to two shillings sixpence by the final number.[9] Moxon's sedate attempt to attract a popular audience imitated the serial publication of Dickens's *Pickwick Papers* (1836) without indulging in the theatrical and financially absurd gesture of Richard Hengist Horne's *Orion* (1841), called the "farthing epic" for

---

[7] Letter ca. March 1840, *Robert Browning and Alfred Domett*, ed. Frederic G. Kenyon (London: Smith, Elder, 1906), pp. 28–29.

[8] Letter of May 22, 1842, *Robert Browning and Alfred Domett*, pp. 35–36. Compare Robert's comment in his letter to Elizabeth of March 22, 1846: "There is no 'côterie' of which I can, by any extension of the word, form a part" (*Letters*, I, 551). Thomas R. Lounsbury has said, "There are many other kinds of education besides that furnished by the university, and for some persons far better. For Browning I doubt if any would have been as good, and his failure to receive it will, it is feared, have in the long run a damaging effect upon his reputation. His writings show throughout the lack of that final result of thorough training, the ability of the communicator of ideas to put himself in the position of the recipient" (*The Early Literary Career of Robert Browning* [New York: Charles Scribner's Sons, 1911], p. 20.

[9] Richard D. Altick notes that penny number trash and cheap periodicals in the 1830s and 1840s "took the form, usually, of an eight-page leaflet, large octavo size, printed in double columns in eye-straining types, minion or brevier" (*The English Common Reader* [Chicago: University of Chicago Press, 1957], p. 292.

being sold at that price. As the preface to the first of the series, *Pippa Passes*, implies, Browning was courting popular success in preparation for returning to the stage. He hoped that *Bells and Pomegranates* would gain him an audience that would, in turn, demand the theatrical production of his work:

> Two or three years ago I wrote a Play, about which the chief matter I much care to recollect at present is, that a Pit-full of goodnatured people applauded it: ever since, I have been desirous of doing something in the same way that should better reward their attention. What follows, I mean for the first of a series of Dramatical Pieces, to come out at intervals, and I amuse myself by fancying that the cheap mode in which they appear will for once help me to a sort of Pit-audience again.[10]

His theatrical aspirations are apparent in the number of plays and closet dramas in *Bells and Pomegranates*. *King Victor and King Charles* (1841), *The Return of the Druses* (1842), and *A Blot in the 'Scutcheon* (1843) were written for Macready, but only the last was accepted for performance. *Colombe's Birthday* (1844) was commissioned in 1843 by the newly married Mr. and Mrs. Charles Kean. But they found it not to their liking, and the play was not produced until Helen Faucit presented it at The Haymarket in 1853. This unpromising career as a would-be playwright effectively ended with the passage of the Theater Reform Act of 1843, which removed the monopoly on legitimate drama held by Covent Garden, Drury Lane, and The Haymarket, put those theaters into direct competition with the music halls, and thus made it financially impossible for producers to offer substantial commissions to playwrights for new work.[11] This made *Luria* (1846) and *A Soul's Tragedy* (1846), the last plays of the series, little more than exercises in closet drama that, when compared to the brilliant flashes of *Pippa Passes* (1841), attest to the nervous exhaustion of his theatrical dreams.

The audience Browning wanted for *Bells and Pomegranates* did not materialize. The reviewers were unsure at first of what Browning intended by his series and were therefore reluctant to discuss the issues piecemeal. Without critical notices, there was little hope of attracting

---

[10]*Complete Works*, III, 7.

[11]See Fred C. Thomson, "A Crisis in Early Victorian Drama: John Westland Marston," *VS* 9 (1966):75–82. Charles Kean, for example, had offered Browning five hundred pounds for an acceptable play; see Robert's letter to Elizabeth of September, 13, 1845, *Letters*, I, 194.

Bells and Pomegranates

a general audience, and none of the issues went into a second edition.[12] Emblematic of his reviewers' bewilderment with Browning's enterprise and his poetry was the *Athenaeum*'s wondering about the significance and purpose of the series' title: "It is reasonable to suppose Mr. Browning knows why, but certainly we have not yet found out—indeed we 'give it up.'"[13] Even Elizabeth Barrett, who caught the allusion to the rabbi's garment in Exodus 28:33–34, could not understand Browning's esoteric symbolism.[14] In answer to her question about it, he explained, "The Rabbis make Bells & Pomegranates symbolical of Pleasure and Profit, the Gay & the Grave, the Poetry & the Prose, Singing and Sermonizing—such a mixture of effects as in the original hour (that is quarter of an hour) of confidence & creation."[15] Given such hermeticism, it is no wonder that the *Athenaeum*'s reviewer remarked on the second issue of *Bells and Pomegranates* as follows: "We have predicted that Mr. Browning's audience would be limited, and, inasmuch as he has doubled the price of admission, we are led to conclude that our prediction has been fulfilled."[16] And there seems little coincidence that the most enduring and endearing work of the series, the songs and short poems of the third and seventh numbers—*Dramatic Lyrics* (1842) and *Dramatic Romances and Lyrics* (1845)—were printed on the advice of Moxon "for popularity's sake."[17] But before examining the intricate manipulations of character and audience in the early lyrics and monologues, it will help to exhume the plays briefly to see how Browning's ideas about character and audience were portrayed on their broad, rough canvases.

I

Browning's association with the English stage is generally viewed as a disappointing blind alley in his career, demonstrating how his attempt to display "Action in Character rather than Character in Ac-

---

[12]Kathleen Tillotson discusses the contemporary reviewers' criticism of and resistance to the serial publication of novels in *Novels of the Eighteen-Forties* (Oxford: Clarendon Press, 1954), p. 39. Moxon printed some copies of *A Blot in the 'Scutcheon* with "second edition" on the title page when he bound the leftover numbers of *Bells and Pomegranates* into one volume in 1846; see *Bibliography*, p. 7.

[13]*Athenaeum*, December 11, 1841, p. 952.

[14]See her letter to Robert, October 17, 1845, *Letters*, I, 239.

[15]Robert to Elizabeth, October 18, 1845, *Letters*, I, 241.

[16]*Athenaeum*, April 30, 1842, p. 376; see also *Gentleman's Magazine*, August 1843, p. 168.

[17]Browning to Domett, May 22, 1842, *Robert Browning and Alfred Domett*, ed. Kenyon, p. 36.

tion," as he says in the preface to *Strafford*, was fatal to the clear plot necessary for a successful stage production but made his dramatic monologues possible.[18] A common theme runs throughout the plays. All concern liberal political and moral sentiment and usually present a tragic view of such sentiment. These tragedies of liberal sentiment are based on the protagonist's feeling that domestic and religious love should be able to solve intricate political and social problems, and they portray the hero's realization that a fundamental opposition exists between his aristocratic inheritance and his desire to act in sympathy with the common man.

In *The Poetry of Experience*, Robert Langbaum suggests that

> nineteenth-century readers read Shakespeare as they read the literature of their own time. They read him not as drama in the traditional Aristotelian sense, not in other words as a literature of external action in which the events derive meaning from their relation to a publicly acknowledged morality, but as literature of experience, in which the events have meaning inasmuch as they provide the central character with an occasion for experience—for self-expression and self-discovery.[19]

Langbaum connects this new way of reading with the decline of poetic drama and the rise of the dramatic monologue. But while this change in reading did occur, and occurred among avant-garde writers like Coleridge, Shelley, and Browning quite early, it did not appear as a widespread phenomenon among general readers until the 1880s and the 1890s and cannot be considered the prevailing way of reading until the early decades of the twentieth century. The greater popularity of Scott, Dickens, and Austen relative to the Brontës in the novel, and of Bulwer-Lytton relative to Browning on the stage, certainly attests to the greater importance that "publicly acknowledged morality" had in relation to "self-expression and self-discovery" for early Victorian readers.

Moreover, the difference in popularity did not stem so much from the writers' emphasis upon either morality or self-expression (though

---

[18]Consider also Browning's comments on *Luria* in a letter to Elizabeth of January 11, 1846: "It is all in long speeches—the *action, proper,* is in them—they are no descriptions, or amplifications—but here . . in a drama of this kind, all the *events*, (and interest), take place in the *minds* of the actors" (*Letters*, 1, 381). On the dramas as preparation for the dramatic monologues, see H. B. Charlton, "Browning as Dramatist," *Bulletin of the John Rylands Library* 23 (1939):33–67.

[19]*The Poetry of Experience: The Dramatic Monologue in Modern Literary Tradition* (New York: Random House, 1957), p. 160.

this was certainly a contributing factor) but more from a difference in their ideas of character. In contrast to the predictable characters created by Scott, Dickens, and Austen and firmly set in their social place, the protagonists of Browning's plays are too unsure of their characters or their proper social roles to act in any predictable fashion. A figure such as Darcy, in *Pride and Prejudice*, has a firm sense of his social status and acts in certain ways which both reveal his character and manifest his awareness that his character is invested in a social role. We may, at first, like Elizabeth Bennet, see only part of Darcy's character, but he will always act consistently, and we and Elizabeth will eventually recognize his sterling qualities. There is little to add to this, since we still base our notion of consistent character upon predictable action, except to say that the nineteenth-century audience did not view a character's social standing and financial circumstances as accidental features. In Bulwer-Lytton's *Money* (1840), for example, the hero cannot marry the gentle heroine until his sound financial footing and his standing as a gentleman are confirmed. The hero has only to act consistently in accordance with the standards of his elevated class and to be careful not to assume the privileges of a gentleman before having his status confirmed. A gentleman could run up debts with tradesmen or marry in expectation of an inheritance, but a would-be gentleman never. So when Browning sought to dramatize in *A Blot in the 'Scutcheon* the impetuous passion of Mertoun by having him risk visiting his betrothed surreptitiously before the wedding as he had done before his engagement, the audience felt Mertoun's action ridiculous and his passion inappropriate to his rank. The play was laughed at in rehearsal, cut by the lord chamberlain, hooted at on stage, and occasioned Browning's final quarrel with Macready.[20]

Measured against a standard of coherent dramatic action, Browning's plays fail, as H. B. Charlton has noted, because the main character's concern for self-realization is at odds with his relations with his fellow man.[21] But when measured on a scale of dramatic tone, Browning's heroes seem trapped by the weight of historical circum-

[20] See Joseph W. Reed, Jr., "Browning and Macready: The Final Quarrel," *PMLA* 75 (1960):597–603.
[21] "Browning as Dramatist," p. 43. Reviewing *Tragedies and Other Plays*, the first volume of the 1863 collection of Browning's works, an anonymous critic said, "But it is true, and it is a pity, that we have no *audiences*—such, at least, as encourage the poet and help form the actor" ("Robert Browning's Poems," *Saturday Review* 16 [1863]:223). See also Mary Rose Sullivan's analysis of the plays as studies in how evasiveness leads to moral degeneration, "Browning's Plays: Prologue to *Men and Women*," *Browning Institute Studies* 3 (1975):17–39.

stances.²² His plays waver between sentimentality and irony and unsuccessfully attempt to achieve a balance between these attitudes. These, then, are the sentimental and ironic poles of interpreting Browning's dramas: on the one hand, we have the view of the plays as internal, psychological dramas having little to do with external events; and on the other we have the view of them as models of historical and psychological determinism.

Pippa Passes, Luria, and *A Soul's Tragedy* paint in black and white the moral opposition between the contending forces of history in much the same way as *Sordello* does: the good masses are in conflict with the bad aristocracy; political freedom struggles against political oppression. If instead of the abstract liberalism in these works Browning had substituted family loyalty, one would have the Hegelian formula for tragedy that is exemplified by Sophocles' *Antigone*: a conflict of the law and authority of the state with family custom.²³ In early nineteenth-century drama this formula fits perfectly Sheridan Knowles's *Virginius*: Virginius kills his daughter to protect her from being ravished by the tyrant. But in Browning's plays (and this is the key to understanding the vacillation of their heroes) the protagonist's family is either directly or indirectly implicated in the aristocratic oppression. The hero is torn between his love for mankind and his love for his own family. Thomas Noon Talfourd's *Ion* (1836), which undoubtedly influenced the spirit of most of Browning's plays, is the chief illustration of this theme in Victorian theater. In the play, the people of Argos are cursed by a plague which a messenger from Apollo says will be lifted only after the line of the tyrant, Adrastus, has been eradicated. Ion pledges to kill Adrastus in the name of the people, but when he discovers he is Adrastus's long-lost son, he refrains from murdering his father, and one of his fellow conspirators must assassinate the king instead. Ion then becomes king, but only in order to commit suicide and thereby fulfill his vow on behalf of the people of Argos.

By killing himself, Ion must also forgo the pleasure of marrying his beloved Clemanthe, a self-denial and sexual pathos which is common in tragedies of liberal sentiment and which suggests an audience of young single men embarking on their careers, who hold liberal politi-

---

²²See Arthur DuBois, "Robert Browning, Dramatist," *SP* 33 (1936):652.
²³G. W. F. Hegel, *Aesthetics: Lectures on Fine Art*, trans. T. M. Knox, 2 vols. (Oxford: Clarendon Press, 1975), II, 1217–18.

cal views despite their families' bourgeois backgrounds and their own good prospects. A Marxist critic like Georg Lukács might argue that these tragedies of liberal sentiment signaled the beginning of the bourgeois individual's acquiescence in the repression stemming from Britain's nascent capitalist economy and expressed his growing awareness, after the Reform Bill of 1832, of his new counterrevolutionary role in British politics. But despite the accuracy of such a political analysis, it seems more likely that the sexual reticence of Browning's and Scott's heroes—as opposed to, say, Fielding's Tom Jones—indicates a change in the bourgeois male image, created by the gradual liberation of women from male dominance and by the restrictive social etiquette men had to observe in a woman's presence—the cultural current of which Dr. Bowdler was perhaps the most extreme expression. The quiet revolution of women in nineteenth-century England is well represented in many ways by Elizabeth Barrett's escape from her father's domestic tyranny. For on the level of sexual politics, Hegel's master/slave relationship can be read as an allegory of man and woman, father and daughter, husband and wife.

Like Talfourd's *Ion*, Browning's tragedies are tragedies of liberal sentiment. Strafford discovers himself trapped between Parliament and the king; Djabal, in *The Return of the Druses*, is caught between the rebellious Druses and the ruling knights of Rhodes; Luria must deal with his beloved Domizia's desire to revenge the Florentines' destruction of her family's noble house and his own love for the free, if untrusting, men of Florence; and Chiappino, in *A Soul's Tragedy*, oscillates between his revolutionary hopes for the people of Faenza and his aristocratic ambitions. One should also recall Browning's treatment of this theme in *Sordello* and Sordello's anguish upon discovering himself a member by blood of the aristocratic Ghibellines when he wishes to be a republican Guelf. But unlike Ion, who makes himself an aristocratic martyr for the people, Browning's protagonists usually die by a kind of emotional asphyxiation when they discover that the language they speak cannot possibly reconcile the conflict between the separate audiences they must face and realize, like Sordello, that there is no "brother's speech" which will satisfy everyone's demands. Sordello, Strafford, Luria, Mertoun, and Djabal all die because in some sense they can say nothing more. Mertoun in *A Blot in the 'Scutcheon*, for example, is caught beneath Mildred's window at night by Thorold Tresham, her brother, who refuses to hear him explain himself:

Robert Browning: His Poetry and His Audiences

> Not one word on your life!
> Be sure that I will strangle in your throat
> The least word that informs to me how you live
> And yet seem what you seem!
>
> [III, i, 73–76]

Mertoun dies when he refuses to defend himself with his sword and in despair lets Tresham kill him. The only audience he has under these circumstances is God:

> And what procures a man the right to speak
> In his defence before his fellow man,
> But—I suppose—the thought that presently
> He may have leave to speak before his God
> His whole defence?
>
> [III, i, 95–99]

Trapped between the demands of private feeling and public honor, he can finally only turn to God.

That God is the last and only true audience is a commonplace in Browning's plays. The most famous, and most discussed, instance occurs in the first vignette of *Pippa Passes*. Sebald and Ottima, having just killed Ottima's husband, are reveling in their bloody lust, when Pippa sings her little song, ending "God's in his heaven— / All's right with the world" (I, 227–28). This song has an incredible effect upon the lovers: first Sebald and then Ottima commit suicide in a fit of recrimination and remorse, both dying with God's name on their lips. What makes this denouement so difficult to accept and to interpret is that these remorseful suicides seem as much an extension of selfish willfulness as a renunciation of it.[24] But one must remember that the psychology of the early Victorians, from Newman's renunciation of the Church of England and his acceptance of the Catholic Church to Arnold's dismissal of aestheticism and his promotion of high moral seriousness, was a psychology of conversion. In a society undergoing great change because of industrial and technological developments, the respect for and belief in moral necessity would make the change in the characters of Ottima and Sebald less incredible. Critics have accused Browning of being sentimentally optimistic and morally obtuse

---

[24] See D. C. Wilkinson, "The Need for Disbelief: A Comment on *Pippa Passes*," *UTQ* 29 (1960):144–46. Jacob Korg suggests that free will leads the characters to moral awareness, in "A Reading of *Pippa Passes*," *VP* 6 (1968):5–19.

in this and other episodes of *Pippa Passes*.[25] But the Victorian convention of villains confessing and pronouncing themselves guilty in the eyes of God and man and delivering themselves to their mercy has not vanished from our society: one need only think of the still existing legal convention whereby someone who confesses to a crime is usually given a lesser sentence than someone who stands trial and is later found guilty.

This psychology of individual conversion has as its logical inverse an assumption of spiritual authority. For if the only true audience a person has is God, the only way for a character to be able to speak to everyone in the world and be everything to them is to become God. But since such a transformation cannot occur, except, Browning would argue, in rare moments, and then only for a moment, the experience of the divine must remain, in political terms, an evanescent ideal of benevolent despotism, and in individual terms a transitory consummation of the personality in love.

To imagine, even for a moment, that an individual could become God would be naive sentimentality at best, and at worst a kind of megalomania. Yet in *Pippa Passes* the songs that Pippa sings at crucial moments in the lives of Ottima and Sebald, Luigi, and the Monsignor reconcile each of them to the ways of God. Even more astonishingly, Pippa predicts that she will become each of these characters. So what appears an awkward attempt on Browning's part to prepare the reader for coming scenes is apparently another manifestation of Pippa's participation in the divine spirit:

> All service ranks the same with God:
> If now, as formerly he trod
> Paradise, his presence fills
> Our earth, each only as God wills
> Can work—God's puppets, best and worst,
> Are we; there is no last nor first.
> [Introduction, 190–95]

---

[25]See J. M. Purcell, "The Dramatic Failure of *Pippa Passes*," *SP* 36 (1939):79, and Wilkinson, "Need for Disbelief," p. 151. The best defense of the usual critical opinion that everyone is saved is made by J. M. Ariail, "Is *Pippa Passes* a Dramatic Failure?", *SP* 37 (1940):125–26. The most cogent analysis of the dramatic problems of *Pippa Passes* is made by Terry Otten in *The Deserted Stage: The Search for Dramatic Form in Nineteenth-Century England* (Athens: Ohio University Press, 1972), pp. 122–40. They stem from the flatness of Pippa's character created by Browning's making her "the structural but not the dramatic locus" (p. 140). Otten also points out that the passionate tour de force of the initial Ottima-Sebald episode unbalances the work's already problematic organization and the linkage of the separate scenes (p. 140).

The series of vignettes will end with the same sentiment. Along the way, though, in the description of the prostitutes lounging in the streets of Asolo and of Bluphocks and the other students drinking in the tavern, one senses a residual skepticism and a pervasive evil that to some readers makes Pippa's triumphs on this her one holiday of the year seem to be little more than small ironies of fate. But to read those triumphs ironically would be to deny the work's sentimental belief that God is part of everyone and everything in the world, and not to see that the accidental, ephemeral nature of Pippa's songs and the miraculous transformations worked in the souls of those who hear them are to be taken not only as evidence of God's work in the world but also as proof that individuals can realize themselves fully only when they face God.

A more problematic view of the consequences of the individual's becoming God appears in the difficulties that Djabal, the protagonist of *The Return of the Druses*, must face. Djabal's predicament economically summarizes Browning's view of his protagonists' struggles to come to terms at once with God and the crowd. Djabal is the hereditary leader of the Druses, who live under the rule of the knights of Rhodes on one of the islands in the lesser Sporades. Despite being an educated man whose aristocratic instincts align him with the ruling knights, he is spiritually committed to leading the oppressed Druses back to their home in Lebanon. But to do so he must assume the role of the people's god, Hakeem. And if he does this, he will lose the love of his beloved Anael, because she will worship him as a god instead of loving him as a man. Moreover, Anael finds herself half in love with the celibate prefect Loys and half in love with Djabal and knows that no matter whom she chooses she will be denied any sexual gratification. At the crucial moment of the play, when Djabal announces to the assembled people that he is their Hakeem, Anael must publicly choose between Loys and Djabal. If she chooses Loys and denies that Djabal is the Hakeem, the Druses will remain under the rule of the knights of Rhodes, while if she chooses Djabal she will surrender him to the people. When she utters the word "Hakeem," she dies, torn between her love of the man and of the god. But by her choice she does allow Djabal to lead his Druses back to Lebanon. Just before Anael's death, however, Djabal wrongly anticipates that she will betray him and tells her:

> See fate! By thee I was seduced, by thee
> I perish: yet do I—can I repent?

> I with my Arab instinct, thwarted ever
> By my Frank policy,—and with, in turn,
> My Frank brain, thwarted by my Arab heart—
> While these remained in equipoise, I lived
> —Nothing; had either been predominant,
> As a Frank schemer or an Arab mystic,
> I had been something;—now, each has destroyed
> The other—and behold, from out their crash,
> A third and better nature rises up—
> My mere man's-nature! And I yield to it:
> I love thee, I who did not love before!
>
> [V, 268–80]

This is extremely complicated. Djabal is willing to accept his failure, which he expects will occur the moment Anael declares him a fraud, on the grounds that it will be symbolic of the conflict between his Frank brain and Arab heart and give him his "mere man's-nature," that he will have a personal, yet tragic, love instead of the popular following he sought. But instead of dying at Anael's hands and finding a personal success in public failure, he is proclaimed Hakeem by the ignorant Druses and, ironically, finds failure in his success. He gains the Druses' freedom but loses Anael. Even becoming a god does not win him everyone's audience; and so, even as he triumphs over the knights of Rhodes, he commits suicide in grief for his lost love.

The sudden, unexpected reversal of fortune in *The Return of the Druses* is a small example of the kind of uncertain interpersonal calculus between the protagonist and his audiences that occurs in Browning's plays. Neither the outcome nor the dialogue has any inevitability; and often his plays seem like the crudest of domestic soap operas in which the only object is the prolonged agony and mental torment of the sufferers. The characters' uncertainty before their audiences produces bizarre paranoiac scenes in which the participants frantically consider what they should say to others to elicit a desired response, and try to imagine what others are thinking. In *The Return of the Druses*, for example, a lengthy, would-be dialogue between Djabal and Anael takes place in asides (II, 269–375). Like diplomats gone mad, Browning's tragic heroes scurry after a language that will appease all sides, and when they find there is no "brother's speech" that will speak to all, they turn to their only true audience, God. They die, despairing of any universal language except God's.

Such a view of the intelligent and sensitive man's audience must lead to a kind of political fatalism, regardless of humanitarian sentiment. And, indeed, *A Soul's Tragedy*, which was published in 1846 along with *Luria* (Browning's pale imitation of *Othello*) in the eighth and final number of *Bells and Pomegranates*, is, as Browning says, "all sneering and *disillusion*."[26] The hope that a brotherhood of love would establish a republican government in which everyone would be equal is declared to be both a megalomaniacal attempt to establish oneself as God and a violation of God's hierarchical ordering of the classes.

In the first half of the play, called the "poetry" of his life, Chiappino curses "whoever loves, above his liberty, / House, land or life" (I, 272–73). Acting in accord with his belief, he has protested against the Provost's rule once too often and has been exiled from Faenza. His friend, Luitolfo, has gone to negotiate for a week's delay in the Provost's enforcement of the sentence. But Luitolfo, failing to win a momentary respite for Chiappino, has killed the Provost and has fled to his own house, where his beloved Eulalia and Chiappino are waiting for him. Hearing the noise of an advancing crowd, Chiappino offers to assume the blame for the murder of the Provost while Luitolfo escapes. His offer is accepted by Luitolfo, but ironically, instead of becoming a martyr to an angry mob, Chiappino is declared the people's hero and told to choose his own reward.

In the second half of the play, or the "prose" of his life, Chiappino decides to assume the provost's office, believing that his "republicanism remains thoroughly / unaltered, only takes a form of expression hitherto / commonly judged (and heretofore by myself) in- / compatible with its existence" (II, 390–93). He declares to Eulalia that

> my soul's capacity for love widens—needs more than one object to content it,—and, being better instructed, will not persist in seeing all the component parts of love in what is only a single part,—nor in finding that so many and so various loves are all united in the love of a woman,—manifold uses in one instrument, as the savage has his sword, staff, sceptre and idol, all in one club-stick.
>
> [II, 273–81]

But his desire for an audience more various than a single woman and his professed love for all of the people of Faenza are shown, by Chiap-

---

[26]Robert to Elizabeth, February 11, 1846, *Letters*, I, 451.

pino's inappropriate comparison of the manifold nature of love to the various uses of a primitive "club-stick," to be nothing more than a thinly veiled desire for tyrannical power. The papal legate, Ogniben, who offers to install Chiappino in the office of provost, skeptically views Chiappino's change of heart about the efficacy of government as an acknowledgment of the "pre-ordained / hierarchies among us" (II, 531–32). He sees Chiappino's action as an early discovery of what all men of genius must realize:

> While you generally began by pulling down God, and went on to the end of your life, in one effort at setting up your own genius in his place,—still, the last, bitterest concession wrung with the utmost unwillingness from the experience of the very loftiest of you, was invariably— would one think it?—that the rest of mankind, down to the lowest of the mass, stood not, nor ever could stand, just on a level and equality with yourselves.
> [II, 537–46]

Ogniben, whose character and rhetoric look forward to Bishop Blougram's, believes that underlying the political order is God's order and that the intellectual's attempt to restructure society radically (and here we are meant to think of the French Revolution) is an overt substitution of man's utopian dreams for God's plan. Chiappino, now thoroughly divorced from his liberal views, substantially agrees with the legate, only arguing that intellectuals have already admitted to "the natural inequality / of mankind, by themselves participating in the / universal craving after, and deference to, the / civil distinctions which represent it" (II, 550–53). These, of course, are self-incriminating words, because Chiappino himself chose the course of political opportunism, instead of manfully admitting to the people of Faenza that Luitolfo, not he, should receive their reward, once it had become clear that Luitolfo had nothing to fear from them. So even though Chiappino asserts "Were 't not for God, I mean, what hope of truth— / Speaking truth, hearing truth, would stay with man?" (I, 28–29), his pride leads him to violate his personal honor and the special relationship he has with God. And once Luitolfo confesses to the murder of the former provost, Chiappino, to retain what honor he has, must undergo a silent, self-imposed exile from Faenza.

As the play comes to an end, Ogniben cynically remarks that he has now known "*Four*-and-twenty / leaders of revolts" (II, 711–12). Although the vindication of Ogniben's worldliness is not the tragedy's main point, it does suggest that these tragedies of liberal sentiment have comic possibilities besides self-parody. This suggestion is borne out by the fact that Browning wrote two comedies of liberal sentiment,[27] *King Victor and King Charles* and *Colombe's Birthday*, in both of which the oppressive tyrant whimsically alters his attitude toward the masses at the last moment, thereby averting the protagonist's self-destructive examination of his or her loyalties. But, barring any such gratuitous alteration of the tyrant's character, Browning's protagonists find themselves trapped between their liberal passions and their aristocratic breeding, unable to reconcile the opposing claims upon themselves and doomed to love without having their love requited. Their situation is tragic only insofar as one believes that social change is necessary and that, while one is misguided in seeking to destroy the natural hierarchy of society, one must alleviate or at least ameliorate the great human suffering which flows directly from the given and unchangeable order of society. Chiappino, for instance, imagines that he can transform the instruments of power into protectors of freedom and no longer has to despair "of ever being able to rightly operate on / mankind through such a deranged machinery as / the existing modes of government" (II, 230–32). He believes that the scale of relationships required to hold power does not necessarily create its own logic. He fails to see that he must betray both his need for a woman's love and his love for the individual man, and, finally, that he must usurp God's place in order to hold power. The darkness of his vision here troubled Browning. He thought of it as a product of his own despair, which was created, no doubt, partly by his growing distrust of the ability of leaders to accommodate the masses, but largely by his being unable to gain an audience for his political plays in particular and his poetry in general—hence his remark that *A Soul's Tragedy* was written two or three years before he met Elizabeth and fell in love with her and therefore had not been touched by the light she had brought into his life.[28] In sharp contrast to Browning's love for Elizabeth, then,

---

[27]Trevor Lloyd convincingly reads *Colombe's Birthday* as sentimental anti–Corn Law propaganda, with "Valence as Cobden-and-Bright, Cleves as Manchester, the courtiers as the Conservative government and the Duchess as Queen Victoria" ("Browning and Politics," in *Major Victorian Poets*, p. 154).

[28]See the letters of Robert to Elizabeth of February 11 and 13, 1846, *Letters*, I, 451–52, 455.

the protagonists' loves in his tragedies of liberal sentiment are cut off from human objects and thus from any self-fulfillment. Unable to satisfy either the world or themselves, even, as in Djabal's case, by becoming gods, they turn at last to God to find an audience that will be able to see the action occurring *within* their characters, will recognize it for what it is, and will let them become themselves in God.

II

Dramatic Lyrics, the third issue of *Bells and Pomegranates*, was published by Moxon in 1842. The collection was hastily gathered together at Moxon's request that Browning print something "for popularity's sake." Browning gave his publisher what odd poems he had on hand, even including "The Pied Piper of Hamelin," which he thought of as a jeu d'esprit, in order to fill out the last sixteen pages of the volume. "The Pied Piper," which had been written for Macready's nine-year-old son to illustrate during an illness, as a favor for the actor; "Waring," which made a kind of mysterious scholar gipsy of the New Zealand-bound Alfred Domett; and "In a Gondola," which began as a poem on a picture by Maclise, were all essentially occasional pieces. "Porphyria's Lover" and "Johannes Agricola," which went together under the title of "Madhouse Cells," had appeared anonymously six years earlier in Fox's *Monthly Repository*. "Artemis Prologizes," which Arnold praised as being in the true classical spirit,[29] was a fragment of a classical tragedy Browning had begun in imitation of Euripides' *Hippolytus* and had abandoned. The rest of the volume's poems seem to have been inspired by the reading he had done for *Strafford*, *Sordello*, *King Victor and King Charles*, and the essay he wrote for the *Foreign Quarterly Review* on Tasso and Chatterton. Yet despite the miscellaneous nature of the collection, the volume displays Browning's obsession with the theme of the audience and in some poems shows him trying to force his readers to judge the speaker's complaints against his audiences or to uncover the moral principle of a tale.

A concern for the captive audience is evident throughout Browning's work and life, and in the figures of the subjected woman and the enslaved mass we have the chief focuses of Browning's sympathy. The plight of the subject audience is perhaps nowhere more chillingly

---

[29]"One of the very best antique fragments I know is a fragment of a Hippolytus by him" (Arnold to Madame du Quaire, February 9, 1858, *Letters of Matthew Arnold*, ed. George W. E. Russell, 3 vols. [London: Macmillan, 1904], I, 80).

portrayed than in "My Last Duchess" or more lightheartedly than in "The Pied Piper of Hamelin." Browning kept a copy of Polidoro's Andromeda on his writing desk, and the theme of rescuing women in distress, whether it be Elizabeth Barrett in real life, Pompilia in history, or the Duchess of "The Flight of the Duchess" in fiction, was one to which he often returned.[30] To decide the fate of a defenseless woman, to restrict the choices of the innocent, and to attempt to control the thoughts of others are anathema to Browning. Johannes Agricola, who claims to be assured of God's audience; the lover who kills Porphyria in order to preserve her love for him; and the Duke of Ferrara, who has his Duchess murdered so that he alone may control the direction of her gaze are all megalomaniacs who have mistaken their physical or mental possession of a person or God for spiritual reinforcement of their self-images. In their own minds they think of themselves as gods: Porphyria's lover ends his monologue with the eerie self-justification, "And yet God has not said a word!" (l. 60); and Agricola gloatingly says, "I have God's warrant, could I blend / All hideous sins, as in a cup, / To drink the mingled venoms up" (ll. 33–35).

In "My Last Duchess," the dangerous parallel between the reader and the controlled audience is examined. The Duke of Ferrara, who is talking to a count's emissary with the purpose of arranging another marriage, has paused before the portrait of his last Duchess and unveiled it in order to discuss his late wife with the envoy before going down to meet the company below. The Duke describes to the emissary how his last Duchess seemed to distribute her smile too democratically, declares he put an end to her unseemly practice, and then pauses before going downstairs to call the envoy's attention to another work in his collection, a Neptune by Claus of Innsbruck.

Readers must first piece this narrative and its attendant circumstances together from the flow of the Duke's talk (something which beginning readers find very difficult). We then must realize not only that the Duke has put an innocent lady to death in order to gratify his possessive nature but also that he does not feel guilty for what he has done. From the Duke's impropriety in discussing his previous domestic dissatisfaction and the disproportionate emphasis he puts upon the lady's lack of proper deference toward him, we are to conclude that she was naive. We are to understand the Duke's complaint that she

---

[30]See W. C. DeVane, "The Virgin and the Dragon," *Yale Review* 37 (1947):33–46.

had a heart "too soon made glad" not as a euphemism for adulterous conduct (l. 22) but as a sign of an insanely possessive jealousy that would control his lady's glance in the same manner he controls the curtain covering her portrait. This inference is to be confirmed by the Duke's casual brutality in passing on to the next work of art in his collection, as if he had said nothing out of the ordinary and were merely playing the role of guide to his gallery.

Browning prompts his reader's response to and understanding of the poem by providing one with a set of circumstances that are internally consistent only if interpreted according to a certain picture of the Duke. For, if one tries to think of him as wronged by his last Duchess, then her praise of a "bough of cherries" and "the white mule / She rode with round the terrace" hardly seems a grave offense against him (ll. 27–29). Browning creates an ironic picture of the Duke's reserved, sophisticated intelligence destroying the Duchess's generous naïveté, as if her innocence were somehow a threat to his elegant worldliness. He shows us how art ironically makes beautiful naïveté into an object possessed by its audience and subject to its whims, how art focuses the generosity of infinite goodness into a single symbolic moment, here in the "spot of joy" on the Duchess's cheek that preserves her reaction to some courtesy of the painter, Fra Pandolf (ll. 14–15). At the same time he leaves us in the Duke's hands to see how it is to have one's attention directed by such a zealous cicerone and to note how the Duke prides himself on his present possession of the Duchess's glance in her portrait: "None puts by / The curtain I have drawn for you, but I" (ll. 9–10). One sees the great contrast between the restricted gaze of her portrait and the wide and varied audience her eyes had before her death:

> She looked on, and her looks went everywhere.
> Sir, 't was all one! My favour at her breast,
> The dropping of the daylight in the West,
> The bough of cherries some officious fool
> Broke in the orchard for her, the white mule
> She rode with round the terrace—all and each
> Would draw from her alike the approving speech,
> Or blush, at least.
> [ll. 24–31]

Her glance is now a privilege granted only by the Duke. He selects her audience, and he explains her meaning. Just as his exegesis of the moment of unveiling provides the reader with the details of his conversation and Browning with the opportunity of presenting those details to the reader, so too the Duke's explanation of the blush on his last Duchess's cheek, the explanation only he can give, guarantees him the captive audience he craves.

Yet, insofar as it portrays a self-satisfied ego ordering the world to fit its desires, "My Last Duchess" is both Browning's most problematic success and the least characteristic of his poems. It is intended, like "Johannes Agricola," "Porphyria's Lover," and the "Soliloquy of the Spanish Cloister," as another negative instance of a self-assured ego attempting to order the world but achieving only madness and moral blindness. A nine-hundred-year-old name is revealed not only as an insufficient and inadequate ground for the self but also as the dangerous voice of a demonic tradition that suppresses the Duchess's genuine individuality. The Duke of Ferrara is ultimately meant to be seen as another nearly anonymous duke subsumed by a long line. From this perspective one can see that to present "My Last Duchess" as Browning's finest achievement or as the perfect monologue is mistaken. The poem assumes too great a knowledge of Browning's point of view by expecting the reader to be suspicious both of formal tidiness and of the absence of a struggle for significant self-discovery through the recognition of others. Indeed, the very attributes that make the poem so pedagogically attractive and seductive—its boundedness and the Duke's apparently secure self-presentation—are what Browning is seeking to attack and to undermine through his irony. It is precisely Browning's point that to see the self as the source of order in life leads to moral fascism. For Browning, the dramatic monologue is ultimately not the expression of a stable, autonomous self but the drama of a speaker's search for the recognition of others that will give the speaker his or her sense of self.[31]

In contrast to such intricate considerations, one is often asked to make much simpler observations about a poem by being forced to

---

[31]One cannot drive this point home too hard. For example, because she sees the self as the ordering principle of the world, Constance W. Hassett consistently resists her best insights in *The Elusive Self in the Poetry of Robert Browning* (Athens: University of Ohio Press, 1982). Although her analysis again and again uncovers the "elusiveness" of the self and the characters' lack of self-knowledge, she assumes that in Browning's poetry a speaker's "existence is organized from within" (p. 139) and so does not see that the moments of significant self-discovery she discusses depend on the recognition of others. Speaking of such moments, she says, "Reciprocal understanding is as intuitive as self-understanding" (p. 126). In truth, for Browning, reciprocal understanding is the intuitive basis of self-understanding.

take a second look at it. One such poem is "Incident of the French Camp." It tells the story of a boy who delivers to Napoleon the message that the French have taken Ratisbon and who then falls dead at Napoleon's feet. But what surprises us is that even after being told, "You looked twice ere you saw his breast / Was all but shot in two" (ll. 23–24), we are as astonished as Napoleon is when the soldier dies. We have fixed our eyes upon the figure of Napoleon surveying the doubtful battle of Ratisbon and thinking how his "plans / That soar, to earth may fall" (ll. 9–10). And when the horseman approaches, we are intent upon the struggle's outcome, so that the description of the soldier's wound doesn't catch our eye. Like Napoleon, we avidly listen to a narrative of the famous victory, only to miss the heroism before us. In our eagerness for news we overlook the soldier's condition and are chastened when in reply to Napoleon's "You're wounded," he exclaims, "Nay, I'm killed Sire!" (ll. 37–39) and falls dead at Napoleon's feet. We are reminded that our distance from the past, like Napoleon's distance from the battle of Ratisbon, often lets us think of history's conflicts in the abstract terms of victory and defeat but that it should never allow us to forget the human pain and suffering of war.

"Count Gismond" is a much more difficult poem that demands at least a second reading. In it Countess Gismond is talking to her maid Adela and telling how Gismond defended her honor against Gauthier's accusation, how Gismond killed Gauthier in a trial by combat, how Gauthier confessed his lie before he died, and how Gismond took her away to Aix-en-Provence to live with him. But at the end of the story, when Gismond appears, the Countess lies to him by saying that she has just finished telling Adela about her tercel and "how many birds it struck since May" (l. 126). This lie comes as something of a shock, and, while one notes the parallel between the tercel and Gismond, one begins to wonder about the Countess's character and goes back to read the poem through more carefully. Some readers who have done this have come to believe that Gauthier was innocent and the Countess guilty.[32]

How successful Browning is in undermining the Duke's self-centeredness has been the subject of critical debate. See B. R. Jerman, "Browning's Witless Duke," *PMLA* 72 (1957):488–93; Laurence Perrine, "Browning's Shrewd Duke," *PMLA* 74 (1959):157–59; and Langbaum, *Poetry of Experience*, pp. 82–85.

[32]See John V. Hagopian, "The Mask of Countess Gismond," *PQ* 40 (1961):153–55; John W. Tilton and R. Dale Tuttle, "A New Reading of 'Count Gismond,'" *SP* 60 (1963):549–53. For a defense of the Countess, see Michael Timko, "Ah, Did You Once See Browning Plain?", *SEL* 6 (1966):731–42.

But the matter doesn't appear to be so simple. The poem begins as a kind of prayer, the Countess asking Christ to save her husband who killed Gauthier. Gauthier, the Countess feels, must have planned to attack her honor, and she believes that her cousins were party to his foul slander. She thinks that her cousins were jealous of her being queen of the tourney on her birthday and that they arranged for Gauthier to make his accusation. But the sole evidence she offers for their complicity is that "all eyes were bent / Upon me, when my cousins cast / Theirs down" (ll. 43–45). This clearly seems to be insufficient evidence on which to convict her cousins of conspiracy. But what do her imaginings suggest? Why would she think her cousins were jealous of her? If one reads carefully, one notices that her cousins are more beautiful than she and that she feels she needs "to be crowned" in order to be a queen (l. 21), while each of them is "a queen / By virtue of her brow and breast" (ll. 19–20). She enjoys the attentions of others and takes great pleasure in "the morning-troop / Of merry friends" who kiss her and call her queen (ll. 31–32), but she doesn't expect admiration and seems particularly sensitive to the possibility of rejection and disappointment. So it would seem, then, that the paranoia induced by Gauthier's challenge of her virtue makes her conclude too quickly that because of some petty jealousy her cousins arranged for Gauthier to impugn her virtue.

Gauthier, nevertheless, must be guilty. He not only confesses to his slander upon his deathbed but also dies in a trial by combat in which it seems clear that Browning sees the hand of God.[33] Whether the poem interested Browning because of the trial so that he felt it unnecessary to reveal Gauthier's motives, or whether Browning had some source in mind and neglected to present all of the details, is unclear. External evidence would seem to suggest, however, that one isn't meant to question the Countess's innocence.

The poem seems to be a study in the lightheaded vanity of a plain woman. The Countess, when queen for a day, was pleased with the attention she received and displeased by any seeming slight. But once the attention paid her turned to scorn, her worst suspicions of her audience took on a nightmarish form in Gauthier's words, "Bring torches! Wind the penance-sheet / About her! Let her shun the chaste, / Or lay herself before their feet!" (ll. 55–57). The attack upon her virtue is too close to an attack upon what beauty and fragile self-esteem

---

[33] Browning thought God intervened on the behalf of the righteous in duels. See his letter to Elizabeth, April 8, 1846, *Letters*, II, 604, quoted below on p. 160.

she has, and she cannot reply to it. She must have a champion and readily accepts Gismond's aid. Her faltering is evident even within her narrative. Invoking his name allows her to begin her story, and, again, when she is about to tell of Gauthier's audacity and "the old mist" blinds her once more (l. 47), she gains courage by noticing that "Gismond's at the gate, in talk / With his two boys: I can proceed" (ll. 49–50). She needs to be assured of a protecting audience even when telling her tale, and so she particularly savors the memory of Gismond's defeating Gauthier.

Perhaps, then, we can account for her lie to Gismond in terms of the psychology of a less than beautiful woman who craves others' attention but fears their scorn. The Countess appreciates and needs the protection and favor of her husband, but her vanity prevents her from admitting it to his face—hence her recourse to the symbolic tercel. Then, too, there is the troubling suggestion (particularly in the remark that her eldest son resembles Gauthier) that she subconsciously wishes she had loved her accuser, a wish she now locates in an Oedipal fantasy and whose vengeance she has already experienced in the form of Gauthier's accusation. But I do not wish to press a psychoanalysis of the Countess any further here (though it would appear the materials are available for one); instead, I merely want to indicate the depth of Browning's psychological insight and to show how he treats the vulnerability of a plain woman's vanity, a theme he will later touch upon in "James Lee's Wife." He shows us how sensitive the Countess is to the eyes of others, how she watches her cousins' "glancing sideways with still head" while she dresses (l. 24), and how her demand for attention borders on paranoia and displays her self-destructive vanity, which is too caught up in itself to attend to its own defense because too afraid it has none.

Gauthier's apparent lack of motive can also be accounted for, then. Even if he had embraced the Countess during the previous night, it seems unlikely that he would be jealous of her being queen of the tourney or that he would reveal their clandestine love at his cost as well as hers. The improbable and gratuitous nature of his action makes him a curiously shadowy figure, who is not so much a character as a representative of fraud, force, and sensuality. The poem, then, seems to suggest that the Countess's desire for attention and love leads her into moral darkness when she faces a man who not only represents the possibility of sexual fulfillment but also stands for sexual love as violation and death. Gismond, who defends her honor and marries her, represents, of course, proper sexual fulfillment. But Gauthier seems to stand for something more primal, more dangerous, and, as the Countess's story tells us, more fascinating.

The tendency to turn the other into a symbol of one's fears and desires is also part of the speaker's deficiency in "Cristina." The poem's speaker imagines that he and Cristina, the queen of Sweden, have fallen in love after their eyes have met once. Although she has left him, he imagines "the secret's mine now! / She has lost me, I have gained her; / Her soul's mine: and thus, grown perfect, / I shall pass my life's remainder" (ll. 57–60). This is love at first sight without any reciprocal feeling. The speaker's vehemence and his emphasis on his having "grown perfect" points to megalomania resembling that of Porphyria's lover and Johannes Agricola. The other, here in the person of Queen Cristina, becomes a symbol of power which the speaker imagines he has added to his soul. "Her soul's mine," he declares, as if he had somehow captured it in the single chance meeting of his eyes and hers.

If one compares "Cristina" with Baudelaire's "À une passante" (1860), which treats a similar subject, one sees how Browning suppresses the sensuality of love in favor of concentrating upon and judging the egocentrism of his speaker's megalomania. In contrast to the circumstances in Browning's poem, those in Baudelaire's are more appropriate, the feelings more plangent, the psychology of modern love more delicate, the passions more objectively observed:

> La rue assourdissante autour de moi hurlait.
> Longue, mince, en grand deuil, douleur majestueuse,
> Une femme passa, d'une main fastueuse
> Soulevant, balançant le feston et l'ourlet;
>
> Agile et noble, avec sa jambe de statue.
> Moi, je buvais, crispé comme un extravagant,
> Dans son oeil, ciel livide où germe l'ouragan,
> La douceur qui fascine et le plaisir que tue.
>
> Un éclair . . . puis la nuit!—Fugitive beauté
> Dont le regard m'a fait soudainement renaître
> Ne te verrai-je plus que dans l'éternité?
>
> Ailleurs, bien loin d'ici! trop tard! *jamais* peut-être!
> Car j'ignore où tu fuis, tu ne sais où je vais,
> Ô toi que j'eusse aimée, ô toi qui le savais!

[The deafening street was howling around me. Tall, thin, in deep mourning, majestic grief, a woman passed, with her gorgeous hand lifting and swinging the scallop and hem; light-footed and noble, with her statue's leg. I drank, twitching like a madman, from her eye, a leaden sky from which the hurricane springs, the sweetness which bewitches and the pleasure which kills. A flash . . . then night!—Fleeting beauty, through whose look I was suddenly reborn, shall I never see you again except in eternity? Elsewhere, far away from here! too late! *never* perhaps! For I don't know whither you flee, and you don't know where I am going, O you whom I would have loved, O you who knew it!][34]

Baudelaire emphasizes the casual, instead of the causal, nature of the speaker's passion; it is something of the moment and not a source of power. The beautiful widow is a woman whose grief makes her vulnerable to her evanescent feelings. So unlike the imperturbable and unapproachable Queen Cristina, Baudelaire's widow momentarily shares and is available to the speaker's desire, even though she quickly flees from it as she passes by him. For Baudelaire this is a delicious experience to be savored in all of its fleeting licentiousness and bewitching beauty, while for Browning the sensual revelry of Baudelaire would have been slightly too daring and too improperly suggestive and the speaker's lingering over his experience not sufficiently self-condemning. In "Cristina," the speaker's one-sided, secret love seems too self-aggrandizing to have anything to do with the woman herself. His is a lust for the complete possession of the other instead of a desire for mutual pleasure.

"Rudel to the Lady of Tripoli," which Browning originally grouped with "Cristina" under the title "Queen-Worship," takes a very different view of the other's gaze, seeing it as the source of self-recognition instead of self-aggrandizement. The poem is the message that Rudel sends to the Lady of Tripoli, telling her that he loves her. It consists of an emblematic picture, followed by a partial explanation of the emblem's meaning. Many readers, however, have been puzzled by the poem and particularly by its curious three-part emblem consisting of the sun which shines on a snow-covered mountain, of the mountain

---

[34]Charles Baudelaire, *Oeuvres complètes,* ed. Claude Pichois, 2 vols. (Paris: Gallimard, 1975–76), I, 92–93. My translation.

On the urban modernity of the poem's sexuality, see Walter Benjamin, "On Some Motifs in Baudelaire," *Illuminations,* ed. Hannah Arendt, trans. Harry Zohn (New York: Harcourt, Brace & World, 1968), pp. 170–72. For a commentary on Benjamin's reading, see Geoffrey H. Hartman, *Criticism in the Wilderness: The Study of Literature Today* (New Haven: Yale University Press, 1980), pp. 66–72.

which does not repay the sun's attention, and of a sunflower beneath the mountain which is unknown to the sun and yet follows it on its daily course through the sky.[35] The identification of the elements of the device has proven difficult for a good reason: the poem appears to be deliberately designed as an example of *trobar clus*—that is, as an imitation of a troubadour emblem the meaning of which is meant to be obscure.

It would seem that the sunflower is Rudel as a private poet, the sun the Lady, and the mountain the monument of tradition formed by literature, of which Rudel's public poetry is a part. The sunflower "has parted, one by one, / With all a flower's true graces, for the grace / Of being but a foolish mimic sun" (ll. 9–11). This suggests a lover attempting to imitate the beauty of his beloved and to become what he beholds, and clearly stands for Rudel as lover and private poet. Since the sunflower loves the sun, the sun, then, is the Lady, even though Rudel refers to the sun as "he" several times. This identification is further supported by the association of the Lady with golden light and the east: Rudel addresses her as "Angel of the East" (l. 19) and implores her to cast "one gold look / Across the waters to this twilight nook" (ll. 19–20).

One might object, however, that the word "twilight" confuses the sense of direction, because the Tripoli of the poem is in present-day Lebanon, to the east of Rudel in Blaye, and so could not be associated with the setting of the sun in the west. But, if one recalls Rudel's story, one understands that "twilight" refers to Rudel himself and not to the sun. Rudel had fallen in love with the Lady of Tripoli after hearing of her beauty and had sailed to Tripoli to see her, writing on the way of his "*amor da lonh*," his "love from afar." He becomes seriously ill during the voyage and had apparently died before arriving in Tripoli. Learning of him and his love for her, the Lady came to see him. Rudel recovered for a moment, thanked God he had lived to see her, and died in her arms. So "twilight" symbolizes the ending of his life. Moreover, in accordance with the legend that Rudel fell in love with the Lady without her knowing anything about him, the sunflower follows the sun but is not recognized by it.

The mountain seems to be the monument of tradition formed by

---

[35]DeVane identifies the mountain as the Lady, the sun as love, and the sunflower as Rudel (*Handbook*, p. 121); in contrast, Eleanor Cook argues that the mountain is the husband in courtly love, the sun the Lady, and the sunflower Rudel (*Browning's Lyrics: An Exploration* ([Toronto: University of Toronto Press, 1974], pp. 83–85).

literature. Since it is the sum of many individual contributions and the result of public acceptance, men "nobly call by many a name the Mount" (l. 13). Rudel's public poetry is apparently to be associated with the mountain, for we learn that "men feed / On songs I sing" (ll. 30–31). The praise men give his songs is, however, different from the derision they accord the sunflower (l. 18). Further, although he receives their praise, he says that "men applaud / In vain this Rudel, he not looking here / But to the East" (ll. 34–36). "This Rudel" does not care for fame but only for love. The word "this" suggests the possibility of two Rudels. It would appear that the sunflower represents Rudel as private poet and lover and that the mountain stands, in part, for Rudel as a public poet. In support of this interpretation, one might point to the parallel distinction between the public and the private poet made in "One Word More" and to Browning's apparent association of the two poems, shown by his placing "Rudel to the Lady of Tripoli" just before "One Word More" in *Men and Women*, beginning with the 1863 edition of his works.

Still the poem's emblem is very difficult and does not form an allegory that is consistent in all of its details:

> See! These inexpert
> And hurried fingers could not fail to hurt
> The woven picture; 't is a woman's skill
> Indeed; but nothing baffled me, so, ill
> Or well, the work is finished.
> [ll. 26–30]

This artistic failure in the service of love represents Rudel's desire to become one with his beloved, just as the sunflower mimics the sun and sacrifices itself to the other. Browning deliberately constructs Rudel's obscure emblem to show the poet finding in the imperfection of his art an adequate symbol for the incompleteness of his soul and for his love for another; he shows Rudel loving without expectation and without an egocentric vision of the world.

The connections between various audiences and proper poetic recognition receive their most fanciful treatment in "The Pied Piper of Hamelin," the poem with which *Dramatic Lyrics* closes. One may remember the alliterative romp of the piper and his followers from hearing it at the local library's Saturday reading hour for children, or may think of it in connection with the delightful anecdote related by Henry James about a children's party at which Hans Christian Andersen "read out to his young friends 'The Ugly Duckling,' after which Browning struck up with the 'Pied Piper'; which led to the formation of a grand march through the spacious Barberini apartment, with Story doing his best on a flute in default of bagpipes."[36] Like Browning's "Cavalier Tunes," which can be read either as heroic marching songs or as elegies for the lost Cavalier cause and so address our loss of historical innocence, "The Pied Piper" shows its more experienced readers how sadly skeptical age has made them and reminds them of their lost childhood and its simple morals. "The Pied Piper of Hamelin" is not only a whimsical threat made by a poet without an audience but also in some sense a nursery tale for adults.

The piper, whose music will spirit away whomever he pleases, makes the tightfisted burghers of Hamelin pay for his destruction of the town's rats by piping their children away. He confirms the townspeople in their ironical, skeptical view of the world by separating them from their vicarious experience of their children's innocence. All that remains for them are their faded memories and the regrets of the poor lame boy who could not make it into the cavern before it closed or those of the rat "who, stout as Julius Caesar, / Swam across and lived to carry / (As he, the manuscript he cherished) / To Rat-land home his commentary" (ll. 123–26). Here Browning not only creates a new version of the Orphic poet, who both lightens and is reponsible for the death of children, but also envisions art as the quest for knowledge and the attempt to preserve a pristine innocence. As in his *Essay on Chatterton*, where he perversely defends Chatterton's poetic project of forging an innocent, archaic poetry against the hostile critics it encountered, Browning sees art here as both a world of ironies and a paradise of dreams—a paradox which is resolved, as it is in *Pippa Passes*, by the audience's naïveté or skepticism. Despite its bourgeois Victorian moral that the piper must be paid his due, the poem's subject, form, and apparent audience seem to threaten our critical high seriousness. It is hard, for example, to quote "Great rats, small rats, lean rats, brawny rats, / Brown rats, black rats, grey rats, tawny rats" in the service of any respectable intellectual enterprise (ll. III–12), but one

---

[36]*William Wetmore Story and His Friends*, 2 vols. (Boston: Houghton, Mifflin, 1903; rpt., 2 vols. in 1, New York: Grove Press, 1958), I, 286. This anecdote has its dark side as well, like the poem itself and the illness of the young Macready that occasioned it. See Elizabeth's comments on Joseph Story's death, on his sister's nearly fatal illness, and on her concern for Pen, in her letter to Mrs. Jameson, December 21, 1853, *The Letters of Elizabeth Barrett Browning*, ed. Frederic G. Kenyon, 2 vols. (London: Macmillan, 1897), II, 147.

can still imagine the joy of a child upon first hearing or reading those lines. If we could forget our critical responsibilities for a moment (or at least pretend to) and enjoy the wonderful chaos Browning sometimes discovers in the language, we would better appreciate Browning's spirit and admire him all the more for writing one of the great poems for children in this or any other language, even while he was despairing because of the indifference toward his poetry shown by the British public.

III

Browning's trip to Italy in 1844–45 inspired him to mine the Italian vein in his poetry more intensively than before and produced his richest descriptive verse. This is apparent in the poems of *Dramatic Romances and Lyrics*, the seventh number of *Bells and Pomegranates*, published in 1845. In the volume Browning also successfully establishes a personal lyric style and displays a renewed interest in narrative poetry, which he had been discouraged from writing by the failure of *Sordello*. At times, though, his subjects seem too much the choice of whimsy and their development too much the product of momentary enthusiasms. It was no doubt this that Matthew Arnold had in mind when he remarked to Clough in 1848 that Browning's poetry was only a "confused multitudinousness," because he did not "begin with an Idea of the world."[37] The very word "multitudinousness" is suggestive here, since it shows Arnold descending for a moment from his seat of critical high seriousness to grapple with the difficulties of the protean Browning. Arnold clearly prefers an informing consciousness that shapes the world to a developing consciousness that seeks form in the

[37] *The Letters of Matthew Arnold to Arthur Hugh Clough*, ed. Howard Foster Lowry (London: Oxford University Press, 1932), p. 31. Walter Bagehot called this same phenomenon Browning's "grotesque," in "Wordsworth, Tennyson, and Browning; or Pure, Ornate, and Grotesque Art in English Poetry," *National Review* 19 (1864):27–67. Anticipating the expressionist interpretation of it, Lily Bess Campbell connects the grotesque with the artist's spiritual freedom to face reality and its ugliness, in *The Grotesque in the Poetry of Robert Browning*, Bulletin of the University of Texas, no. 92, Humanistic Series no. 5 (Austin: University of Texas, 1907). Carol T. Christ sees the grotesque as both a stylistic and a thematic expression connected with Browning's perception of energy in individuals and the particularities of life: *The Finer Optic: The Aesthetic of Particularity in Victorian Poetry* (New Haven: Yale University Press, 1975), pp. 65–89. See also Hegel's comments on the connection between the spiritual freedom of Romantic poetry and its embrace of the ugly in contrast to the effort of Classical poetry to fix the soul in a beautiful world, *Aesthetics*, II, 526–27. The best extended discussion of the grotesque in Browning is J. Hillis Miller's chapter on him in *The Disappearance of God*.

world. If we attempt to translate his criticism into a more precise analysis of Browning's thematics, we will see that Arnold is indirectly describing how Browning's and his speakers' uncertainties about themselves and their relations with their audiences fragment their visions and desires, and also how his speakers pour out a flood of description in an attempt to compensate for the attention and recognition they do not receive from others.

Take, for instance, a simple poem such as the first of the "Garden Fancies" entitled "The Flower's Name," a poem which anticipates "Love in a Life" in the speaker's pursuit of the material reminders of a loved one's having been where he is now. The speaker says the garden reminds him of the woman with whom he was walking there "such a short while since" (l. 2). His thoughts about her make the poem a collection of her traces: the shrub she must have reached before letting the wicket gate swing back (ll. 5–6), the snail she moved out of harm's way (ll. 7–8), the box her robe brushed against (l. 10), and the flower she stopped at (l. 17). She gave him the flower's "soft meandering Spanish name" (l. 20), but he has forgotten it. His lapse of memory is an emblem of how beauty slips away from him when she isn't there: "Where I find her not, beauties vanish; / Whither I follow her, beauties flee" (ll. 41–42). Like the flower's name, she and the beauty she creates around her are somehow foreign and unavailable to him; and he can only register the traces of their passing, since the roses of the garden seem much less beautiful in her absence.

"The Flower's Name" is a domesticated version of the *Pauline*-poet's desire to be everything in nature when he can't be one with God, Shelley, or Pauline. It is a better poem than *Pauline* because it provides motivation for the poem's natural description: the speaker looks for the woman with whom the garden's objects are associated and finds that he somehow cannot recover her beauty or that of the garden's roses. We see a similar substitution in "The Englishman in Italy." The Englishman is talking to a little Italian girl named Fortù, is trying to comfort her with his voice while the sirocco blows itself out, and is amusing himself by recalling the beauties of the Italian countryside.

The speaker's indulgent description gains momentum from the storm's motion and then rapidly moves from one image of Sorrento's autumnal bounty to another and yet another:

> Meantime, see the grape bunch they've brought you:
> The rain-water slips

Bells and Pomegranates

> O'er the heavy blue bloom on each globe
>   Which the wasp to your lips
> Still follows with fretful persistence:
>   Nay, taste, while awake,
> This half of a curd-white smooth cheese-ball
>   That peels, flake by flake,
> Like an onion, each smoother and whiter;
>   Next, sip this weak wine
> From the thin green glass flask, with its stopper,
>   A leaf of the vine;
> And end with the prickly-pear's red flesh
>   That leaves thro' its juice
> The stony black seeds on your pearl-teeth.
>   Scirocco is loose!
> Hark, the quick, whistling pelt of the olives
>   Which, thick in one's track,
> Tempt the stranger to pick up and bite them,
>   Tho' not yet half black!
> How the old twisted olive trunks shudder,
>   The medlars let fall
> Their hard fruit, and the brittle great fig-trees
>   Snap off, figs and all,
> For here comes the whole of the tempest!
>   [ll. 101–25]

Like the olives, medlars, and figs blown before the storm, his words describing the scene no longer savor themselves but fly quickly in the tempest's wind from one delight to another.

Yet the speaker always finds a viewpoint from which he can see the landscape at a distance. Yesterday evening he had gone up into the mountains around Sorrento and looked out to the Mediterranean, where he had seen the Galli Islands and had been reminded that the sirens lived there who called to Ulysses and told him of "this life's secret" (l. 227). But, like the three Gallis, which are separated from the mainland and from each other, and like Ulysses tied to the mast of his ship, the speaker surveys the plain of Sorrento from afar, viewing it from the distant peak of Calvano. And even among the mountains he is a stranger, because they make him feel like an intruder in the same way that the hills surrounding the Dark Tower make Childe Roland feel like one (ll. 181–87). He finds the mountains harsh and unfruitful, imagines they are envious of the fertile plain of Sorrento below (ll. 188–196), and through the perspective's power is indirectly reminded that Italy is "but a slave" of Austria (l. 196). This realization makes his own isolation all the more poignant, because at Sorrento's harvest festival he cannot help comparing the happiness and bounty of subjugated Italy with the misery and neediness of his free England, where the poor starve because of the Corn Laws (ll. 287–90). So, while he sees the abundance of the land and sea around him, he thinks of how he is, like Ulysses, separated from it, a wanderer unable to live Italian life fully because he is an Englishman.

As the figure of the sleeping Fortù touchingly shows, the speaker has no real audience in Italy, and so his sense of being a foreigner causes him to overcompensate, as travelers will often do, by lavishly describing the landscape and the people around him. In contrast, there is nothing of this productive tension between the stranger's alienation and his compensatory description in Gerard Manley Hopkins's "Pied Beauty," a poem that one feels is nevertheless deeply indebted to Browning's poem:

> Glory be to God for dappled things—
>   For skies of couple-colour as a brinded cow;
>   For rose-moles all in stipple upon trout that swim;
>   Fresh-firecoal chestnut-falls; finches' wings;
>   Landscape plotted and pieced—fold, fallow and plough;
>   And áll trádes, their gear and tackle and trim.
>
> [ll. 1–6][38]

In Hopkins's poem the description arises from a perception of God's order in the world. Even nature's pied variegation fits into a "plotted and pieced" pattern and is reflected in the language's alliteration and assonance. But because he is so sure of his divine audience, Hopkins's hymn to God's arrangement of nature's variation lacks the creative spontaneity, the delectable chaos, and the emotional engagement of the description in "The Englishman in Italy." Sensing the troubled uncertainty in Browning's descriptions, J. Hillis Miller has interpreted this "confused multitudinousness" as an attempt on Browning's part to become the God who has disappeared from the world: "Browning is both diffused through his body and the world, as water is absorbed by a sponge, and at the same time is withdrawn from them, an infinitesimal spark of distinct life at the middle point."[39] Yet it is easier to think of this psychological fragmentation and its accompanying descriptive compensation as being created by a speaker's uncertainty

---

[38]*The Poems of Gerard Manley Hopkins*, ed. W. H. Gardner and N. H. Mackenzie, 4th ed. (London: Oxford University Press, 1967), p. 69.

[39]Miller, *Disappearance of God*, p. 91.

about, and distance from, any audience—not just God. This point is clearly illustrated in "The Bishop Orders His Tomb at St. Praxed's Church."

The dying Bishop addresses his sons, who are gathered around him, and describes the tomb he wants them to build for him. His deathbed delirium and his growing fear that his sons will deny his final request not only provide, as Ruskin long ago pointed out,[40] a remarkable mirror of the consciousness that gave rise to the Renaissance combination of pagan and Christian art but also make his descriptions of his tomb seem hopelessly fanciful resolutions of the conflicts between his desires and his audiences. The Bishop imagines that a magnificent antique-black marble sarcophagus amid nine peach-blossom marble columns, a choice Latin epitaph, a bas-relief frieze on the tomb's side showing Christ, St. Praxed, and Pan, and a lump of lapis lazuli between his statue's knees will reconcile him with his sons, avenge Gandolf's "snatch from out the corner South" for his final resting place (l. 18), and will place him closer to salvation because he will be able to "see God made and eaten all day long" in the church (l. 82). But he fears that his sons are not paying attention to him (ll. 62–63) and that they will brick him over "with beggar's mouldy travertine / Which Gandolf from his tomb-top chuckles at" (ll. 66–67) or consign his corpse to "Gritstone, a-crumble!" (l. 116). So he tries to point out to them not only that he has given them his villas and could easily give them to the pope instead (ll. 102–3), but also that in the church he will have "Saint Praxed's ear to pray / Horses for ye, and brown Greek manuscripts, / And mistresses with great smooth marbly limbs" (ll. 73–75). But his sons seem unimpressed by his promised intercessions on their behalf, and we are left with the nightmarish vision of the Bishop slowly turning into stone before our eyes as his sons leave him to the ghosts of the ages in St. Praxed's church:

> For as I lie here, hours of the dead night,
> Dying in state and by such slow degrees,
> I fold my arms as if they clasped a crook,
> And stretch my feet forth straight as stone can point,
> And let the bedclothes, for a mortcloth, drop
> Into great laps and folds of sculptor's-work:
> And as yon tapers dwindle, and strange thoughts
> Grow, with a certain humming in my ears,

[40]*Modern Painters* (London: Smith, Elder, 1856), IV, 377–79.

> About the life before I lived this life,
> And this life too, popes, cardinals and priests,
> Saint Praxed at his sermon on the mount,
> Your tall pale mother with her talking eyes,
> And new-found agate urns as fresh as day,
> And marble's language, Latin pure, discreet.
>
> [ll. 85–98]

His dreaming about life in death is a paratactic phantasmagoria in which one image quickly replaces another. The Bishop finally can take comfort only in imagining how old Gandolf had wished that he had had the Bishop's mistress:

> And leave me in my church, the church for peace,
> That I may watch at leisure if he leers—
> Old Gandolf, at me, from his onion-stone,
> As still he envied me, so fair she was!
>
> [ll. 122–125]

There is some suggestion here that the Bishop's love for his mistress is the most enduring and the most satisfying of his relationships with other people; but there is also much melancholy in his voice as he is forced to turn to his memory of his mistress to assure himself of his importance in Gandolf's eyes.

The sons' betrayal of the Bishop is one of many in *Dramatic Romances and Lyrics*. The poet of "The Lost Leader" (Wordsworth) has betrayed his audience "for a handful of silver" and "a riband to stick in his coat" (ll. 1–2). Sir De Lorge, in "The Glove," first betrays his vanity when he throws a lady's glove in her face after being forced to prove his boast that he would do anything for his love by retrieving her glove from the den of the king's lion, and he subsequently must betray his pride by going in pursuit of his new mistress's gloves when the king and she wish to be with one another. The wife in "The Confessional" betrays her husband's political activities to her priest, and her priest betrays her husband to the authorities, who hang him. In "The Italian in England," the speaker, who has escaped from the Austrian soldiers through the help of a patriotic Italian woman, thinks how he has betrayed her and himself by fleeing to England and going into business there instead of continuing to fight for the liberation of Italy. And the reader in "Sibrandus Schafnaburgensis" lightheartedly abandons Sibrandus's boring tome in the water-filled crevice of a plum tree, where it endures the indignity of being invaded by amorous efts and bugs; he then turns to Rabelais and only a few weeks later fishes out the soaked volume and puts it on his shelf to "dry-rot at ease till the Judgment-day" (l. 120).

Even an apparently simple poem like "'How They Brought the Good News from Ghent to Aix'" is pervaded with the feeling that there is no audience for one's true accomplishments. While its rollicking rhythm does remind one that Browning liked to ride horses, the poem also illustrates Browning's belief that struggle is more important than success and that public applause for one's efforts is not to be expected.

The speaker and his companions, Joris and Dirck, gallop apace from Ghent to Aix, but only the speaker astride his stout Roland completes the journey of 120 miles. The poem underlines the abstractness of Browning's meditation on the difference between striving and succeeding, because one never learns what the "good news" is.[41] Instead of wondering what the good news is, one should turn one's attention to the last stanza, which describes the people's celebration after the speaker and Roland have arrived in Aix:

> And all I remember is—friends flocking round
> As I sat with his head 'twixt my knees on the ground;
> And no voice but was praising this Roland of mine,
> As I poured down his throat our last measure of wine,
> Which (the burgesses voted by common consent)
> Was no more than his due who brought good news from Ghent.
> [ll. 55–60]

The reward for this gallant ride is an anticlimax to the ride itself. The tired speaker remembers his friends gathering around him, but the language of his reminiscence undercuts their praise in a curious way—"And no voice but was praising." The force of the "no" is not completely controlled by the "but." The crowd's acclaim seems all the more empty when we learn that the speaker pours "our last measure of wine" down Roland's throat. One might suppose at first that this wine was from the burgesses and the crowd of Aix, but as one naturally reads the line, the "our" applies to the speaker and his horse; and so the parentheses of the penultimate line are meant to alert us to the irony of the burgesses' vote commending Roland and saying that the

---

[41]Browning insisted that the poem describes "*no* historical incident whatever" (letter to Charles D. Browning, March 22, 1883, *Letters*, ed. Hood, p. 215).

wine he received was "no more than his due." Browning's negative construction implies that it was much less and that the reward Roland received, when both Dirck's Hasselt and Joris's Roos gave their all and died trying to reach Aix, was incommensurate with the service rendered and finally insignificant.

So even in this seemingly slight jeu d'esprit, Browning returns to a theme that pervades his poetry: namely, that the earthly reward we receive from our fellow men when we render them a great service is much less than we deserve or expect. Just before Joris's horse gives out, the speaker shouts, "How they'll greet us!" (l. 43). But one feels that the speaker's patting of Roland's ear (l. 51), calling him "his pet-name" (l. 52), and giving him his wine far surpass the comparatively cool welcome given by the people and burgesses of Aix, which heightens in Browning's eyes the great accomplishment of Roland and the speaker.

"Pictor Ignotus" is another meditation on fame. The poem's cloistered painter has chosen to paint anonymous religious paintings for his church instead of framed paintings for the private market.[42] He tells how he once dreamed

> Of going—I, in each new picture,—forth
> As, making new hearts beat and bosoms swell,
> To Pope or Kaiser, East, West, South, or North.
> [ll. 26–28]

Like the poet of *Pauline*, he dreams about a blissful state of earthly fame emanating from the dissemination of himself in his art. For a moment he even imagines this fame replacing heaven itself:

> Oh, thus to live, I and my picture, linked
> With love about, and praise, till life should end,
> And then not go to heaven, but linger here,
> Here on my earth, earth's every man my friend.
> [ll. 36–39]

But his view of the friendly audience created by fame has changed. He now regards his visions of it as glimpses of "revels through a door / Of some strange house of idols at its rites" (ll. 42–43), reminiscent of

---

[42]J. B. Bullen has suggested that the painter is Fra Bartolommeo, in "Browning's 'Pictor Ignotus' and Vasari's 'Life of Fra Bartolommeo di San Marco,'" *Review of English Studies* 23 (1972):313–19.

the slave worship imagined by the *Pauline*-poet. This nightmarish interpretation of attention has replaced the admirers with the "cold faces" of critics (l. 46) and has moved him to withdraw from the world. He has substituted for an appreciative audience the monotonous task of painting "Virgin, Babe and Saint" again and again (l. 60). But unlike Fra Lippo, he feels that in dedicating himself to church decoration he is at least not selling his soul: "No merchant traffics in my heart" (l. 62). Even though his paintings will blacken and die unseen in the sanctuary's gloom, he can be sure that he paints only for himself and for God. So he says to the young painter whose work men love:

> O youth, men praise so—holds their praise its worth?
> Blown harshly, keeps the trump its golden cry?
> Tastes sweet the water with such specks of earth?
> [ll. 70–72]

The unknown painter looks forward to the praise of heavenly rather than earthly trumpets and to the judgment of God instead of men.

This modest poem represents a tremendous advance in Browning's ability to portray objectively his subjective perception of his being an artist who can only "give you truth broken into prismatic hues."[43] Previously he had insisted upon presenting poets as examples of failed artists and forced himself to write in a disconnected fashion to show the subject-poet's internal conflict, thus making his own poetry an inchoate image of the psychological and artistic turmoil he depicts and, ironically, creating in the failures of his subjects his own poetic disasters. Here in "Pictor Ignotus" he has turned to another art form for an image of failure and found in painting a proper objective correlative for his theme. One cannot talk for long about the inadequacy of language to express the condition of a poet's spirit, as Browning does in *Sordello*, without having the tenor of the portrayed philosophical and psychological predicament affect the artistic vehicle of words one is trying to create. But once the poet emerges from his narcissistic fascination with himself (as Browning feels he needs to if he is to develop his soul), the poet can turn outside himself to forms of artistic representation using media other than language and to artists other than poets.

Even Browning's subjective lyrics, such as "Home-Thoughts, from

---

[43]Robert to Elizabeth, January 13, 1845, *Letters*, I, 7.

the Sea" and "Home-Thoughts, from Abroad," gain from the multitudinousness of detail that substitutes for the missing assurance of an audience. While the English public denies him a poetic or heroic fame, Browning finds that his love of England gives him his imaginative being and vision in the midst of foreign lands. In "Home-Thoughts, from the Sea" the speaker looks out from his ship to the sun setting upon Trafalgar, the scene of Nelson's victory over the French navy in 1805. And he asks, "Here and here did England help me: how can I help England?" (l. 5). Thinking of Nelson's great service to England, he wonders how in a time of peace he can do anything as heroic and, implicitly, as deserving of fame, and he answers himself by turning toward God: "Whoso turns as I, this evening, turn to God to praise and pray, / While Jove's planet rises yonder, silent over Africa" (ll. 6–7). He becomes for a moment a priest of nationalism, directing his audience to give thanks to God for England and reminding them through the reference to "Jove's planet" and to Africa that there are dark, pagan countries over against which England stands. So in his very worship of Nelson's victory, England's nationhood, and God, he finds the poetic task he had been looking for.

"Home-Thoughts, from Abroad" is another of Browning's poems in which the speaker is talking to someone who isn't where he is, to an audience he wishes he were close to. As in many other poems in *Dramatic Romances and Lyrics*, the rush of description is in some ways a compensation for the audience he doesn't have as a traveler abroad: "Oh, to be in England / Now that April's there" (ll. 1–2). He goes on to evoke a spring landscape which is unavailable to him but which, paradoxically, he alone in his imaginative vision can see. For "whoever wakes in England / Sees, some morning, unaware" that spring has come (ll. 3–4), and it is the poet who makes us aware that it has. Moreover, he self-consciously employs the overflow of detail as a sign of emotion attempting to substitute for vision: "That's the wise thrush; he sings each song twice over, / Lest you should think he never could recapture / The first fine careless rapture" (ll. 14–16). It is a poem not only about trying to live up to the conscious greatness of its first two lines but also about our needing the compensatory excess of the lonely poet's imaginative song in order to feel that an English spring has come.

When Charles Kingsley reviewed the poems of *Dramatic Romances and Lyrics*, along with the other work Browning published in the *Poems* of 1849, he gave voice to a narrower kind of poetic nationalism:

There are fine ballads in the second volume, healthy and English, clear of all that Italianesque pedantry, that *crambe repetita* of olives and lizards, artists and monks, which the English public, for its sins, has been spoon-fed for the last half century, ever since Childe Harold, in a luckless hour, thought a warmer climate might make him a better man, and that the way to raise one's own spirit was to escape to a country where humanity has sunk below the beasts.

And he enjoined:

How can Mr. Browning help England? By leaving henceforth "the dead to bury their dead," in effete and enervating Italy, and casting all his rugged genial force into the questions and the struggles of that mother-country to whom, and not to Italy at all, he owes all his most valuable characteristics.[44]

But Kingsley did not appreciate how the "gaudy melon-flower" of Italy helped Browning to see the English buttercups better ("Home Thoughts, from Abroad," l. 20), nor did he understand how the "*crambe repetita* of olives and lizards" was symptomatic of a larger poetic and psychological problem at the heart of Browning's work, a problem which had its roots in his lack of an audience and which was to be ameliorated only by Browning's love for Elizabeth Barrett and hers for him.

[44]"Mr. and Mrs. Browning," *Fraser's Magazine* 43 (1851):175–76.

3

Elizabeth Barrett and Robert Browning

> And now, my Audience, my crown-bearer, my path-preparer—I am with you again and out of them all—there, *here*, in my arms, is my *proved palpable success!*—My life, my poetry,—gained nothing, oh no!—but this found them, and blessed them.

Their story begins with each of them reading the other's poetry and then writing about it.[1] Elizabeth praised the "veined humanity" of *Bells and Pomegranates* in "Lady Geraldine's Courtship";[2] and, after perusing the two-volume collection of her *Poems* (1844), Robert said in his first letter to her, "I do, as I say, love these books with all my heart—and I love you too."[3] The ensuing two-year correspondence not only constitutes a valuable biographical and historical record but also stands as a literary monument. The letters themselves are epistolary monologues with a poetic density arising from the drama of Robert and Elizabeth's courtship as it is acted out and reflected in them. It is in these letters that Robert first discovers a discourse which both expresses himself and leads him to love another, that he finds his audience in Elizabeth, and that he recognizes himself to be as complete as a mere man can be through her love of him and his poetry.

They corresponded for more than five months before Robert first visited Elizabeth in her sitting room at 50 Wimpole Street on Thursday, May 20, 1845. In his second letter after this visit he apparently

---

[1] The quotation that heads the chapter is from a letter by Robert to Elizabeth dated January 11, 1846, *Letters*, I, 382.

[2] *The Poems of Elizabeth Barrett Browning*, ed. Harriet Waters Preston (Boston: Houghton Mifflin, 1900), p. 122.

[3] Robert to Elizabeth, January 10, 1845, *Letters*, I, 3.

proposed marriage to her. Elizabeth declined this first impulsive proposal but accepted his second some four months later, married him the following year, and eloped with him to Italy where they lived for the sake of her health. After the first five months, their letters became an extension of Robert's visits to and conversations with Elizabeth, and arranging their next meeting and discussing their last became constant topics that give their letters much of their intensely private character. Robert visited her about once a week, usually for an hour and a half at the beginning, gradually lengthening his stay to two hours in the middle and three hours at the end of their courtship, and increasing the frequency of his visits to once every five days.[4] As their meetings became more frequent, so did their letters. They usually wrote at least every other day to one another in response to the letter the other had sent the day before and often wrote twice a day when matters seemed especially urgent. They met at Wimpole Street for the last time on Wednesday, September 9, 1846, were married in St. Marylebone's Church on Saturday, September 12, wrote their last letters to one another on September 18, and left for France and Italy the next day.

Readers of their love letters must admit that the sentimental and literary expectations raised by *Sonnets from the Portuguese* and *Men and Women* are a little disappointed. Both Robert's and Elizabeth's letters are written in a breathless and involuted prose (his more than hers); they are prolix, and yet maddeningly elliptical and allusive; and, as most letters seem to retrospective readers, they are burdensomely trivial. One often experiences pleasure in perusing them, but to read them at length and straight through is a labor of scholarly love. The most dramatic event narrated in them is the dognapping of Flush and Elizabeth's ransoming of him, which delays the Brownings' marriage and elopement. This Dickensian episode stirs up a tempest in the Barrett household, has Robert sharing one of Mr. Barrett's financial principles, shows Elizabeth in her most sentimental, agitated, and determined mind, and, above all, as Virginia Woolf recognizes in her whimsical biography of Flush, underlines the extreme seclusion of Victorian bourgeois domestic life from the world's affairs. London does occasionally intrude in other ways: Robert is asked to get Dickens to endorse a brand of cough drops and once on an omnibus has his forehead and eye admired by a phrenologist; Elizabeth visits Hyde Park and Hampstead Heath and is taken by Mr. Kenyon to see the

---

[4]Robert recorded the dates and times of his visits on the covers of Elizabeth's letters; see *Letters*.

Robert Browning: His Poetry and His Audiences

Great Western train arriving at Paddington Station. Nevertheless, their letters rarely escape from the smell of the study and the gossip of the literary gazettes. The writers always seem agitated, observe little society outside their families or their sitting rooms, have little taste for British public life, and spend most of their time when they are not writing letters either writing poetry or reading. They have liberal views, but the distant struggles of Italy against Austria seem more romantic and more important than the continuing Corn Law debates and the plight of the poor at home. Their letters lack the familiar easiness of Arnold's letters to K, his wife, and his mother, and have nothing of the classic prose and critical observation of Arnold's letters to Clough. But both writers possess great reservoirs of epistolary energy, whether in discussing the day's events or in analyzing their own psychological states, and their letters display a range of operatic passion that puts even the tortured casuistry of Richardson's *Clarissa* to shame.

Their attention to their evanescent passions resembles that of a coloratura soprano singing bel canto and embellishing the most trivial of libretti with grace notes and finely spun trills. Here is Elizabeth:

> Dearest beloved, when I used to tell you to give me up, & imagined to myself how I should feel if you did it, . . & thought it would not be much worse than it was before I knew you . . (a little better indeed, inasmuch as I had the memory for ever . .) the chief *pang* was the idea of another woman . . ! From THAT, I have turned back again & again, recoiling like a horse set against too high a wall. Therefore if I talk of what all women *would* do, I do not mean that they SHOULD. "Thirty-six Bas," we shall not have,—shall we? or I shall be like Flush, who, before he learnt to be a philosopher, used to shiver with rage at sight of the Flush in the looking-glass, and gnash his teeth impotently, & quite howl.[5]

And here is Robert in reply:

> In your last letter you spoke of "other women," and said they might "love" me—just see! They might love me because of something in me, lovingness in me, which they never could have evoked . . so the effect produces the cause, my dear "inverter!" If there had been a vague aimless feeling in me, turning hither & thither for some object to attach itself to

---

[5]Elizabeth to Robert, April 23, 1846, *Letters*, II, 650. In their letters both Elizabeth and Robert used a two-dot ellipsis as a rhetorical pause, somewhere between a dash and a period. In quoting from their letters, I have followed Kintner's use of " . . " throughout to indicate their ellipses and so avoid any confusion.

and spend itself on, and you had chanced to be that object . . I should understand you were very little flattered and how a poplar does as well for a vine-prop as a palm tree—but whatever love of mine clings to you was created by you, dearest,—they were not in me, I believed—those feelings,—till you came: so that, mournful & degrading as it sounds, still it would, I think, be more rational to confess the possibility of their living on, tho' you withdrew,—finding some other,—oh, no, it is,—*that* is as great an impossibility as the other,—they came from you, they go to you—what is the whole world to them.[6]

The possibility of Robert's loving some other woman both makes Elizabeth jealous and gives her the courage to keep and marry him. While, on the other hand, Robert asserts that his feelings of love for her circumscribe his sexual desire, even in the midst of submitting to the logic that if he could love one woman he could love another, he passionately protests she is "the whole world" of his love, the true and only audience of his amorous attentions. This self-analysis also takes place in a hypothetical vacuum: neither one gives the other woman a name or flesh and blood, and neither supposes that anything but memory could substitute for the other. Then, too, the heavily rhetorical punctuation—the dashes, ellipses, and underlinings—attests to their ongoing conversation behind their letters, to their familiarity, their effusiveness, and their suddenly discovering what it is they are saying while speaking or writing.

Many still think of the Browning's marriage in the sentimental and evangelical terms made popular by the religious, bourgeois society that celebrated their marriage and their work as examples of Christian wholesomeness and found symbols of hope in them. Although the days of *The Barretts of Wimpole Street* (1930) are fast fading, along with the popular memory of their marriage, almost every Browning scholar will testify that the name of Browning, among the slightly read, will prompt the disconcerting question "Do you mean Elizabeth Barrett Browning?", even if, perhaps, more because of the euphony of her name than any knowledge of her work. And there seems little doubt that Elizabeth's *Sonnets from the Portuguese* still outsells Robert's poems among a certain kind of reader and that for them he is still Elizabeth Barrett Browning's husband. But such nostalgia should not distress us. For the symbolic union of romance and marriage and the balance of intellectual equality with the maintenance of male and fe-

---

[6]Robert to Elizabeth, April 26, 1846, *Letters*, II, 656.

male natures that their marriage represents were progressive in terms of their intellectual culture and still are in ours. Moreover, their marriage gave their poetry a sense of lived experience, making it less fanciful and more deeply felt. Elizabeth's best poetry, in fact, is her record of their love's progress in *Sonnets from the Portuguese*. And Robert's marriage to Elizabeth confirmed that he had found the audience he had been looking for, as one can see in "One Word More."

Browning was attracted to Elizabeth because she had praised his poetry and because she was a poet both of some merit and of popular acclaim. She appeared to him to possess a certain poetic power he desired and had always despaired of acquiring:

> Your poetry must be, cannot but be, infinitely more to me than mine to you—for you *do* what I always wanted, hoped to do, and only seem now likely to do for the first time. You speak out, *you*,—I only make men & women speak—give you truth broken into prismatic hues, and fear the pure white light, even if it is in me: but I am going to try . . so it will be no small comfort to have your company just now.[7]

He wanted to be able to "speak out," to give voice to his own beliefs, and to address his audiences directly. But he instinctively avoided the nakedness of religious and moral statement, preferring to indicate his own point of view indirectly and to let his readers make their own judgments of his monologues' speakers. Victorian readers, however, were never so sure of such judgment in complicated circumstances, and, as shown by their preference for his "Prospice," for Elizabeth's poetry over his, and for sententious touchstones in books of quotations, they enjoyed the poetry of statement and found Browning's indirectness puzzling and disturbing. Browning, too, felt this:

> What I have printed gives *no* knowledge of me—it evidences abilities of various kinds, if you will—and a dramatic sympathy with certain modifications of passion . . *that* I think: But I never have begun, even, what I hope I was born to begin and end,—"R.B. a poem." And next, if I speak (and God knows, feel) as if what you have read were sadly imperfect demonstrations of even mere ability, it is from no absurd vanity, though it might seem so—these scenes and song-scraps *are* such mere and very escapes of my inner power, which lives in me like the light in those crazy Mediterranean phares I have watched at sea, wherein the light is ever re-

[7]Robert to Elizabeth, January 13, 1845, *Letters*, I, 7.

volving in a dark gallery, bright and alive, and only after a weary interval leaps out, for a moment, from one narrow chink, and then goes on with the blind wall between it and you.[8]

The parenthesis here, "(and, God knows, feel)," is one of these momentary escapes of his inner light, and not the throwaway it would appear. For what he feels and God knows can only be communicated to others in brief moments at intermittent intervals. He wants to write poems with the religious vision of "Cowper's Grave" and the directness of another of Elizabeth's poems, "Cheerfulness Taught by Reason," which begins: "I think we are too ready with complaint / In this fair world of God's."[9] Again and again in his letters one finds variations on this theme: "I desire in this life (with very little fluctuation for a man & too weak a one) to live and just write out certain things which are in me, and so save my soul. I would endeavor to do this if I were forced to 'live among lions' as you once said—but I should best do this if I lived quietly with myself and with you."[10] The same sentiment appears in an earlier letter:

> I don't even care about reading now—the world,—and pictures of it, rather than writings about the world! but you must read books in order to get words and forms for "the public" if you *write*, and *that* you needs must do, if you fear God. I have no pleasure in writing myself—none, in the mere act—tho' all pleasure in the sense of fulfilling a duty—whence, if I have done my real best, judge how heartbreaking a matter must it be to be pronounced a poor creature by Critic This and acquaintance the other. But I think you like the operation of writing as I should like that of painting or making music, do you not?[11]

For Browning, Elizabeth takes on the roles of his first audience, of his mediator in the world of lions and critics, and of his partner in his quest to save his soul. This last divine duty entails the burden of writing for the public and the risk of critical disapproval, and, since his pleasure comes from self-recognition and not from the process of writing itself, he needs a loving audience. In Elizabeth he finds, he says, "my Audience, my crown-bearer, my path-preparer." She is to play nothing less than John the Baptist to his Christ.

[8] Robert to Elizabeth, February 11, 1845, *Letters*, I, 17.
[9] *Poems of Elizabeth Barrett Browning*, ed. Preston, p. 102.
[10] Robert to Elizabeth, September 18, 1845, *Letters*, I, 206.
[11] Robert to Elizabeth, March 11, 1845, *Letters*, I, 39.

Robert Browning: His Poetry and His Audiences

Why, then, didn't Browning become a bourgeois nineteenth-century Cowper, as so many of his later readers wished and thought he had become? And why didn't his love for Elizabeth allow him to overcome his reserve and embrace the confessional mode for himself instead of doing the police in different voices? There were two reasons. First, as his narrative poems and his dramas show, he believed in the ultimate inability of man to communicate his true passions for more than a moment to anyone other than God. Second, since for Browning it is only through the love of another that one discovers and can speak with assurance of God's love and since one cannot humanly love more than a few others, revelation remains a private matter that can only be hinted at by analogy and through symbols to those outside the circle of love. Browning believes that only God can express love for all of mankind in terms that everyone can understand. From this standpoint only God or one's beloved can know a man's feelings, while a man only glimpses his true feelings and his true self through his love of another or God; and, furthermore, our "fallen" language cannot express these feelings or make the struggle for individual salvation intelligible to others who would save their souls. As a consequence, Browning's heroes often practice a strange emotional celibacy which prevents them from engaging either in sexual intercourse or in normal conversation—for these relationships, in their eyes, distract them from their ultimate communion with God. There is, then, in Browning an extreme version of Protestant inwardness akin to that of the Nazarite and of Milton's Samson.

This kind of doctrine, even when as loosely held and as incoherent as in Browning's case, makes the point of writing poetry problematic and certainly makes the role of any human audience difficult to define. Browning had not retreated into a private mythology, as Smart and Blake had done, but he had deliberately written difficult poetry: "You do not understand what a new feeling it is for me to have someone who is to like my verses or I shall not ever like them after! So far differently was I circumstanced of old, that I used rather to go about for a subject of offence to people; writing ugly things in order to warn the ungenial & timorous off my grounds at once. I shall never do so again at least!"[12] With Elizabeth as his reader he will have a sympathetic muse and an understanding poet to whom and for whom he can

[12] Robert to Elizabeth, June 14, 1845, *Letters*, I, 95.

Elizabeth Barrett and Robert Browning

write. Indeed, in *Dramatic Romances and Lyrics*, the first issue of *Bells and Pomegranates* published after he had met Elizabeth, one sees some signs of this new deference to his audiences.

Whatever accommodations he makes to others, however, one senses in all of Browning's talk that he has developed a marked defensiveness in order to conceal his deep dismay concerning his critics' attacks upon him and his lack of popular success. Elizabeth felt this too, and, when she once inquired about his "sensitiveness to criticism," Browning replied with this thin-lipped attempt at nonchalance:

> I write from a thorough conviction that it is the duty of me, and with the belief that, after every drawback & shortcoming, I do my best, all things considered—that is for *me,* and, so being, the not being listened to by one human creature would, I hope, in nowise affect me. But of course I must, if for merely scientific purposes, know all about this 1845, its ways and doings, and something I do know, as that for a dozen cabbages, if I pleased to grow them in the garden here, I might demand, say, a dozen pence at Covent Garden Market,—and that for a dozen scenes, of the average goodness, I may challenge as many plaudits at the theatre close by; and a dozen pages of verse, brought to the Rialto where verse-merchants most do congregate, ought to bring a fair proportion of the Reviewers' gold-currency, seeing the other traders pouch their winnings, as I do see: well, when they won't pay me for my cabbages, nor praise me for my poems, I may, if I please say "more's the shame," and bid both parties 'decamp to the crows,' in Greek phrase, and YET go very lighthearted back to a garden-full of rose-trees, and a soul-full of comforts; if they had bought my greens I should have been able to buy the last number of "Punch," and go thro' the toll-gate of Waterloo Bridge, and give the blind clarionet-player a trifle, and all without changing my gold—if they had taken to my books, my father and mother would have been proud of this and the other 'favourable critique,' and . . at least so folks hold . . I should have to pay Mr. Moxon less by a few pounds—whereas . . but you see! Indeed, I force myself to say ever and anon, in the interest of the market-gardeners regular, and Keats's proper,—"It's nothing to *you,*—critics & hucksters, all of you, if I *have* this garden and this conscience,—I might go die at Rome, or take to gin and the newspaper, for what *you* would care"![13]

---

[13]Robert to Elizabeth, February 11, 1845, *Letters,* I, 18–19. Compare Kierkegaard's undated journal entry from 1846: "That there are publishers, that there are men whose entire existence expresses the fact that books are merchandise and an author a merchant, is a completely immoral state of affairs" (*The Journals of Søren Kierkegaard,* ed. and trans. Alexander Dru [London: Oxford University Press, 1938], p. 155). Later in the same entry he adds: "The insolence lies in viewing the spiritual production quite without reserva-

After this remarkable unburdening of his feelings under the cover of his market-garden analogy, he then says that he is not aiming at the intelligence of the postman or the merchants who knock at the door and that he is reasonably satisfied with his critics, as if to reassure Elizabeth that although he could wish for better notices, the ones he has received have not unduly affected him.

Despite his distrust of and disdain for his readers' opinions, one senses his great desire for approval and sees in his letters a growing trust in Elizabeth. He shows her his work in manuscript, gives her copies of his old poems to read, and discusses plans for new ones. Betty Miller, seizing upon this sort of personal confidence, has suggested that Browning was a psychologically weak man who sought the company of strong-willed women.[14] But this is a mistaken analysis, attributable in part to the fact that the important collections of Browning's surviving correspondence are addressed to women—Elizabeth Barrett, Isabella Blagden, Julia Wedgwood, and Mrs. Fitzgerald. Moreover, the deference paid to women by men of some taste in the Victorian age may seem today more than merely polite, since epistolary affection went much further then, before it became romance, than it does now. Further, it seems to be a sociological phenomenon often overlooked that after the 1820s the letters of literary men are addressed primarily to women and not to other men. This is true in Byron's *Letters*, Keats's *Letters*, and Arnold's *Letters*, just to name the most prominent letter writers of the period. Surviving correspondence among major literary figures during this period is very rare in comparison with the eighteenth century, notwithstanding the greater volume which

---

tions as merchandise" (p. 155). Morse Peckham points out that the technological revolution in papermaking had made books cheap by 1830, and so "the nineteenth-century author was culturally alienated from his society; at the same time he was being progressively forced out of the immensely expansive market by the consequences of the revolution in paper making. The cheaper publishing became, as it was harnessed into the industrial age, the more profit depended on exploitation of the mass market, and the more high-level cultural writing became economically marginal. A kind of Gresham's law took over: inferior culture drives out superior" (*Beyond the Tragic Vision: The Quest for Identity in the Nineteenth Century* [New York: George Braziller, 1962], p. 28). See also p. 67 and n. 9 above.

[14]Consider, for example, her comments on his friendship with Eliza Flower: "Half consciously, already, his quest was for a woman whose attributes would enable him not only to love and respect in the same person—(what happiness could I find in 'allying myself with a woman to whose intellect, as well as goodness, I could *not* look up?')—but who would restore to him the paradise of trust, of submissiveness, from which prematurely he had found himself severed" (Miller, *Robert Browning*, p. 29). She cites from Robert's letter to Elizabeth, August 13, 1846, *Letters*, II, 960.

survives. Literary men who lived in or near London had easy access to one another because of better roads and the railways and so had little need for writing letters to one another and had little of the mania of Boswell or Eckermann for recording their conversations. But while men attended dinners and talked at their clubs, women did not. There was no English institution equivalent to the Parisian salon; consequently, literary women of the period became voluminous letter writers, and much of the discourse that one would expect to occur between men and women in society became enshrined in letters, especially the men's, since women, then as now, keep letters longer than men do.

Robert's letters to Elizabeth also reflect his great sympathy for and fascination with the woman as the captive of others. Indeed, the rhetorical submissiveness in Browning's courtship of Elizabeth stems largely from his projection of himself into the woman's place. His second proposal of marriage, which Elizabeth conditionally accepted, was prompted by Mr. Barrett's tyranny in refusing to allow her to go to Italy: "You are in what I should wonder at as the veriest slavery."[15] He feels moved to offer himself as a compensatory sacrifice and to become her slave: "I would marry you now and thus—I would come when you let me, and go when you bade me."[16] She will order, and he will obey. Elizabeth, in a letter written shortly after their marriage, tells him that she thinks there has been too much of this: "And now, you still go on—you persist—you will be the woman of the play, to the last; let the prompter prompt ever so against you. You are to do everything I like, instead of doing what *you* like, . . and to 'honor & obey' *me*, in spite of what was in the vows last saturday,—is *that* the way of it and you?"[17] But it is hard to imagine how Elizabeth could have been otherwise persuaded of his love for her, especially when she had great fears of trading the at least familiar parental tyranny of her father for the unknown restrictions of marriage. She is comforted because she sees in Robert "none of the common rampant man-vices which tread down a woman's peace—& which begin the work often long before marriage. Oh, I understand perfectly, how as soon as ever

---

[15]Robert to Elizabeth, September 25, 1845, *Letters*, I, 214.

[16]Ibid. Constance W. Hassett acutely analyzes the moral and psychological "neediness" of Browning's rescuers in relation to the defenseless innocents who are rescued, in *The Elusive Self in the Poetry of Robert Browning* (Athens: University of Ohio Press, 1982), pp. 38–45.

[17]Elizabeth to Robert, September 14, 1846, *Letters*, II, 1073.

a common man is sure of a woman's affections, he takes up the tone of right & might . . & he *will* have it so . . & he *won't* have it so!"[18] She recognizes that Robert's sense of self is consistently to be found not in asserting his power over another but in striving imaginatively to become one with the other. In mythic terms, he sees his marriage as Perseus' rescue of Andromeda, instead of as Perseus' battle with Medusa. For the reverse of the Andromeda myth is the myth of Medusa, with whose head Perseus turns all who would steal Andromeda from him into stone. Medusa is the ravished and ravishing woman who reduces men to their erection; she is the woman whose beauty is horrible; the woman who demands the attention of men, and whose captive audience men are; the woman who leads men to their sexual and physical death. One glimpses this vision in Guido's view of Pompilia in *The Ring and the Book* and in Don Juan's thoughts about Fifine in *Fifine at the Fair*. But, by fixing his eyes on the woman whom death always threatens—on Andromeda, on Pompilia, on Alcestis in *Balaustion's Adventure*, and, of course on Elizabeth—Robert creates the audience he needs in order to become the resuscitating poet who rescues spirit from the tomb of history and the tyranny of time.

I

In becoming his audience, Elizabeth also becomes his critic, writing some fifty-six manuscript pages of commentary on the drafts of *Dramatic Romances and Lyrics, Luria,* and *A Soul's Tragedy,* which are printed (with the exception of twelve pages on "The Flight of the Duchess") in the *New Poems by Robert Browning and Elizabeth Barrett Browning* (1914) edited by Frederic Kenyon.[19] In agreeing to criticize his work as he had her *Prometheus Bound,* she finds herself losing her poetic self to him in a most curious way. After receiving her criticisms on "The Flight of the Duchess," Browning had complained about her having blotted out some of her remarks, and she explains to him:

> When I had done writing the set of annotations & reflections on your poem I took up my pencil to correct the passages reflected on with the reflections, by the crosses you may observe, just glancing over the writing as I did so. Well! and, where that erasure is, I found a line purporting to

[18] Elizabeth to Robert, July 4, 1846, *Letters,* II, 844.
[19] (London: Smith Elder, 1914), pp. 140–76; for the comments on "The Flight of the Duchess," see Edward Snyder and Frederic Palmer, Jr., "New Light on the Brownings," *Quarterly Review* 269 (1937):48–63.

be extracted from your "Duchess," with sundry acute criticisms & objections quite undeniably strong, following after it,—only, to my amazement, as I looked & looked, the line so acutely objected to & purporting, as I say, to be taken from the "Duchess," was by no means to be found in the Duchess, . . nor anything like it, . . & I am certain indeed that, in the Duchess or out of it, you never wrote such a bad line in your life. And so it became a proved thing to me that I had been enacting, in a mystery, both poet & critic together—& one so neutralizing the other, that I took all that pains you remark upon to cross myself out in my double capacity, . . & am now telling the story of it notwithstanding. And there's an obvious moral to the myth, isn't there?—for critics who bark the loudest, commonly bark at their own shadow in the glass, as my Flush used to do long & loud, before he gained experience & learnt the γνῶθι σεαυτόν in the apparition of the brown dog with the glittering dilating eyes, . . & as *I* did, under the erasure. And another moral springs up of itself in this productive ground; for, you see, . . "quand je m'efface il n'y a pas grand mal."[20]

In the mirror of the other poet she sees her own reflection, and, as the Greek phrase indicates, learns to know herself. Her projection of her own line upon his poem becomes evidence of a desire to make the other into a lesser version of oneself, a desire which must be repressed so that there can be self-recognition.

Robert, too, realizes that her reading and criticism of his poems underline her having become his audience. He begins to think of his writing to her as being somehow an unmediated expression of his feelings:

> One thing vexed me in your letter—I will tell you, the praise of *my* letters: now, one merit they have—in language mystical—that of having *no* merit. If I caught myself trying to write finely, graphically &c &c, nay, if I found myself conscious of having in my own opinion, so written—all would be over! yes, over! I should be respecting you inordinately, paying a proper tribute to your genius, summoning the necessary collectedness,—plenty of all that!—But the feeling with which I write to you, not knowing that it is writing,—with *you*, face and mouth and hair and eyes opposite me, touching me, knowing that all *is* as I say, and helping out the imperfect phrases from your own intuition—*that* would be gone—and *what* in its place?[21]

More than relying on her intuition to supply the meaning to his "imperfect phrases," he depends upon her for a sense of his reader's per-

---
[20]Elizabeth to Robert, August 8, 1845, *Letters*, I, 145.
[21]Robert to Elizabeth, February 19, 1846, *Letters*, I, 474.

spective. He not only adopts most of the particular changes in wording she urges on him in her remarks on *Dramatic Romances and Lyrics* but, in response to her comments, also makes larger structural changes and supplies the reader with a clearer view of the poems' content. She suggests that "The Englishman in Italy" without the coda on the Corn Laws is an "unfinished poem."[22] And, in a tone that shows she knows what it is to be perplexed by a particularly thistly patch of Browning, she wonders whether adding titles to his fragments might not help his readers:

> And now when you come to print these fragments, would it not be well if you were to stoop to the vulgarism of prefixing some word of introduction, as other people do, you know, . . a title . . a name? You perplex your readers often by casting yourself on their intelligence in these things—and although it is true that readers in general are stupid & cant understand, it is still more true that they are lazy & wont understand . . & they dont catch your point of sight at first unless you think it worth while to push them by the shoulders & force them into the right place. Now these fragments . . you mean to print them with a line between . . & not one word at the top of it . . now don't you!—And then people will read
>
> "Oh to be in England"
>
> and say to themselves . . "Why who is this? . . who's out of England?" Which is an extreme case of course; but you will see what I mean . . & often I have observed how some of the very most beautiful of your lyrics have suffered from your disdain of the usual tactics of writers in this one respect.[23]

So Browning titled the fragments "Home-Thoughts, from Abroad," which, while not wholly answering Elizabeth's objections, was at least a change for the better. And in reprinting *Dramatic Lyrics* in his *Poems* of 1849, Browning also retitled a number of others: "My Last Duchess" and "Count Gismond," which had first appeared together under the unhelpful general title of "Italy and France"; "Incident of the French Camp" and the "Soliloquy of the Spanish Cloister," which were originally paired under the title "Camp and Cloister"; and "Johannes Agricola in Meditation" and "Porphyria's Lover," which had been called "Madhouse Cells."

[22] *New Poems*, p. 143.
[23] Elizabeth to Robert, October 4, 1845, *Letters*, I, 222.

Elizabeth offers her best suggestions for revisions of rhythm. She supplies "Morning, evening, noon and night" for "Morning, noon, eve and night" ("The Boy and the Angel" l. 1), objects to the broken original line "What was in store" and points to the final "What change was in store" in "The Englishman in Italy" (l. 34), and in the same poem suggests that his original "Oh when shall we sail there together" is rhythmically better than "When shall we sail together," a line which Browning finally changes to "Fortù, shall we sail there together" (l. 209).[24] Her comments on "The Laboratory," in particular, demonstrate her understanding that Browning's ability to hear the underlying rhythm of a poem even when it is severely or haphazardly counterpointed creates great difficulties for his readers.[25] Indeed, he confesses to Elizabeth, that he sometimes composes carelessly, saying of "The Flight of the Duchess," "I shall let it lie, (my poem) till just before I print it; and then go over it, alter at the places, and do something for the places where I (really) wrote anyhow, almost to get done."[26] Elizabeth's tempering of his impatience, if not suddenly transforming him into a great poet, as Snyder and Palmer enthusiastically claim,[27] does at least make him more aware of his readers' difficulties and a little more willing to take into account exactly how much he is asking of them.

Browning's need for an audience was especially brought home to him by others' recognition of it and particularly by Landor's poetic tribute to him and by one of Elizabeth's in *Sonnets from the Portuguese.* Walter Savage Landor (1775–1864) was by 1845 an aging poet who

---

[24]*New Poems*, pp. 143, 147, 149.

[25]"And the Laboratory is hideous as you meant to make it:—only I object a little to your tendency .. which is almost a habit .. & is very observable in this poem I think, .. of making lines difficult for the reader to read .. see the opening lines of the poem. Not that music is required everywhere, nor in *them* certainly, but that the uncertainty of rhythm throws the reader's mind off the *rail* .. & interrupts his progress with you and your influence with him" (Elizabeth to Robert, July 21, 1845, *Letters*, I, 131). On Browning's versification, see Harlan Henthorne Hatcher, *The Versification of Robert Browning* (Columbus: Ohio State University Press, 1928). On the roughness of his verse, see Park Honan, "The Iron String in the Victorian Lyre: Browning's Lyric Versification," in *Browning's Mind and Art*, ed. C. R. Tracy (Edinburgh: Oliver & Boyd, 1968), pp. 82–89. And on his verse's approximation of conversation, see Russell Astley, "Browning's Logaoedic Measures," *VP* 16 (1978):357–68.

[26]Robert to Elizabeth, July 25, 1845, *Letters*, I, 135.

[27]Snyder and Palmer, "New Light on the Brownings," pp. 62–63. On Browning's increasing rhetorical accommodation of the reader, see Roy E. Gridley, "Browning and His Reader, 1855–1869," *The Nineteenth-Century Writer and His Audience*, ed. Harold Orel and George J. Worth, Humanistic Studies, no. 40 (Lawrence: University of Kansas, 1969), pp. 75–92.

sought to ingratiate himself with a younger generation of poets by praising them all and by writing poems hailing their genius.[28] Almost as if anticipating the future appreciation of the younger poet who later acted as the older poet's guardian when his irascibility and senility made him too difficult for his family to care for, Landor wrote one of his finest poems after reading *Dramatic Romances and Lyrics*:

To Robert Browning

> There is delight in singing, though none hear
> Beside the singer; and there is delight
> In praising, though the praiser sit alone
> And see the prais'd far off him, far above.
> Shakespeare is not *our* poet, but the world's.
> Therefore on him no speech; and short for thee,
> Browning! Since Chaucer was alive and hale,
> No man hath walk'd along our roads with step
> So active, so inquiring eye, or tongue
> So varied in discourse. But warmer climes
> Give brighter plumage, stronger wing; the breeze
> Of Alpine heights thou playest with, borne on
> Beyond Sorrento and Amalfi, where
> The Siren waits for thee, singing song for song.[29]

In reading "The Englishman in Italy," to which the last two lines here allude, Landor, unlike Kingsley, sensed that Browning had discovered his true subject in the Italian landscape, and he also understood how lonely Browning was as a poet, how he had no audience, how he took delight in singing even though no one beside himself heard, and how he hoped for some siren who would sing with him "song for song." But although he was right that Browning would find his heart and learn to sing freely in Italy, Landor's identification of this siren with Italy was too easy. For, as Browning correctly interpreted Landor's prophecy, his siren was Elizabeth:

> Dearest, whatever change the new year brings with it, we are together—I can give you no more of myself—indeed, you give me now—(back again if you choose, but changed and renewed by your possession—) the powers that seemed most properly mine: I could only mean that, by the ex-

---

[28]*Landor's Poetical Works*, ed. Stephen Wheeler, 3 vols. (London: Oxford University Press, 1937), II, 378–479.
[29]Ibid., II, 387–88.

pressions to which you refer—only could mean that you were my crown and palm branch, now and for ever, and so, that it was a very indifferent matter to me if the world took notice of that fact or no—Yes, dearest, that *is* the meaning of the prophecy—which I was stupidly blind not to have read and taken comfort from long ago—You ARE the veritable Siren—and you "wait me," and will sing "song for song"—And this is my first song, my true song—this love I bear you—I look into my heart and then let it go forth under that name—love—I am more mistrustful of many other feelings in me: they are not earnest enough; so far, not true enough—but this is all the flower of my life which you call forth and which lies at your feet.[30]

Browning understood, as Landor did not, that Elizabeth was to be his audience, and that his love for her would be his "true song."

Elizabeth, too, recognizes in Browning's poetry his need for a loving reader, and in the fourth of her *Sonnets from the Portuguese* sees with some quiet trepidation that she is his audience:

> Thou hast thy calling to some palace-floor,
> Most gracious singer of high poems! where
> The dancers will break footing, from the care
> Of watching up thy pregnant lips for more.
> And dost thou lift this house's latch too poor
> For hand of thine? and canst thou think and bear
> To let thy music drop here unaware
> In folds of golden fulness at my door?
> Look up and see the casement broken in,
> The bats and owlets builders in the roof!
> My cricket chirps against thy mandolin.
> Hush, call no echo up in further proof
> Of desolation! there's a voice within
> That weeps . . . as thou must sing . . . alone, aloof.[31]

Here in the ruined house of the sonnet Elizabeth finds shelter for her voice, while acknowledging Robert's poetic greatness by comparing his music to Jove's golden rain that impregnated Danaë. Moreover, in becoming the audience for a poet without one, who had become discouraged in his efforts to reach a wider public, she enabled Robert to recognize that his voice could be listened to even though he was isolated from others.

---

[30] Robert to Elizabeth, December 31, 1845, *Letters*, I, 351–52.
[31] *Poems of Elizabeth Barrett Browning*, ed. Preston, p. 215.

II

Despite the confidence that having an audience in Elizabeth gave him, the inspiration of Elizabeth's poetry does not seem in retrospect to have had a salutary effect upon Robert's work. Despite his reluctance to speak in his own voice, he had for a long time wanted to write "R.B. a poem," which would be a public confession of his religious beliefs; and with Elizabeth's encouragement and example he wrote and published *Christmas-Eve and Easter-Day* (1850).[32] There was certainly a market for religious sentimentality in 1850, whether for Martin Tupper's *Proverbial Philosophy* (1838–42), Tennyson's *In Memoriam*, or for his own wife's poetry. Browning knew this and was inclined to attribute the failure of *Christmas-Eve and Easter-Day* to the accidental circumstances of publication, advertising, and reviews.[33]

But upon looking into the work, one can see that despite Browning's desire to address the public at large, the poems have little audience other than the poet himself. This is particularly true of *Christmas-Eve*. The speaker enters a Dissenters' chapel on Christmas Eve and after observing the motley and ill-assorted mob assembled within and its incompetent pastor is so provoked that he walks out of the meeting into the rain. He then sees Christ and follows him to the outside of a Roman basilica, where the speaker criticizes Catholic ceremony without attending mass. He then goes to a dry lecture given by a Göttingen professor on Christ's possessing a profound moral vision despite lacking divinity. When the speaker's journey ends, he suggests that he has fallen asleep during the dissenting pastor's sermon and declares that though the Dissenters' worship has its shortcomings, it is better than Catholic pomp or ethical rationalism. But because of the sudden swerving from the original Hudibrastic satire, this pronouncement strikes one as no more than sentimental condescension.

This contradiction underlines the structural weakness of the poem. Browning wants to survey the range of contemporary religious thought, from dissenting Calvinism to moral atheism, but in order to provide narrative links between the various discussions he has the speaker miraculously transported by the hem of Christ's robe in a way reminiscent of Scrooge's journeys with the spirits of Christmas in Dickens's *Christmas Carol* (1843). The speaker finally calls these vision-

---

[32]Robert to Elizabeth, February 11, 1845, *Letters*, I, 17; also see *Handbook*, pp. 195–97.
[33]See Browning's letters to Edward Chapman of September 23, 1851 and January 16, 1852, *New Letters*, pp. 52, 54.

ary flights into question when he reveals that he has been dreaming, but not the tenor of their revelation, which ultimately reconciles him to the Dissenters' fervor. This narrative sleight of hand diminishes the reader's sympathy with his change of heart. Our principal difficulty as readers of *Christmas-Eve* (apart from any difficulty of religious belief) is that Browning offers no objective correlative for the abstract love of God in the form of humanitarian action as either evidence of the Dissenters' faith or an ethical ground on which to reverse our earlier aesthetic judgment. Instead, the speaker unaccountably bases his preference for the Dissenters on the implicit ground that he can most easily exercise the condescension of his ecumenical sentimentalism when they are its object. Despite his likes and dislikes, he holds out hope for everyone:

> And I exult—
> That God, by God's own ways occult,
> May—doth, I will believe—bring back
> All wanderers to a single track.
> Meantime, I can but testify
> God's care for me—no more, can I—
> It is but for myself I know;
>   The world rolls witnessing around me
>   Only to leave me as it found me.
>   [ll. 1181–89]

This last couplet, which revolves around the word "me," is a very haunting one. For if the world's testimony offers no message to him, he cannot offer his own testimony to anyone other than God.

This gives rise to a religious belief akin to abstract expressionism, since the formal surface of our utterance is held to have no connection with our intentions or our meaning; what we say has no ultimate significance. From this perspective, the formalism of Roman Catholic worship is only concrete confusion, for in Browning's view to believe in that form of worship is to believe that there is a proper mediation of man's love for God and that man can express that love perfectly. But still, according to his view that all worship of God is in some sense love of God, Browning feels that one's democratic appreciation of someone else's intentions must overcome one's doctrinal and dogmatic prejudices. This doctrinal democracy is then translated into aesthetic terms and occasions a digression on one of Browning's favorite aperçus—the perfect expressiveness of artistic imperfection. He asks us to "applaud the great heart of the artist" (l. 740), who not only makes statues of "a perfect symmetrical man" (l. 746) but also attempts to create a colossus and "uses the whole of his block for the bust, / Leaving the mind of the public to finish it" (ll. 751–52). The artist who, like the sculptor of colossus, understands that his execution must be less than what he has imagined is the most nearly perfect artist, because he consciously acknowledges the inherent imperfection of human artistic expression.

But both Browning and the speaker of *Christmas-Eve* have difficulty translating this doctrine of aesthetic and religious democracy into a criterion for critical judgment. The speaker finally chooses to worship in the Dissenters' chapel for the most condescending of reasons:

> Ask, else, these ruins of humanity,
> This flesh worn out to rags and tatters,
> This soul at struggle with insanity,
> Who thence take comfort—can I doubt?—
> Which an empire gained, were a loss without.
> [ll. 1317–21]

He prefers their worship because he feels they need God's love in their struggle with insanity more than others do. But one could surely find Catholic or Anglican congregations as poor or poorer whose worship was more restrained. The confusion of sociological and aesthetic criteria, moreover, leads the speaker to attribute his perception of their imperfection, of their being a grotesque collection of the "ruins of humanity," to them as well. Further, he confuses his condescending pity of their condition with an imaginative justification of their form of worship. But how are we to make a meaningful distinction between singing the "last five verses of the third section / Of the seventeenth hymn of Whitfield's Collection, / To conclude with the doxology" (ll. 1357–59) and listening to *Te Deum*? We cannot claim that either would be a more formally imperfect and thus more expressively perfect form of worship, if only because the claims of exclusive righteousness advanced for both forms of worship preclude any consciousness of imperfection. Whatever one's sympathies with the Dissenters' worship may be, one cannot by the poem's standards attribute any conscious imperfection to them, nor can one equate the unconscious grotesquerie of the congregation with the expressive imperfection of the sculptor's bust.

One finds the same lack of an audience for the speaker's meditations in *Easter-Day* as in *Christmas-Eve*. The speaker declares, "How hard it is to really be / A Christian, and in vacancy / I pour this story!" (ll. 363–65). The speaker is afraid that no one hears him, that the "Easy Christian" to whom he gives arguments and with whom he debates in the first twelve sections of the poem is not listening to him,[34] and that because everyone wishes to believe that faith is easy he will have no audience. He thinks it is so difficult to be a Christian that to profess his own faith is logically useless. Although he implicitly appeals to his reader's sense of being one of the elect, he seems to "stand in a cloud" of prophecy which isolates him from everyone (l. 351), as he recalls a vision of Judgment Day that he had three years ago. He sees that hell is the reward for whose who prefer earthly to heavenly pleasure and understands how easy it is to enjoy "earth's exquisite / Treasures of wonder and delight" (ll. 702–3) instead of loving God, and so to be condemned to hell.

The severity of this vision, together with the abstraction of its rhetoric, make *Easter-Day* a dry and dull theological poem. Elizabeth gently complained of the poem's "asceticism" and was assured by her husband that it was only "one side of the question."[35] But there is little comfort in *Christmas-Eve and Easter-Day*. In *Christmas-Eve* Browning displays the egalitarian nature of his belief; he feels that everyone has a chance to be saved and that God may extend his grace to anyone. The speaker's preference for the Dissenters' chapel at the poem's end and Browning's choice of Hudibrastic rhyme are evidence of the poet's good faith: they show Browning believes that man's love for God manifests itself in many ways and that man's salvation is not determined by any intellectual, aesthetic, social, or religious form but instead by man's love for God. But in *Easter-Day* he suggests that being a Christian, and so deserving of salvation, is almost impossible because it is so difficult to think of heavenly rather than earthly rewards. In short, Browning believes that salvation is possible for everyone but probable only for a few, that many are called but few chosen.

Given this modified Calvinism, it is no wonder that Browning would appear so uncomfortable in *Christmas-Eve and Easter-Day* with the idea of preaching to everyone. His distrust of a general salvation finally makes an address to the public at large on the subject of reli-

---

[34]On the "Easy Christian," see *Handbook*, pp. 202–4.
[35]Elizabeth to Mrs. Jameson, May 4, 1850, *Letters of Elizabeth Barrett Browning*, ed. Kenyon, I, 449.

gious doctrine a futile exercise for him. He is much more comfortable telling stories about individual salvation such as "The Boy and the Angel" and expressing his hopes for his own in such poems as "The Guardian Angel: A Picture at Fano." Reviewing *Christmas-Eve and Easter-Day* in *Revue des deux Mondes*, Joseph Milsand said, "Pour apprécier M. Browning, on est forcé de prophétiser, comme lorsqu'il s'agit d'une réligion naissante."[36] Milsand thought that Browning's great poetic accomplishment would be of epic scope, in contrast to Tennyson's lyrics. But, as one can see in *Christmas-Eve and Easter-Day*, Browning lacked both the corporate vision and the prophetic and nationalistic aims of the epic poet. It is difficult for any writer to make his or her work prophetic of the times, and it is especially so in the case of an individual's profession of faith. In nineteenth-century England, John Henry Newman, not Browning, made the most momentous religious confession. The Catholic emancipation, the turmoil among the clergy caused by the Reform Bill of 1832, and the slow diffusion of German textual criticism of the Bible gave to Newman's *Tract XC* and *Apologia pro Vita Sua* the air of prophecy and made the moment when he stared into his mirror and realized he was theologically a Monophysite a model of Victorian religious conversion. Yet in the light of biblical textual criticism, Newman's conversion was a retrograde movement in England's political and religious history, while Matthew Arnold's *Culture and Anarchy* and his career as a school inspector were truer prophecies of England's future course. Browning had neither Newman's nor Arnold's vision. He possessed the belief that one's fullest expression of oneself—one's love of God—was never wholly intelligible to oneself or to others but only to God; and given this belief, prophecy is impossible.

III

As his misunderstanding in *Christmas-Eve and Easter-Day* of the nature of Elizabeth's inspiration suggests, Browning's poetic difficulties usually stem from an insufficient grounding of his own and his speak-

---

[36]"La Poésie Anglaise depuis Byron: Browning," *Revue des deux Mondes*, n.s. 11 (1851):661. ("In order to appreciate Mr. Browning, one is forced to prophesy, as when considering a nascent religion"—my translation.) As a corrective to the enthusiasm of Milsand and of many late-Victorian readers for Browning's religion, see the somewhat disdainful but often insightful account of Browning's religious beliefs in Hoxie N. Fairchild, *Religious Trends in English Poetry*, 6 vols. (New York: Columbia University Press, 1939–68), IV, 132–67.

ers' voices in dramatic contexts. His lyric poetry, unlike Tennyson's, is not so much concerned with establishing and generalizing a mood by finding an objective correlative for it as with showing a speaker in search of an audience that will give him a sense of self. For Browning, the poetry of life is created from a dramatic and biographical density of detail, and, as Browning explains in his account of the objective and subjective poets in the *Essay on Shelley*, poetic consciousness is defined in relationship to its audiences.

In the two poems of "Night and Morning," Browning, like Tennyson in "Break, Break, Break," uses the sea to symbolize the separation of the speaker from his desired audience. But, in contrast to Tennyson, who finds in the sea's dull roar an image for the private isolation and loneliness created by the speaker's loss, Browning sees a certain beauty in separation that compensates for his speaker's chosen isolation and that has a deep resonance in the context of the great emigration from Great Britain in the 1840s, as he imagines the farewells of a voyager—most likely Alfred Domett, who sailed to settle New Zealand in 1842.

"Meeting at Night," the first of the companion poems, begins with a description of the sea and then modulates through the pathetic fallacy into a personification of the landscape, as if to create an audience in the absence of another:

> The grey sea and the long black land;
> And the yellow half-moon large and low;
> And the startled little waves that leap
> In fiery ringlets from their sleep,
> As I gain the cove with pushing prow,
> And quench its speed i' the slushy sand.
> [ll. 1–6]

There is in the picture of the waves being abruptly awakened from sleep and in the boat's almost sexual landing a sense of the speaker's desire to be with the person he meets in the second stanza. Their encounter is symbolized by "the quick sharp scratch / And the blue spurt of a lighted match" (ll. 9–10), which in its sudden flaring underscores the great passion and brevity of the pair's meeting. Moreover, the subdued sounds of their greeting—the "tap at the pane" (l. 9), the match's scratch (l. 9), the soft voice (l. 11), and the beating of the two hearts (l. 12)—heighten the feelings of the two in their reunion. And yet, although the speaker rushes from detail to detail as if to express the great urgency he feels, the force of so much description is to produce a certain detachment.

In "Parting at Morning," the second of the poems, the description of the sea reinforces our impression of the speaker's detachment. But, as some have felt, its immediate relation to "Meeting at Night" is puzzling. In 1889 Browning answered questions posed to him by the Day's End Club of Exeter and was asked if the final line of "Parting at Morning"—"And the need of a world of men for me"—was the expression of a woman's sense of loss or "the despairing cry of a ruined woman," to which he replied: "Neither: it is *his* confession of how fleeting is the belief (implied in the first part) that such raptures are self-sufficient and enduring—as for the time they appear."[37] From this A. Allen Brockington concluded that when the speaker mentions "him" in the poem's third line, he refers to the sun, extending the sun's personification that occurs in the second line.[38] This reading assumes that the speaker is saying good-bye to a woman, an assumption for which there is no internal evidence. But if the "parting" in the title makes any sense, it seems highly unlikely that the speaker would be pointing to divergent paths taken by him and the sun. Instead, it seems that he and his friend are dedicated to different purposes in life: the speaker on his ship to "a world of men" and the sea (l. 4), and his friend to "the path of gold" created by the sun (l. 3). In terms of Browning's personal allegory, Domett gives voice to his pioneering spirit, "happy as Waring then, / Having first within his ken / What a man might do with men" ("Waring," ll. 179–81), and Domett also associates Browning with the poetic path of the sun and with Shelley, the "Sun-Treader." The difference between the two men not only gives the speaker his melancholy insight into the brevity of fellowship with others but also creates his awareness that they need different audiences from each other in order to satisfy themselves.

Browning's feeling for Domett was never what Domett's was for Browning. As the thinly veiled voice of "Time's Revenges" says, "I've a Friend, over the sea; / I like him, but he loves me" (ll. 1–2). Yet, despite his departure for New Zealand, Domett turns up in "Waring," "Night and Morning," "Time's Revenges," and later in "The Guardian

---

[37]A. Allen Brockington, "Robert Browning's Answers to Questions Concerning Some of His Poems," *Cornhill Magazine* 109 (1914):317. The article is reprinted in *New Poems*, pp. 177–82, and also in Brockington's *Browning and the Twentieth Century* (Oxford: Clarendon Press, 1932), pp. 117–18.
[38]Brockington, "Browning's Answers," p. 317. His interpretation is noted in *Handbook*, p. 178. Most annotators of the poem follow Brockington.

Angel" and as "my old fellow" in " 'De Gustibus—'."³⁹ Still Browning is clearly more comfortable imagining Domett in "Waring" as a newborn Byron or the next avatar of Vishnu-land than he is with him in "Time's Revenges" as his nurse. Browning was never really a man for other men, partly because he grew up within the small circle of his family's society, but largely because he was not educated in a public school or at Oxford or Cambridge, where the friendships of Arnold and Clough and of Tennyson and Hallam flourished. Instead he was a poet of the relationships between men and women, between men and God, and between human and divine love.

The justification for and necessity of such biographical interpretation is addressed by Browning in his *Essay on Shelley*, which prefaced a collection of spurious Shelley letters that Moxon published in 1852 and withdrew when he discovered they were forgeries. As the introduction to the letters of a poet, the essay defends the publication of such private communications on the grounds that they provide the foundation for understanding Shelley's life and thus for interpreting his poetry: "Letters and poems are obviously an act of the same mind, produced by the same law, only differing in the application to the individual or collective understanding" (1007).⁴⁰ Browning argues that in the case of an objective poet such as Shakespeare we welcome biographical information without needing it to understand his work, but that in the case of a subjective poet such as Shelley we may need access to the facts of his life in order to comprehend his work fully, even though we should be able to intuit the worth of his moral purpose without fully understanding that purpose or the poetry.

The difference between the objective and subjective poets, Browning says, does not lie so much between their respective faculties, artistic methods, or subjects (though these count too) as between the objective poet's "appeal to the aggregate human mind" and the subjective poet's appeal "through himself to the absolute Divine mind" (1003). The objective poet speaks to be understood by his fellow man, while the subjective poet writes only for God. The objective poet is

---

³⁹For the identification of Domett in "'De Gustibus—,'" see James McNally, "The Lover of Trees in 'De Gustibus—,'" *Studies in Browning and His Circle* 3, no. 1 (1975):124–27. For a discussion of "Waring" in terms of Browning's position as a poet without an audience and of his relationship with Domett, see John F. McCarthy, "Browning's 'Waring': The Real Subject of the 'Fancy Portrait,'" *VP* 9 (1971):371–82.

⁴⁰My text is *Robert Browning: The Poems*, ed. John Pettigrew and Thomas J. Collins, 2 vols. (New Haven: Yale University Press, 1981). All citations refer to page numbers in the first volume of this text.

one whose endeavor has been to reproduce things external (whether the phenomena of the scenic universe, or the manifested action of the heart and brain), with an immediate reference, in every case, to the common eye and apprehension of his fellow-men, assumed capable of receiving and profiting by this reproduction. [1001]

This poet provides a poetic history of the world from which readers of all capacities may learn:

> The auditory of such a poet will include, not only the intelligences which, save for such assistance, would have missed the deeper meaning and enjoyment of the original subjects, but also the spirits of a like endowment with his own, who, by means of his abstract, can forthwith pass to the reality it was made from, and either corroborate their impressions of things known already, or supply themselves with new from whatever shows in the inexhaustible variety of existence may have hitherto escaped their knowledge. [1001]

The objective poet, then, presents the world as it is, recording faithfully what he sees for the enjoyment and enlightenment of both those who cannot see as well as a poet can and also for those who can. So, although one may like to know about the life of the objective poet, the "work speaks for itself as we say; and the biography of the worker is no more necessary to an understanding or enjoyment of it than is a model or anatomy of some tropical tree to the right tasting of the fruit we are familiar with on the market-stall" (1002). Since one has immediate access to the poet's subject, which is the world as it appears to everyone, one has no need of a biographical anatomy to uncover the concealed structure and hidden operation of the recorded experience.

The subjective poet, on the other hand, gives readers great difficulty. Unlike the objective poet, the subjective poet

> is impelled to embody the thing he perceives, not so much with reference to the many below as to the one above him, the supreme Intelligence which apprehends all things in their absolute truth,—an ultimate view ever aspired to, if but partially attained to, by the poet's own soul. Not what man sees, but what God sees,—the *Ideas* of Plato, seeds of creation lying burningly on the Divine Hand,—it is toward these that he struggles. [1002]

This poet speaks to and about God, not to and about his fellow men. Further, he discovers his poetry within his own soul: "Not with the combination of humanity in action, but with the primal elements of humanity, has he to do; and he digs where he stands,—preferring to seek them in his own soul as the nearest reflex of that absolute Mind, according to the intuitions of which he desires to perceive and speak" (1002). His social task is to prepare "for the forthcoming stage of man's being" by further extending his own relationship with God (1005), just as Zarathustra does in proclaiming the *Übermensch* in Nietzsche's *Thus Spake Zarathustra*. And, since a reader's understanding of the subjective poet's spiritual advancement depends not on a knowledge of the world but on the degree of individual spiritual enlightenment, there will be a concomitant delay in the subjective poet's reception and effect upon the world.

Browning's description of the connection between the subjective poet's life and art closely corresponds to Hegel's account, in his *Aesthetics*, of the content of Romantic art:

> The entire content is therefore concentrated on the inner life of the spirit, on feeling, ideas, and the mind which strives after union with the truth, seeks and struggles to generate and preserve the Divine in the subject's consciousness, and now may not carry through aims and undertakings in the world for the sake of the world but rather has for its sole essential undertaking the inner battle of man in himself and his reconciliation with God; and it brings into representation only the personality and its preservation along with contrivances towards this end.[41]

In contrast to Hegel, Browning does suppose that it is possible for a poet to alternate between objective and subjective modes and points to Shelley's *Cenci* and "Ode to Naples" as examples (1003, 1012). But the general force of Browning's distinction is to drive a wedge between private meditation leading to individual salvation and the advocacy of public action leading to institutional reform. In keeping with this implicit division, Browning sees the errors of Shelley's youth as the results of misapplied idealism. He feels that Shelley concerned himself too much with practical rather than spiritual matters (especially in *Queen Mab*), confusing the institutional oppression of the church and marriage with their spiritual foundations and urging their radical demolition instead of their spiritual reform. Nevertheless, Shelley not only represents for Browning the possibility of the poet's awakening and turning toward God but also reminds him of his own

---

[41]G. W. F. Hegel, *Aesthetics: Lectures on Fine Art*, trans. T. M. Knox, 2 vols. (Oxford: Clarendon Press, 1975), I, 525.

youthful renunciation of atheism in *Pauline*. For Browning believes men will not "persist in confounding, any more than God confounds, with genuine infidelity and atheism of the heart those passionate, impatient struggles of a boy towards distant truth and love, made in the dark, and ended by one sweep of the natural seas, before the full moral sunrise could shine out on him" (1007). By studying Shelley's life and so learning to love him and his poetry, Browning thinks men will see that Shelley was engaged not in a misguided social revolution but in a private struggle to reconcile himself with God.

For Browning, the biblical archetype of the subjective poet and his spiritual awakening is David the psalmist (1010). His treatment of David in "Saul" attempts to show when and how a subjective poet's private experiences become public therapy. "Saul" dramatizes the question of whether or not David's perception of beauty in God's nature can become Saul's. This question is rendered all the more problematic by Browning's imposition in the 1855 version of a Christian allegory on the poem's Hebraic subject.[42] The 1845 version of "Saul" would seem at first a fragmentary attempt to illustrate the poet's role as the unacknowledged legislator of mankind, which has as its source the following biblical text: "And it came to pass when the evil spirit from God was upon Saul, that David took an harp, and played with his hand: so Saul was refreshed, and was well, and the evil spirit departed from him" (1 Samuel 17:23). But because the question of Saul's recovery really arises from the great aesthetic pressure the drawn-out medley of David's songs places upon any dramatic resolution, Browning's original interest in "Saul" appears instead to have been in describing the various moods of the pieces David plays. And it is possible that, like *Fifine at the Fair*, which was in part inspired by Schumann's *Carnaval*, "Saul" was suggested by hearing a performance of Schumann's collection of dances for the piano, *Davidsbündlertänze* (1837).[43]

In the 1845 version, David's songs culminate in this declaration of his and the people's love for Saul:

[42] For discussions of this problem, see W. David Shaw, "The Analogical Argument of Browning's 'Saul,'" *VP* 2(1964):277–82; Ward Hellstrom, "Time and Type in Browning's *Saul*," *ELH* 33 (1966):370–89; Victor A. Neufeldt, "Browning's 'Saul' in the Context of the Age," *JEGP* 73 (1974):48–57; and Elizabeth Bieman, "The Ongoing Testament in Browning's 'Saul,'" *UTQ* 43 (1974):151–60.

[43] Like Browning, Schumann was interested in projecting different voices and moods from a single perspective. In *Davidsbündlertänze* the piano alternates between the voices of Florestan and Eusebius, the first passionate and the other reflective. One might also note that this work was written while Schumann was courting Clara, whose parents disapproved of the composer.

> Thou art grown to a monarch; a people is thine;
> And all gifts, which the world offers singly, on one head combine!
> On one head, all the beauty and strength, love and rage (like the throe
> That, a-work in the rock, helps its labour and lets the gold go)
> High ambition and deeds which surpass it, fame crowning them,—all
> Brought to blaze on the head of one creature—King Saul!
> [ll. 91–96]

Yet the word "rage" suggests that the evil spirit still possesses Saul and points to Browning's difficulty in deciding whether to show Saul exorcised of it or to show that despite David's efforts to soothe his soul the king remained full of sin and in need of God's grace.

In the 1855 version of "Saul," Browning will have decided that David cannot cleanse Saul's soul but that in his prophecy of Christ's coming David can envision the possibility of restoring the monarch's peace of mind. Browning will hold out hope for some communication between men on this earth in the incarnation of God's love in Christ.[44] Insofar as this doctrine avoids the solipsistic didacticism of *Christmas-Eve and Easter-Day*, it clearly provides a sounder poetic grounding for Browning's addressing his fellow men, and along with his courtship and marriage of Elizabeth it shows Browning coming to believe that one person's love for another can be something more than an ironic commentary upon the imperfections of language and the impossibility of a soul-fulfilling love between human beings. Like the subjective poet, David may sing his songs for God rather than for any one Saul; yet, Browning seems to say, in recognizing David's love for the world and for Saul, the reader, too, is afforded a glimpse of the poet's private love for God. But as "Saul" illustrates, one sees in *Dramatic Romances and Lyrics* only hints of and hopes for the ecstasy present in Robert and Elizabeth's letters. It is not until *Men and Women* that Browning is able to express fully his discovery of himself as a poet and a man in Elizabeth's love for him and his love for Elizabeth, in whom he found both his wife and, as he says, his audience.

---

[44] See Thomas J. Collins's discussion of the incarnation of Christ in connection with "Saul," in "Browning's *Essay on Shelley*: In Context," *VP* 2 (1964):121–23.

4

Men and Women:
Background and Audiences

Open my heart and you will see
Graved inside of it, "Italy."
Such lovers old are I and she:
So it always was, so shall ever be!

—"'De Gustibus—'"

From 1846 until Elizabeth died in 1861 the Brownings lived in Italy for the most part. They resided in Florence at Casa Guidi but spent one year in Paris and travelled in the summers for the sake of Elizabeth's health, and, while their financial resources were not great, they led a comfortable bourgeois life.[1] If their marriage was not quite, as romanticizers have imagined, the perfect picture of marital bliss (largely, I think, because of the natural strain created by the shadow of death darkening Elizabeth's eyes in her portraits), their fifteen years together were undoubtedly happy ones. Robert had found a woman he could both love and serve; and Elizabeth had escaped from her father's domestic tyranny, had married, and had had a child, when the prospect of becoming a mother must have seemed impossible to her before meeting Robert. Moreover, despite feeling the intellectual and social isolation of English society in Italy, they missed England very little, since they were both essentially solitary persons—Elizabeth because of her illness, Robert because of his public reserve. They did not

---

[1] Elizabeth had an income from an investment in shipping funds and a smaller one from her poetry, and John Kenyon, who thought of himself as their matchmaker, had given them a hundred pounds a year after they had married (*New Letters*, p. 47, n. 1; also see Browning's letter of June 12, 1850, to Reuben Browning, *New Letters*, pp. 47–49). Kenyon left them eleven thousand pounds when he died in 1856, which eventually made Robert's worrying over his meticulous accounts a purely formal exercise (*New Letters*, pp. 47–48, n. 2).

132

Men and Women: Background and Audiences

require the society of literary London and found the source of their imaginative inspiration in their chosen Italy and in each other.

Robert produced his best poetry in these years—ironically, because he had so little time to write. Talking with and caring for Elizabeth, writing to publishers, managing his meticulous accounts, and traveling required most of his energy. He had revised his poems for the two-volume collection Moxon had published in 1849 and had suffered yet another disappointment when *Christmas-Eve and Easter-Day* failed to win him the popular audience he had aimed for. But while *Christmas-Eve and Easter-Day* seemed yet another misdirection of his energies in an attempt to write for an audience he knew nothing about, *Men and Women* (1855) was an artistic, if not a critical, triumph.[2] Part of the reason for its success is that he wrote its poems to please Elizabeth, not to impress his family, gain fame, or prepare for the stage. Despite the relative obscurity of some of his subjects, nothing seems recherché in the way that *Paracelsus, Sordello,* and all of his plays do. His poetry is often not any easier to read for his being sure of his audience, since private biographical references make it even more obscure, but at least Browning does not confuse us so often by projecting his own difficulty in establishing a relationship with an audience onto the imagined relationship between a poem's speaker and his or her audiences. The speakers still struggle to find themselves in terms of their audiences, but they now come to terms with their analysis, instead of wildly grasping for compensatory substitutes for God or their beloved.

Victorian readers did not find the new Browning much different from the old. Although William Morris, reviewing *Men and Women* in the *Oxford and Cambridge Magazine* (1856), placed Browning "high among the poets of all time, and I scarce know whether first, or second, in our own," he was forced to acknowledge that almost everyone else thought him "a careless man, writing down anyhow anything that comes into his head."[3] Arthur Hugh Clough, for example, in a letter to William Allingham, said that *Men and Women* displayed Browning's "most reckless, de-composite manner."[4] And John Ruskin wrote

---

[2] See Charlotte C. Watkins, "Browning's *Men and Women* and the Spasmodic School," *JEGP* 57 (1958):57–59.

[3] "*Men and Women* by Robert Browning," *Collected Works of William Morris,* 24 vols. (London: Longman, Green, 1910), I, 347.

[4] Clough to Allingham, January 14, 1856, *Correspondence of Arthur Hugh Clough,* ed. Frederick L. Mulhauer, 2 vols. (Oxford: Clarendon Press, 1957), II, 514. Clough alludes here to *Sordello,* v, 619.

to Browning about the volume, complaining: "You are worse than the worst Alpine Glacier I ever crossed. Bright, deep enough surely, but so full of clefts that half the journey has to be done with ladder and hatchet."[5] In reply to Ruskin, Browning gave one of his fullest accounts of his artistic principles:

> For the deepnesses you think you discern,—may they be more than mere blacknesses! for the hopes you entertain of what may come of subsequent readings,—all success to them! For your bewilderment more especially noted—how shall I help *that*? We don't read poetry the same way, by the same law; it is too clear. I cannot begin writing poetry till my imaginary reader has conceded licences to me which you demur at altogether. I know that I don't make out my conception by my language; all poetry being a putting the infinite within the finite. You would have me paint it all plain out, which can't be; but by various artifices I try to make shift with touches and bits of outlines which *succeed* if they bear the conception from me to you. You ought, I think, to keep pace with the thought tripping from ledge to ledge of my "glaciers," as you call them; not stand poking your alpenstock into the holes, and demonstrating that no foot could have stood there;—suppose it sprang over there? In *prose* you may criticize so—because that is the absolute representation of portions of truth, what chronicling is to history—but in asking for more *ultimates* you must accept less *mediates*, nor expect that a Druid stone-circle will be traced for you with as few breaks to the eye as the North Crescent and South Crescent that go together so cleverly in many a suburb.[6]

The aim of poetry, according to Browning, is to put "the infinite within the finite." For this reason, he tells us, we can't expect to learn about ultimate truths in an ordered chronicling of versified events. We must instead rely upon an impressionism, which, by its very method of conveying experience in bits and pieces, suggests the existence of the infinite, of God, of entities otherwise beyond the capacities of coherent expression to describe. Consequently, if the reader doesn't understand the juxtaposition of the touches, of the fragmented brush strokes on the canvas, the painter-poet Browning considers himself to be can do nothing to help, for to expect an ordered, logical exposition of incidents and their meanings when talking about ultimates is already to misunderstand their nature. Hence readers can say that a par-

---

[5] Ruskin to Browning, December 2, 1855, published in David J. DeLaura, "Ruskin and the Brownings: Twenty-five Unpublished Letters," *John Rylands Library Bulletin* 54 (1972):326–27.

[6] Browning to Ruskin, December 10, 1855, in W. G. Collingwood, *The Life and Work of John Ruskin*, 2 vols. (London: Methuen, 1893), I, 200.

ticular series of images does not succeed in conveying a message to them, but, according to Browning, they can't quarrel as Ruskin does with the method, for that is a sine qua non.

Although he does not present his speaker's arguments in a logical fashion, Browning still has his readers in mind, because he still conceives of writing poetry in the same way that Paracelsus conceived of teaching medicine; that is, as an attempt to communicate esoteric knowledge to the common man. Later in the same letter to Ruskin he says:

> Do you think poetry was ever generally understood—or can be? Is the business of it to tell people what they know already, as they know it, and so precisely that they shall be able to cry out—"here you should supply *this*—*that*, you evidently pass over, and I'll help you from my own stock?" It is all teaching, on the contrary, and the people hate to be taught. They say otherwise,—make foolish fables about Orpheus enchanting stocks and stones, poets standing up and being worshipped,—all nonsense and impossible dreaming. A poet's affair is with God, to whom he is accountable, and of whom is his reward: look elsewhere, and you find misery enough.[7]

Browning's thinking contrasts sharply with the Neoclassical dictum of Samuel Johnson expressed by Imlac in *Rasselas*:

> "The business of a poet," said Imlac, "is to examine, not the individual, but the species; to remark general properties and large appearances; he does not number the streaks of the tulip, or describe the different shades in the verdure of the forest. He is to exhibit in his portraits of nature such prominent and striking features as recall the original to every mind, and must neglect the minuter discriminations."[8]

And it differs from Shelley's Neoplatonic emphasis upon the revelatory power of poetry:

> Poetry lifts the veil from the hidden beauty of the world, and makes familiar objects be as if they were not familiar; it reproduces all that it represents, and the impersonations clothed in its Elysian light stand thenceforward in the minds of those who have once contemplated them, as

[7]Ibid., I, 201.
[8]*The History of Rasselas, Prince of Abissinia*, in *The Works of Samuel Johnson*, ed. Arthur Murphy, 12 vols. (London: S & R. Bentley, 1823), V, 448.

memorials of that gentle and exalted content which extends itself over all thoughts and actions with which it coexists.⁹

Browning not only thinks the poet should express thoughts in an original manner but that the poet should have original thoughts, neither appealing to a common stock of observations nor recalling the unfamiliar essence of the familiar. The poet, therefore, will have difficulty being understood and can only dream of a popular fame. Indeed, Browning fears fame: "I shall never change my point of sight, or feel other than disconcerted and apprehensive when the public, critics and all, begin to understand and approve me."¹⁰ In the face of Ruskin's criticism, in particular, and of harsh public comment in general, Browning retreats into a doctrine of prophetic esoterism. He feels that a "poet's affair is with God" and that the true meaning of poetry will "act upon a very few, who react upon the rest."¹¹

By the time of *Men and Women*, then, Browning, who had attempted in his early narratives, his plays, and the lyrics of *Bells and Pomegranates* to reach a wider public and achieve a financial and poetic success, had abandoned this project as wishful thinking. The thought of a wider public makes him think of "foolish fables about Orpheus enchanting stocks and stones, poets standing up and being worshipped"; he now believes that this is an audience which cannot be had. Further, even communication with a single reader about his private experience of the infinite in the finite must be haphazard. Browning can never be sure that his fragments will be understood by anyone, whether it be Ruskin or even his favorite reader, Elizabeth.

I

As a useful heuristic device, one may schematically categorize the imaginary and real audiences within Browning's poetry as either one or many, and as either present or absent. The ideal audience in *Men and Women* is both single and present: the speaker will usually be a lover, his audience his beloved. This ideal relationship will somehow transcend time and nature and exist in an infinite moment outside the

---

⁹*A Defence of Poetry*, in *The Complete Works of Percy Bysshe Shelley*, ed. Roger Ingpen and Walter E. Peck, 10 vols. (London: Ernest Benn, 1926–30), VII, 117–18.
¹⁰Browning to Ruskin, December 10, 1855, in Collingwood, *Life and Work of Ruskin*, I, 202.
¹¹Ibid.

natural world. The two will implicitly become one with God. No poem, of course, could represent such a state, nor does this perfect relationship exist in Browning's poems as anything other than an ideal, evanescent moment recollected in memory. Browning allows his readers access to these moments by juxtaposing disparate details to indicate the active presence of God in the natural world, and his impressionistic method of presentation seeks to reproduce this experience in his readers by requiring them to "connect the scattered light into one constellation—a Lyre or a Crown," as Browning says in the preface to *Paracelsus*.[12] According to Browning, then, the reader, as the correlative of the ideal audience, has the task of synthesizing the poem's luminous details and discovering the meaning intended by their structure. The reader, in short and by extension, must find God on his or her own.

This image of the ideal audience undercuts Browning's earlier notions about the poet's possibly becoming a prophet whose audience is manifold and present. In *Pauline, Paracelsus,* and *Sordello* we are given the image of the boy Nature-poet who communes with Nature and whose identity becomes virtually indistinguishable from it. This poet claims to experience a special union of himself with the world and everyone in it because he desires to "be all, have, see, know, taste, feel all" (*Pauline*, l. 278). In *Paracelsus* this poet, whom one cannot disentangle from his audiences, has difficulties because he must attempt to mediate between a private, privileged audience with God and his public. And later, in *Sordello* and Browning's tragedies, the political or religious prophet's attempted mediation between his audiences is associated with liberal bourgeois sentiment, while in *Christmas-Eve and Easter-Day* this mediation is associated with an ecumenical spirit.

Once Browning's dreams of offering prophecy to an avid Victorian public dissipated, the always troubling nightmare vision of the absent or ghostly crowd comes to the fore in his imagination and is identified in many ways as an image of the mass consumption of poetry. In *Pauline* this appears in the image of the slave readers; in "'Childe Roland to the Dark Tower Came'" the ghostly crowd becomes the Band—that group of fellow adventurers on the quest—in short, tradition. These images are nightmarish because they are associated with the historical death and living petrification of the poet, with the crystallization of the living person in the poet's work as he or she

---

[12]*Complete Works*, I, 65.

becomes a historical monument, or part of the "practico-inert."[13] In terms of classical myth, this destruction of the poet recalls the Maenads' dismemberment of Orpheus. One expects, then, that given Browning's interest in the poet as prophet, he would be obsessed with the poet's revolutionary self-sacrifice for the people. But because of the private nature of his religious beliefs and the bourgeois association of political salvation with religious enlightenment, this image of the Promethean poet is nightmarish. Consequently, Browning's political poems come to concentrate on the relationship between his speaker and a single, absent lover, thus making them lyrics of nationalist sentiment instead of heroic eulogies and laments of the golden age just past. The poet celebrating his absent mistress writes "Home Thoughts, from Abroad" ("Oh to be in England, / Now that April's there,") and "Home Thoughts, from the Sea." The country is thought of as an abstract entity instead of a mass of people. For Browning, the crowd becomes something ghostly and is associated with the grotesque. "The Heretic's Tragedy" and "'Childe Roland to the Dark Tower Came,'" for example, burgeon with disconnected detail and monstrous rhymes and have crowds celebrating the death of an adventurous soul.

In much of Browning's minor poetry the speaker addresses a single, absent audience—the lover who has gone, the God who seems to have disappeared. Here the poetry becomes a tenuous discourse in which the speaker explains his actions and expresses his feelings to himself; the dramatic monologue becomes lyric. In Browning's later poetry and in many of his shorter lyrics this audience will be invoked and then disappear (literally so in *Prince Hohenstiel-Schwangau*), and the poems become abstract, private lyrics, of which "My Star" is the most famous. This poetry is filled with expressly private symbolism, biographical allusions, and esoteric meanings, which we may annotate by referring to Browning's life and his letters but can never be sure of completely understanding.

---

[13]This is Jean-Paul Sartre's term for any "worked-over matter" in the public domain and outside one's personal control; see *Search for a Method*, ed. and trans. Hazel E. Barnes (New York: Alfred A. Knopf; rpt. New York: Random House, 1968), p. 173. Browning associates fame with cannibalism in a letter to Elizabeth of June 19, 1846: "As if it were not the best privilege one finds in being 'known' never so little, that it dispenses one from having to make oneself known: when you are shipwrecked among Caribee Indians you are forced to begin professing 'I can make baskets, and tell fortunes, and foresee eclipses—so don't eat me!' And even there if they threatened nothing of the kind, I should be content to live and die as unhonoured as one of their own cabbage-trees" (*Letters*, II, 801). Note the parallel with Browning's market-garden analogy quoted on p. III.

Men and Women: Background and Audiences

To put in perspective Browning's poetic practice of concentrating upon the relationship of the poem's speaker to his audiences, it will be useful to compare his poetry briefly with Shelley's and to notice both the structural similarities between their images of audience and also the substantial differences between the tenors of their vehicles. In Shelley's poetry one sees man in relationship to a powerful and destructive Nature and also sees that images of this relationship usually partake of a sublime irony. In "Ozymandias," to take a simple example, a traveller from an antique land tells the sonnet's speaker how he saw a ruler's broken statue in the middle of nowhere and read the inscription on its pedestal:

> "My name is Ozymandias, king of kings:
> Look on my works, ye Mighty and despair!"
> Nothing besides remains. Round the decay
> Of that colossal wreck, boundless and bare
> The lone and level sands stretch far away.[14]

One sees how time and Nature have made a melancholy mockery of the ancient tyrant's boast. While Ozymandias's words once counseled the less powerful to consider their relative unimportance in the face of his magnificence, they now remind one that the fate of all human endeavor and vanity is to return to dust. Where there was once a great civilization, one sees only a wrecked piece of sculpture and an unintentional memento mori in the midst of an empty, endless desert. Ironically, then, the head of Ozymandias speaks to us of that sublime Nature which will engulf us all.

Shelley's sonnet represents a cultivated search for the sublime in Nature, an attempt to recapture the elemental forces of Nature through a Romantic exaggeration which reduces man to an insignificant figure in the landscape. In John Martin's painting, *Sadek in Search of the Waters of Oblivion* (1815), for example, the precipitous mountains and an angry, red sky are pressed so much into the foreground that at first one overlooks the small figure of Sadek stretched over a rock in the raging torrent and reaching for the roaring waters below him. Associated with this aesthetic of the natural sublime is a kind of counter-sublime in which one self-consciously realizes that there would be no sublimity without the human imagination, that without the figure of Sadek in the foreground for the landscape to dwarf, Martin's painting

---

[14] *The Complete Poetical Works of Percy Bysshe Shelley*, ed. Thomas Hutchinson (London: Oxford University Press, 1904), p. 550.

would seem empty and meaningless.¹⁵ Shelley gives his fullest expression to this counter-sublime in "Mont Blanc." He begins by comparing the relation of the human mind to "the everlasting universe of things" with the sound of "a feeble brook" in "the wild woods, among the mountains lone, / Where waterfalls around it leap for ever, / Where woods and winds contend, and a vast river / Over its rocks ceaselessly bursts and raves" (ll. 1, 7–11).¹⁶ Shelley meditates in the remainder of the poem on the powerful serenity of Mont Blanc, which has seen civilizations come and go, but he finally reflects triumphantly upon the controlling power of the human imagination: "And what were thou, and earth, and stars, and sea, / If to the human mind's imaginings / Silence and solitude were vacancy?" (ll. 142–45). While on the one hand Shelley humbly contemplates the awesome power of Nature which Mont Blanc represents, he also points out that without man's apprehension of it there would be no sublimity about Mont Blanc, only an essential blankness, that man's relationship to Nature is predicated in terms of a dialectic of the sublime and counter-sublime.

Browning, in contrast, discovers the sublime in everyday life. The infinite moment, for Browning, depends on the barrenness of common life and occurs when one comes into communion with either God or the divine presence in another person. In "Memorabilia" he juxtaposes two visionary moments: one in which he hears someone mention having seen and spoken with Shelley, and a remembered occasion when he found an eagle's feather while walking across a moor. Browning wonders at someone's having seen Shelley and survived, as if that person had returned from the dead: "But you were living before that, / And also you are living after" (ll. 5–6). To Browning, who had idolized Shelley as the Sun-Treader in *Pauline*, the idea that Shelley led a real life seems somehow beyond the imagination. The thought of having seen and spoken with Shelley astonishes him so much that he recoils from the difference between his idealized vision and the idea of an everyday, flesh and blood Shelley as if he has seen a ghost: "And the memory I started at— / My starting moves your laughter" (ll. 7–8). His association of Shelley with a kind of inaccessible divinity paradoxically makes Browning's demystifying experience into a sublime revelation:

---

¹⁵The term *counter-sublime* is Harold Bloom's, in *The Anxiety of Influence: A Theory of Poetry* (New York: Oxford University Press, 1973), pp. 99–112. See also Thomas Weiskel's discussion of this term in *The Romantic Sublime: Studies in the Structure and Psychology of Transcendence* (Baltimore: Johns Hopkins University Press, 1976), p. 27.

¹⁶*Complete Poetical Works of Shelley*, p. 535.

Men and Women: Background and Audiences

> I was one day in the shop of Hodgson, the well-known London bookseller, when a stranger came in, who, in the course of conversation with the bookseller, spoke of something that Shelley had once said to him. Suddenly the stranger paused, and burst into laughter as he observed me staring at him with blanched face; and . . . I still vividly remember how strangely the presence of a man who had seen and spoken with Shelley affected me.[17]

The anecdote places Browning's surprise in an everyday setting. It presents us with a London bookshop, an overheard conversation, and Browning's embarrassing public display of his private astonishment. There are three confrontations here: one between the stranger and Shelley, one between Browning and the stranger, and one between Browning and Shelley. But the poem isolates the sublime encounter that takes place between Browning and Shelley, letting the easy conversational exchange indicate the ordinary circumstances and almost projecting Browning into the stranger's place and the stranger into Shelley's. It emphasizes Browning's subjective difficulty in coping with two audiences at once, both with his private Shelley and with the public Shelley represented by the stranger he is speaking to and shows him momentarily confusing the one with the other.

The poem makes strangers of us, too, by unsettling us with its opening line: "Ah, did you once see Shelley plain?" The awkwardness of "plain," a word which seems at first glance chosen solely for the sake of rhyme, and the clumsily poetic "Ah" may remind us of Arnold's voice straining for a note beyond its range. But this awkwardness is deliberate and ironic: who would have thought of seeing Shelley plain? This Shklovskyan "making strange" or "defamiliarization" stemming from the deliberately roughened language serves to demystify us.[18] The difficult, mellifluous poet of ethereal love becomes a man seen in the light of day. So what appears at first to be strained poetic diction modulates into a conversational rhyme which neatly and ironically expresses Browning's sense of wonder at discovering that Shelley had once lived and breathed: "And did he stop and

---

[17]Browning's remarks as recalled by W. G. Kingsland in "Robert Browning: Some Personal Reminiscences," *Browning Baylor Interests,* no. 2 (Waco, Texas: University of Baylor Press, 1931), p. 33. On the relation between memory and imagination in Shelley and Browning, see Herbert F. Tucker, Jr., "Memorabilia: Mnemonic Imagination in Shelley and Browning," *Studies in Romanticism* 19 (1980):285–325.

[18]Victor Shklovsky, "Art as Technique," in *Russian Formalist Criticism: Four Essays,* trans. Lee T. Lemon and Marion J. Reis (Lincoln: University of Nebraska Press, 1965), pp. 12, 22.

speak to you / And did you speak to him again?" (ll. 2–3). To our surprise, the ordinary, everyday event of meeting someone in public and speaking with him suddenly acquires a poetic content.

The status of the last two stanzas with respect to the first two seems uncertain. They ostensibly represent the "memory I started at," the speaker's explanation of his surprise; for, after telling us about finding an eagle's feather in the middle of a moor, to cover up his faux pas and his inexplicable astonishment, he breaks off: "Well, I forget the rest" (l. 16). But the second incident doesn't explain the first in any commonly received way. Hence, it would seem, the lame excuse. We have all been in the same predicament of having to try to explain away some trivial yet overpowering private association whose visible sign has caused us public embarrassment and have all had to yield to the tyranny of social convention by excusing ourselves, dismissing our private thoughts as unimportant and inconsequential, and mulling over our recollection in silence. Yet, although "Memorabilia" takes the form of a failed poem, of a few lines which must end without having made their point, the second half of the poem in fact celebrates allegorically the discovery of this found memory:

> I crossed a moor, with a name of its own
> And a certain use in the world no doubt,
> Yet a hand's-breadth of it shines alone
> 'Mid the blank miles round about:
>
> For there I picked up on the heather
> And there I put inside my breast
> A moulted feather, an eagle-feather!
> Well, I forget the rest.
> [ll. 9–16]

In the middle of a bare moor, the name of which he cannot remember and the purpose of which escapes him, is the place where he found an eagle's feather. It makes the place strange in the same way Shelley's imagined presence makes Browning's encounter with the man who had met Shelley strange; and, through its juxtaposition with the first moment, it plunges us into Browning's private associations and so "defamiliarizes" the natural process of personal recollection by making art of it. The reminder of the sublime eagle creates a kind of shrine "'mid the blank miles round about," in the same way the jar placed on a hill in Tennessee does in Stevens's "Anecdote of the Jar." But while

Men and Women: Background and Audiences

Stevens makes a statement about meaning being given by artistic framing and not by the inherent properties of what is being framed, Browning, in "Memorabilia," places two framed moments next to each other to show us how he had had a sublime vision in the course of an ordinary conversation.

In Shelley's poems we find, first, the human engulfed by a sublime Nature and then, counterbalancing this vision, the poet's realization that without the human imagination Nature means nothing. We find we have an adequate psychic defense against Nature's terrible sublimity but that it is purchased at the cost of looking at man from Nature's point of view and seeing life as "a dome of many-coloured glass" staining "the white radiance of Eternity" ("Adonais," ll. 462–63).[19] The price of our freedom from Nature is a scientific viewpoint and a thoroughgoing skepticism.

To go very rapidly, then: instead of seeking to control the Byronic search for self-forgetfulness in Childe Harold's and Manfred's contemplation of sublime Nature through an urbane irony, as Shelley does, Browning tries to control irony by isolating persuasive moments of transcendental experience. Unlike Shelley, he is not interested in isolating subjectivity as such but instead is worried about whether or not subjective, spiritual experience can be communicated to others. The difference in their management of poetic tone stems from their divergent cultural motivations: while Shelley seeks to control and express the alienation of frustrated revolutionary vision, Browning tries to preserve the hopes of ecumenical religion and bourgeois liberal sentiment amidst the social reorganization and the great spiritual alienation created by industrial rationalization. In "Memorabilia," Browning attempts to reveal the content of his subjective experience by grounding the transcendental moment in objective circumstance, making the discovery of an eagle's feather the vehicle for the Shelleyan tenor. What at first appears to be the juxtaposition of two unrelated epiphanies is revealed to be an identity of two experientially disconnected moments. This identity not only reminds us that our memories single out particular events in such a way that their context disappears but also suggests that poetry is the collection and assemblage of such events with a view towards confirming the existence of a world beyond this one. The danger of such a method is that readers will view the speaker's ecstatic experience as a purely private one not available to them. But in

[19]*Complete Poetical Works of Shelley*, p. 443.

Robert Browning: His Poetry and His Audiences

"Memorabilia" Browning curiously plays upon our transcendental expectations by requiring us to imagine a flesh and blood Shelley as an impossibility when we know very well that Shelley once lived and by making us realize that it is somehow more difficult to picture the living Shelley than the Shelley whose poetry we read.

There is, I think, a curious epilogue to "Memorabilia" in Wallace Stevens's "Anecdote of the Prince of Peacocks":[20]

> In the moonlight
> I met Berserk
> In the moonlight
> On the bushy plain.
> Oh, sharp he was
> As the sleepless!
>
> And, "Why are you red
> In this milky blue?"
> I said.
> "Why sun-colored,
> As if awake
> In the midst of sleep?"
>
> "You that wander,"
> So he said,
> "On the bushy plain,
> Forget so soon.
> But I set my traps
> In the midst of dreams."
>   [ll. 1–18]

This appears to be Browning's encounter with Shelley, the Sun-Treader, generalized and rendered surrealistically. As in most of his poems, Stevens exploits the ambiguities of syntax in a dreamlike logic: the speaker meets Berserk "in the moonlight," but the repetition of the phrase in the poem's third line suggests that what is meant by "in" is not clear. Is Berserk equivalent to the moonlight? To a kind of lunacy? Or what? This dream, which perhaps dramatizes the poet's anxiety about poetic influence that Harold Bloom talks about,[21] works by

---

[20] Quoted with the permission of the publisher from *The Collected Poems of Wallace Stevens*, copyright 1954 by Wallace Stevens (New York: Alfred A. Knopf, 1954), pp. 57–58.

[21] *Anxiety of Influence*; see also his *Map of Misreading* (New York: Oxford University Press, 1975).

distorting any sense of a proper reference. It makes the speaker's question, "Why are you red / In this milky blue?" seem to suggest that it would be perfectly normal to meet Berserk in the moonlight if he weren't red. In short, here as elsewhere in Stevens, the imagination is the prince of peacocks, creating a private world from the colors of its own moonlit language.

For Browning, poetry is neither the unveiling of the world's essence in the mind's imagination, as it is in Shelley, nor the creating of a language for the imagination, as it is in Stevens; instead, it is the discovery of the divine in the mundane and the preservation of a memory of the divine. For Browning, poetry is again and again an attempt to ground the experience of the transcendental world in the context of a speaker's relationship with his audiences, in order to record and reduplicate that experience. Or, in Browning's words, poetry puts "the infinite within the finite." In "Memorabilia" we see the tension between the individual's private contact with the divine in the other and the need to make this ecstatic vision public. As the speaker's hesitancy in the poem so richly suggests, the poet's apprehensiveness concerning his audience's understanding of his private experience prevents him from fully expressing his feelings. He needs to find the proper audience to address and to feel he has a chance of being understood, before he speaks. In "Memorabilia" the proper audience appears to be Shelley, who is paradoxically made available to Browning's imagination just when he is transformed from an ideal figure into a dead man. This appears to make Browning feel that Shelley would have understood him, even as he is realizing that Shelley isn't there. For Browning, then, the poetic problem is neither the ontological status of the imagination, as it is in Shelley, nor the referentiality of language as it is in Stevens; instead, it is the creation of a self-conscious identity in the moment of recognizing the divine in the audience to whom one is speaking.

II

But Browning, too, can retreat into private symbolism and does so consciously in "My Star":

> All that I know
> Of a certain star
> Is, it can throw

> (Like the angled spar)
> Now a dart of red,
> Now a dart of blue;
> Till my friends have said
> They would fain see, too,
> My star that dartles the red and the blue!
> Then it stops like a bird; like a flower, hangs furled:
> They must solace themselves with the Saturn above it.
> What matter to me if their star is a world?
> Mine has opened its soul to me; therefore I love it.

We first need a little annotation: "spar" refers to any shiny, crystalline mineral, such as feldspar, that cleaves in chips or flakes. And Geoffrey Tillotson helpfully explicates the image "then it stops like a bird" as meaning that the star stops twinkling just as a bird ceases to move its wings when it comes down to earth.[22] Browning claims to have a private audience with his star; he can tell others about its twinkling until they want to see it too, but it does not twinkle for them. So they must be content with Saturn. He, on the other hand, doesn't care "if their star is a world," because, he says, "mine has opened its soul to me; therefore I love it." What is this star that only he can see? To the first reader of *Men and Women* it was probably no mystery; it was she —Elizabeth Barrett Browning. He works a much more elegant variation on this same theme when he compares her to the moon in "One Word More" (ll. 188–97), but in "My Star" the metaphor remains esoteric. One may want to understand precisely what he means, may "fain see, too," may even be satisfied with having worked out that his star is Elizabeth, that the twinkling is her love for him, that the Saturn above her is her poetry; and one may think that the moon and Saturn are surprisingly condescending, if just, images for his wife's poetry in comparison with his own. But the distance between Browning and his star is even greater for the reader: Browning feels only the effluence of its soul, not the soul itself; and the reader cannot even do that.

The esoteric color symbolism and the cross-referencing of one metaphor with another—the star with the spar, for example—are common features of Browning's later poetry, and so it is not surprising that when he published the *Selections from the Poetical Works of Robert Browning* in 1872, one of the most popular volumes of his poetry to appear during his lifetime, he placed "My Star" first. Its preëminence

---

[22]"A Word for Browning," *Southern Review* 72 (1964):394. On the image of the star in general, see C. Willard Smith, *Browning's Star Imagery* (Princeton: Princeton University Press, 1941).

Men and Women: Background and Audiences

and its obvious reference to Robert's love for Elizabeth made it a favorite poem of his readers and also contributed to making it the signature piece that he wrote in the albums of admirers who wanted something from him.[23]

If in this poem Browning speaks of a single, absent audience that is not readily accessible to himself and not at all to others, in "'Childe Roland to the Dark Tower Came'" he presents a remarkable portrait of a mad quester after fame who converts his paranoiac delusions of mass persecution into a vision of self-transfiguration. The image of the ghostly, multitudinous audience risen from the dead to preside over the destruction of the hero had first appeared in *Paracelsus*:

> Here stand my rivals; Latin, Arab, Jew,
> Greek, join dead hands against me: all I ask
> Is, that the world enrol my name with theirs,
> And even this poor privilege, it seems,
> They range themselves, prepared to disallow.
> Only observe! why, fiends may learn from them!
>   [V, 161–66]

Paracelsus projects his students' dissatisfaction with his quackery onto the past and imagines that the world and the famous doctors of the centuries are conspiring against his posthumous fame. Like Paracelsus, Childe Roland, too, desperately desires fame and like Paracelsus has wandered throughout the world in a "search drawn out thro' years" (l. 20). Roland's long quest for the Dark Tower has made him bizarrely paranoid as well: he imagines that the "hoary cripple" he meets at the beginning of the poem "lied in every word" and has gained "one more victim" (ll. 1–6). But, as Harold Bloom has pointed out, Roland immediately contradicts himself by noting that the old man has directed him into "that ominous tract which, all agree, / Hides the Dark Tower" (ll. 14–15).[24] The fear of failing in his quest to become a member of the Band causes him to anticipate malevolence in everyone

---

[23] Katherine de Kay Bronson, "Browning in Venice: Being Recollections by the Late Katherine de Kay Bronson with a Prefatory Note by Henry James," *Cornhill Magazine*, ser. 3, 12 (1902):165, 169. The poem may have something to do with Browning's learning of Elizabeth's middle name and his response to it: "I have a flower here—rather, a star, a mimosa, which must be turned and turned, the side to the light changing in a little time to the *leafy* side, where all the fans lean and spread . . so I turn your name to me, that side I have not last seen: you cannot tell how I feel glad that you will not part with the name—Barrett—seeing you have two of the same—and must always, moreover, remain my EBB!" (*Letters*, I, 329–30).

[24] *Map of Misreading*, pp. 108–9.

and everything around him, and he thinks of himself as a dying man whose friends have all abandoned him (ll. 25–36).

At first, Roland finds himself surrounded by a Nature which refuses to pay attention to him. All of the landscape seems engaged in an internecine war: the grass leaves quarrel with the thistle stalks (ll. 67–69); some brute oppresses the dock's leaves (ll. 69–72); a blind, uncomprehending horse stands stupefied (ll. 76–84); and the alders and willows participate in some profane communion with the river, "which had done them all the wrong" (l. 119). The incestuous narcissism that Roland projects upon the landscape finds its most intricate convolution in the circular confinement of a battlefield, where there is "no foot-print leading to that horrid mews, / None out of it" (ll. 135–36). But as its demonic qualities increase, the landscape seemingly begins to notice Roland. An oak appears almost to cry out to him, and a great black bird brushes his cap. The pathetic fallacy here seems to function as a satanic parody of the communion with all of creation that Paracelsus, like the *Pauline*-poet, believes man's imaginative sympathy will guarantee:

> The new glory mixes with heaven
> And earth; man, once descried, imprints for ever
> His presence on all lifeless things: the winds
> Are henceforth voices, wailing or a shout,
> A querulous mutter or a quick gay laugh,
> Never a senseless gust now man is born.
> [*Paracelsus*, v, 718–23]

Roland seeks such a communion with Nature and wishes to unify creation around himself, but he can only make the landscape hate him. The poem's description seems no more than a surrealistic jumble of bits and pieces, the appearance and disappearance of which make no sense. One notes, for instance, that when Roland fords the river his mind shifts among various interpretations of what he speared:

> Which, while I forded,—good saints, how I feared
>   To set my foot upon a dead man's cheek,
>   Each step, or feel the spear I thrust to seek
> For hollows, tangled in his hair or beard!
> —It may have been a water-rat I speared,
>   But, ugh! it sounded like a baby's shriek.
>   [ll. 121–26]

"A dead man's cheek" becomes "a water-rat" and then a baby. The details of the landscape seem to have a meaning that is inaccessible to him. And the Dark Tower is the ultimate symbol of the landscape's apparent inaccessibility; its meaning for Roland becomes its mystery. To see his own being implicated in the mystery of Nature and to imagine its enigma to be a conspiracy against him gives the landscape its unity and confirms Roland in his paranoid identity.

Indeed, his paranoid fantasies effect a transformation in Nature that appears in the alteration of the similes used to describe the hills surrounding the Dark Tower. Upon first glance, they appear "crouched like two bulls locked horn in horn in fight" (l. 177). But after Roland sights the tower, "The hills like giants at a hunting, lay, / Chin upon hand, to see the game at bay" (ll. 190–91). And by further imaginative transformation these giants become the ghosts of the Band, whose members have died in the quest of the Dark Tower. These antagonistic ghosts rise from the alien landscape, and at that moment Roland defiantly declares himself separate from Nature and transfigures himself in song:

> There they stood, ranged along the hill-sides, met
> To view the last of me, a living frame
> For one more picture! in a sheet of flame
> I saw them and I knew them all. And yet
> Dauntless the slug-horn to my lips I set,
> And blew *"Childe Roland to the Dark Tower came."*
> [ll. 199–204]

This is Orpheus being dismembered by the gathered Maenads and the poet merging into his own poetry, becoming his own song, and singing, as Orpheus's head does, in defiance of death. Hence the ambiguity critics have sensed about whether Roland dies or lives to tell the tale.[25] In one sense he must die, because the Band has come to view

---

[25]Mrs. Sutherland Orr has it right when she says Childe Roland "lives to tell the tale" (*A Handbook to the Works of Robert Browning*, 6th ed. [London: G. E. Bell & Sons, 1892], p. 273). Langbaum ingeniously argues that the knight uses the past tense to intensify his immediate experience, and he rejects the possibility of Roland's retrospection on the grounds that "the utterance develops as in other dramatic monologues without preordained direction—the knight does not, articulately at least, seem to know the outcome" (*Poetry of Experience*, p. 198n). Yet one page later, comparing Roland with T. S. Eliot's Prufrock, Langbaum states, "Both Prufrock and the knight know from the start that they will fail" (p. 199). John King McComb argues that Roland's "voice in the poem is Browning's most forceful presentation of the futility of all attempts to suppress or escape memory," the last memory being the poem itself ("Beyond the Dark Tower:

the last of him, while in another sense he does not die but instead becomes his own objectification, the "other" the Band sees in him, part of the Dark Tower's history. Roland speaks the last line, then, to begin telling his tale. By having the last line repeat the poem's title, and by having Roland speak in the past tense throughout the poem to reexperience his triumph, Browning has made the poem into a narrative that tries to, but cannot, recapitulate its own telling and that consequently becomes a demonic parody of the infinite moment—a *mise en abîme*. In its inversion of the good moment the poem presents a nightmare vision of the poet's audience and a petrification of the self into the historical monument of its own poetry.

This dark image of the crowd contrasts sharply with Browning's early ideal poetry of natural religion in which the young poet, like Wordsworth, tries to extend his communion with Nature to a fellowship with mankind but finds his ambitions beyond his capability and must satisfy himself with the comfort of a few close friends and God. In the early narratives the protagonists' failure to find fellowship with mankind is seen as the product of historical circumstances and their own characters. But in *Men and Women* Browning seems to see the prospect of any general fellowship with man as not only beyond his reach, as in *Christmas-Eve and Easter-Day*, but also beyond anyone's. The few poems showing the affection of a group for an individual are fraught with ironies: the grammarian of "A Grammarian's Funeral" is dead; the hero of "The Patriot" is first feted and then later hanged; and the Jews of "Holy-Cross Day" attend the Roman bishop's annual sermon to them but thumb their noses at the doctrine preached.

The best index of this shift in Browning's poetics is "Saul." Browning defers the possibility of David's enlightenment of Saul to the Last Judgment and to Christ's coming. This deferral represents a rewriting of the story in Samuel, since there we are told that David did comfort Saul. The question for Browning in 1845, when he ended the

---

Childe Roland's Painful Memories," *ELH* 42 [1975]:469). Harold Bloom has a much more imaginative view of Childe Roland's temporal position in *Map of Misreading*, pp. 106–22. Bloom believes that Browning, in working out his anxiety over Shelley's influence on him, runs through a series of tropic defenses before finally having Roland assert through the trope of metalepsis his priority over the Band (Roland's precursors). Roland thus at once repudiates the weight of historical influence and valorizes the past as metaleptically rewritten. In short, for Bloom the problem of writing poetry under the influence of a tradition is how to dramatize, psychologically and rhetorically, a "Whiggish" historical dialectic of tradition such as the one T. S. Eliot discusses in "Tradition and the Individual Talent," *Collected Essays*, 3d ed. (London: Faber & Faber, 1951), pp. 13–22. See also chapter 1, n. 62, above.

poem with section 9, was how David would or could soothe Saul's soul. Before publishing the poem, Browning had shown it to Elizabeth when he visited her on August 26, 1845. She thought that the poem could be published as it was: "The consolation is not obliged to be definite . . is it?"[26] But Browning did finish the poem eventually and published the completed version in *Men and Women*.

The first version portrays David, the youthful Nature-poet, trying to bring the greenness of the natural world to the desert of Saul's soul. The figure of the young Nature-poet (seen before in *Pauline* and *Sordello*) appears here in a story that would appear to affirm the myth of a poet at one with his audience and Nature. When David first appears, he is literally in tune with the spirit of the natural world. Abner exclaims, "Yet now my heart leaps, O beloved! God's child with his dew / On thy gracious gold hair, and those lilies still living and blue / Just broken to twine round thy harp-strings" (ll. 11–13). The extension of this natural imagery to Saul gives us reason to hope that Saul will be comforted, especially when David describes him as "waiting his change, the king-serpent all heavily hangs, / Far away from his kind, in the pine, till deliverance come / With the spring-time" (ll. 31–33). David, then, feels that Saul's recovery will flow directly from the cycles of Nature and that like the serpent Saul will slough off his old skin when spring comes. As the youthful poet of spring and "the wild joys of living" (l. 70), he believes that he only needs to remind Saul of Nature's beauty and strength to heal his soul. By singing of the world's beauty David will be reminding Saul of God's part in creating it and will, or so he thinks, bring Saul back into God's family: "God made all the creatures and gave them our love and our fear, / To give sign, we and they are his children, one family here" (ll. 47–48). David hopes to sing to Saul in the same way he plays his harp to his sheep, soothing them "so docile they come to the pen-door till folding be done" (l. 37). Given the biblical text and the poem's development through section 9, one expects Saul to be comforted in the poem's continuation.

But for Browning it would be at once too easy and too hard to follow the biblical story: too easy, because it would imply that a poet can have an intimate relationship with all audiences, and too hard because to make the poem's denouement and Saul's reawakening believable, the second part of the poem would logically have to have given us

[26]Elizabeth to Robert, August 17, 1845, *Letters*, I, 173. Also see *Letters*, I, 185, 252.

Saul's instead of David's point of view, just as the vignettes in *Pippa Passes* do. The whirl of images and songs which are the representation of God's bountiful presence in the world should, one thinks, draw Saul from his private agony. In terms of the biblical story, the cascading flow of beautiful word pictures would certainly appear to be enough:

> Oh, the wild joys of living! the leaping from rock up to rock,
> The strong rending of boughs from the fir-tree, the cool silver shock
> Of the plunge in a pool's living water, the hunt of the bear,
> And the sultriness showing the lion is couched in his lair.
> And the meal, the rich dates yellowed over with gold dust divine,
> And the locust-flesh steeped in the pitcher, the full draught of wine,
> And the sleep in the dried river-channel where bulrushes tell
> That the water was wont to go warbling so softly and well.
> How good is man's life, the mere living! how fit to employ
> All heart and the soul and the sense for ever in joy!
>
> [ll. 70–79]

In the burgeoning fullness of these lines one hears a more mature version of the poet of *Pauline*, who would "be all, have, see, know, taste, feel, all" (l. 278), and one expects something more than a groan and a shudder from Saul in response (ll. 61, 63), for Saul's motions would seem to be sounds and gestures preliminary to his acknowledging and sharing David's grand vision of life. One might even think here of Mr. Kenyon, who, according to Elizabeth, found the poem a mental restorative: "He reads it every night, he says, when he comes home & just before he goes to sleep, to put his dreams into order."[27] Testimony such as this, it would seem, would certainly have given Browning the courage to play David to other Sauls besides Mr. Kenyon.

But Browning violates our expectations by not having David cure Saul and by substituting instead a proleptic vision of Christ's spiritual resurrection. This refashioning of the biblical story attempts both to preserve the salvation implicit in the Bible and also to remain true to Browning's feeling that no poet can be everything to everyone without being God. It does so by reformulating and updating the Old Testament in the traditional terms of an anagogic allegory. David does not heal Saul's soul but instead envisions Christ healing it in heaven. David wishes "to save and redeem and restore him" but admits he cannot (l. 277). All he can offer is the Christ to come:

[27]Elizabeth to Robert, December 9, 1845, *Letters*, I, 315.

Men and Women: Background and Audiences

> O Saul it shall be
> A Face like my face that receives thee; a Man like to me,
> Thou shalt love and be loved by, for ever: A Hand like this hand
> Shall throw open the gates of new life to thee! See the Christ stand!
> [ll. 309–12]

The poet, who desires an audience and a response from it, defers to the myth of the great Poet of poets whom, he tells Saul, "Thou shalt love and be loved by." The reciprocal love between David and Nature does not carry over into David's fellowship with mankind and is displaced by the more encompassing vision of Christ's love which provides the promise of such fellowship.

This ecstasy then transforms David's old communion with Nature into something faintly ominous:

> I know not too well how I found my way home in the night.
> There were witnesses, cohorts about me, to left and to right,
> Angels, powers, the unuttered, unseen, the alive, the aware:
> I repressed, I got through them as hardly, as strugglingly there,
> As a runner beset by the populace famished for news—
> Life or death. The whole earth was awakened, hell loosed with her crews;
> And the stars of night beat with emotion, and tingled and shot
> Out in fire the strong pain of pent knowledge: but I fainted not,
> For the Hand still impelled me at once and supported, suppressed
> All the tumult, and quenched it with quiet, and holy behest,
> Till the rapture was shut in itself, and the earth sank to rest.
> [ll. 313–23]

This is the image of the runner surrounded by crowds as he brings news home from Marathon, which reminds us of Browning's "Pheidippides," the Marathon runner, in *Dramatic Idyls* (1879) and of his lighter treatment of a similar subject in "'How They Brought the Good News from Ghent to Aix.'" The earlier communion with Nature is replaced by this threatening image of a crowd hungry for news and indifferent to its bearer's fate and then by one of hell and its crews. The poet's relationship with his audience changes from communion to disturbing uncertainty and then to antagonism. But God's hand puts this image out of David's mind by quieting Nature until "the rapture was shut in itself." After having had his vision of Christ, David no longer seems to be at one with Nature as the birds and beasts shrink away and he hears only its whispered affirmation of his vision, "E'en so, it is so!" (l. 335).

With "Saul," then, Browning underlines the shift of the privileged audience in and for his poetry from all of God's creation to God alone. After trying to find adequate subjects and metaphors for the attempt to transform his love of nature into a love of mankind and for the noble success in the failure of the attempt, Browning returns to considering brief, seemingly apocalyptic moments which afford some communication with, or some vision of, divinity. This moment of reciprocal response and recognition makes all other appreciation unnecessary and leaves the poet undisturbed by his inability to soothe Saul's troubled soul, because he can rejoice in the memory of that ecstatic instant of seeing Christ and in discovering his true audience, God.

5

Men and Women:
The Self and Others

Take them, Love, the book and me together.
—"One Word More"

In *The Phenomenology of Mind* Hegel says, "Self-consciousness exists in itself and for itself in that, and by the fact that it exists for another self-consciousness; that is to say, it *is* only by being acknowledged or 'recognized.'"[1] The dialectic of self and other reflected in Hegel's definition can help us understand the relationships between the speakers of Browning's dramatic monologues and their audiences

---

[1] G. W. F. Hegel, *The Phenomenology of Mind*, trans. J. B. Baille, 2d ed. (New York: Macmillan, 1931), p. 229. Hegel's definition of self and self-consciousness is idealistic in the philosophical sense of the word and ultimately depends upon an apprehension of Absolute Spirit. This intersubjective idealism was first challenged within a Christian perspective by Kierkegaard in *Either/Or*. Nietzsche's notion of the *Übermensch* in *Thus Spake Zarathustra* represents a secular repudiation of Hegelian self-definition and is the forerunner of Lacan's critique of self and Derrida's critique of presence and being. From any of these modern positions one could easily lay philosophical waste to Browning's naive metaphysics, not to mention his poetry. But my task here is to understand the dramatic workings of Browning's poems in *Men and Women*, not to see how much or how little of modern philosophical or psychoanalytic thought the poems anticipate. Further, I am not claiming that Hegel is the source of Browning's ideas. Browning had little interest in things German and tackled the language only in the early 1840s when he was closest to Carlyle. Michael Mason provides a sketch of possible sources of Germanic influence on Browning's early aesthetic thought in "The Importance of *Sordello*," in *Major Victorian Poets*, pp. 143–45. In 1882 John Bury read a paper to the London Browning Society in a section of which he sketched some very general parallels between Browning and Hegel's ideas of Being, "Browning's Philosophy," *Browning Society Papers*, I, 270–72. In response to Bury's preliminary thoughts for this paper, Browning said in a letter to Frederick J. Furnivall of October 2, 1881: "As for Hegel—I am rejoiced if our wits should jump—but I never read a word of his—caring as little as you for elaborate metaphysics" (*Browning's Trumpeter: The Correspondence of Robert Browning and Frederick J. Furnivall, 1872–1889*, ed. William S. Peterson [Washington, D.C.: Decatur House Press, 1979], p. 29.

and also allow us to read Browning's poems with a deep appreciation of their dramatic aspects and psychological intricacies. Further, in the light of a few of Hegel's remarks on romantic poetry and art in his *Aesthetics*, one can see how this dialectic of self and other is worked out dramatically and symbolically within Browning's *Men and Women* in the form of the speakers' loving and being loved. One can see how Browning uses the dramatic monologue in *Men and Women* to show audiences making the speakers' image of themselves possible; how Robert's love for Elizabeth serves as an ideal form of this self-realization in the dedicatory poem "One Word More"; and how the poems in the volume dramatically unveil the speakers' awareness of their audiences' shaping of their self-conscious selves.

This Hegelian approach will remind readers that Browning's dramatic monologues are profoundly dramatic. One might think that such tautological emphasis is unnecessary. But it is not. Most modern criticism has concentrated on the solipsistic aspects of the monologue and has tended to simplify the problematic drama of Browning's poems by reducing the speakers' audiences to emanations of speakers' personalities, when, in fact, those very audiences both affect and in some ways determine the speakers' selves. Park Honan, for example, has suggested that "every auditor exists only through a few, select, emphasized characteristics" and so "the auditor element may be said to be an objectified representation of the speaker's own being."[2] In his discussion of "The Pope" from *The Ring and the Book*, Honan goes so far as to say that this holds true for a character's relationship with God: "It is incidental that God has created everything and everyone, for God is revealed as an embodiment merely of the love and devotion to truth that are, in turn, only characteristics in a more complex sum of characteristics constituting Innocent's character."[3] This strategy of reducing the other to a projected version of the speaking self ignores Browning's repeated and self-evident concern with the irreducibility of the other to the speaking self: the speaker, despite his or her desires, cannot become one with God, a lover, a crowd, or ghosts from the past. In "Two in the Campagna," for instance, the speaker tries to en-

[2]*Browning's Characters: A Study in Poetic Technique* (New Haven: Yale University Press, 1961), p. 156. Robert Langbaum stresses the speakers' insufficient motivation in the dramatic occasion of the monologue and sees them as talking to themselves in *The Poetry of Experience*, pp. 182–91. Dorothy S. Mermin also makes this point about the speakers' solipsism and, as her use of the term *auditor* suggests, views the audience as a passive screen upon which the speaker projects his or her self-consciousness and self-expressive language, in "Speaker and Auditor in Browning's Dramatic Monologues," *UTQ* 45 (1976):139–57.

[3]*Browning's Characters*, p. 155.

gage his beloved in the activity of his thoughts and to become closer to her, but then the good minute of amorous union goes, and he is left observing the "infinite passion, and the pain / Of finite hearts that yearn" (ll. 59–60).[4] What does he yearn for? He wants to internalize his love so he and she may become an infinite one instead of a finite two. But he cannot fulfill his desires: there will always be two in the Campagna. Moreover, in dramatizing the ethical consequences of man's finite self-consciousness and his dependence upon others for self-realization, Browning's poems imply that to project one's will and self upon another, as Porphyria's lover does with Porphyria, is an immoral act, an attempt to gratify the self in the way the master does in Hegel's master/slave relationship—by killing the other (the slave) and reducing it to nothingness.[5]

The way in which Browning's monologuists must gain the true recognition of another self-consciousness follows the general pattern for romantic art that Hegel outlines in his *Aesthetics*: "The romantic Ideal [of Beauty] expresses a relation to another spiritual being which is so bound up with depth of feeling that only in this other does the soul achieve this intimacy with itself. This life in self in another is, as feeling, the spiritual depth of love."[6] And this love finds its ultimate model in God's love for the world and in an awareness, finally, of what Hegel calls Absolute Spirit.[7] Browning's speakers, too, gain some measure of self-consciousness by confronting others, but must love another and be loved in order to become intimate with and know themselves. Yet given their inevitable human frailty and finitude, they can achieve only a limited self-consciousness which readers must fill out for themselves, partially, as Langbaum suggests, by mediating between the sympathy we feel for a speaker and the judgment we make of him or her,[8] and partially by remembering that Browning emphasizes man's incompleteness in relation to God's perfect fullness and

---

[4]William O. Raymond interprets such "good" or "infinite" moments in terms of an aesthetic of concentration expressing Browning's gusto and energy, not in terms of the speaker's seeking self-definition in relationship with another, in *The Infinite Moment and Other Essays on Robert Browning*, 2d ed. (Toronto: University of Toronto Press, 1965), pp. 3–18. See also the discussion of the good moment and its connection to the individual's experience of particularity and spiritual transcendence through the energetic embracing of the finite in Carol T. Christ, *The Finer Optic: The Aesthetic of Particularity in Victorian Poetry* (New Haven: Yale University Press, 1975), pp. 111–27.

[5]See the discussion of the master/slave relationship in *Phenomenology of Mind*, pp. 234–40.

[6]G. W. F. Hegel, *Aesthetics: Lectures on Fine Art*, trans. T. M. Knox, 2 vols (Oxford: Clarendon Press, 1975), II, 533.

[7]See *Phenomenology of Mind*, pp. 789–808.

[8]*Poetry of Experience*, pp. 75–159, 182–209.

man's inability to progress completely toward becoming one with God on earth. When, for example, Browning stresses "the development of a soul" in his 1863 preface to *Sordello*,[9] he refers to Sordello's gradually realizing the impossibility of resolving the competing claims made upon him by his warring countrymen and so finally turning to his true audience, God.

The importance for Browning's poetry of his belief in an immanent God and in the necessity of speakers' finding themselves in God's eyes through loving and being loved by another should not be discounted; otherwise Browning's doctrine of the incompleteness of the soul and a speaker's desire to love and be loved may then be confused with a Keatsian poetics:

> A Poet is the most unpoetical of any thing in existence; because he has no Identity—he is continually in for—and filling some other Body—The Sun, the Moon, the Sea and Men and Women who are creatures of impulse are poetical and have about them an unchangeable attribute—the poet has none; no identity—he is certainly the most unpoetical of all of God's creatures.[10]

It is a measure of Keats's poignant desire and of Browning's great achievement, that Keats wrote this but that the poet he describes reminds us more of Browning than of Keats. From this perspective, J. Hillis Miller in his *Disappearance of God* sees Browning's poetry as psychic compensation for both Browning's strongly felt lack of a poetic personality and his (supposed) feeling that God has deserted the world.[11] Paradoxically, then, Miller both reduces Browning's characters to various versions of Browning's poetic self, thereby extending Honan's reduction of the audiences to the characters (radically so, by referring to the poetry by volume and page number in *The Works of Robert Browning* instead of individual poems), and also speaks of a desire called "Browning" which wishes to be everything in general and God in particular. Or, from the same perspective and given a voluntaristic psychology, it is possible to see Browning's poetry as a deliberate strategy of self-repression and self-fragmentation, as E. D. H. Johnson does in *The Alien Vision of Victorian Poetry*. Johnson argues that Browning's embarrassment and disappointment with the response to his

---
[9] *Works*, II, 123.
[10] Keats to Richard Woodhouse, October 27, 1818, *The Letters of John Keats*, ed. Hyder S. Rollins, 2 vols. (Cambridge, Mass.: Harvard University Press, 1958), I, 387.
[11] *The Disappearance of God*, pp. 81–156.

early work led him to exploit "all the devices of objectivity at his command in an effort to capture the attention of his age."[12] The dramatization of individual cases histories, Johnson thinks, allowed Browning to attack flawed contemporary values piecemeal and indirectly, while concealing his "opposition to existing values and hence the extent of his alienation from Victorian society."[13] And because of the ensuing discussion of the views Browning wishes to express indirectly, Johnson's analysis of individual poems, like Miller's, scants the interaction of the characters with their audiences within the poems.

If we are to account for the internal dynamics of Browning's monologues, we must not look away so quickly from their dramatic context and character. Instead, we must be careful to triangulate the self-consciousness of Browning's speakers and see it not merely as the product of a Hegelian dialectic of self and other, of master and slave (though this can sometimes be useful), but as the self-recognition created by the discovery of God and the other, of the other as participating in God's spirit, and of God as irreducibly Other. We need to acknowledge that Browning's poems have their foundation in the Christian practice of seeing evidences in others of God's spirit and upon Christ's words, "Inasmuch as ye have done it unto the least one of them, my brethren, ye have done it unto me" (Matthew 25:40). According to Christ and to Browning, to love another is to love God, and to sin against another is to sin against God. Therefore one's salvation is gained through the love of God and the love of others: "Thou shalt love thy neighbour as thyself" (Matthew 22:39). This doctrine and its consequences are clearly apparent in many of Browning's poems in *Men and Women*. The speaker of "The Last Ride Together," for example, believes that while he can be with his beloved for "one day more am I deified" (l. 21). And Karshish, through his admiration of Lazarus's faith, catches sight of the Christian vision that salvation might come through the love of Christ and that the omnipotent God might be "the All-Loving, too" (l. 305).

To the extent that love reflects the spiritual depth of romantic poetry as Hegel suggests, we see in *Men and Women* (1855) a subtle tempering of self-righteous judgment in anticipation of God's that stems in part from Browning's love for Elizabeth and his personal experience of the powers of loving forgiveness. The condemnations we are ex-

---

[12]*The Alien Vision of Victorian Poetry: Sources of Poetic Imagination in Tennyson, Browning, and Arnold* (Princeton: Princeton University Press, 1952), p. 91.
[13]Ibid., p. 96.

pected to make in *Dramatic Lyrics* (1842) of the Duke of Ferrara, Porphyria's lover, and Johannes Agricola are not clearly called for with Andrea del Sarto and Fra Lippo Lippi. The duelling poems "Before" and "After" will briefly illustrate this point. In "Before" one of the seconds tells another, "Let them fight it out, friend! things have gone too far. / God must judge the couple" (ll. 1–2). As we have seen, Browning had earlier believed that God oversees affairs of honor and that their outcomes represent God's judgments, and Elizabeth had taken up arms against Robert's idea of honor: "Who believes in such an honour . . liable to such amends, & capable of such recovery! YOU cannot, I think—in the secret of your mind, Or if *you can* . . *you*, who are a teacher of the world . . . poor world—it is more desperately wrong than I thought."[14] And Robert had replied, "But I must confess that I can conceive of 'combinations of circumstances' in which I see two things only . . or a Third: a miscreant to be put out of the world, my own arm and best will to do it; and, perhaps, God to excuse; which is approve. Mr. Ba, what is Evil, in its unmistakeable shape, but a thing to suppress at any price?"[15] Here in this letter he not only expresses his belief in God's providential intervention in the affairs of men but also sees the relationship between duellers as an allegorical confrontation between good and evil. In addition, Robert momentarily transforms Elizabeth into a would-be adversary by addressing her as "Mr. Ba," condescendingly and pompously reminding her that she is not a man of the world, and for this one disconcerting moment self-consciously resorts to the rhetoric of duelling to put her in what he thinks is her proper place, reminding one of the residual master/slave, man/woman thinking in Browning. But the second of the duelling poems in *Men and Women*, "After," shows that Elizabeth had later convinced him of the moral inefficacy of duelling. The victor surveys the face of his dead opponent for the last time and laments that duelling teaches nothing: "He recks not, he heeds / Nor his wrong nor my vengeance" (ll. 6–7). There is no recognition of one's righteousness to be gotten from the dead man, no spiritual intimacy to be had with a corpse.

The most common sign in Browning's dramatic monologues of a character's underdeveloped self-consciousness is pride. Unwilling or unable to see himself and his actions through another's eyes, he will aggrandize himself at the expense of others and act, not as he thinks

[14]Elizabeth to Robert, April 7, 1846, *Letters*, II, 596.
[15]Robert to Elizabeth, April 8, 1846, *Letters*, II, 604.

Men and Women: The Self and Others

all others should act, not in terms of the categorical imperative, but as if exempt from all laws and moral restrictions. The prideful prepossession that characterizes this ethical confusion manifests itself ultimately in a speaker's presumption of God's favor and final judgment. In *Dramatic Lyrics* Porphyria's lover, after strangling Porphyria, exults "And yet God has not said a word" (l. 60), and Johannes Agricola, while revelling in his sins, ignores the universal application of God's laws and complacently states, "'Tis to God I speed so fast" (l. 7). Though both look expectantly toward God, they do so with an unwarranted self-assurance and consequently transform what one would expect to be a prayer into a boast. And in *Men and Women* the guilty dueller is thought by one of the seconds of "Before" to be the epitome of satanic pride and mockery: "Who's the culprit of them? How must he conceive / God—the queen he caps to, laughing in his sleeve" (ll. 9–10). The hypocritical scorn attributed to the guilty man is seen to be finally mockery of God.

For Browning the prideful man deludes himself as to his self-sufficiency before both God and his fellow men and women, while the man who seeks to know himself must love another to be loved and so gain his soul; for Browning the drama of the dramatic monologue lies in the speaker's struggles for recognition in the eyes of others and of God. And reading the poems of *Men and Women* illuminates the differences Browning imagines between a self-consciousness based on love and one based on fame, explains the relation Browning sees between love and artistic expression, and reveals in the structure of the poems' symbolism Browning's artistic representation of his characters' needs for reciprocal recognition in love in order to come to terms with themselves and their God.

I

In an 1853 letter to Joseph Milsand, Browning says, "I am writing a sort of first step toward popularity (for me! 'Lyrics') with more music and painting than before so as to get people to hear and see."[16] This aesthetic program to make his readers hear and see in *Men and Women* is reflected in a few poems but is largely belied by the work's great diversity and by Browning's rounding out its two volumes with exactly fifty poems: "There they are, my fifty men and women / Naming me

---

[16]Browning to Milsand, February 24, 1853, "Deux lettres inédites de Robert Browning à Joseph Milsand," ed. W. Thomas, *Revue Germanique* 12 (1921):251.

the fifty poems finished" ("One Word More," ll. 1–2). As these lines suggest, his men and women shadow forth another otherness among them and speak the name of their poet—Robert Browning. Indeed, the otherness of his poems and their fifty different selves does name him, as he playfully says, because he is preëminently the poet of *Men and Women*. Yet Browning had always felt that his ventriloquist's gift never allowed him to express his own self-conscious recognition of his loving and being loved. As we have seen, in an early letter to Elizabeth he had written: "You speak out, *you*,—I only make men and women speak—give you truth broken into prismatic hues, and fear the pure white light, even if it is in me: but I am going to try . . so it will be no small comfort to have your company just now."[17] He feels that in Elizabeth's company he can have a voice of his own and that she will allow him to see his personal myth about his voice from the outside. So in *Men and Women* he is also the poet for Elizabeth Barrett Browning, as the dedication of "One Word More"—"To E.B.B."—proclaims and as he says for once in his own voice: "Take them, Love, the book and me together: / Where the heart lies, let the brain lie also" (ll. 3–4). The work is for her, just as Rudel's poem in "Rudel to the Lady of Tripoli" is for the unseen lady. "One Word More" acknowledges and celebrates the sense of audience which Browning feels both protects and gives purpose to his scattering of himself in his art. In Elizabeth he finds a union of sympathy and judgment, of "heart" and "brain," and also the guarantee of his self which is otherwise dissociated by the analysis required to render the impressions of his characters in *Men and Women*.

"One Word More" speaks of an artist's private art as being different from his public art because it appears in something other than his established form. Browning thinks of Raphael's sonnets to his lady and Dante's painting of Beatrice as examples of how one wants to create a private, separate art to describe the intimate experience of loving another. By working in another medium (one remembers that Browning took sculpture lessons from William Wetmore Story in the 1850s), the painter or poet symbolizes the private character of his experience: "Cheek, the world was wont to hail a painter's, / Rafael's cheek, her love had turned a poet's" (ll. 16–17). Browning similarly recalls from *La Vita Nuova* Dante's being interrupted by some visitors while drawing an angel and thinking of Beatrice on the first anniversary of her

---

[17] Robert to Elizabeth, January 13, 1845, *Letters*, I, 7.

death (ll. 55–57). And so we have *The Inferno* instead of Dante's drawing of his angel. The world cannot have this private art, for it is not art created in the service of fame. Raphael's sonnets, too, have disappeared: "All Bologna / Cried, and the world cried too, 'Ours, the treasure!' / Suddenly, as rare things will, it vanished" (ll. 29–31). The artist in love creates a private language that is outside his art and expresses his feelings naturally:

> No artist lives and loves, that longs not
> Once, and only once, and for one only,
> (Ah, the prize!) to find his love a language
> Fit and fair and simple and sufficient—
> Using nature that's an art to others,
> Not, this one time art that's turned his nature.
> [ll. 59–64]

He would do this to "save the man's joy, miss the artist's sorrow" (l. 72). Browning thinks of the fresco painter who "fills his lady's missal-marge with flowerets" (l. 125) and of the trumpet player turned singer—"He who blows thro' bronze, may breathe thro' silver, / Fitly serenade a slumbrous princess" (ll. 126–27). The artist as lover wants both an unmediated and an unmeditated art. It is unmediated art because it is not created with an eye on the general public and its past criticism of one's efforts, and it is unmeditated because it is natural rather than artistic expression. In terms of Browning's poetry, this means that in "One Word More" he will speak in his own voice: "Let me speak this once in my true person, / Not as Lippo, Roland or Andrea" (ll. 137–38). So "One Word More" in unmediated. And it is unmeditated because it is written from his heart: "Where my heart lies, let my brain lie also" (l. 141).

As Paul Turner notes in his helpful explication of stanza 9, the artist's "awareness of a hostile audience interferes with his art, causing anxiety (o'er-importuned brows) which prevents the free expression of his inspiration (mandate), and makes his manner (gesture) either self-conscious or careless (from feeling: 'What's the use of trying?')."[18] If the poet's mission in the world is indeed to bring divine truth to it, to put the infinite in the finite, it is difficult for him to endure the indifference and mocking of the crowd, just as Moses found it when he remembered the Israelites' previous complaints as he struck the Rock of

---

[18]*Men and Women* (London: Oxford University Press, 1971), p. 387.

Horeb and produced water from it for them (ll. 79–82). Browning imagines that Moses, if he had to save his wife's life, would envy the camel, "keeping a reserve of scanty water / Meant to save his own life in the desert" (ll. 104–5), because Moses' marriage to the Ethiopian woman had created a religious and political controversy in the racially conscious tribe (Numbers 12). Moses has no private self as a prophet: "Never dares the man put off the prophet" (l. 99). For Browning, to be a prophet is to know God's commandments and suffer both God's wrath and the people's without ever having a private life.

Like the prophet, the artist receives rough treatment from the public, but unlike the prophet he does have a private life that brings him joy: "God be thanked, the meanest of his creatures / Boasts two soul-sides, one to face the world with, / One to show a woman when he loves her!" (ll. 184–86). The moon, usually an image of otherness, becomes an image of the self. Browning supposes he is "the moon's self," not only in the sense of being "thrice-transfigured" and waxing and waning according to his poetic inspiration by borrowing light from another (ll. 144–56) but also in the sense of remaining unknown to others, just as the moon never revealed her other side to Zoroaster, Galileo, Homer, or Keats (ll. 161–65). And he imagines that seeing the other side of the moon would be equivalent to seeing God in the way that Moses, Aaron, Nadab, and Abihu did (ll. 174–79). The other side of the moon, then, which remains unseen by the famous men of history but is revealed to God, symbolizes the artist's private self. The moon's other side, its hidden self, cannot be seen by the public or Elizabeth unless, as in the Endymion myth, the moon falls in love and turns "a new side to her mortal" (l. 161).

But since the moon is at least constant in her feminine associations in English literature, it seems curious that Browning should refer to himself as if he were a woman. Yet in a certain sense he is, because not only does he claim that his poetry reflects Elizabeth's light and love, but he also takes his being as a poet and a man from her:

> This I say of me, but think of you, Love!
> This to you—yourself my moon of poets!
> Ah, but that's the world's side, there's the wonder,
> Thus they see you, praise you, think they know you!
> There, in turn I stand with them and praise you—
> Out of my own self, I dare to phrase it.
> But the best is when I glide from out them,
> Cross a step or two of dubious twilight,

Men and Women: The Self and Others

> Come out on the other side, the novel
> Silent silver lights and darks undreamed of,
> Where I hush and bless myself with silence.
>
> Oh, their Rafael of the dear Madonnas,
> Oh, their Dante of the dread Inferno,
> Wrote one song—and in my brain I sing it,
> Drew one angel—borne, see, on my bosom!
> [ll. 187–201]

He incorporates her, carries a picture of her in his heart, and crosses over from himself to her. When he talks of himself as being the moon and having two sides, he can do so only because of her. He reflects the light of her love, just as she reflects the light of his love. She, too, has her moon poetry to show the world and which the world praises. Browning can stand and look in admiration as the world does, can read her poetry, and can praise it like other men "out of" his own self—both in the sense of *outside* his real self and also in the sense of *from* his true self. But "best" of all he can also cross over and come out "on the other side" of himself and her and enter into a silent communion with her that is unmediated by the alienation of words. In "this realm of novel / Silent silver lights and darks undreamed of," he and she can love one another. The intertwining of self and other in love is complete: Browning gains his sense of self and self-consciousness from Elizabeth, and his poetry reflects his love for her, just as her *Sonnets from the Portuguese*, which first appeared in her *Poems* of 1850, had reflected her love for him. And, unlike the public and the ghosts of the past who cannot understand him, she can see his other side. With her appreciative audience Browning can gain the awareness he needs to be himself both as a poet and as a man, for only through his love for Elizabeth, according to his private Endymion myth, does he gain an insight into his own heart and see there his "one angel."

II

The artist's desire for a private, comforting audience which will both provide him access to the other side of love's moon and also let him see the otherness of God is the center of "Andrea del Sarto." But unlike Browning, who has been fortunate in his love of Elizabeth, Andrea loves the grasping Lucrezia and cannot find the private recess in the moonlight which will inspire his art. He thinks instead, while he paints her portrait as the Madonna, how she is "My face, my moon, my everybody's moon, / Which everybody looks on and calls his" (ll. 29–30). Like the Victorian public which admired Elizabeth's poetry, the Florentine public adores Andrea's wife in the form of the Madonna. But for Andrea the gain produced by having her serve as the model for all of his portraits is more than erased by the knowledge that the owners of his paintings possess her as much as he does: she is really "no one's: very dear, no less" (l. 32). The play on "dear" and its meanings of "expensive" and "loved" points to Andrea's wistfulness as he contemplates the cost to him in relation to the cost of the paintings to his customers. There is nothing behind her beautiful face:

> But had you—oh, with the same perfect brow,
> And perfect eyes, and more than perfect mouth,
> And the low voice my soul hears, as a bird
> The fowler's pipe, and follows to the snare—
> Had you, with these the same, but brought a mind!
> [ll. 122–26]

Her personality has no other side. And so while he longs for some sort of intimacy with her, Andrea discovers himself trapped like a bird in a snare.

As Eleanor Cook has pointed out in *Browning's Lyrics*,[19] the imagery of enclosure is crucial to an understanding of the poem. In general, Andrea's desire for an audience is reflected in his obsession with imagery of closure. He holds Lucrezia's hand and thinks, "Your soft hand is a woman of itself, / And mine the man's bared breast she curls inside" (ll. 20–21). And he wishes that he could hold her soul as easily as he can hold her hand. To compensate for this lack, his hand and eyes seek to encircle part of the world and so provide the audience he feels he does not have. He notes that the "length of convent-wall across the way / Holds the trees safer, huddled more inside" (ll. 42–43), tells her "Love, we are in God's hand" (l. 49), and exclaims, "So free we seem, so fettered fast we are! / I feel he laid the fetter: let it lie!" (ll. 51–52). He both longs for the security of being enfolded in

---

[19]*Browning's Lyrics*, pp. 126–27. See also the discussion of the temporal aspects of this enclosure imagery in Herbert F. Tucker, Jr., *Browning's Beginnings*, pp. 198–200. See also Richard D. Altick's fine, sympathetic reading, "'Andrea del Sarto': The Kingdom of Hell is Within," in *Browning's Mind and Art*, ed. C. R. Tracy (Edinburgh: Oliver & Boyd, 1968), pp. 18–31. One should also note the claustrophobic character of Browning's cramped study at Casa Guidi, which had the blank, brick wall of the church San Felice outside its window.

God's hand and also feels restrained by it. He thinks of himself as "the weak-eyed bat no sun should tempt / Out of the grange whose four walls make his world" (ll. 169–70).

His obsession with enclosure has led to an overcompensation in his art. His great accomplishment is his ability to paint without preliminary sketching, because the outlines he paints are so perfect; hence, he is called "The Faultless Painter." While other artists labor to get their preliminary drawings right, he dispenses with such preparation (ll. 68–71). When he looks at a painting by Raphael, he quickly sees how he would have gotten the outline right: "Give the chalk here—quick, thus the line should go!" (l. 196). But his concern for the encompassing power of exterior form has produced a grievous lack of soul in his art:

> Somebody remarks
> Morello's outline there is wrongly traced,
> His hue mistaken; what of that? or else,
> Rightly traced and well ordered; what of that?
> Speak as they please, what does the mountain care?
> Ah, but a man's reach should exceed his grasp,
> Or what's a heaven for?
>
> [ll. 92–98]

Andrea's mastery of form reflects his desire to enclose and secure the world; consequently he avoids striving for any artistic effect which would violate formal constraints. Like Adam reaching out to God in Michelangelo's painting on the ceiling of the Sistine Chapel, Andrea can stretch his arm out full length until his finger just touches heaven, but he cannot grasp it. The distance he can reach describes a limit, since he can have no control over objects at his fingertips, only a liminal experience of them. In a literal way Browning's metaphor represents another version of the infinite moment: we can reach heaven for a moment; we can touch it, but cannot hold onto it. For if we could grasp it, it would by definition no longer be heaven, no longer be the limit of our mortal being. Andrea painfully realizes this but has sacrificed such striving in the service of Lucrezia: "Come from the window, love,—come in, at last, / Inside the melancholy little house / We built to be so gay with" (ll. 211–13). He has sought both an artistic and emotional security within a closed space.

This desire for confinement recalls the feeling of the speaker of *Pauline*, who longs for an audience and, lacking one, retreats to the metaphorical interiors of "those living hedgerows where / The bushes close and clasp above and keep / Thought in—I am concentrated—I feel" (*Pauline*, ll. 806–8). Andrea dreams of a similar retreat when he imagines his reward in heaven:

> What would one have?
> In heaven, perhaps, new chances, one more chance—
> Four great walls in the New Jerusalem,
> Meted on each side by the angel's reed,
> For Leonard, Rafael, Agnolo and me
> To cover.
>
> [ll. 259–64]

Although it is conventional since Revelation to think of heaven as a walled city, Andrea's use of the image suggests that he cannot move beyond the constriction of his earthly thoughts and can only imagine heaven as a bounded, enclosed space within which he would be both happy and famous. The danger, as Browning sees it, lies not only in the confinement of Andrea's dreams but also in his presumption in assuming that God will be his audience. Andrea takes too much comfort in thinking that failure in art guarantees success in God's eyes (ll. 140–44). He is also inclined to believe that his being underestimated as an artist excuses his callous treatment of his parents (ll. 246–57). Andrea's resignation, coupled with his fatalistic balancing of his painting and his neglect of his parents, leads the reader to eye Andrea's moral accounting less forgivingly.[20]

We even see his "long festal year at Fontainebleau" (l. 150), when he painted for King Francis and his court, as less of an accomplishment. And though we are originally inclined to sympathize with Andrea's melancholy (particularly considering his wife's impatience with him and her amorous restlessness), we ultimately find ourselves agreeing with his judgment of himself in comparison with other artists:

> I am judged.
> There burns a truer light of God in them,
> In their vexed beating stuffed and stopped-up brain,
> Heart, or whate'er else, than goes on to prompt
> This low-pulsed forthright craftsman's hand of mine.
>
> [ll. 78–82]

---

[20]See Langbaum's harsh judgment in *Poetry of Experience*, pp. 148–54.

Men and Women: The Self and Others

There is something too self-satisfied in his self-deprecation. He has given up trying to compensate for the lack of spirit in his paintings and has contented himself with the silver-grey of his art, because it represents an artistic compensation for the lack of an audience and for his own lack of love as shown by his neglect of his parents. He is content with his failure and inclined to locate the reasons for it not in himself but in his audience. He laments Lucrezia's mindlessness and partially blames her for not urging him on to glory (ll. 127–32). But he also thinks, "Perhaps not. All is as God over-rules" (l. 133). Not only does he excuse himself by thinking of Lucrezia's superficiality, but he also feels that God controls all of man's actions and suggests that by ruling too much God has prevented him from achieving the fame he had hoped for. And not satisfied with these explanations of his failure, he points to the criticism he must endure from the Parisian lords (ll. 145–48). He comforts himself with the paranoia of feeling persecuted and so doesn't venture from the safe confines of his home. He had earlier claimed to be "unmoved by men's blame / Or their praise" (ll. 91–92), but he seems to think of little else: he talks of the legate and what "they used to say in France" (l. 66), how someone says others do "so much less" than he (l. 76), the praise of King Francis and the French court (ll. 151–61), general public opinion (ll. 177–80), Michelangelo's praise (ll. 184–94, 198–200, 231–33), and of his fancied fame in heaven (ll. 259–64).

We are inclined, then, to judge Andrea very harshly. A man who pities himself gets little sympathy from us, and a self-pitying cuckold even less. Yet it is important to see that Andrea's success, despite his artistic failure, is a great one. He loves Lucrezia. She may not pay attention to him, may not have a mind to go with her beauty, may not care for Andrea's art, but he loves her nevertheless: "So—still they overcome / Because there's still Lucrezia,—as I choose" (ll. 265–66). Even though he knows that his love for his wife has limited his art and makes him much less of a painter than Leonardo, Raphael, and Michelangelo, he refuses to relinquish his love, his true audience. He chooses to love her at all costs, even, we see, at the cost of the completion of his self-knowledge that her love would bring, knowing that she injures his art, and knowing that she is "everybody's moon" and that he only as a part of her. He can tell her, "Go, my Love" (l. 267), letting her go to her lover, in a triumphant gesture expressive in a way more than he knows of his loss in loving her and of his love for her.

Browning's triumph in "Andrea del Sarto" stems partially from his portrayal of the painter's quiet anxiety about his art and Lucrezia: he catches the tone of resignation in Andrea's thinking about his art and his love without having recourse to the wild, self-conscious ravings of Sordello or Strafford. Instead of attempting to reflect artistic and political failure through incomprehensible rhetoric or fractured, coruscating metaphors, Browning discovers more objective and less dangerous symbols of Andrea's failure in the descriptions of his paintings and his relations with his audiences. When Andrea sees all he "was born to be and do, / A twilight-piece" and later comments on how "all is silver-grey / Placid and perfect" in his art (ll. 48–49, 98–99), we have natural, objective images for Andrea's abject resignation to his falling short of spiritual greatness in his art. And when he says, "I am grown peaceful as old age to-night. / I regret little, I would change still less" (ll. 244–45), we see the degree to which Andrea's failure follows from his fatalism and complacency, from his desire to be enclosed within another's gaze, and his satisfaction, despite his desire, with the artificial enclosures of his art. We must realize, though, that his renunciation of greatness is based for better or worse upon his love for Lucrezia and is made with the knowledge that she doesn't love him in return. So despite our judgment of Andrea, we finally are meant to forgive him his failures because "love is best," as the speaker of "Love Among the Ruins" exclaims, and because in Browning's eyes our love for another, like Andrea's love for Lucrezia, is what defines our being and makes us what we are.

III

Browning's poems usually portray their speakers' subjective experience of being caught between public and private audiences, between fame and love, and between natural desires and spiritual needs. But sometimes Browning seeks to underline the differences between fame and love, and between nature and spirit, by having his speakers inveigh against fame and its attendant tyranny and evils and extol love and its inherent divinity and virtues. This does encourage rhetorical obviousness and produces touchstone poetry, but it also allows for strangely poetic transformations and sublimations of the speakers' desires. For example, "Love Among the Ruins," the first poem in the first volume of *Men and Women*, is seen upon examination to be more than a touchstone poem to be quoted only for its idealistic assertion that "love is best" (l. 84) or to be noticed for its easy contrasts be-

Men and Women: The Self and Others

tween love in the present and ruins of the past, between the open pasture and the closed city, between the peaceful sheep and the warring men, and between the adoring girl in the crumbling turret and the arrogant king in his high tower.

The shepherd of "Love Among the Ruins" speaks to a fellow herdsman as they slowly follow their sheep homeward in the evening, telling him a story about the landscape's past. The pasture, he says, is supposedly the site of a long-ruined city which had at its center a powerful prince, who "held his court in, gathered councils, wielding far / Peace or war" (ll. 11–12). This image of audience control contrasts sharply with the random, somnambulistic progress of the sheep in the twilight. The speaker then, in the next three stanzas, compares the enclosures of the city and the king's council with the landscape's seamlessness. The city is characterized by its boundaries: its hundred-gated wall on which men could march twelve abreast (ll. 21–24) and its chariot stadium where the monarch, his women, and his minions viewed the races (ll. 45–48). The landscape, on the other hand, impresses the viewer with its unity: the rills and the hills seem to "run / Into one" (ll. 17–18).

In the fifth stanza the simple contrast between the self-enfolding, unitary landscape and the imagined glories of the country's king and men suddenly gives way to the speaker's revelation that he is meeting his love in the turret to which he has directed his companion's and our attention. Instead of the king watching his charioteers from his tower, this girl now looks and waits for the shepherd among the ruins of that tower. The shepherd sets his and his love's spiritual communion against the king's rule over his men. While the king's power and gold could command the hearts and minds of his men, he imagines that the two lovers will "extinguish sight and speech / Each on each" (ll. 71–72), finding themselves in the immediacy of the other's embrace. And he declares that the power over an audience founded upon gold is illusory, because time has claimed the king and his men, and the earth has "Shut them in, / With their triumphs and their glories and the rest" (ll. 82–83).

If the hurrying wings of Time's chariot gave a sense of urgency to the speaker's voice, one might find some poignancy in his final proclamation of the superiority of love. And if the shepherd had been speaking to his love in anticipation of their rendezvous (thus making the poem a kind of serenade), one would find some rhetorical point in the assertion of love's triumph. But, as it is, the shepherd's discussion of his love with his companion instead of his beloved makes the sentiment seem the product of a complacency which the landscape's serenity reinforces. It appears that Browning has bled the poem of passionate love and substituted a curiously obsessional rant. "Love Among the Ruins," then, becomes a stranger poem the more we read it, largely because the wild closing crescendo seems so out of place in the quiet pastoral setting. Eleanor Cook has commented on this disjunction and felt uneasy about it: "The lover does not pay much attention to his lady though he is on his way to a meeting. Perhaps I am being perverse: he is thinking of something else. But oddly enough the closer he comes to his beloved, the greater his vehemence grows, as if the city posed a direct threat to the lovers."[21] She is right and not being perverse. Furthermore, it seems that the "something else" the speaker is thinking of is death and that the city of the past is not only the symbolic displacement of death in the present but also explicitly a city of the dead. Yet it is important to note that while the city is symbolic of death, it is nature itself which brings death to the city and has entombed it. Think, for example, of the turret "by the caper overrooted, by the gourd / Overscored" (ll. 39–40). Then, too, the girl with eager eyes resembles a corpse, since she is "breathless, dumb" (l. 61). By Victorian convention, of course, this breathlessness represents her passion, but it also suggests the presence of death, as does the violence of their meeting in which they "extinguish sight and speech." Indeed, "Love Among the Ruins" is an example of what happens in the age to the energy that classically goes into carpe diem poetry; as in Arnold's "Dover Beach," a Victorian decorum displaces the image of time by transforming it into history which only threatens love from a distance, instead of forcing its bloom.[22] Seen in this light, "Love Among the Ruins" becomes at once a much more complex poem and a much less successful one. We see that the poem's indirectness in its address creates a rhetorical blindness: the vehemence directed against the city of the past seems obsessional, and the poem's urgency is turned inward upon the shepherd's discourse and backward in time, instead of toward the girl.

But instead of ascribing the poem's failure to Victorian reticence,

---

[21]*Browning's Lyrics*, p. 168.
[22]Anthony Hecht's parody of Arnold's "Dover Beach," "The Dover Bitch," brings the subterranean eroticism to the surface; see *The Hard Hours: Poems by Anthony Hecht* (New York: Atheneum, 1967), p. 17.

Men and Women: The Self and Others

we do better to consider it the result of two closely related obsessive associations: a feeling that nature is closely tied to death, and a belief that earthly fame is a kind of tyranny. What unbalances "Love Among the Ruins" is the way in which the concern with death in nature coincides with Browning's obsession with fame and the audience that creates fame. The subconscious carpe diem motif which supplies the poem's energies is subsumed by the surface invective hurled against the all-powerful king and his control of his warriors and by Browning's affirmation that the private world of the lovers triumphs over the machinations of political power. The imagery of the ruins and the terrible past, which one would expect the speaker to employ in order to persuade his love to make love immediately, demonstrates instead that earthly fame becomes nothing more than a historical remainder. Instead of a large audience controlled by tyranny, which he thinks of as an emblem of the self's death, Browning prefers the intimate audience and life for the self provided by love.

This reduction of the self's struggle for an audience to a historical reification is perhaps most clearly symbolized in "The Statue and the Bust." Although they have fallen in love at first sight, the lady and the duke, instead of consummating their love in defiance of public opinion, memorialize their love in a bust and a statue which gaze at one another across a square in Florence. This reduction of love to symbol at the cost of experience elicits Browning's contempt: "And the sin I impute to each frustrate ghost / Is—the unlit lamp and the ungirt loin, / Though the end in sight was a vice, I say" (ll. 246–48). Browning rejects the art which expresses the subjugation of the lovers' private audience to the conventions of society.

One can contrast the lovers' failure in "The Statue and the Bust" with the paradoxical success of the dusty scholar in "A Grammarian's Funeral." The grammarian spurns "the world's way" (l. 41), but his final accomplishment is surely forgettable: "He settled *Hoti's* business—let it be!— / Properly based *Oun*— / Gave us the doctrine of the enclitic *De*, / Dead from the waist down" (ll. 129–32). Certainly, if the grammarian had been in quest of earthly fame and had arrived at this, one would have here another instance of how a man's work on earth is as dust to the ages, how his fame grows dimmer, how this particular grammarian has no name to be remembered by.

But though the encircling and reductive powers of death have paralyzed him and made his accomplishments a mockery of his scholarly desire to know everything, his great thirst for learning for learning's sake stands as a reminder of his success.²³ It is the purity of the grammarian's quest that his students celebrate in their eulogy as they journey from the common crofts, bearing his pall, to seek the "sepulture / On a tall mountain" (ll. 14–15) where they plan to lay him to rest. Their song describes the gradual narrowing of the grammarian's life, in contrast with his great energy and promise. When the procession begins at the bottom of the mountain, the pallbearers sing of the grammarian as if he were a god: "He was a man born with thy face and throat, / Lyric Apollo!" (ll. 33–34). But as the students approach the mountain's peak, he becomes less of a god and more of a corpse, his health deteriorating and his studies focusing on minute grammatical difficulties. Yet his seeking to understand makes him deserving of a high place in men's estimations and of his lofty burial ground: "Here—here's his place, where meteors shoot, clouds form, / Lightnings are loosened, / Stars come and go!" (ll. 141–43). The grammarian's pursuit of heavenly knowledge instead of earthly fame saves him from being reduced to the fragmented nature of his accomplishments.

One can also see Browning's association of a group of voices with death and with art's reification of life and truth in "Master Hugues of Saxe-Gotha." The organist of the poem is trying to interpret Hugues's metaphysical fugue and argues with Hugues's ghost about the ultimate meaning of the composition. Seated before the organ in the church loft, he summons Master Hugues from the dead and asks him, "What do you mean by your mountainous fugues?" (l. 4). But the dead Hugues will not answer. Nor will the voices of Hugues's fugue, who wrangle among themselves without ever addressing the listening organist.²⁴ As he describes it and as the reader attempts to imagine it,

---

[23] In his reading of the poem, Richard D. Altick has seen a satire on the dusty scholar; see "'A Grammarian's Funeral': Browning's Praise of Folly?", *SEL* 3 (1963):449–60. Martin J. Svaglic argues that the grammarian is an example of Browning's paradoxically finding success in failure, in "Browning's Grammarian: Apparent Failure or Real?", *VP* 5 (1967):93–104. This latter view seems borne out by Browning's saying in a letter to Tennyson of July 2, 1863, that he thought of the grammarian as one of the "Tritons among minnows" (Christopher Ricks, "Two Letters by Browning," *TLS*, June 3, 1965, p. 464).

[24] See Wendell Stacy Johnson's comparison of the stanza structure to fugal arrangement in "Browning's Music," *Journal of Aesthetics and Art Criticism* 22 (1963):205. Also see Richard D. Altick, "The Symbolism of Browning's 'Master Hugues of Saxe-Gotha,'" *VP* 3 (1965):1–7. John Hollander sees Browning's consciousness of the structure of music as new and significant in the history of poetry's portrayal of music, in "Browning: The Music of Music," in *Robert Browning*, ed. Bloom and Munich, pp. 100–122.

Men and Women: The Self and Others

the fugue is an alien, self-entangled structure, which he in exasperation compares to a spider web covering the roof's gilt molding and groining. It obstructs his vision of "God's gold": "But where's music, the dickens? / Blot ye the gold, while your spider-web strengthens" (ll. 98–99). The variations of the fugue cause him to lose track of the melody; and, as he interprets it, the fugue shows how we weave a cobweb over life and thus separate ourselves from the union of heaven and earth: "So we o'ershroud stars and roses, / Cherub and trophy and garland" (ll. 116–17). The lonely figure sadly confronts the multitude of conflicting voices which obscure his vision of God and heaven:

> One is incisive, corrosive;
>   Two retorts, nettled, curt, crepitant;
> Three makes rejoinder, expansive, explosive;
>   Four overbears them all, strident and strepitant:
> Five . . . O Danaides, O Sieve!
>
> [ll. 76–80]

Like the daughters of Danaus, who are condemned to Hades for murdering their husbands and must gather water with a sieve forever, the voices of the fugue will never arrive at the truth the organist seeks. But like the Victorian reader of *The Ring and the Book* whom Browning hopes for, the organist continues to assert the existence of the truth despite the fragmenting multiple perspectives of a baroque work. Over against the demonic voices from the past, though, the organist can only offer his belief in, rather than any proof of, an eternal verity. When the candle he has been playing by gutters out and he must climb down the rotten ladder from the organ loft, he querulously asks: "Do I carry the moon in my pocket?" (l. 149). The organist's question admits to his unenlightened condition and yet also imaginatively claims that the merger of the mundane and the divine and also the perfect communion of man with God and truth are possible.

IV

The question of the proper relationship between life and art is also at the heart of "Fra Lippo Lippi." Does painting tie its audiences to the earth if it imitates life too slavishly, as the Prior suggests? Or is Lippo right when he argues that we don't see God in creation until we see it painted? While the Prior believes that painting which seeks to represent the world in detail threatens to "put all thoughts of praise out of our head" (l. 191), the good brother would have us believe that the love of beauty leads to the love of God (ll. 217–20).

For Fra Lippo the sort of painting the Prior has in mind is equivalent to artistic death. We discover him, after all, cornered by the Florentine guards while trying to scurry back to his quarters after exploring "an alley's end / Where sportive ladies leave their doors ajar" (ll. 5–6). He is now feeling trapped by the patrol, just as he had felt confined in his room "a-painting for the great man, saints and saints / And saints again" (ll. 48–49). Indeed, poor brother Lippo views his entire life as a kind of trap: he was orphaned at birth (ll. 81–82), taken by his old aunt Lapaccia to the convent (ll. 88–91), and there dressed in the "warm serge and the rope that goes all round" (l. 104). Then, too, his betters force him to paint in the constricted manner he chafes at: "So, I swallow my rage, / Clench my teeth, suck my lips in tight, and paint / To please them—sometimes do and sometimes don't" (ll. 242–44). He views his art, then, as a struggle between conventional restraint and fine inspirational excess. He thinks "the cup runs over, / The world and life's too big to pass for a dream" (ll. 250–51). He also remembers how his first artistic efforts were furtive doodlings in his school books (ll. 129–35) and how his marginal art, his making of letters and words into representations of the world that seemed less arbitrary to the poor, young Latin scholar, violated his superiors' conventional expectations. So Lippo feels caught in the act of going beyond the bounds in both life and art.

Lippo's identity is somehow determined by being caught by others, not only within the monologue's moment but also within his life and art. We remember that in answer to the soldiers' question, "Who are you?", which precedes the monologue, Lippo replies: "I am poor brother Lippo, by your leave" (l. 1). We also think of him describing how he accommodated himself to the gaze of passers-by when he was living in the streets as a young boy (ll. 112–25). The "look of things," in the sense of both their appearance and their gaze (l. 125), which has defined the world's relationship with him, is reflected in his paintings. In them he comments on the dialogue of reflected glances: "I had a store of such remarks, be sure, / Which, after I found leisure, turned to use" (ll. 127–28). And we note the complicated organization of different viewpoints and implied relationships among them in his art when he describes his painting of a murderer who once found sanctuary in a church:

Men and Women: The Self and Others

> The breathless fellow at the altar-foot,
> Fresh from his murder, safe and sitting there
> With the little children round him in a row
> Of admiration, half for his beard and half
> For that white anger of his victim's son
> Shaking a fist at him with one fierce arm,
> Signing himself with the other because of Christ
> (Whose sad face on the cross sees only this
> After the passion of a thousand years).
>   [ll. 149–57]

This matrix of vision has at its center not only the representation of Christ's passion on the cross but also his all-seeing face, which draws the people together and grants them forgiveness. We also remember the forgiveness granted to Fra Lippo when he is caught by everyone's eyes in his own painting (which he is planning for Sant' Ambrogio's church):

> I, in this presence, this pure company!
> Where's a hole, where's a corner for escape?
> Then steps a sweet angelic slip of a thing
> Forward, puts out a soft palm—'Not so fast!'
>   [ll. 368–71]

Here in his plan for his painting, as explained to the commander of the guard, he thinks of himself "caught up" with his "monk's things by mistake" (l. 366) and associates his being surprised with one of his more roguish escapades (ll. 378–83). This transgression of artistic and moral expectations becomes his personal myth, his artistic signature: "*Iste perfecit opus!*" (l. 377). His identity is created by his viewers' gaze, both by that of his "bowery flowery angel-brood" within the painting (l. 349) and by the spectator who examines his work:

>   Up shall come
> Out of a corner when you least expect,
> As one by a dark stair into a great light,
> Music and talking, who but Lippo! I!—
> Mazed, motionless and moonstruck—I'm the man!
>   [ll. 360–64]

He is frozen in the spectator's gaze both by the static nature of the medium and by his surprise. The evocation of light and dark, this chiaroscuro of art and life, of roguishness and good intentions, reminds us of our first discovery of Lippo in the soldiers' torchlight and makes us look forward to his surprised exclamation when he discovers himself caught by the light of the day's "grey beginning" (l. 392).

We should pay particular attention to the word "moonstruck" here. For as in "One Word More" and "Andrea del Sarto," the moon symbolizes the crossing over of life into art. The word not only suggests the artistic effect of chiaroscuro which highlights Lippo's face amid a dark background and points to the moment of religious enlightenment he experiences in St. Lucy's divine presence, but it also signifies the reification of the artist in his art, his being captured by it through the gaze of his audience. The imagery of encirclement which fills the poem—the soldiers around Lippo, the rope around Lippo's waist, the children around the murderer, the monks "closed in a circle" around Lippo's painting (l. 166), the bounds he has broken, the rings on Cosimo de Medici's house on the corner (ll. 228–30)—all this becomes transformed into a myth of artistic entrapment and creation. Like the encircled Childe Roland, Fra Lippo turns his predicament into a personal statement, an expression of his self, and a hope for some kind of transcendence, a wish that he could "interpret God to all" (l. 311). But because of his lusty, bestial nature, he can't forget the "value and significance of flesh" (l. 268) and deplores the pious crowd's defacing of the devils in his painting of St. Lawrence—"Hang the fools!" he says (l. 335). He is trapped between the crowd's conventional piety and his own sense that the "world and life's too big to pass for a dream" (l. 251). His uneasy compromise between his feelings and his audiences' expectations becomes a mark of the failure of his artistic intentions: neither the monks nor the Prior see that "God made it all" when they look at his paintings (l. 285) but instead that Lippo paints "faces, arms, legs and bodies like the true" (l. 177).[25] He consequently gets caught up in his paintings, unable to separate the soul from the flesh, unable to separate his private experience from his painting, though he realizes "how much more, / If I drew higher things with the same truth!" (ll. 308–9). Like Lippo, one may find the

---

[25] See the analysis of "Fra Lippo Lippi" as a response to the aesthetic doctrines of Alexis François Rio, in David J. DeLaura, "The Context of Browning's Painter Poems: Aesthetics, Polemics, Historics," *PMLA* 95 (1980):378–82. On distinguishing Browning's views from Fra Lippo's, see David Sonstroem, "On Resisting Brother Lippo," *TSLL* 15 (1974):721–34. Both DeLaura and Sonstroem are undoubtedly right in stressing the unsavory aspects of Lippo's escapades in the context of Browning's Victorian views of proper passion.

Prior's artistic sensibility too narrow, but one sees that for better or for worse the good brother must define himself in terms of a shared spiritual and artistic ideal which he at once acknowledges and yet cannot fulfill, because he cannot forget "the value and significance of flesh" that were impressed upon him when he was living on the streets as a boy and had to beg from others to stay alive.

V

The reification of the soul the Prior complains about in Fra Lippo's work has its pagan counterpart in Cleon's lament that the condition of his art is not the condition of his life: "I can write love-odes: thy fair slave's an ode" (l. 296). From Cleon's classical perspective, his work and art are nothing more than the unhappy reification of his soul and experience, and they are not, as the king to whom he is mentally replying thinks, the guarantee of his immortality:

> "But," sayest thou—(and I marvel, I repeat,
> To find thee trip on such a mere word) "what
> Thou writest, paintest, stays; that does not die:
> Sappho survives, because we sing her songs,
> And Æschylus, because we read his plays!"
> Why, if they live still, let them come and take
> Thy slave in my despite, drink from thy cup,
> Speak in my place. Thou diest while I survive?
> Say rather that my fate is deadlier still,
> In this, that every day my sense of joy
> Grows more acute, my soul (intensified
> By power and insight) more enlarged, more keen;
> While every day my hairs fall more and more,
> My hand shakes, and the heavy years increase.
> [ll. 301–14]

The beauty of his poems and pictures makes Cleon all the more melancholy as he contemplates his own beauty and powers falling away just as his hair does. He thinks of his accomplishments in relationship to his approaching death, then, as the shoring of fragments against his eventual ruin and as the necessarily hopeless attempt to imagine a perfect fullness in life:

> Long since, I imaged, wrote the fiction out,
> That he [Zeus] or other god descended here

> And, once for all, showed simultaneously
> What, in its nature, never can be shown,
> Piecemeal or in succession;—showed, I say,
> The worth both absolute and relative
> Of all his children from the birth of time,
> His instruments for all appointed work.
>
> [ll. 115–22]

In his fiction Cleon has thought that life can logically have meaning only if man has some connection with divine and immortal being, and if this connection is demonstrated by God's granting an audience to mankind, thus giving him "worth both absolute and relative." Cleon believes that only through that special audience of divine incarnation granted to man is it possible for us to know life has meaning because our souls possess immortality. But since Cleon has "written three books on the soul, / Proving absurd all written hitherto, / And putting us to ignorance again" (ll. 57–59), his fiction of incarnation remains nothing more than an impossible hope and a figment of his imagination.

Because he has rejected what for Browning is the only ground of man's being, Cleon is doomed to an earthly fame that is associated with tyranny and empty monumentality. He addresses his poem to "Protus in his Tyranny" (l. 4) and casually accepts the institution of slavery. He also identifies Protus with a "tower that crowns a country" (l. 235) but laments that Protus's soul "now climbs it just to perish there!" (l. 236). Further, only a "brazen statue" overlooking the tyrant's grave will survive him (l. 175), reminding one of the emperor of "Protus," who ends a period of rulers remembered by "these latter busts we count by scores, / Half-emperors and quarter-emperors, / Each with his bay-leaf fillet, loose-thonged vest, / Loric and low-browed Gorgon on the breast" (ll. 1–4). The busts, statues, and towers serve only to remind one of the futility of attempting to establish one's kingdom here on earth, where everything decays and where one's struggle to achieve a lasting fame becomes reduced to the mocking petrification of stone by the face of that dreaded Gorgon, time.

In "Popularity," one sees a poet who is loved privately by the speaker and God—"My star, God's glow-worm!" (l. 6)—but not by others: "I'll draw you as you stand, / With few or none to watch and wonder" (ll. 21–22). But, on the other hand, the retailers of the poet's art, who water down his style, profit handsomely from their efforts: "There's the extract, flasked and fine, / And priced and saleable at last!" (ll. 56–57). Keats's poetic imitators have reduced his style to a commodity which can be reproduced and sold; it is as if they had cannibalized him and were feasting on his poetic remains: "Hobbs hints blue,—straight he turtle eats: / Nobbs prints blue,—claret crowns his cup" (ll. 61–62).[26] In contrast with their public gorging, the speaker praises the splendor of Keats's poetry in a concatenation of images that connects the brilliant coloring of his style with the privacy of wedded bliss:[27]

> Enough to furnish Solomon
>   Such hangings for his cedar-house,
> That, when gold-robed he took the throne
>   In that abyss of blue, the Spouse
> Might swear his presence shone
>
> Most like the centre-spike of gold
>   Which burns deep in the blue-bell's womb,
> What time, with ardours manifold,
>   The bee goes singing to her groom,
> Drunken and overbold.
>   [ll. 41–50]

The intimacy of the relationship between the reader and the poet that Browning describes here in echoing the Song of Solomon, with the poet as Solomon and the reader as bride, is too rich for the world, which "stands aloof" (l. 55). Only when art becomes associated with tradition and the mummification of the market does it come to popular attention:

> And each bystander of them all
>   Could criticize, and quote tradition
> How depths of blue sublimed some pall
>   —To get which, pricked a king's ambition;
> Worth sceptre, crown and ball.
>   [ll. 31–35]

[26] See Jerome Thale, "Browning's 'Popularity' and the Spasmodic Poets," *JEGP* 54 (1955):348–54; and also see Richard D. Altick, "Memo to the Next Annotator of Browning," *VP* 1 (1963):65–66.
[27] Browning had a decided preference for strong, dark colors, especially in Elizabeth's clothes. See Elizabeth's letter to Arabella of May 19, 1847, *Elizabeth Barrett Browning: Letters to Her Sister, 1846–1859*, ed. Leonard Huxley (London: John Murray, 1929), p. 29.

Only when art becomes associated with the death of the soul and with its market value, only when it is abstracted from life does it enter the consciousness of the general public.

For Browning the true meaning of life and art lies in the experience instead of its popular acceptance. Further, he emphasizes the privacy of experience, particularly insofar as it is, or can be interpreted as being, divine revelation. This theme is treated again and again in his poetry but nowhere so poignantly as in "An Epistle Containing the Strange Medical Experience of Karshish, the Arab Physician." Despite his scientifically skeptical account of Lazarus's being raised from the dead as just one of many bits of curious medical lore acquired in his travels through Israel, Karshish seems strangely moved by his experience. He is especially impressed that Lazarus does not try to convince scoffing audiences of "his great truth":

> Hence, I perceive not he affects to preach
> The doctrine of his sect whate'er it be,
> Make proselytes as madmen thirst to do:
> How can he give his neighbour the real ground,
> His own conviction? Ardent as he is—
> Call his great truth a lie, why, still the old
> "Be it as God please" reassureth him.
> [ll. 213–19]

Lazarus's passivity is for Karshish an emblem of inner peace. Unlike Cleon, Karshish clearly believes in God and the immortality of the soul and is drawn toward the idea of God coming to earth in the flesh to dwell "on it awhile" and acquaint man with the divine ground of his being (l. 270).

While Cleon feels the great disjunction between earthly fame and the immortality of the soul (the unsatisfactory nature of the first and the doubtfulness of the second), Karshish wonders at the difference between an omniscient, omnipotent God and a loving God: "So, the All-Great, were the All-Loving too" (l. 305). Yet one doesn't feel that Karshish's becoming a Christian instead of an Arabian monotheist would add anything to his life, because he seems to have no particular need of Christianity in the way Cleon does. His monologue tangentially addresses the problem of the incarnation's being a historical event that only a handful of people knew about firsthand but doesn't consider this problem of faith as directly as Browning's later "A Death in the Desert" does; instead, like "Saul," the poem examines indirectly

Men and Women: The Self and Others

Browning's belief in the incommunicable nature of divine revelation. In the place of David's despairing of ever soothing Saul's tortured soul, one sees Karshish puzzling over Lazarus's enlightenment. Through Karshish's eyes one perceives the exterior signs of some revelation but cannot envision its content. Consequently, like Karshish, one tends to explain this experience in terms of an empirical psychology and to reduce it to a fanciful inscription on the walls of Lazarus's soul:

> But, flinging (so to speak) life's gates too wide,
> Making a clear house of it too suddenly,
> The first conceit that entered might inscribe
> Whatever it was minded on the wall
> So plainly at that vantage, as it were,
> (First come, first served) that nothing subsequent
> Attaineth to erase those fancy-scrawls
> The just-returned and new-established soul
> Hath gotten now so thoroughly by heart
> That henceforth she will read or these or none.
> And first—the man's own firm conviction rests
> That he was dead (in fact they buried him)
> —That he was dead and then restored to life
> By a Nazarene physician of his tribe.
> [ll. 87–100]

Anything less than firsthand experience of God's incarnation seems insufficient, since it is confined in history to a few unreproducible individual experiences. Hence the desire to incorporate the incarnation of God within the sign as representation becomes a poetic problem as well. The "fancy-scrawls" of the soul upon the body and the mind that contain it can be nothing more than a private credo. From an exterior point of view like that of Karshish, Lazarus is reduced to an incredible bit of medical lore about psychological imprinting. Lazarus becomes an emblem of the living dead or of revelation seen not in the spirit but in the letter and so open to misinterpretation and misunderstanding by those who would read it without supplying the proper spirit.

VI

The best of Browning's poems dealing directly with the contemporary problem of man's faith in God is "Bishop Blougram's Apology."[28] The Catholic bishop presents himself as a mediator between man and God, as one who is in communion with both of them and who speaks to both. But to Browning's Protestant thinking, this duality is an impossibility; he believes that Blougram has given himself to the crowd's superstition and credulity in exchange for wealth, popularity, and power:

> Of course you are remarking all this time
> How narrowly and grossly I view life,
> Respect the creature-comforts, care to rule
> The masses, and regard complacently
> "The cabin," in our old phrase. Well I do.
> I act for, talk for, live for this world now,
> As this world prizes action, life and talk.
> [ll. 764–70]

Blougram's disarming admission of his desires does not in any way ennoble his character. He is not motivated by love and charity but by a Nietzschean will to power:

> There's power in me and will to dominate
> Which I must exercise, they hurt me else:
> In many ways I need mankind's respect,
> Obedience, and the love that's born of fear.
> [ll. 322–25]

And, as a corollary to this, Blougram thinks of the miracles and absurd beliefs of the Catholic Church in terms of their political and sociological purpose: to control the masses and give the church its power.

> The steadfast hold
> On the extreme end of the chain of faith
> Gives all the advantage, makes the difference
> With the rough purblind mass we seek to rule:
> We are their lords, or they are free of us,
> Just as we tighten or relax our hold.
> [ll. 753–58]

For Blougram, then, the faith of others is not primarily a question of salvation but of temporal and personal power.

---

[28]For commentary on the poem, see Rupert Palmer, Jr., "The Uses of Character in 'Bishop Blougram's Apology,'" *MP* 58 (1960):108–18; also see Robert G. Laird, "'He Did Not Sit Five Minutes': The Conversion of Gigadibs," *UTQ* 18 (1976):295–313.

Men and Women: The Self and Others

Gigadibs, the skeptical journalist, for this reason presents a challenge to Blougram's inherent desire to bring others under his dominion; and at the same time he offers Blougram an audience to whom the bishop can safely reveal his worldliness. One might at first wonder at Blougram's frankness in his interview with Gigadibs. But one soon realizes that Blougram need not fear any reprisal from the writer. Gigadibs's association with freethinking makes the bishop's hypocrisy into a kind of idealism, inasmuch as the bishop professes to believe in something he would like to be true, and then the agnostic Gigadibs cannot but wish to validate and recognize the skeptic in the bishop, so that any skepticism attributed to Blougram by him in public would be immediately discounted. Realizing his security, Blougram can freely devote himself to undermining the frail defenses of the journalist's doubt.

Blougram takes Gigadibs's point of view for the sake of argument—"And now what are we? unbelievers both" (l. 173)—and tries to show that one ironically comes to doubt one's doubt. In fact he discovers that faith is paradoxically the residue of skepticism:

> How can we guard our unbelief,
> Make it bear fruit to us?—the problem here.
> Just when we are safest, there's a sunset-touch,
> A fancy from a flower-bell, some one's death,
> A chorus-ending from Euripides,—
> And that's enough for fifty hopes and fears
> As old and new at once as nature's self,
> To rap and knock and enter in our soul,
> Take hands and dance there, a fantastic ring.
> Round the ancient idol, on his base again,—
> The grand Perhaps! We look on helplessly.
> [ll. 180–90]

The marvellous metamorphosis of doubt into faith, which Browning symbolizes by capitalizing "perhaps" and so converting the word into an idolized god, is typical of Blougram's rhetorical tactics. He treats skepticism as something to be guarded, as something endangered by feeling, when the prevailing intellectual endeavor was to defend faith against the incursions of doubt; that is, if it was not to attack it. Blougram imagines how happy Gigadibs would be, for example, if he were transported back six hundred years:

> How you'd exult if I could put you back
> Six hundred years, blot out cosmogony,

185

> Geology, ethnology, what not,
> (Greek endings, each the little passing-bell
> That signifies some faith's about to die),
> And set you square with Genesis again,—
> When such a traveller told you his last news,
> He saw the ark a-top of Ararat
> But did not climb there since 't was getting dusk
> And robber-bands infest the mountain's foot!
> [ll. 678–87]

In the midst of the exegetical wreckage of the Germans and the geologists, Blougram conjures up another strange monument to faith: he envisions the ruins of Noah's ark "a-top of Ararat." And like the idol of Perhaps, it is encircled by a strange, threatening crowd in a way which recalls the Band and the Dark Tower of "'Childe Roland to the Dark Tower Came.'" Faith for Blougram is appropriately reified in icons and images worshipped by the masses, the "Naples' liquefaction" that Newman had accepted as a miracle being one particular example among many.[29]

The greatness of "Bishop Blougram's Apology" both as a monologue and as an anatomy of the modern religious soul rests, I think, in Blougram's consciousness of the complicated network of audiences in which religion, and the Catholic Church in particular, are embedded. He appreciates the political and sociological uses of dogma when it comes to dealing with the masses; he understands as well the usefulness of doctrinal authority when many people do not know what to think; he sympathizes with the desire for divine revelation and feels its absence from his life; and he knows how the Christian faith must depend upon an uncertain historical inheritance as its foundation. And last, but not least, Blougram is conscious of his immediate audience, Gigadibs.[30] He knows Gigadibs despises him (l. 13), he senses the journalist's dissatisfaction with the world (l. 233), and he recognizes that Gigadibs's ideals are of a more heroic and literary order than those the church and religion have to offer—"You would like better to be Goethe, now, / Or Buonaparte" (ll. 52–53). On a mundane level

---

[29]Newman's remarks in the *Morning Chronicle* of October 21, 1851, quoted in C. R. Tracy, "Bishop Blougram," *MLR* 34 (1939):423. The legend that Wiseman had reviewed *Men and Women* and "Bishop Blougram's Apology" for the *Rambler* has been disproven by Esther R. Houghton, "Reviewer of Browning's *Men and Women* in the *Rambler* Identified," *Victorian Newsletter* 33 (1968):46.

[30]Laird persuasively identifies Gigadibs as Richard Henry Horne, in "Conversion of Gigadibs," pp. 295–313.

he is simply the good host, feeding Gigadibs (l. 16), advising him which is the cooler jug of wine (l. 132), and pouring out his last glass (ll. 918–19). But in keeping with the occasion of Corpus Christi day, Blougram is also leading Gigadibs to communion with the Host of Hosts, speaking at once in the writer's terms and in the language of the Catholic religion.

Browning, nevertheless, makes it clear that he prefers, as always, a conception of religious faith that is based upon love. He says in the poem's epilogue that Blougram "said true things, but called them by wrong names" (l. 996), and he implies that the bishop's strategy of arguing the case for Christianity from the worst of premises and so justifying the opulence and worldliness of his priesthood is better than Gigadibs's undisciplined skepticism. He has greater hopes, though, for the outward-bound Gigadibs, who eschews the comfortable enclosed cabin of the bishop for the rigors of pioneer life in Australia and who, Browning would like to think, feeds his spiritual sheep, as Christ urges in the "last chapter of St. John," with more concern than the bishop does (l. 1014). Browning places the discourse of love above theological casuistry and consequently appears to claim more for a poem like "By the Fire-side" than for "Bishop Blougram's Apology," as great a poem as it is.

The speaker of "By the Fire-side" curiously embeds in a maze of temporal perspectives the experience of a walk through an Italian landscape.[31] And at the center of the poem is the infinite moment, the privileged instance of the speaker's union with his love, which warps his sense of time. This moment, which the speaker seeks to prolong by his reminiscence, occurs during a confrontation with Nature and removes the barrier which existed between him and his beloved, putting their love on a spiritual plane and outside time.

Throughout the poem the speaker has difficulty in keeping track of time. While one can be sure that he speaks continuously, one cannot be sure from what temporal perspective he speaks. The tenses shift without warning, as if he imagines in recollection that he is at times actually on the walk he is recalling. He begins in the first six stanzas by predicting how he will some November's day be reading Greek and

---

[31]For biographical parallels, see Jean Stirling Lindsay, "The Central Episode of Browning's *By the Fire-Side*," *SP* 39 (1942):571–79. For a reading of the poem in the light of possible Shelleyan sources, see Leslie Brisman, "Back to the First of All: 'By the Fire-Side' and Browning's Romantic Origins," in *Robert Browning*, ed. Bloom and Munich, pp. 39–58. See also the discussion of the connection between continuity and the good moment in Christ, *Finer Optic*, pp. 119–27.

fall into a reverie over a stroll he and his wife once took in Italy. And in the last stanza he begins to begin again, saying "the whole is well worth thinking o'er / When autumn comes: which I mean to do / One day, as I said before" (ll. 263–65) and pretends to have forgotten that he has just finished going over it. This momentary forgetting of time paradoxically insures the repetition of future reminiscences and future forgettings, because the infinite moment is interwoven throughout past, present, and future.

He talks of their love as an anticipation of the apocalypse of Revelation, of the moment "when our one soul understands / The great Word which makes all things new, / When earth breaks up and heaven expands" (ll. 131–33). For example, when the speaker first interrupts his reverie to address his wife, he anticipates that moment in this landscape of time:

> Whom else could I dare look backward for,
> With whom beside should I dare pursue
> The path grey heads abhor?
>
> For it leads to a crag's sheer edge with them;
> Youth, flowery all the way, there stops—
> Not they; age threatens and they contemn,
> Till they reach the gulf wherein youth drops,
> One inch from life's safe hem!
>
> [ll. 103–10]

For others, time divides old age from youth and implicitly from love. But for the speaker this will not be so. He can "slope to Italy at last / And youth, by green degrees" (ll. 24–25); for him the path of reminiscence is smooth and unobstructed by any gulf of sensibility. And the interfusion of their love makes all of this possible. Their two spirits have been "mixed at last / In spite of the mortal screen" (ll. 234–35); and so, unlike other lovers, who "are one and one, with a shadowy third" and for whom "one near one is too far" (ll. 229–30), their love transcends physical and temporal barriers and exists in a spiritual realm.

The poem describes how the forest removed Nature's shadowy third from their souls' communion when they were taking a walk through the countryside. The Nature they see is concerned only with itself: a stream feeds a lake below; "lichens mock / The marks on a moth, and small ferns fit / Their teeth to the polished block" (ll.

Men and Women: The Self and Others

48–50); and "a freaked fawn-coloured flaky crew / Of toadstools" spy on the rose-flesh mushrooms (ll. 64–65).

> The place is silent and aware;
> It has had its scenes, its joys and crimes,
> But that is its own affair.
>   [ll. 98–100]

The reader sees that the landscape is not only indifferent to the lovers but also inimical to man and his works. The "lichens fret / And the roots of the ivy strike" the stones of the chapel and the crumbling bridge (ll. 74–75). And the rustic chapel itself stands as an emblem of the ravages of Nature and time. In comparison with the struggle of Nature against the chapel, the opposition of Nature to the lovers is a fairly gentle one; nevertheless, it does make them aware of their love's spiritual essence. As their stroll proceeds, the personification of the landscape becomes stronger:

> The silence grows
> To that degree, you half believe
> It must get rid of what it knows,
> Its bosom does so heave.
>   [ll. 157–60]

And as the speaker retraces the moment after the silence's passage, he says the "lights and shades made up a spell / Till the trouble grew and stirred" (ll. 189–90). Later, one discovers that the forests transfigured the lovers and then "relapsed to their ancient mood" (l. 240). One cannot say precisely what the forests did in that moment. But the reader can understand that because of what they have done, the speaker's heart has lost its last "touch of the woodland-time" which prevented him from shaking "the whole tree in summer-prime" and thus removing the last leaf of the tree (ll. 201–4). When he finally realizes his separation from Nature, the mortal screen drops away and the lovers become one for a moment. Just as the children's cutting of the "hazels by the creek" closes the space between the fireside and Italy, so a similar opposition of the lovers to Nature closes the distance between the man and the woman and produces that "moment, one and infinite" (l. 181).

This infinite moment, which reveals the lovers to each other in their immortal souls and so reveals their relationship to God, is Browning's poetic ideal. The absent audience of "The Statue and the Bust," the image of the statue and the bust facing one another across the square, is a reification of ideal love, just like the earthly worship of such idols as the "grand Perhaps." One may believe like Bishop Blougram that an intimate relationship with the populace will give one the power one desires, but Browning again and again tries to show in his poetry that earthly fame and power reduce the soul to a petrified icon and make art into an empty, historical monumentality, for he believes that the love for another is man's only evidence of his love for God and his only hope for coming to terms with himself. The dramatic and problematic status of the other in Browning's dramatic monologues arises because a character must not only mediate between various audiences on earth but must also think about God in his effort to find and define himself. Through the love of another, in "One Word More" through the love of Robert for Elizabeth and her love for him, Browning feels that self-knowledge approaching that available through God's love is possible. But to make sense of such an experience in art is difficult at best. As in "Fra Lippo Lippi," "Andrea del Sarto," and "One Word More," art is necessarily an imperfect register for communicating the experience of the infinite, of one's learning through love about oneself and others in God's light. In his letter to Ruskin, Browning says: "I *know* I don't make out my conception by my language; all poetry being a putting the infinite within the finite. You would have me paint it all plain out, which can't be; but by various artifices I try to make shift with touches and bits of outlines which *succeed* if they bear the conception from me to you."[32] Browning gives us "bits of outline" which we must connect and fill in through the operation of our imaginative sympathy, an operation made more difficult today by the secular tenor of our thinking. In order to understand the workings of Browning's dramatic monologues, we need to be readers who, like the Elizabeth Barrett Browning of "One Word More," can envision the other side of the artistic moon, who can imagine the characters of his monologues living among and loving other people, and who can sympathize in some way with their struggles to find themselves in terms of their audiences and their God.

[32]Browning to Ruskin, December 10, 1855, in W. G. Collingwood, *The Life and Work of John Ruskin*, 2 vols. (London: Methuen, 1893), I, 200.

6

Dramatis Personae

"Quest' anima benedetta e passata!"

After Elizabeth died at Casa Guidi in Florence on June 29, 1861, Robert wrote several letters to relatives and close friends in England informing them of her death, made arrangements for her funeral, closed up their apartment, and left for Paris on July 27 with Isabella Blagden and Pen, never to return.[1] Despite his later metamorphosis into one of London's literary lions, Browning would live and write throughout the remainder of his life in the shadow of Elizabeth's death and lament the loss of his "soul's companion."[2]

Browning devoted much of his energy in the next two years to overseeing his wife's literary estate. He corrected the fifth edition of her *Poems* (1862), edited her *Last Poems* (1862), and republished as *The Greek Christian Poets and the English Poets* (1863) two series of essays which had originally appeared in the *Athenaeum* in 1842. His own work made two significant reappearances during this period: John Forster and Bryan Waller Proctor, with Browning's assent, edited a selection of his poetry which was published in December 1862 (dated 1863); and Browning issued a three-volume edition of his *Poetical Works* in 1863.[3] As Charlotte Crawford Watkins has pointed out, the

---

[1] The quotation that heads this chapter is the exclamation of Annunziata, Elizabeth's maid, upon Elizabeth's death, recalled in Robert's letter to his sister Sarianna of June 30, 1861, *Letters*, ed. Hood, p. 62.

[2] Browning to Wedgwood, June 25, 1864, *Robert Browning and Julia Wedgwood: A Broken Friendship as Revealed by Their Letters*, ed. Richard Curle (New York: Frederick A. Stokes, 1937), p. 7.

[3] Browning began to rearrange his poems with this edition under the generic names suggested by the titles of his collected verse. Such rearranging had a lengthy vogue in the nineteenth century, because the Romantic poets had blurred the distinctions between the poetic kinds and had tried to redefine the form of a poem in terms of its content, with unsatisfactory results. For the historical background of this problem and an

191

publication of these volumes led to a revaluation of Browning's work and to the growth of his reputation.[4] The new editions and the favorable reviews they occasioned also led to a large increase in sales: *The Poetic Works of Robert Browning* reached its third edition in 1863 and required a fourth in 1865. Only *Ferishtah's Fancies*, which was published at the height of the Browning Society craze in 1884 and went through five editions, had a greater sale during his life than the *Works* of 1863. More than finally drawing public attention to his poetry, the reviews of these collections also established a general critical consensus concerning Browning based on the grounds first surveyed by a retrospective consideration of his work that appeared in the *North British Review* in 1861.

The writer for the *North British Review* begins his discussion of Browning's *Poetical Works* of 1849, *Christmas-Eve and Easter-Day*, and *Men and Women* by examining the reasons why a great poet he considers second only to Tennyson among living poets has not been read by the public. Part of the blame for this unfavorable reception, he concludes, rests with the general mind of the Victorian reader: "We live in what has been called the Mudiæval era. A time that is well calculated to produce a run-and-read sort of mind; or rather, a mind that may run-and-ride at the rate of forty miles an hour!"[5] But his being "A Poet without a Public," as *Chamber's Journal* called him in its review of the 1863 *Selections*,[6] was also due to Browning's poetic peculiarities. The critic of the *North British Review* points to Browning's un-English preference for things recondite, historical, and Italian, to his taste for psychological subtlety and difficult readings of dramatic circumstances, and, above all, to his disconcerting habit of always assuming his reader understands him and can leap to the same conclusion he does:

---

attempt to discover some fixed generic deep structure among the poems Browning finally chose to call *Dramatic Lyrics*, *Dramatic Romances*, *Men and Women*, *Dramatis Personae*, and *Dramatic Idyls*, see Donald S. Hair, *Browning's Experiments in Genre* (Toronto: University of Toronto Press, 1972). On Browning's rearrangement for the 1863 edition of his works, see also Laurence Poston, III, "Browning Rearranges Browning," *Studies in Browning and His Circle* 2 (1974):39–54.

[4]"Browning's 'Fame within These Four Years,'" *MLR* 53 (1958):492–500.

[5][Gerald Massey], "The Poems and Plays of Robert Browning," *North British Review* 34 (1861):184. Sir John Skelton echoes this analysis, saying that "to those that read while they run he is commonly obscure, and often incomprehensible" ("Robert Browning," *Fraser's Magazine* 67 [1863]:240). Browning incorporates this criticism into his address to the British public in *The Ring and the Book*: "Perchance more careful whoso runs may read / Than erst when all, it seemed, could read who ran" (1, 1381–82).

[6]"A Poet without a Public," *Chamber's Journal* 39 (1863):91–95.

Dramatis Personae

Not only does he take too much for granted in the way we have indicated and pass on with chirping cheeriness; but, with his quick habit of leaping to conclusions, he often fails to carry the mind of the reader with him. There is a bright flash, a blank, and then a bright flash again; but all so sudden is the process that the midway is not illuminated. We are left in the middle, in the dark.[7]

While the reviewer then goes on to praise Browning for the great range of characters displayed in his poetry and for the depth of his religious feeling, one should note that the critic here describes in his impressionistic manner the same sort of experience that Ruskin had written about in his letter to Browning when he said that reading him was like crossing an "alpine glacier"—"bright, deep enough surely, but so full of clefts that half the journey has to be done with ladder and hatchet." It also recalls Browning's famous lighthouse metaphor for his poetry: "These scenes and song-scraps *are* such mere and very escapes of my inner power, which lives in me like the light in those crazy Mediterranean phares I have watched at sea, wherein the light is ever revolving in a dark gallery, bright and alive, and only after a weary interval leaps out, for a moment, from the one narrow chink, and then goes on with the blind wall between it and you." But while this suggestive scattering of brushstrokes and colors upon the critical canvas has its attractions, one should stand back and notice the general agreement among contemporaries that Browning's poetry created a problematic relationship between him and his readers which prevented him from becoming as popular as Tennyson was with the Victorian public. Sir John Skelton, writing in *Fraser's Magazine,* could say, "It is about time that we began to do justice to Robert Browning."[8] The reviewer for *Chamber's Journal* could say, "It is probable that no man of our times has written so much and so well without general acknowledgment as Robert Browning."[9] And their praise would sell his books better than they had ever been sold before. But Browning's problems with his audiences both inside and outside his poetry remained, and, after Elizabeth died, even worsened.

I

Ironically enough, the critic of the *North British Review* in 1861, echoing Kingsley's remarks made in 1849, had felt confident that

[7][Massey], "Poem and Plays of Browning," p. 186.
[8][Skelton], "Browning," p. 240.
[9]*Chamber's Journal* 39 (1863):91.

Robert Browning: His Poetry and His Audiences

Browning could "write such poems as shall bring his books home to many" and had called for his return to England: "He has lived long enough abroad, figuratively speaking; let him come home and dwell a while."[10] But even though Browning literally came home after Elizabeth died, one only has to think of *The Ring and the Book* to realize that he never really lived in England in a figurative or poetic sense, because his heart was buried in Italy. And how to "bring his books home to many" or to decide whom he was writing for had become even more difficult puzzles for him than they had been before:

> It is one of the facts of my experience that one limits sorrowfully one's pretension to influence other people for good: I live more and more — what am I to write? — for God not man — I don't care what men think now, knowing they will never think my thoughts; yet I need increasingly to tell *the truth* — for whom? Is it that *I* shall be the better, the larger for it, have the fairer start in next life, the firmer stand? Is it pure selfishness or the obedience to a natural law?[11]

Here, in writing to Julia Wedgwood, Browning questions the purpose of his poetry. He feels that now more than ever he needs to tell "the truth" (whatever that may be) but does not know to whom and for whom he is telling it. In *Men and Women* he could lovingly consider Elizabeth as his first reader, and in "One Word More" he could believe that his poetry symbolized the public face of their private intercourse and give thanks for the love of God and Elizabeth. After her death and by the time of *Dramatis Personae*, he is almost reduced, as he implies in his letter, to writing poetic confessions of his faith in God: he no longer lives to persuade men and have them think his thoughts, but instead lives for God. Yet, as his questions show, he suspects that the lack of an audience other than himself undermines the efficacy of his telling the truth and threatens to make his poetry a purely selfish and wholly hermetic enterprise. He seems headed at best toward a critique of confessional poetry, holding that the only proper poetic task is to demonstrate how untrustworthy any individual interpretation of "the truth" is and how it is subordinate to the larger truth of God's love. He seems compelled, at worst, to write not knowing the answers to the questions "What am I to write" and "For whom?"

---

[10][Massey], "Poems and Plays of Browning," p. 195.
[11]Browning to Wedgwood, July 28, 1864, *Browning and Wedgwood*, ed. Curle, pp. 33–34.

and to drift into a private symbolic universe. He is not only beginning to write and to think about *The Ring and the Book* but also to point self-consciously to reasons for his poetic decline.

Browning's poetry in *Dramatis Personae* attempts to compensate both for his loss of Elizabeth and also for the apparent futility of addressing anyone else in her absence. The poem of the volume which parallels "One Word More" and which most programmatically reveals the difference between the imagined audiences of *Men and Women* and *Dramatis Personae* is "Epilogue." The poem presents three speakers—David, Renan, and Browning—each of whom offers a distinct, individual vision of man's relation to God. The poem's brief survey of the development of religious doctrine emphasizes the primary importance of individual as opposed to corporate vision and distinguishes between the Old Testament belief that God's spirit is external to man and the New Testament belief that God's spirit is within man.

David describes the dedication of Solomon's Temple (II Chronicles 5) in which the priests, Levites, and the people became "as a single man / (Look, gesture, thought and word) / In praising and thanking the Lord" (ll. 8–10). The image of the united audience is then reflected and magnified by God's presence:

> Then the Temple filled with a cloud,
>   Even the House of the Lord;
> Porch bent and pillar bowed:
>   For the presence of the Lord,
> In the glory of His cloud
>   Had filled the House of the Lord.
>   [ll. 16–21]

In this historical moment God and his chosen people join in perfect union.[12] While David envisions a perfect harmony between a multitudinous congregation and God, Renan feels the personal absence of God. While David tells us of God's glorious cloud filling the Temple, Renan regrets that the star of Bethlehem which announced the coming of Christ to the Magi is no longer visible to us, that God has since "gone across the dark" (l. 22). Because man has been deprived of God's presence, man discovers himself, Renan says, in a universe sprinkled with faint, glimmering reminders of God:

---

[12]For an analysis of the poem as a comment on Anglo-Catholic ritualism, see Watson Kirkconnell, "The *Epilogue* to *Dramatis Personae*," *MLN* 61 (1926):213–19.

Robert Browning: His Poetry and His Audiences

> We, lone and left
> Silent through centuries, ever and anon
> Venture to probe again the vault bereft
> Of all now save the lesser lights, a mist
> Of multitudinous points, yet suns, men say—
> And this leaps ruby, this lurks amethyst,
> But where may hide what came and loved our clay?
> [ll. 43–49]

God's absence from the world reduces man's experience of the divine to brief flashes of ruby and amethyst from distant stars and finally to a private nostalgia.

Speaking in his own voice, Browning supposes that from the wholly private experiences of each individual we can reconstruct the face of God. Unlike Renan, he does not despair of the refracted light through which man perceives divinity, because for Browning man's very separation from God, man's irreducible individuality, and man's private experience of God's nature all become signs of God. He believes that

> That one Face, far from vanish, rather grows,
> Or decomposes but to recompose,
> Become my universe that feels and knows.
> [ll. 99–101]

This doctrine, then, becomes both a justification for and evidence of Browning's artistic method which asks his readers to

> Take the least man of all mankind, as I;
> Look at his head and heart, find how and why
> He differs from his fellows utterly.
> [ll. 69–71]

This aesthetic can be traced to the preface to *Paracelsus*: "It is certain, however, that a work like mine depends on the intelligence and sympathy of the reader for its success,—indeed were my scenes stars, it must be his cooperating fancy which, supplying all chasms, shall collect the scattered lights into one constellation—A Lyre or a Crown." From this perspective an individual character becomes a kind of magnetic force field which makes "nature dance / About each man of us" (ll. 87–88). This individual vision, which orders the world around itself and then passes away, mirrors the activity of "that one Face" which "decomposes but to recompose." The poet also engages in a kind of creative decomposition by taking "the least of all mankind, as I," discovering "how and why / He differs from his fellows utterly," and so indirectly demonstrating that each individual's experience, every work of the poet, and God's creation are reflections and refractions of one another. This, then, is the program of *Dramatis Personae*. Indeed, Browning goes so far as to suggest that "that one Face" has become "my universe that feels and knows."

In "One Word More" Browning thinks of his love for Elizabeth as the ground of his art and as the mediation between his public truth telling and his private dedication to and love of God. But in the epilogue to *Dramatis Personae* there is a curious ambiguity and worrisome solipsism, reflected in the phrases "as I" and "my universe." Browning seems to feel he must subordinate his characters' expression of their feelings to an exposition of a general principle concerning his view of God's existence and does not feel at all concerned with establishing within the poem's context and dramatic situation a common metaphorical ground for such theological discourse. Although the dramatic setting of the dedication of Solomon's Temple described by David is not available to him, and although in many ways he, like Renan, cannot discover the star of Bethlehem in the heavens and can only imagine for a moment God's presence in the twinkling of a distant star, Browning unhesitatingly asserts that the decomposition of the templar experience of God into fragmented shards of individual faith is paradoxically the creation of plenitude and that one can naturally assume direct parallels between "my universe that feels and knows" and God's. Consequently, with the notable exceptions of "Caliban upon Setebos" and "Abt Vogler," one too often finds oneself, while reading *Dramatis Personae*, bemoaning the absence of an audience and of dramatic conflict in the monologues, the lack of particular description stemming from dramatic deficiencies, and the corresponding increase in unadorned homiletic.

Browning's emphasis upon the individuality of his speaker's experience leads to a greater solipsism, a greater abstraction, and, most noticeably, a greater loneliness in the monologues than before. The love poems of *Dramatis Personae*—"James Lee's Wife," "The Worst of It," "Dîs Aliter Visum; Or Le Byron de nos jours," "Too Late," "Confessions," "May and Death," and "Youth and Art"—depict the bitter regrets and stolen pleasures of modern love instead of the delicious, half-veiled intimacies of his and Elizabeth's love for one another evident everywhere in *Men and Women,* or the idealized romances of love and loyalty in Tennyson's *Idylls of the King* (1859–85). The speakers of these melancholy poems address either someone who has died, someone who has abandoned them, or someone who has ignored them, and so in lieu of attempting to establish some kind of fellowship between themselves and their wished-for or would-be audience, they indulge themselves in fanciful recollection and moody recrimination. The absence of an audience or the felt lack of sympathy between themselves and their audience leads to inaccessible symbolic reveries like that of "My Star."

II

"James Lee's Wife," which Browning placed first in *Dramatis Personae,* ushers the reader into a somber, grey world of lost loves and melancholy reflections. In the nine lyrics which make up the poem, the woman expresses her fear of losing her husband, realizes their marriage has died, regrets that she has lost her husband, sadly contemplates her lost beauty, and then turns toward God as her only consolation for her loss. The sorrows of James Lee's wife concern particular circumstances from which Browning can keep his distance and which still allow him to give voice to his own grief without making a public display of his emotions. But he has great difficulty creating a language of grief for the woman that is separate from his own and does not successfully objectify his personal sorrow in the woman's lament upon being abandoned by her husband.[13]

The first two lyrics, "James Lee's Wife Speaks at the Window" and "By the Fireside," show her fearing that as the weather and the seasons change, so will her husband's love for her. The first lyric moves from examining the weather outside the window to seeking the reassurance of an intimate, enclosed order not available in Nature except as it is idealized. The woman desires the enclosure of an embrace in order to escape from the processes of time and the changes they may work on the love between her and her husband. In the second lyric she imagines that their fire is made from the wood of wrecked ships, and she pictures a group of sailors on their sinking boat, catching a

---

[13]Browning said in a letter to Julia Wedgwood of December 31, 1864, "I have expressed it all insufficiently and will break the chain up, one day, and leave so many separate round rings to roll each its own way, if it can" (*Browning and Wedgwood,* ed. Curle, p. 109).

glimpse of the light from their window and, possessed by despairing envy, gnashing their teeth as they drown. The picture of disordered Nature sketched in the first lyric becomes transformed into an image of a hostile crowd leering in at the lovers, wanting to possess the warmth and comfort of their safe fireside. The thought suggests to her that there is a corresponding shipwreck of the soul in her own marriage: "All through worms i' the wood, which crept, / Gnawed our hearts out while we slept" (ll. 43–44). She fears that she will fall from the safe ship of "love's voyage" into the devouring sea (l. 51), from the comfortable fireside into the hell of the fire and its teeth-gnashing demons, as the ardor of her husband's love burns out.

The third lyric, "In the Doorway," again looks outward to the disorder of Nature in autumn and contrasts it with the comfort of home. She discerns in Nature a desire for shelter from the changing seasons, hears in the wind an unhappiness with things as they are, and points again to the symbolic refuge provided for her and her husband by their love: "Yet here are we two; we have love, house enough" (l. 68). Their relationship, like their house, protects them from the harshness of the autumn weather.

At the end of the lyric the image of coldness intrudes upon the poem and is considered in a peculiarly religious light:

> But why must cold spread? but wherefore bring change
>   To the spirit,
> God meant should mate his with an infinite range,
>   And inherit
> His power to put life in the darkness and cold?
> Oh, live and love worthily, bear and be bold!
>   [ll. 75–80]

She imagines that like God she should be ready to love the cold and give life to it, both in the sense of bringing children into the world and also in the sense of loving a man whose love for her seems to be cooling as the weather is. This coldness is a monitory sign of death, of things growing cold and the life going out of them, as well as a symbol of the absence of soul. She later speaks of a rock on the beach as

> Baked dry; of weed, of a shell, no trace:
> Sunshine outside, but ice at the core,
> Death's altar by the lone shore.
>   [ll. 131–33]

The bare, cold rock symbolizes the icy petrification of their love and is a much more final and terrifying image of love's reification than the statues of "The Statue and the Bust," where love is at least transformed into art.

According to Browning, though, the true God, the true poet, the true hero, and the true lover give themselves to the cold. Like the heroes of old, the speaker of "Prospice" wants to "Bear the brunt, in a minute pay glad life's arrears / Of pain, darkness and cold" (ll. 19–20). In "Caliban upon Setebos" Caliban sets the limits to the powers of Setebos, who "dwelleth i' the cold o' the moon" (l. 25), when he notes that the god has created the sun, moon, and earth from "being ill at ease: / He hated that He cannot change His cold" (ll. 31–32). Instead of this personified coldness and heartless, aleatory justice, Browning prefers the men and women who give life to the cold and in the "Epilogue" asks us to watch each of his characters,

> when nature by degrees
> Grows alive around him, as in Arctic seas
> (They said of old) the instinctive water flees
>
> Toward some elected point of central rock,
> As though, for its sake only, roamed the flock
> Of waves about the waste: awhile they mock
>
> With radiance caught for the occasion,—hues
> Of blackest hell now, now such reds and blues
> As only heaven could fitly interfuse.
> [ll. 72–80]

This image of a character resembling a rock that gives color and order to the Arctic sea and so imitates God's creation, as the woman of "James Lee's Wife" suggests, is both an image of being petrified in the face of a ghostly multitude—the waves "find and flatter, feast and finish there" on the rock's peak (l. 86)—and also an image of an art in which the artist relies on symbolic colors and bare icons instead of dramatic situations to portray his meaning.[14]

---

[14] There is a complicated web of associations with the images of water breaking on a rock and of light being broken into its colors by water in Browning's letters and poetry. See, for instance, Robert's letter to Elizabeth of March 6, 1846, replying to her playful claim to have chained a Promethean poet to the rock of marriage: "The words were only words and the playful feelings were play—while the *fact* has always been so irresistibly obvious as to make them *break* on and off it, fantastically like water turning to

Dramatis Personae

The meditation on giving life to the cold in "James Lee's Wife" also has a biographical parallel. After Elizabeth died, Browning habitually vacationed in the summers on the French Atlantic coast and took up sea bathing, and many of the places where he vacationed and swam find their way into his poetry—Pornic, Cambo, Croisic, and St. Aubin among others. Browning's sea bathing probably suggested this almost Conradian idea of submitting oneself to the destructive element, of giving oneself to the cold sea, and his thinking about this relationship to the sea is one of the central reflections of *Fifine at the Fair* (1872):

> "That rise into the true out of the false—explain?"
> May an example serve? In yonder bay I bathed,
> This sunny morning: swam my best, then hung, half swathed
> With chill, and half with warmth, i' the channel's midmost deep:
> You know how one—not treads, but stands in water? Keep
> Body and limbs below, hold head back, uplift chin,
> And, for the rest, leave care! If brow, eyes, mouth should win
> Their freedom,—excellent! If they must brook the surge,
> No matter though they sink, let but the nose emerge.
> [ll. 1008–16]

The false, the sea in its blank destructiveness, submerges all but the poet's nose, which, because it preserves him from drowning, represents the true spirit, the true breath of life and poetry. Still, this emblematic forerunner of existential drama, this replacement of dramatic confrontation with an abstract struggle against Nature and time, leads to the flaccid, prosy poetry of *Fifine at the Fair* and in "James Lee's Wife" seems to dilute the poem's force, since the abstract image of living in and against the cold cannot adequately express the pain of having been abandoned by one's love.

In "Along the Beach," the fourth lyric, the wife tells James that their love has revealed God in the world and in each other:

---

spray and spurts of foam on a great solid rock—*Now* you *call* the rock, a rock, but you must have known what chance you had of pushing it down when you sent all those light fancies and free-leaves, and refusals-to-hold-responsible . . to do what they could" (*Letters*, 1, 518–19). Also see the play of "the radiant cripple" of light upon a splash of water from Pippa's ewer in *Pippa Passes*, Introduction, ll. 77–87. And see "With Francis Furini": "There did I plant my first foot. And the next? / Nowhere! 'T was put forth and withdrawn, perplexed / At touch of what seemed stable and proved stuff / Such as the coloured clouds are: plain enough / There lay the outside universe: try Man— / My most immediate! and the dip began / From safe and solid into that profound / Of ignorance I tell you surges round / My rock-spit of self-knowledge" (ll. 402–10).

> I will be quiet and talk with you,
>   And reason why you are wrong.
> You wanted my love—is that much true?
> And so I did love, so I do:
>   What has come of it all along?
>
> I took you—how could I otherwise?
>   For a world to me, and more;
> For all, love greatens and glorifies
> Till God's a-glow, to the loving eyes,
>   In what was mere earth before.
>   [ll. 82–91]

The first stanza is a quiet, extraordinary triumph in working the bareness of conversation into verse while preserving the rhythms of natural speech, a poetic ground which Hardy and Frost were later to cultivate more intensively. The diction and rhythm are as classically spare and natural as any touchstone Arnold cites in "The Study of Poetry," but the sentiment and subject are not. This is modern love—not the love of an ideal beauty but a love of "mere earth." It is Christianized Romanticism without the visionary and mythic pyrotechnics of Blake. The discovery of God in the other because of one's love for the other is a Romantic idea, but here it has been domesticated and turned into a myth of plenitude. So, when she talks about her disappointment in marriage, James Lee's wife laments the unfulfilled promise of the Bible's flowing "rivers of oil and wine" (l. 105). Nevertheless, despite their failure to produce children and despite his tiring of her and ceasing to love her, she wants to go on with their marriage. Its physical and spiritual barrenness is better than nothing at all.

Since to lose her husband and her love makes her fear that she will then lose her faith in God and go insane, she seeks refuge in a private fantasy. In the fifth lyric, "On the Cliff," she sees on top of a cold rock on the beach a butterfly which she feels symbolizes love that is not appreciated by the rock. The comforting fancy in which she imagines the butterfly as a war-horse for a chivalrous knight and as an emblem of her own love for the rocklike James Lee begins to take the place of her hope for a spiritual union between her soul's desire and the other. Her soul becomes a butterfly, an image of love, and her husband, who cannot hear her, becomes an unfeeling stone. She speaks of her love as a "blue and red grace" (l. 150), which recalls Browning's use of these colors in "My Star" as symbols of love and its privacy. But there is nothing inherently wonderful about these colors, nor are blue and red necessarily associated with grace. The only basis within the poem for this association is the woman's fancy; and only the colors' private significance for Browning, only their symbolizing for him Elizabeth's true love, explains the lyric's meaning fully. So, while he can indirectly comment here on his not having fully appreciated Elizabeth's love for him before she died, he can do so only because of the private nature of the woman's fantasizing.

In the sixth and seventh sections of the poem, "Reading a Book, under the Cliff" and "Among the Rocks," one senses the greatest strain between Browning's desire to express his sense of loss and the mask through which he chooses to speak. In "Reading a Book, under the Cliff," James Lee's wife is perusing "Still Ailing, Wind?", a poem Browning had published anonymously in 1836 in the *Monthly Repository*. This early exercise explores the ambiguity of the pathetic fallacy by asking whether the poet in his contrived misery speaks for the wind or the wind for the poet. The woman objects to the young poet's use of a dying nun and a hungry dog in stanzas 4 and 5 as objective correlatives for his emotion and is obviously thinking of the immediacy of her own pain in comparison to the young poet's collection of distant, contrived analogues for his discontent. But her criticisms seem out of proportion to the slightness of the poem and so make the scene itself seem recherché. It appears that in the light of his grief over Elizabeth's death Browning is indirectly and ironically commenting upon the inadequacy of his youthful expression and is pointing to the more exact registration of emotion he can now produce through the character of James Lee's wife in comparison with the etiolated romanticism of "Still Ailing, Wind?".

One's feeling that Browning has dropped his mask for a moment to speak *in propria persona* is confirmed by the eighth lyric, "Among the Rocks." Suddenly a great brawny line of pure Browning sprawls before us: "Oh, good gigantic smile o' the brown old earth" (l. 232). While one might have heard his voice before in such phrases as "God's a-glow" (l. 90), "the old woe o' the world" (l. 217), and "God does: endure his act!" (l. 226), the expansiveness and weight of this line present a sharp contrast to the delicate fancy, close observation, and cultivated diction and phrasing of the rest of the poem's lyrics. Although James Lee's wife has expressed her faith in God previously, it seems that the felt need to provide something more substantial than doctrinal consolation has driven Browning to speak in his heartiest voice to show the woman regaining hope from Nature, from seeing how the old earth "sets his bones / To bask i' the sun" (ll. 233–34). The resulting contrast with the bitter resignation of the surrounding sections is more than one of tone: it is one of persona.

From the image of mirthful Nature, James Lee's wife turns in "Beside the Drawing Board" to the image of a clay cast of a perfect, "princess-like" hand (l. 272). She draws the hand and extracts from her action an illustration of God's love. The ring placed upon the cast by the previous artist represents "for him on earth, his art's despair, / For him in heaven, his soul's fit bride" (ll. 290–91). The ring is an emblem of the failure of art in imitating the "limit-line" of the hand (l. 257), an image which, in turn, recalls Andrea del Sarto's "a man's reach should exceed his grasp." The hand becomes a symbol not only of God's hand in creation but also of the artist's hand in imitating God, and so a symbol of the marriage of God and man. The artist's ring is a "token of marriage rare" (with an ironic play upon "rare") and of "his art's despair" (ll. 289–90). It is proof of his having acknowledged God's presence in the world.

Despite the lesson of the hand, the final lyric, "On Deck," seems unrestrained in its bitterness. At its end she imagines that James Lee might age and grow to look like her:

> Why, fade you might to a thing like me,
>   And your hair grow these coarse hanks of hair,
> Your skin, this bark of a gnarled tree,—
>   You might turn myself!—should I know or care
> When I should be dead of joy, James Lee?
>
>   [ll. 368–72]

She fancies that if he came to resemble her in outward appearance, he would also love her as she loves him. This crossing over of speaker into audience, reminiscent of the transition between Robert and Elizabeth in "One Word More," is ominous here. It does not represent a shared private world but instead a retreat into the secret world of her self at the cost of any audience other than God. But her fancies and her faith do not seem adequate substitutes for James Lee's love. She fashions at the end the grotesque image of James Lee grown old and his skin become like the "bark of a gnarled tree" and so returns the reader to the disorder of Nature with which the poem began. But this disorder is now fully internalized. She has abandoned her earlier vision of her husband and his love for her as a refuge from natural change

Dramatis Personae

and substituted a mirror image of herself as her audience and her proper lover. In commenting on the poem and so indirectly explaining the woman's obsession with the ravages of Nature, Mrs. Sutherland Orr long ago pointed out that James Lee's wife is "a plain woman" and rather gnomically suggested that this "may throw some light on the situation."[15] Like the countess of "Count Gismond," who was not as fair as her sisters and was extremely sensitive to any rejection by her audience, James Lee's wife fears she will be left alone without a lover. From the beginning of her marriage she worries that James Lee may leave her because she is not beautiful, and at the end she bitterly thinks, "There is nothing to remember in me" (l. 333). The loss of James Lee threatens her sense of self so much that it forces her to turn toward God and also inward upon herself in a search for an audience to replace her husband. Her fancy, though, cannot compensate for his forgetting her except by paradoxically transforming him into a reflection of herself and so allowing her to renounce him as he has renounced her. It is no accident that she has no name or identity other than her tie to James Lee. Only by creating this self-image, which represents her at once in the most spiritually attractive and in the most physically repulsive light, can she both revenge herself upon him by making him into herself and also console herself by imagining someone who loves her, thus allowing her to love herself.

The idea of two newly married people "trying to realize a dream of being sufficient to each other" reminds one of Robert and Elizabeth's honeymoon in Pisa and of the private references in poems such as "A Lover's Quarrel" and "My Star" of *Men and Women*.[16] But the unhappy misalliance of James Lee and his wife more closely resembles that of the couple in George Meredith's *Modern Love* (1862). James Lee's desertion of his wife would also have likely made a Victorian reader think of the Marriage Act of 1857, which, besides placing divorce cases under the jurisdiction of civil rather than ecclesiastical courts, had added separation or desertion to adultery and cruelty as grounds for divorce. The new significance of marital separation and desertion, then, along with his own loss of Elizabeth, encouraged Browning to write "The Worst of It," "Dîs Aliter Visum; Or Le

---

[15]Mrs. Sutherland Orr, *Handbook*, p. 246. For a discussion of the poem in terms of the Victorian recognition of the often hard realities of love, see Patricia M. Ball, *The Heart's Events: The Victorian Poetry of Relationships* (London: Athlone Press, 1976), pp. 145–66.

[16]Browning to Wedgwood, December 31, 1864, *Browning and Wedgwood*, ed. Curle, p. 109.

Byron de nos jours," "Too Late," "Youth and Art," "A Likeness," and "May and Death" in the same vein as "James Lee's Wife," and also influenced "Confessions" and "Prospice."

Throughout these poems the metaphors associated with separation tend to overpower any dramatic situation. In "Confessions," for example, the speaker, who is lying on his deathbed, reconstructs the scene of his clandestine meetings with a young girl, using the objects of his sickroom: "And that farthest bottle labelled 'Ether' / Is the house o'er-topping all" (ll. 15–16). In "Dîs Aliter Visum" an embittered woman, speaking to a man she feels should have married her ten years ago but who did not ask her, recalls the seaside landscape of the walk they took at the height of their love and allegorizes it in terms of their failure. She imagines him thinking to himself, "Climb high, love high, what matter? Still, / Feet, feelings, must descend the hill: / An hour's perfection can't recur" (ll. 68–70). And in "Youth and Art" a married woman remembers her bohemian days when she lived on the same street with a painter who has since been knighted and has received his membership in the Royal Academy. She compares the two of them to a pair of sparrows: she singing and he building his sculpture with "sticks and clay" (l. 5). But their acquaintance from afar did not turn into a nesting together in the spring, when the stalls in the "street looked rare / With bulrush and watercresses" (ll. 35–36). Like the speaker of "Dîs Aliter Visum," she cannot successfully extend the metaphor derived from the landscape to their lives, because they never had the intimate love she wishes they had had.

The speaker of "Prospice," unlike the one of "Youth and Art," is able to forecast a future union with his dead beloved. But, as in the poems of modern love in *Dramatis Personae*, the absence of an audience lets the speaker follow his fancy and allegorize his metaphors. He proleptically compares dying to climbing a mountain in bad weather: the fog, snow, and wind of the storm symbolize "Arch Fear in a visible form" (l. 7). Through the operation of the pathetic fallacy, "the elements' rage" becomes a group of "fiend-voices that rave" (l. 23). By struggling with those voices he recovers his lost love: "Then a light, then thy breast, / O thou soul of my soul! I shall clasp thee again, / And with God be the rest!" (ll. 26–28). He imagines recovering those perfect audiences: God and his love. Yet his optimism seems too smug and his fancy too unself-consciously desperate. Knowing that Browning is surely speaking in his own voice of Elizabeth here, one finds this crossing over into "the soul of my soul" even more movingly troubled and self-deceived than that in "James Lee's Wife."

III

How one can hold on to the experience of the divine so that one has a convincing intertwining of event and history, of a text and the commentary on it, is a central issue in "A Death in the Desert." Like "Cleon" and "Karshish," "A Death in the Desert" considers the ephemeral nature of man's testimony about Jesus Christ and explores the dividing line between those who heard Christ's words and those who must depend on the testimony of others. The poem presents an imaginary account of the death of St. John the Evangelist, who, according to legend, was the last man living to have seen and heard Christ. The poem frames St. John's testimony by surrounding it with the remarks of a host of commentators. The anonymous owner and editor of the text, whose initials are given as mu and epsilon (or, to transliterate, "me"), says in his introduction that the story is supposedly told by one Pamphylax the Antiochene (l. 1), describes the manuscript which contains the story (ll. 2–7), and gives us the manuscript's provenance (ll. 8–12). He inserts the glossa of Theotypas concerning John's preaching (ll. 82–104), reports the impressions of the heretic Cerinthus (l. 665), and records, in an appendix to the story (ll. 665–87), the hopeful interpretation of the text by an anonymous reader. This framing and mediation of St. John's discourse on his witnessing Christ dramatizes and accentuates the question to which St. John addresses himself: how can those who have not seen or heard Christ themselves believe?

Not only does the manuscript have a history of readers and commentators, but there is also an oral tradition anterior to it. Christ had spoken to St. John, St. John in turn preached to his followers, and Pamphylax, one of these disciples, tells his story to Phoebas before going the next day to "fight the beasts" (l. 652). The fragility and tenuousness of this oral transmission is emphasized by the fate of the others who had heard St. John's last words: Xanthus "escaped to Rome, / Was burned, and could not write the chronicle" (ll. 56–57); Valens "is lost" (l. 648); the Bactrian, who guarded the cave while the others listened, "was but a wild childish man, / And could not write nor speak, but only loved" (ll. 649–50); and the boy, who woke St. John to speak his last words by intoning the words of Christ, "I am the Resurrection and the Life" (l. 64), was presumably too young to remember such a lengthy sermon. Then, too, Pamphylax observes that such human testimony is not altogether trustworthy, since many still believe St. John to be alive (ll. 654–60). One must hope that despite the inacurate, inconsistent, and incoherent testimony of others, "He will grow incorporate with all, / With me as Pamphylax, with him as John, / Groom for each bride!", as the anonymous commentator of the appendix believes (ll. 682–84). One's true audience is not composed of other human beings but of Christ himself; and the devoutly desired consummation with this single and perfect audience is imagined in terms of the metaphor of marriage, of groom and bride, Christ being the husband of each individual soul.

As scholars have pointed out, Browning was addressing himself indirectly to the harsh criticism of St. John's gospel in Strauss's *Leben Jesu*, translated by George Eliot (1846), and in Renan's *La Vie de Jésus* (1862).[17] But his poem does not try to defend the gospel of John or to refute the criticisms of Renan and Strauss. Instead, Browning's St. John argues that we need not rely on anyone's testimony for our access to God, that God is within us. Charlotte Porter and Helen A. Clarke focus on this key point in their notes on the poem: "John's own spiritual faith transcends the idea of evidence as dependent upon witness or memory of signs and wonders. He has been nourished on such external evidence to the end that his faith now rests on internal evidence,—has become one with the desires and aspirations of his soul."[18] In the poem, St. John describes how after traveling and evangelizing, being exiled on Patmos, and writing his Revelation, he wondered how best to testify to others about Christianity so that their love for Christ and God would not be a secondhand love that would inevitably weaken when handed on from one generation of believers to another and found a way to do so: "And reasoning from my knowledge, merely taught / Men should, for love's sake, in love's strength believe" (ll. 147–48). In his letters St. John said that through this love men

---

[17]See Raymond, *Infinite Moment*, pp. 32–38; and DeVane, *Handbook*, pp. 295–98. Elinor Shaffer corrects the view that Browning's poem was solely a reaction to higher criticism by showing how his apologetics incorporated the perspective of higher criticism itself, in "Browning's St. John: The Casuistry of the Higher Criticism," VS 16 (1972):205–21.

[18]Charlotte Porter and Helen A. Clarke, eds., *The Complete Works of Robert Browning*, 12 vols. (New York: Thomas Y. Crowell, 1898), v, 311. Elinor Shaffer also shows that John's faith depends upon and is incorporated with the community of believers, in "Browning's St. John," pp. 219–20.

would come to know God and would strive to be one with him. In the first epistle of John, which Browning follows here, we find St. John saying,

> We are of God: he that knoweth God heareth us; he that is not of God heareth not us. Hereby know we the spirit of truth, and the spirit of error.
> Beloved, let us love one another: for love is of God; and every one that loveth is born of God, and knoweth God.
> He that loveth not knoweth not God; for God is love. [1 John 4:6–8]

Instead of promulgating a doctrine holding that the truth is communicable and dependent primarily upon the historical fact of Christ's Resurrection, John, in response to the needs of those who have not seen and heard Christ themselves, believes that one's individual actions and experiences are sufficient testimony of God's and Christ's love for man in this world, as long as these actions and experiences are accompanied by a profession of faith in Jesus Christ.

There is danger, however, in relying upon one's own insight for revelation, because one might then conclude that God is not an irreducible other but merely a figment of man's imagination and that St. John's testimony is no better than fiction. One might well ask, "Is John's procedure just the heathen bard's?" (l. 530). By appealing to psychology instead of history as a means of resolving man's doubts about his faith and about God, John lays himself open to the objection that we must already be one with Christ, since we are forced to imagine him, instead of being able to rely upon the evidence of his presence or his miracles: "Has He been? Did not we ourselves make Him? / Our mind receives but what it holds, no more" (ll. 377–78). This Romantic Platonizing is dangerous because it threatens to obscure the difference between God and man and to let man imagine himself to be God. From our knowledge of nature and our mastery of the world, we might mistakenly conclude that "man proves best and highest—God, in fine" (l. 567). This mistake would lead to the destruction of one's soul, because one would then not strive to model oneself after God but, assuming oneself to be God, would instead stagnate in self-satisfaction and not rise toward God in an unending progress:

> And in this striving, this converting air
> Into a solid he may grasp and use,

> Finds progress, man's distinctive mark alone,
> Not God's, and not the beasts': God is, they are,
> Man partly is and wholly hopes to be.
> Such progress could no more attend his soul
> Were all it struggles after found at first
> And guesses changed to knowledge absolute,
> Than motion wait his body, were all else
> Than it the solid earth on every side,
> Where now through space he moves from rest to rest.
>
> [ll. 584–94]

This image of absolute knowledge petrifying the very air around man and so entombing him in solid rock is a curious imaginative consequence of having become the center of all things, of supposing in one's delusion that one has become God. But, like the bare rock in "James Lee's Wife," this frozen, solid knowledge is really an image of death, an image of the soul's constriction and of a false monumentality of the spirit. Man in Browning's mind is not a monument for the ages but a desire for the future.

The poem appears to pose in its form grave questions about the possibility of any audience's being sure that it has access to the truth, least of all the reader of Browning's poem. The confused allegory which Theotypas makes out of John's simple introductory remarks, the Chinese box of speakers, and the worrisome questions John asks and then answers in his catechism appear to be formal grounds for our being skeptical of the reliability of St. John's word and for asking, "Was John at all, and did he say he saw?" (l. 196). One fears that the complicated and obscure transmission of his words and the text of them is cause enough to doubt their validity. But what would logically seem reason for doubt is, according to John, a sign to man that that "help, he needed once, and needs no more, / Having grown but an inch by, is withdrawn" (ll. 425–26). Now man must depend upon himself to imitate God, to strive after "the ultimate, angels' law" (l. 631). St. John's view accords with the Protestant belief in the individual's inner light and in his not needing recourse to the mediation of priests or to an apostolic succession which transmits God's truth. Unlike Newman, in *An Essay in the Aid of a Grammar of Assent* (1870), Browning's John brushes aside the troublesome difficulties of being persuaded of the truth, convincing others of it, and teaching it to them so they can repeat it to others, by appealing to the doctrine that the existence of love "proveth Christ" (l. 510). And so the question of

Christ's existence is begged and the difficulty of persuading others of his existence answered in a similarly circular manner: "He that knoweth God heareth us; he that is not of God heareth not us" (1 John 4:6). This view reflects Browning's feeling that after Elizabeth's death he was living and writing more "for God not man." Writing poetry for God instead of Elizabeth, and showing St. John answering the objections of a phantom audience outside the circle of disciples gathered in a cave near Ephesus instead of imagining him facing his persecutors directly, seem sufficient to Browning. One does notice, however, that, instead of recalling Christ's life and teachings and the acts of the apostles in order to reassure the persecuted Christians around him that they will receive their reward in heaven, St. John appears to address his relatively abstract discourse to a much more complacent and skeptical audience: the Victorian public. St. John does not call for any corporate action but intimates instead that it is enough to desire to become like God and to express one's love for him; he also suggests that this desire and love are by themselves evidence of Christ's presence in the world and that to worry about what others think is unnecessary.

IV

The complacency and simplicity of the doctrine evident within the tortured casuistry and complicated perspectives of "A Death in the Desert" have their counterparts in the optimism and bareness of the beliefs expressed in "Rabbi Ben Ezra." But in "Rabbi Ben Ezra" there is almost no sense of audience; one has no clear idea to whom the rabbi is speaking. Like St. John, Rabbi Ben Ezra is a historical figure, a biblical scholar in Spain who lived from around 1097 to 1167. But the poem doesn't place him within either his historical circumstances or a dramatic context. He asks his readers to grow old along with him and proclaims, "The best is yet to be" (ll. 1–2). He thinks that whatever doubt we have is a spark to the soul which gives us evidence of God (stanzas 2–5). This observation leads him to reflect upon Browning's favorite doctrine that man's failure to attain God's perfection is, paradoxically, essential to his spiritual success: "What I aspired to be, / And was not, comforts me" (ll. 40–41). This dogma orients man toward the future as an unformed desire rather than as a creature of brute satisfactions, as a hopeful old man rather than a despairing youth, and as an active rather than a passive soul.

He holds to these tenets in the face of the world's scorn and complains that to try to express his thoughts to others around him is an impossible task, because he thinks "thoughts hardly to be packed / Into a narrow act, / Fancies that broke through language and escaped" (ll. 145–47). For Rabbi Ben Ezra there is a world outside and beyond language for which words are a poor substitute, and only his fancy of being a cup fashioned by God on the wheel of life, fixed "'mid this dance / Of plastic circumstance" (ll. 163–64), can in any way express his sense of his private communion with God. According to the rabbi, each man is individually fashioned by God into a cup on the wheel of life; so it is to the God who has made him that man should pay attention, rather than to the whirling "shapes and colors" surrounding him (l. 185). This communion in its purest form takes place in death, when God drinks from the cup of one's body and gathers back one's soul; so Rabbi Ben Ezra looks forward to death and even implores God, in the poem's final two stanzas, to use him by drinking from his life.

While the directness of "Rabbi Ben Ezra" made it a favorite poem with the Victorian readers of Browning, its shrill declamation now seems to catch the tone of a troubled country vicar, temperamentally unfit for his pastoral duty and familiar in a vague way with the German higher criticism of the Bible, attempting to convince himself of his faith in God by shouting it in the pulpit on Sunday morning, and so really talking only to himself and not his congregation. The poem's bluff optimism, together with the lack of a dramatic context, make "Rabbi Ben Ezra" a relatively weak poem. Its blithe dismissal of the loneliness, fear, and physical decay of old age becomes not so much vigorous testimony to Browning's belief in a life after death as a troubling intimation of his subsequent retreat from the observation of human experience into a poetic world of private colors and murky language.[19]

In contrast to the strained metaphor of the potter's wheel in which Rabbi Ben Ezra finally finds the proper image for describing the formlessness of man's striving after God, Abt Vogler has the more convenient ambiguity and slipperiness of music with which to describe his private experience of God's presence. As the poem begins, Abt Vogler imagines that the piece he has just finished extemporizing on the musical instrument of his invention resembled the palace Solomon built for Bathsheba, and he wishes that "it might tarry like his, the beautiful

---

[19]See the comparison of the poem with Arnold's "Growing Old" in John Huebenthal, "'Growing Old,' 'Rabbi Ben Ezra,' and 'Tears, Idle Tears,'" *VP* 3 (1965):61–63.

building of mine" (l. 9). It is a symbol of his creative power, "claiming each slave of the sound" (l. 3), which in its glory appears to "match man's birth" (l. 25). He envisions his work as a kind of magnificent apocalypse:

> And the emulous heaven yearned down, made effort to reach the earth,
>   As the earth had done her best, in my passion, to scale the sky:
> Novel splendours burst forth, grew familiar and dwelt with mine,
>   Not a point nor peak but found and fixed its wandering star;
> Meteor-moons, balls of blaze: and they did not pale nor pine,
>   For earth had attained to heaven, there was no more near nor far.
>   [ll. 27–32]

In his vision, each part of nature acquires its own private part of heaven.

One might expect that such a revelation would lead to megalomania in Abt Vogler, but the ephemeral nature of his performance prevents him from taking on the role of a musical tyrant. He humbly recognizes in his music "the finger of God" and understands that God has granted the gift of music to man so that "out of three sounds he frame, not a fourth sound, but a star" (ll. 49, 52). He also expects nothing from his fellow men in the way of fame, for as his "palace of music" fades away, "the good tears start, the praises that come too slow" (ll. 57–58). Because their praise, like his music, is evanescent, he cannot rely upon men and women to be his audience, but only upon God. For only God can perceive the artist's intentions: "On earth the broken arcs; in the heaven, a perfect round" (l. 72). Again:

> The high that proved too high, the heroic for earth too hard,
>   The passion that left the ground to lose itself in the sky,
> Are music sent up to God by the lover and the bard;
>   Enough that he heard it once: we shall hear it by-and-by.
>   [ll. 77–80]

Neither his fellow men nor Abt Vogler himself heard clearly or understood fully his extemporaneous composition; only God, his true audience, has both heard and understood. So, in the way all pasts become golden as the dross in them is forgotten, the remembered infinite moment of his performance acquires a heavenly halo—a halo all the more beautiful in the drabness of reflection, in the "C Major of this life" (l. 96).

Robert Browning: His Poetry and His Audiences

The relationship between private, spiritual revelation and its public exhibition, glanced at in "Rabbi Ben Ezra" and "Abt Vogler," is examined in detail and at length in "Mr. Sludge, 'The Medium.'" The poem, by far the longest in *Dramatis Personae*, at 1525 lines, considers the defensive and exculpatory arguments of a medium caught manufacturing the spirit rappings he has attributed to souls from beyond. As Isobel Armstrong has pointed out,[20] the poem pleases few readers, partly because of its sordidness but above all because of the extended casuistry concerning the medium's and audience's relative shares of responsibility for the spiritual phenomena (ll. 83–663), concerning the dividing line between religion and superstition (ll. 664–1279), and concerning the relation between lies and truth (ll. 1280–1477). But pointing to Sludge's parodies of many of Browning's aesthetic principles, Armstrong also shows that Browning examines "the religious and aesthetic problems arising from the medium's claim to authentic insight and spiritual vision" and raises "the problem of the integrity of the creative imagination."[21] There is also an implicit criticism of the emptiness of the American self and the historical vacuum of American culture that the medium's spirits and the ghost stories of Hawthorne and James sought to fill. The problem of the medium's integrity is connected to the nature of the relationship between him and his audience. Browning's feelings about this relationship and, in particular, about Mr. Hume, the spiritualist who was the model for Sludge, were vehemently expressed in a letter to Mrs. William Burnet Kinney: "Indeed, I have got to consider such a beast as the proper associate and punishment of those who choose to shut their eyes and open their arms to bestiality incarnate."[22] He sensed something unnatural and improper in the medium's prostitution of himself and whatever insight he had.

Sludge pretends that the spirits of the dead speak through him to satisfy the wishes and fancies of his audiences, and he exploits their desires to contact the spirit world for his own psychological and material gain. In compensation for others' demonic possession of his soul, he projects a monstrously inflated ego. At the beginning of the poem he

---

[20] "Browning's *Mr. Sludge, 'The Medium,'*" *VP* 2 (1964):1. In a letter of December 25, 1845 to Elizabeth, Robert speaks of his "foolish concentrating of thought and feeling, for a moment, on some one little spot of a character or anything else indeed, and—in the attempt to do justice and develop whatever may seem ordinarily to be overlooked in it,—that over vehement *insisting* on, and giving an undue prominence to, the same—which has the effect of taking away from the importance of the rest of the related objects which, in truth, are not considered at all" (*Letters*, I, 343).

[21] "Browning's 'Mr. Sludge,'" p. 8.

[22] Browning to Kinney, January 6, 1871, *New Letters*, p. 199.

is striking a bargain with Hiram H. Horsefall of Boston in which Sludge agrees to tell the truth about himself. Horsefall has discovered Sludge's cheating, has threatened to expose him by writing to "Greeley's newspaper" (l. 54), and, enraged by Sludge's insolence, has tried to choke him (l. 17). After accepting money and passage to England, Sludge tells his patron how it is his audience's fault that he is what he is. Society's conceit "that ghosts may be" makes it listen to a vulgar boy who could not otherwise hold their attention (l. 140); he needs only to act like "an epileptic dervish" because the gathered circle "will lay down spiritual laws, read wrong things right / By the rule o' reverse" (ll. 305, 308–9). He describes how he can marshal social pressure to force any doubting Thomas to choose between Sludge's spirits at one house and some Captain Sparks's "hunting-stories, scalping-scenes, / And Mexican war exploits" at another (ll. 232–33). And he tells how those who believe in him "put up with having knowledge strained / To half-expression through his ignorance" (ll. 337–38). Sludge, then, raises not only voices from the dead but also audiences from society. By turns he entertains them, reinforces their faith in an afterlife, and titillates them with the "naked truth"—that is, with a picture of heaven similar to an old Italian print a judge has on which one spies "three nymphs conversing with a cavalier, / And never a rag among them" (ll. 615, 626–27).

Sludge has acquired great popularity by providing access to the greatness of the past and especially by assuring séance participants that there is another world beyond this one. Despite being a servant to his audiences and their whims, he receives their rapt attention and imagines himself as a protean god who becomes what they want him to be:

> I shut my eyes and fancy in my brain
> I'm—now the President, now Jenny Lind,
> Now Emerson, now the Benicia Boy—
> With all the civilized world a-wondering
> And worshipping.
>
> [ll. 1267–71]

By being a medium he becomes more than himself and so makes his audiences more than themselves:

> What would you have? Just speak and, there, you see!
> You're supplemented, made a whole at last,

> Bacon advises, Shakespeare writes you songs,
> And Mary Queen of Scots embraces you.
>
> [ll. 1406–9]

He makes the circle of culturally deprived Americans around him feel more important by filling the emptiness of their selves with the ghosts of famous people for a moment, and he, too, feels more important because he can imagine that these spirits are his slaves:

> And all depose their natural rights, hail you
> (That's me, sir) as their mate and yoke-fellow,
> Participate in Sludgehood—nay, grow mine,
> I veritably possess them.
>
> [ll. 1426–29]

He satisfies his own wish to control the audience which condescends to him socially and morally by picturing himself, as the *Pauline*-poet does, as the tyrant of enslaved ghosts, able both to summon spirits from the vasty deep and, unlike Glendower, to make them come.

Sludge also justifies himself as a "seer of the supernatural" (l. 875) who can provide spiritual experience to those who believe or wish to believe in religion, and who can also divine the various interventions of providence in human affairs. But his reading of Nature's signs is transparently based upon absurd superstition rather than religious insight and is a sign of his uncultured American upbringing. In such moments Sludge the charlatan gives one an idea of what Huck Finn would have had to become in order to retain something of his backwoods nature and still enter into high society. In the most outrageous instance, he claims that if he sees Charles's Wain in the sky at midnight, it is a sign that he should have his hair cut (ll. 919–23). To the natural rebuttal that God seems more likely to act in extraordinary rather than ordinary events, Sludge responds by reminding his patron of his special standing in the spirit world and his interest in any event that will affect him (ll. 943–45). He compares himself to the writer who embellishes the truth with his imagination and considers it evidence of his "godlike craft" (l. 1469):

> It's fancying, fable-making, nonsense-work—
> What never meant to be so very bad—
> The knack of story-telling, brightening up
> Each dull old bit of fact that drops its shine.
>
> [ll. 190–93]

He feels that by creating the voices and signs of the spirits he is at worst only engaging in an imaginative ornamentation of the commonly accepted truth about life after this one and that this elaboration is proof of his divine inspiration.

Despite advancing these sophistical arguments, Sludge admits that he lies for his own self-interest:

> My care is for myself;
> Myself am whole and sole reality
> Inside a raree-show and a market-mob
> Gathered about it.
> [ll. 908–11]

This comparison of Mr. Sludge to a raree show and its audience, and Sludge's boast that he is the "whole and sole reality," make him a demonic parody of God. His pretension to being both God and his own audiences is finally a delusion, a compensation for his being unable to establish a legitimate relationship with an audience. This leads him in the coda (ll. 1500–25) (which shows the "gratitude, forsooth, of a prostitute / To the greenhorn and the bully" [ll. 783–84]), to curse his patron. Like the prostitute who dominates the greenhorn and in turn is controlled by the bully in the most transient of intercourse, Sludge cannot envision a lasting relationship between himself and his audiences based upon mutual respect, because he has sold his soul to the world.

V

In contrast to the tedious "Mr. Sludge, 'The Medium,' " which at one-fifth its length could have been among Browning's best poems, "Caliban upon Setebos; or, Natural Theology in the Island" has long been a favorite among Browning's readers. The poem's curious profusion of natural detail, its beasts and creeping things, and its picture of Caliban in his cave sprawling on his belly, "both feet in the cool slush" during the heat of a summer's day (l. 4), remind one of the grotesque descriptions in "Sibrandus Schafnaburgensis" and the "Soliloquy of the Spanish Cloister" but are still properly subordinated to the program of *Dramatis Personae* and its reflections on God and love.

Caliban believes in an immanent god, Setebos, who, because of his discomfort and distress, has "made all we see, and us, in spite" (l. 56). Setebos is not the God who out of the goodness and fullness of his being created the world and whose creation represents the perfect, overflowing expression of his not needing to keep himself to himself. Instead, Setebos is a god who wishes to be other than he is and yet, hating this imagined otherness for revealing his own imperfections, creates only to destroy. So, when we hear Caliban at the beginning of the poem thinking within brackets (ll. 1-23), we are listening to Caliban silently convincing himself of his safety from Setebos's reprisals before letting his "rank tongue blossom into speech" (l. 23); and when the brackets appear again at the end (ll. 284-95), Caliban has stopped his foolish "prattling" (l. 287) and is lying low, cursing himself for expressing himself so intemperately and so openly. He believes that Setebos has placed Prospero above him, but his imagination allows him to picture Setebos only as a more powerful version of himself.[23] Caliban supposes that all parts of creation belong to a hierarchy and that the relationships between the levels of this order are relations of dominance. He reasons, for example, that Setebos is to him as he is to the crabs he sees:

> He is strong and Lord.
> 'Am strong myself compared to yonder crabs
> That march now from the mountain to the sea;
> 'Let twenty pass, and stone the twenty-first,
> Loving not, hating not, just choosing so.
> [ll. 99-103]

He sees no morality or emotion existing in the relation of any one being to any other—only the arbitrary expression of their relative power.

Caliban's failure is a failure of the imagination. This is indicated by the poem's epigraph, taken from Psalms 50:21: "These things hast thou done, and I kept silence; thou thoughtest that I was altogether such an one as thyself: but I will reprove thee, and set them in order before thine eyes." Like the Israelites to whom these words were addressed, Caliban thinks of Setebos as a larger and more powerful version of himself. He does not perceive Setebos's wrath as an expression of the world's moral order but instead as Setebos's hatred of his own imperfection: "He hated that He cannot change His cold" (l. 32). Beyond Setebos, he speculates, is something he calls the Quiet and that represents a principle of plenitude and satisfaction: "This Quiet, all it hath a

---

[23]See John Howard, "Caliban's Mind," *VP* 1 (1963):250.

Dramatis Personae

mind to, doth" (l. 137). But his Quiet also represents a principle of indifference, because it "feels nor joy nor grief" (l. 133) and ultimately has nothing to do with Caliban.

Caliban's self-expression, therefore, becomes confined to his self-objectification. He constantly refers to himself in the third person in an attempt to create the illusion of another, to try to place himself in some sort of perspective and so come to terms with his existence. But, confined within the dialectic of master and slave without the possibility of rebellion, Caliban can think only of his being obliterated, crushed by a meteorite (ll. 211–12) or, like a certain newt, "shut up inside a stone" (l. 215). Only when hidden from Setebos's eye (the sun by day, the moon by night) within his cave or in complete darkness can he express himself and give voice to his fears and desires:

> Wherefore he mainly dances on dark nights,
> Moans in the sun, gets under holes to laugh,
> And never speaks his mind save housed as now:
> Outside, 'groans, curses.
>
> [ll. 266–69]

Like the sea beast he has captured and blinded and which plays his role as slave while Caliban plays Prospero, Caliban has a "bitter heart that bides its time and bites" (l. 167). He is outside *The Tempest*'s world of love and significant self-discovery, because he unknowingly has fashioned the world's laws and its gods from a projection of himself; instead of coming to terms with others and so with himself by appreciating others for what they are, Caliban tries to put himself in their place and constructs the world from various versions of himself.

In terms of the project for *Dramatis Personae*—that is, seeing how "heaven's high with earth's low should intertwine" and watching "when nature by degrees / Grows alive around him" ("Epilogue," ll. 66, 72–73)—"Caliban upon Setebos" is by far the most successful poem. One penetrates in the poem to the principle of dominance which orders Caliban's mind and world and understands that this principle obscures from him the fact that he is without another being against which he can properly define himself, that he has no one to love, and that to supply his need for an audience he has projected himself into all the nature around him, only to gain a vision of his own nothingness. Other poems in *Dramatis Personae* come face to face with the psychological fact that in the absence of either divine or human love, in the absence of an audience, we tend to substitute a private symbolism that will supply our need and ultimately construct an audience from ourselves: in an attempt to revenge ourselves upon the other, as in "James Lee's Wife"; to raise our self-esteem as in "Caliban upon Setebos"; or to express the relative insignificance of our accomplishments in the face of God's, as in "Abt Vogler." But only in "Caliban upon Setebos" does Browning find the necessary consciousness with which to portray the horrors of losing that other person or that God whose recognition of oneself guaranteed one's having fully understood oneself. Only in "Caliban upon Setebos" do we see that the horror present in Mr. Sludge and Caliban is that in their envy of power they have both egocentrically assumed themselves and their desires to be the law of the universe and have also blinded themselves to their own emptiness by replacing all possible audiences with versions of themselves.

Elsewhere in the volume there are interesting speculations about the worth of men's testimony in relation to the truth, most notably in "A Death in the Desert," and one can see Browning moving to the position that one cannot trust what anyone says about the truth and can only discover from others after careful evaluation what their heart's affections are, a position that will receive its fullest exposition in *The Ring and the Book*. One can also appreciate in a poem like "James Lee's Wife" Browning's delicate if somewhat flawed treatment of modern love and can understand why his handling of relations between men and women is considered by far the most mature, progressive, and adventurous in Victorian poetry. But only "Caliban upon Setebos" in this volume ranks with the finest poems of *Men and Women*, *Dramatic Lyrics*, and *Dramatic Romances and Lyrics*—partly because it is the only poem that displays Browning's genius in natural description to any great extent, partly because the roughness of Browning's blank verse needs only a few more burrs and brambles to be the beastly Caliban's speech, and, above all, because it is the volume's only poem whose circumstances let Browning forget for a moment that Elizabeth has died and so allow him to imagine dispassionately and unself-consciously the consequences of not having an audience to help one define oneself.

7

The Ring and the Book

But human promise, oh, how short of shine!
—I, 295

One can still enter the local bookstore, examine the poetry shelves, and find a copy (if bound in paper) of Browning's *Ring and the Book*. But while this certainly attests to our general estimation that Browning is a major English poet, one may well wonder whether this isn't merely a sign of our lingering attachment to the Victorian sages and whether Browning's magnum opus isn't doomed to be relegated to the darker shelves of our literary museums as one of the curiosities of the age, like many other Gothic monuments to the voraciousness and patience of Victorian readers that have been found unsuited to modern taste. Indeed, few readers today have done more than taste from a layer or two of this Victorian wedding cake of a poem in a selected edition of Browning's poetry, which has provided, perhaps, the Pope, Pompilia, or Caponsacchi, and now and then even Guido, or at worst "O Lyric Love" for the readers' sampling. And, when one reads the poem carefully, one can perceive signs that Browning's poetic powers were decaying; one sometimes painfully realizes that after Elizabeth died in 1861 Browning, instead of doing nothing but attending dinner parties, as the biographical myth would have it, spent most of his time writing poetry (three-fifths of his complete works as they stand on the shelf). But the poem's modern experimental form, its spiritual imagination, and its poetic power make it one of the great long poems in English, being, I think, behind only Milton's *Paradise Lost*, Wordsworth's *Prelude*, both Chaucer's *Canterbury Tales* and *Troilus and Criseyde*, and Spenser's *Faerie Queene*, and ahead of Byron's *Don Juan* because of its more impressive architectonics. One may find fault with it, as one often does with other great poems, but it merits careful reading and study both for its intrinsic qualities and because it is the last great long poem written in the language before the modern symbolist aesthetic effectively guaranteed in advance the failure of such poetic enterprises. In particular, Browning's idealization of the Old Yellow Book and its relation to the governing poetic of *The Ring and the Book,* his attempt to accommodate his readers in his opening monologue, the larger social implications of the poem's form, and that form's relation to the epic deserve our special attention.

I

On a June day in 1860, while looking over the contents of a bookstall in Florence, Browning discovered the Old Yellow Book containing the various pamphlets and manuscripts, which one Francesco Cencini had collected and bound together, relating to the trial of Guido Franceschini and his henchmen for the murder of Pompilia, Pietro, and Violante Comparini. Reading through its contents—the summaries of charges and the tedious legal arguments—one finds it easy to understand why Elizabeth expressed no interest in it, why Miss Ogle, A. C. Cartwright, and Anthony Trollope declined Browning's offer of the material for adaptation into a novel, and why Tennyson didn't think it would make a poem.[1] The story is sordid; the motives of all the participants questionable; and the imaginative effort required to fashion the trial's records into narrative poetry an enormous one. But Pompilia fascinated Browning.[2] She appeared to him an innocent woman in great distress who was, for a moment, rescued by St. George in the guise of Caponsacchi. The parallels between Elizabeth and Pompilia, himself and Caponsacchi, and Guido and Elizabeth's father must have suggested themselves to him, especially after Elizabeth's death, and he naturally idealized Pompilia, thinking of her as the perfection of womanly innocence.

But many readers have opposed Browning's view of his material. Carlyle said of the poem, "The real story is plain enough on looking

---

[1]Elizabeth's lack of interest, noted in a letter of Browning to Wedgwood of January 21, 1869, *Browning and Wedgwood,* ed. Curle, p. 154; the offers to Mrs. Ogle and A. C. Cartwright, noted in W. Hall Griffin and Harry Christopher Minchin, *The Life of Robert Browning* (New York: Macmillan, 1910), p. 229; the offer to Trollope, noted in *William Allingham: A Diary,* ed. H. Allingham and D. Radford (London: Macmillan, 1907), p. 180; to Tennyson, ibid., p. 326.
[2]See William C. DeVane, "The Virgin and the Dragon," *Yale Review* 37 (1947):33–46.

into it; the girl and the handsome young priest were lovers."[3] And scholarship on the background of *The Ring and the Book* has driven a wedge between the historical truth concerning Pompilia's actions and Browning's idealized perception of them. Judge John Marshall Gest and Beatrice Corrigan have shown, for example, that the historical Pompilia could write, that she no doubt wrote the letters to Caponsacchi and almost without doubt committed adultery with him; and they have shown this both from the partial evidence offered in the Old Yellow Book and from the fuller record of the trial in the Cortona codex.[4] What emerges from their accounts is that in the eyes of the seventeenth-century Italians the cowardly Guido failed to avenge his honor when he didn't kill Pompilia and Caponsacchi after overtaking them in their flight at Castelnuovo; that Guido's family deservedly became the laughingstock of Arezzo; and that when driven by public disgrace to kill Pompilia, he both overstepped the laws protecting his honor as a husband and a nobleman by murdering Pietro and Violante Comparini, and also displayed his incompetence in executing his revenge by cheating his henchmen and by failing to make proper arrangements for his escape from Rome. Guido's case excited interest among contemporary Italian lawyers (among them Cencini, the compiler of the Old Yellow Book) because Guido had not killed the adulterous couple when he had overtaken them and when by law he would have been exonerated, and the case therefore promised to offer arguments and perhaps precedents concerning how long a man could delay in avenging his honor. This interest is evident in the lawyers' arguments in the Old Yellow Book and in the subtitle of the case: "Wherein it is disputed if, and when, / Husbands may kill adulterous wives, yet 'scape / The customary forfeit" (I, 129–31).[5] Browning was certainly free to alter and even to misread the Old Yellow Book for his poetic ends (a less than innocent Pompilia would have made *The Ring and the Book* irretrievably vulgar), and while early Browning scholars like Charles Hodell mistakenly defended Browning's essential faithfulness to the historical and psychological truth of his source and his magnification of the characters' good and evil through his tragic per-

---

[3] Quoted in Allingham and Radford, *William Allingham*, p. 207.
[4] *The Old Yellow Book: Source of Browning's "The Ring and the Book,"* ed. and trans. John Marshall Gest (Boston: Chipman Law Publishing Co., 1925), pp. 605–06; Beatrice Corrigan, *Curious Annals: New Documents Relating to Browning's Roman Murder Story* (Toronto: Toronto University Press, 1956), p. xxx.
[5] For a discussion of the lawyers' interest in the case, see Corrigan, *Curious Annals*, p. xxxvii.

spective, recent critics, following J. E. Shaw, have rightly emphasized instead Browning's faithfulness to his own idealizing imagination.[6]

To impose upon Browning a standard of historical realism, on the other hand, and to expect, as Judge Gest does, for example, that Browning not caricature the hard-working lawyers Hyacinthus and Bottini is to subject imagination to the tyranny of circumstance and, in the case of the lawyers, is to ignore the need for comic relief in *The Ring and the Book* and to appeal to a standard of dully perfect artistic representation.[7] Art, as Browning understands very well, will inevitably be symbolic, be a mixture of "fact and fancy," to use his favorite terms. And, when he talks about creating art, Browning employs as an analogy for his poetic process the making of a ring from pure gold and an alloy:

> That trick is, the artificer melts up wax
> With honey, so to speak; he mingles gold
> With gold's alloy, and, duly tempering both,
> Effects a manageable mass, then works.
>
> [I, 18–21]

The pure gold is pure, crude fact, the alloy Browning's imagination without which the material cannot be shaped into a form. With the breath of his poetic fancy he makes "dead" truth into "living" art, resuscitates the past, and gives form to shapeless fact.

There are, then, two competing metaphors in "The Ring and the Book" (the title of the first book of the larger work) for Browning's poetic method: one of poetic making or fashioning, and another of poetic resuscitation. These correspond roughly to Browning's understanding of the difference between the objective and subjective poets, discussed in his *Essay on Shelley*. In his formulation there, his definition seems to rest on a distinction between mimetic and expressive poetry: "He [the subjective poet] is rather a seer, accordingly, than a fashioner, and what he produces will be less a work than an effluence. That effluence cannot be easily considered in abstraction from his personality,—being indeed the very radiance and aroma of his personality, projected from it but not separated."[8] This comes, one remem-

---

[6]Charles Hodell, *The Old Yellow Book*, 2d ed. (Baltimore: Lord Baltimore Press, 1908); J. E. Shaw, "The 'Donna Angelicata' in *The Ring and the Book*," *PMLA* 41 (1926):55–81.

[7]Gest, *Old Yellow Book*, p. 16.

[8]*Robert Browning: The Poems*, ed. John Pettigrew and Thomas J. Collins, I, 1002.

bers, in defense of the usefulness of Shelley's biography to an understanding of his poetry, and specifically in defense of publishing the letters supposedly by Shelley to which the essay served as preface. But in "The Ring and the Book," Browning deftly joins the creative processes of the objective and subjective poets—at least in metaphor, if not in practice.

According to Robert Langbaum, this gives rise to a new poetic theory of the poet as a "resuscitator," the poet who "is the superlatively effective psychologist and historian, the arch-empiricist who works toward greater concreteness and not, as in traditional poetic theory, toward general truths."[9] In imitating God the Creator, man does not create, "but resuscitates, perhaps" (I, 719):

> man, bounded, yearning to be free,
> May so project his surplusage of soul
> In search of body, so add self to self
> By owning what lay ownerless before,—
> So find, so fill full, so appropriate forms—
> That, although nothing which had never life
> Shall get life from him, be, not having been,
> Yet, something dead may get to live again,
> Something with too much life or not enough,
> Which, either way imperfect, ended once:
> An end whereat man's impulse intervenes,
> Makes new beginning, starts the dead alive,
> Completes the incomplete and saves the thing.
> Man's breath were vain to light a virgin wick,—
> Half-burned-out, all but quite-quenched wicks o' the lamp
> Stationed for temple-service on this earth,
> These indeed let him breathe on and relume!
> For such man's feat is, in the due degree,
> —Mimic creation, galvanism for life,
> But still a glory portioned in the scale.
> [I, 722–41]

This will remind one of Shelley, a looser, prosier Shelley, and of this passage from *A Defence of Poetry*: "A man cannot say, 'I will compose poetry.' The greatest poet even cannot say it: for the mind in creation is as a fading coal, which some invisible influence, like an inconstant wind, awakens to transitory brightness: this power arises from within, like the colour of a flower which fades and changes as it is developed,

---

[9]*Poetry of Experience*, p. 134.

and the conscious portions of our natures are unprophetic either of its approach or its departure."[10] But while the image of the fading coal or dying lamp is the same, Browning's application differs from Shelley's: Browning refers to a dying, material world awakened by the poet's visionary breath, while Shelley is talking about a Neoplatonic kind of imaginative inspiration that highlights the mind's fleeting impressions and fugitive sensations. For Browning, it is not the poet's mind but something outside the poet that comes to life. Browning's theory of poetic creation makes the pathetic fallacy into an aesthetic principle: artists first sympathize with the world in general and the past in particular and then record their re-creations in their poetry. In its supreme application the pathetic fallacy can perform spiritual miracles. Just as Elijah raised the widow's son from the dead (I Kings 17), so his successor Elisha raises the Shunamite's son to life again (II Kings 4) (I, 760–72). And so it is with Browning and the Old Yellow Book. His imagination finds some object in the world, "some fragment of a whole, / Rag of flesh, scrap of bone in dim disuse, / Smoking flax that fed fire once" (I, 752–54), adds to it "his surplusage of soul," and brings it back to life again. But by this transference the artistic product will no longer be the reflections and intimations of the Platonic ideas but another being possessing another identity: "Enough of me!" says the poet (I, 773). For Browning, then, the poet seeks to supplement God's creation and does so through his imagination by bringing some other consciousness to life and by effacing himself in the other's voice.

From the standpoint of the metaphor of ring making, Browning arrives at the same result:

> This was it from, my fancy with those facts,
> I used to tell the tale, turned gay to grave,
> But lacked a listener seldom; such alloy,
> Such substance of me interfused the gold
> Which, wrought into a shapely ring therewith,
> Hammered and filed, fingered and favoured, last
> Lay ready for the renovating wash
> O' the water. "How much of the tale was true?"
> I disappeared; the book grew all in all.
>
> [ll. 679–87]

---

[10]*The Complete Works of Percy Bysshe Shelley*, ed. Roger Ingpen and Walter E. Peck, 10 vols. (London: Ernest Benn, 1926–30), VII, 135.

There is little doubt that Browning disappears from the face of the poem and that the voices of *The Ring and the Book* replace his voice, just as the diluted acid bath removes the alloy from the face of the ring and leaves a smooth surface of gold behind. But why does Browning do this? He does so in anticipation of his audience's question, "How much of the tale was true?"[11] In Browning's view, "Art may tell a truth / Obliquely, do the thing shall breed the thought, / Nor wrong the thought, missing the mediate word" (XII, 859–61). Art is not a mediation but an articulated action that reveals the truth with the aid of the reader's interpretation. For this reason, it is necessary to remove the possible obstruction of the poet's personality from other men's access to the truth:

> How look a brother in the face and say
> "Thy right is wrong, eyes hast thou yet art blind,
> Thine ears are stuffed and stopped, despite their length:
> And, oh, the foolishness thou countest faith!"
> Say this as silverly as tongue can troll—
> The anger of the man may be endured,
> The shrug, the disappointed eyes of him
> Are not so bad to bear—but here's the plague
> That all this trouble comes of telling truth,
> Which truth, by when it reaches him, looks false,
> Seems to be just the thing it would supplant,
> Nor recognizable by whom it left:
> While falsehood would have done the work of truth.
>
> [XII, 845–57]

By leaving the "mediate word" of interpretation to his readers, Browning's poetry allows one to recognize oneself in the other. Unlike a sermon or a moral essay that foregrounds a shaping self, *The Ring and the Book* offers a sequence of voices, each of which readers must judge for themselves and so make the truth their own.

II

The first of the poem's twelve books, "The Ring and the Book," is intended to function as a formal argument summarizing the action

---

[11]On the ring metaphor, see Paul A. Cundiff, "The Clarity of Browning's Ring Metaphor," *PMLA* 63 (1948):1276–82; George R. Wasserman, "The Meaning of Browning's Ring Figure," *MLN* 76 (1961):420–26; and Mary Rose Sullivan's useful discussion of these studies, and other remarks on the ring metaphor, in *Browning's Voices in "The Ring and the Book": A Study of Method and Meaning* (Toronto: University of Toronto Press, 1969), pp. 19–20.

and the plan of the entire poem and also as a formal apology for Browning's artistic method. What makes the first book so remarkable is the effort Browning makes to explain himself to his audience and to involve them in an active reading of his work by describing the process of its creation. He addresses us: "Do you see this Ring?" (l. 1), "Do you see this square old yellow Book?" (l. 33), "Examine it yourselves!" (l. 38), and "Give it me back!" (l. 89). He makes explanations to his readers and tries to anticipate possible objections they may have: "I found this book, / Gave a *lira* for it, eightpence English just" (ll. 38–39); "'*Romana Homicidiorum*'—nay, / Better translate—'A Roman murder-case'" (ll. 120–21); "You know the tale already: I may ask, / Rather than think to tell you, more thereof" (ll. 377–78); and

> What's this then, which proves good yet seems untrue?
> This that I mixed with truth, motions of mine
> That quickened, made the inertness malleolable
> O' the gold was not mine,—what's your name for this?
> Are means to the end, themselves in part the end?
> Is fiction which makes fact alive, fact too?
> The somehow may be thishow.
>
> [ll. 700–706]

Browning displays much more rhetorical deference to his readers here than he does anywhere else in his poetry. But the bitterness he feels shows itself in his mocking references to his audience, taken not as individuals but as a whole: "Well, British Public, ye who like me not, / (God love you!) and will have your proper laugh / At the dark question, laugh it! I laugh first" (ll. 410–12); "British Public, ye who like me not, / (God love you!)—whom I yet have laboured for" (ll. 1379–80). The bitterness even shades into hints of ominous prophecy:

> Perchance more careful whoso runs may read
> Than erst when all, it seemed, could read who ran,—
> Perchance more careless whoso reads may praise
> Than late when he who praised and read and wrote
> Was apt to find himself the self-same me.
>
> [ll. 1381–85]

Browning here recalls the reference of the *North British Review* to the second chapter of Habakkuk in criticism of Browning's readers:[12] "I

---

[12][Gerald Massey], "The Poems and Plays of Robert Browning," *North British Review* 34 (1861):184. For the quotation, see p. 192 above.

will stand upon my watch, and set me upon the tower, and will watch to see what he will say unto me, and what I shall answer when I am reproved. / And the Lord answered me, and said, Write the vision and make it plain upon tables, that he may run that readeth it" (2:1–2). But what is gnomically prophetic in Habakkuk is self-consciously ironic here. Browning hopes that his readers, who read him only when they are running for their trains or to work, will now slow their pace.[13] He hopes that his labor to be clear, to keep his readers in mind, will prevent them from criticizing him for being forgetful of them and that someone beside himself, "the self-same me," will praise his poetry. Perhaps even more ironic is the appeal to Elizabeth as the first reader of his work: "Some whiteness which, I judge, thy face makes proud, / Some wanness where, I think, thy foot may fall!" (ll. 1415–16). For there is a sense of public confession of his love for his dead wife and yet a creation of a private ground upon which the common reader may not tread. The public audience may have the "ultimate Judgment" on the merits of Guido's case (ll. 1220–21), but, as he has done in "One Word More" of *Men and Women*, he has in some sense written for Elizabeth, and it is only to her judgment on the merits of his poetry that he will defer. One should note, however, that in the absence of her physical presence Browning substitutes a private color symbolism and explains that because she has taken "sanctuary within the holier blue" he does not have access to her (l. 1394). So it is with some sadness that one watches him attempting to distinguish between the whiteness of her approval and the wanness of her disapproval, thus deliberately isolating himself from his public by taking refuge in his memory of her.

III

The great formal innovation of *The Ring and the Book* is to have Half-Rome, the Other Half-Rome, Tertium Quid, Guido, Caponsacchi, Pompilia, Arcangeli, Bottini, the Pope, and again Guido all present arguments about various aspects of the case from their points of view. Since these monologues together are supposed to constitute a whole, it is necessary and quite helpful that Browning provides us in

---

[13]Curiously enough, the Official Guide of the Chicago and Alton Railroad published the complete works of Robert Browning from December 1871 through June 1872 in consecutive monthly numbers; see *Bibliography*, pp. 32–33; see also Richard D. Altick, "Robert Browning Rides the Chicago and Alton," *New Colophon* 3 (1950):78–81.

the first book with a ready-made summary of each character's relationship to every other. This, after all, is the kind of summary that we find ourselves having to construct while trying to read and make sense of Browning's other monologues. The implications of this sequence of monologues, however, are very disturbing. On a superficial level we are asked to distinguish between prejudiced opinion and correct judgment, between the sophistical balancing act of Tertium Quid and the evenhanded justice of the Pope. There is also the slightly more complicated matter that Langbaum raises: are ethical judgments of actions dependent on an understanding of the circumstances in which they took place? Browning's answer is yes, as Langbaum suggests. But Langbaum is wrong to call this "relativism" and thereby invite confusion regarding the distinction between opinion and judgment.[14] Instead, Browning is really asking us to believe in the possibility of what Kierkegaard calls "the teleological suspension of the ethical."[15] In the context of *The Ring and the Book*, Browning asks us to believe that despite our ethical judgment Guido might be saved by God:

> Man, like a glass ball with a spark a-top,
> Out of the magic fire that lurks inside,
> Shows one tint at a time to take the eye:
> Which, let a finger touch the silent sleep,
> Shifted a hair's-breadth shoots you dark for bright,
> Suffuses bright with dark, and baffles so
> Your sentence absolute for shine or shade.
>
> [ll. 1367–73]

This again is the prismatic poetry of colors that is symbolic of the inaccessible, private audience—here of man with his God who will restore the broken colors to a single light. Once one must consider a man's character in relation to his final end, to "the silent sleep," one can no longer be sure of the brightness or darkness of his soul or whether he is ultimately destined "for shine or shade." One is asked to understand that whatever one's ethical judgment or one's view of God's ultimate judgment, our opinion (and that is the right word, be-

---

[14]Langbaum himself points out the confusion likely to be caused by his choice of the term; see *Poetry of Experience*, p. 112; an even less successful suggestion is the word *pluralism*, used by E. D. H. Johnson in "Robert Browning's Pluralistic Universe: A Reading of *The Ring and the Book*," *UTQ* 31 (1961):20–41. John Killham argues against both Langbaum's and Johnson's formulations as being too modern, in "Browning's 'Modernity': *The Ring and the Book*, and Relativism," in *Major Victorian Poets*, pp. 153–75.

[15]Søren Kierkegaard, *Fear and Trembling: A Dialectical Lyric*, ed. and trans. Walter Lowrie (Princeton: Princeton University Press, 1941), pp. 64–77.

cause one has no more of an understanding of God's actions than the word *opinion* suggests) finally counts for nothing and is significant only when accompanied by this understanding.

This radical discounting of human judgment in the face of God's is, however, less disturbing than the implications that this ring of monologues has for society and human relations. One comes to understand that each monologuist can really only act as his or her own advocate and cannot dispassionately argue someone else's case. Bottini, for example, is shown to be working at cross-purposes with Pompilia's interests in his prosecution of Guido because he is handling the Convertites' claim on Pompilia's inheritance and therefore has a vested interest in defaming her character. Arcangeli, on the other hand, is shown conceding Guido's guilt in advance but persevering in embellishing his Latin with choice phrases and arguments about honor in hopes of drawing attention to himself and gaining a promotion. One senses that in this respect Browning's sense of the law is not far removed from Kafka's. One can only laugh at Bottini and Arcangeli insofar as one understands them to be self-interested. Were they to become disinterested advocates of the law itself, they would transform ethical and legal questions into formal, aesthetic ones; they would arrange facts and arguments not in an attempt to arrive at any deep understanding of the case but in order to produce the best theatrical performance. Worse yet, we come to feel that any sense of community beyond marriage itself is for Browning nothing more than an agreement to go on trial before everyone else, that human relations outside love are legal, not organic, bonds.

The monologue form admirably suits not only the view that human relationships within society are agreements to go to trial but also this particular murder case in which all arguments were in written form and all testimony was taken in the form of depositions and sworn affidavits. Without the trappings of courtroom drama to give us a sense of society, one can easily be tempted, as Browning was, to see this form of trial as a metaphor of every man's trial before God and of every monologuist's true audience's being God. And in this sense Guido's second monologue is indeed the climax of the poem, because he moves from the stoic view of death as something that "mows here, mows there, makes hay of juicy me" (XI, 148) to his final cry —"Pompilia, will you let them murder me?" (XI, 2427). One can only wonder whether this is somehow parallel to Browning's invocation of his dead wife's aid at the end of book I or a demonic parody of such a request. Is this plea from the half-crazed Guido sufficient to raise one's doubts about his damnation? If one tries to decide what counts as a sincere eleventh-hour change of heart and what if any actions preclude God's forgiveness, one is likely to inquire about motivations and character in a way Browning thinks one simply can't since one isn't God. Browning seems to think that Guido's appeal to Pompilia does hold out hope for his salvation, and in his introduction suggests that this is so when he describes how he will conduct his reader's descent from this summit of *The Ring and the Book*:

> Finally, even as thus by step and step
> I led you from the level of to-day
> Up to the summit of so long ago,
> Here, whence I point you the wide prospect round—
> Let me, by like steps, slope you back to smooth,
> Land you on mother-earth, no whit the worse,
> To feed o' the fat o' the furrow: free to dwell,
> Taste our time's better things profusely spread
> For all who love the level, corn and wine,
> Much cattle and the many-folded fleece.
> Shall not my friends go feast again on sward,
> Though cognizant of country in the clouds
> Higher than wistful eagle's horny eye
> Ever unclosed for, 'mid ancestral crags,
> When morning broke and Spring was back once more,
> And he died, heaven, save by his heart, unreached?
> Yet heaven my fancy lifts to, ladder-like,—
> As Jack reached, holpen of his beanstalk-rungs!
> [I, 1330–47]

There is a certain violence done here in the butchered rhythm of "and he died, heaven, save by his heart, unreached?", in the bizarre introduction of Jack and his magic beanstalk as an image of eternal salvation, and in the awkwardly archaic diction of "holpen of." Is Browning serious? Why does he risk injuring his reader's good opinion of the poet's decorum at what would seem to be a crucial point? Is Guido's confession before the Company of Death the climax of the work, and how so? Does Browning think readers are to be led like so many sheep from one pasture to another and are not to question what they eat? These questions about decorum are helpful only insofar as they let us understand that Browning's poetry and his theology are based upon an aesthetic sympathy which strives for inclusiveness, instead of a doctrine of exclusiveness and strict decorum, because it is precisely at those moments in which Browning displays his theological generosity that he relaxes in his language and encourages his readers to "feed o' the fat o' the furrow," to enjoy the unconstrained life of his poetry, to ignore considerations of decorous constraint, and, finally, to forgive Guido as his fancy does.[16]

Browning is bent on his fairytale ending—"Yet heaven my fancy lifts to." But the reader, I think, is not likely to care much. The climax Browning hopes for, the eleventh-hour salvation of the villain, is an imposition of the narrative expectations of a novel or the conventional reversal of melodrama upon the essentially static form of the monologue that recalls the narrative problems of *Pippa Passes*. Browning tries to fit the monologues into a narrative of sorts, each monologue taking place on a different day and representing a different part of the trial. This schematic narrative is clear enough in book I, but gets lost in reading the other monologues. Indeed, the banal textbook absurdity that *The Ring and the Book* is the same story told from ten different points of view, obscures the real narrative weakness of the poem. This weakness does not lie in an overdetermination of the central story, because the monologues gradually shift their focus upon the details of the Guido-Comparini affair, moving from background of the case given in Half-Rome's account to the aftermath of the murders described in Guido's second monologue. The weakness is not an overdetermination of internal events but an underdetermination of external events. Browning has attempted to provide his Roman murder story with an exterior framework in the monologues of Half-Rome, the Other Half-Rome, and Tertium Quid, thereby putting Guido's trial and the monologues of the chief actors within the context of divided and uninformed public opinion. But Guido Franceschini's trial was not for the late seventeenth-century Papal States what Dreyfus's trial was for late nineteenth-century France; it was not a focal point of political opinion and internal divisions. Moreover, the nature of Guido's trial precludes any dramatic narrative involving and influencing the telling of each individual tale and also does not provide for narrative closure. There is really no good reason, for example, why a few more

---

[16]Browning at least leaves the question open. See Robert Langbaum, "Is Guido Saved?: The Meaning of Browning's Conclusion to *The Ring and the Book*," VP 10 (1972):289–305. James F. Loucks marshals the arguments against Guido's salvation (as if it could be determined in advance) in " 'Guido "Hope?" ': A Response to 'Is Guido Saved?,' " *Studies in Browning and His Circle*, 2, no. 2 (1974):37–48.

people weren't allowed to get a word in (imagine a poem on the scale of Balzac's *Comédie Humaine*!), or why there weren't fewer speakers, or why Guido got a second hearing. The form is almost frighteningly open-ended. As the trailing off of the reports in "The Book and the Ring" shows, there is always the possibility of considering yet another point of view. Indeed, the form is designed to leave the work open to interpretation by readers who bring their perspectives to bear upon it or who offer more historical evidence for others to consider.[17] Yet Browning's struggle to bring *The Ring and the Book* to an interpretive crisis—Guido is surely guilty, but can he be saved?—and the need to manage this crisis without ever putting Pompilia's innocence into serious question unbalance the poem. Readers who read only to decide the innocence and guilt of each party will most likely finish the poem feeling that *The Ring and the Book* tested only their endurance and not their judgment; for, as Browning has arranged the opinions, testimony, and evidence, we can never really doubt Pompilia's innocence, nor can we ever become much attracted by the prospect of Guido's salvation.

IV

Why isn't *The Ring and the Book* an epic? This question hasn't really been asked. Contemporary reviewers were quick to note the poem's epic length but pursued the comparison no further, nor have critics since then.[18] They haven't done so largely, I think, because the convergence of the long poem and the novel in the middle of the nineteenth century and their divergence afterwards with the advent of

---

[17]Corrigan, *Curious Annals*, pp. xix–l.

[18]See the *Saturday Review*, December 26, 1868, quoted in *Browning: The Critical Heritage*, ed. Boyd Litzinger and Donald Smalley (London: Routledge & Kegan Paul, 1970), p. 297; and see John Addington Symonds, review of *The Ring and the Book*, *Macmillan's Magazine* 19 (1869):258. One should also note G. K. Chesterton's figurative use of the word in calling *The Ring and the Book* an "epic of free speech" (*Robert Browning* [London: Macmillan, 1903], p. 173). Richard D. Altick and James F. Loucks argue against calling the poem an epic: "But the poem's matter lacks epic scope: the action is confined to Arezzo and Rome in a brief period of the late seventeenth century. The only epic action is Caponsacchi's rescue of Pompilia, and the only victory is the vindication, by a Pope thought to be in his dotage, of the fame of a Roman prostitute's illiterate daughter. The central subject, in fact, is a domestic plot of the sort which in the true epic is relegated to secondary importance and even used for comic relief. Nor does the language possess epic grandeur, except in certain exalted passages of philosophical commentary" (*Browning's Roman Murder Story: A Reading of "The Ring and the Book"* [Chicago: University of Chicago Press, 1968], p. 7). See also the comments on Browning and the epic on p. 124 above.

symbolism has centered most theoretical interest around the relationship of realism to symbolism and the social and moral ramifications of these aesthetic positions. Readers interested in the realism of *The Ring and the Book* have asked about Browning's adherence to the historical truth of his subject and about whether or not the poet's imagination can get at the truth in a factual sense. And from a formal, psychological, and symbolist approach, best exemplified by Langbaum, *The Ring and the Book* has been seen as a modernist and relativist work, symbolically demonstrating the ephemeral, subjective nature of truth.[19] But seeing Browning's poem as a meditation on the balance between historical and psychological truth does not adequately explain the form the poem takes nor fully account for its successes and failures.

The aesthetic excesses of *The Ring and the Book* resemble those of the period's sprawling novels; and one can understand why Henry James, who was generally interested in streamlining narrative to focus sharply on the psychological complexity of character, would have considered making a novel from the romantic centerpiece of Browning's polyptych, the love of Pompilia and Caponsacchi.[20] The poem's multiplication of perspectives, on the other hand, is often taken to be an anticipation of the modern fragmentation of artistic point of view. But the size and complexity of *The Ring and the Book* do not make it an epic, and by examining its governing aesthetic more closely we will see why. Such an examination will shed more light on the disturbing social implications of the poem's form and will perhaps account for the poem's successes and failures in terms of Browning's feeling that there is, finally, no satisfactory audience available for an individual outside love other than God.

The Ring and the Book adheres to a Romantic aesthetic, which, instead of classically viewing character as a function of national ethos, envisions national ethos as a function of character development and subject to revolutionary change. But the poem does not furnish any national or institutional correlative to its individual psychology of love and salvation. In short, it does not have epic scope. As Hegel says in his *Aesthetics*, when he discusses the contingency of romantic love in relationship to the universality of social institutions, "In the family,

[19] *Poetry of Experience*, pp. 109–36.
[20] Henry James, "The Novel in 'The Ring and the Book,'" in *Notes on Novelists with Some Other Notes* (London: J. M. Dent, 1914), pp. 306–26. This essay was originally presented as an address to the Academic Committee of the Royal Society of Literature in Commemoration of the Centenary of Robert Browning, May 7, 1912, and was first printed in *The Transactions of the Royal Society of Literature*, 2d ser., 31 (1912):269–98.

marriage, duty and the state, it is not subjective feeling as such and the consequential unification with just *this* individual and no other, which should be the chief thing at issue."[21] In other words, romantic love, because of its particular and accidental character, does not possess the universality necessary to make it the focus of an epic. Browning's subordination of history to love and the soul in *The Ring and the Book* has its foundation in the 1863 preface to *Sordello*, which dismissed the history of the struggle between the Guelfs and the Ghibellines as mere "decoration" and stressed the poem's emphasis on "the development of a soul."[22] This psychological romanticism which emphasizes the individual soul at the expense of social history finds its ultimate grounding not in the unfolding of events but in God's creation:

>   I find first
> Writ down for very A B C of fact,
> "In the beginning God made heaven and earth";
> From which, no matter with what lisp, I spell
> And speak you out a consequence—that man,
> Man,—as befits the made, inferior thing,—
> Purposed, since made, to grow, not make in turn,
> Yet forced to try and make, else fail to grow,—
> Formed to rise, reach at, if not grasp and gain
> The good beyond him,—which attempt is growth,—
> Repeats God's process in man's due degree,
> Attains man's proportionate result,—
> Creates, no, but resuscitates, perhaps.
>   [1, 707–19]

The "good" beyond man is God, not a utopian society. The final goal of man's progress is an imitation of God's creation. But this means the resuscitation of the past's life, not, as in Shelley and his *Prometheus Unbound*, the fanning of the mind's fugitive sensations into flame and the projection of the poet's hopes for mankind into an imaginary, if not political, reality. Although it has Romantic elements, the concern

---

[21] Hegel, *Aesthetics: Lectures on Fine Arts*, trans. T. M. Knox, 2 vols. (Oxford: Clarendon Press, 1975), I, 567.

[22] *Complete Works*, II, 123. Morse Peckham, in his resolute attempt to make Browning as modern as possible, attributes to Browning the methodology and the self-conscious, self-effacing historical irony of Ranke, in "Browning's Historiography and *The Ring and the Book*," *VP* 6 (1968):243–57. Peckham's arguments are convincingly refuted by Roger Sharrock in "Browning and History," in *Robert Browning*, ed. Armstrong, pp. 77–103. Sharrock instead sees Browning attempting "to bind his own intensely personal vision to the world of facts" (p. 90).

for individual passion in *The Ring and the Book* runs counter, then, to the Romantic concentration upon the extraordinary individual as a vehicle for expressing revolutionary hopes. The epic impulses underlying Napoleon's dream of a personal empire and his transformation of France have parallels in *Sordello* but none in *The Ring and the Book*.

Indeed, it is the very historical insignificance of Guido's trial that attracts Browning. The archivists may snicker at him, saying "names and facts thus old / Are newer than Europe news we find / Down in today's *Diario*" (I, 429–31). But he sees that the triviality of the circumstances surrounding the love of Pompilia and Caponsacchi and the trial of Guido somehow puts the human passions into relief and allows them to be freed from the "pure crude fact" by his imagination (I, 35). His imagination aims at making the act of reading poetry a hermeneutical act of resuscitating the past, and so virtually identical with the imaginative act of creating the poem. He presents the characters from their own point of view in order to bring the bare fact that they once existed to the reader's experience in a concrete, psychological form, and also suppresses his own commentary on the "truth" of each character, leaving readers to determine it for themselves. Because the reader must discover the particular "truth" of each monologue, the reader resuscitates (if in a secondhand way, as the poet himself does) the spirit of each individual character from the past. In this way both Browning and his readers rescue a human meaning that lies beneath and is always threatened by history. Browning feels that in his poem is "the final state o' the story" (XII, 827), because there it "lives, / If precious be the soul of man to man" (XII, 833–34). He believes he has written a book that "shall mean beyond the facts, / Suffice the eye and save the soul beside" (XII, 866–67).[23]

---

[23] Also consider Browning's reply to Julia Wedgwood's complaints about the evil in *The Ring and the Book*: "But remember, first that this is God's world, as he made it for reasons of his own, and that to change its conditions is not to account for them—as you will presently find me try to do so. I was struck with the enormous wickedness and weakness of the main composition of the piece, and with the incidental evolution of good thereby,—good to the priest, to the poor girl, to the old Pope, who judges anon, and, I would fain hope, to who reads and applies my reasoning to his own experience, which is not likely to fail him" (Browning to Wedgwood, December 19, 1868, *Browning and Wedgwood*, ed. Curle, pp. 144–45). I agree with L. J. Swingle that *The Ring and the Book* is meant to be read from an ontological, not an epistemological point of view, as he argues in "Truth and *The Ring and the Book*: A Negative View," *VP* 6 (1968):259–69. As Swingle eloquently puts it, "We are not reading the poem in order to discover the truth; after all, we know the truth already. Rather we are reading the poem in order to trace the disappearance of truth" (p. 267). For Browning, Swingle says, "This one bit of life has flashed into being only to disappear back into the darkness of history" (p. 268).

Yet, since Browning's poem, like the *Iliad*, revolves around a single action, one may think of Homer's poem in connection with *The Ring and the Book*. Guido's trial, like the Trojan War, serves as the force affecting the lives and the expressions of the individual characters. In the *Iliad*, individual actions are reflections of the forces of war, of killing and dying, of victory and defeat, and the manner of a man's death is often his sole raison d'être. There is nothing like this in *The Ring and the Book*. Instead, every voice asks for a judgment on Guido, but a judgment that is necessarily colored by each speaker's relationships with others. One learns that the speaker of "Half-Rome" is jealous "of a certain what's-his-name and jackanapes / Somewhat too civil of eyes with lute and song / About a house here" where Half-Rome keeps his wife (II, 1544–46). And so one understands why he defends Guido. The speaker of "Other Half-Rome," who defends Pompilia, has a grudge against Guido, who had objected to his "administration of effects" of a will to which both he and Guido were heirs (III, 1688). Tertium Quid, who appears to plump for Guido after having argued both sides of the case, hopes that his declaration that "presumptive guilt is weak / I' the case of nobility and privilege" will advance him with Her Excellency and Her Highness, who are playing cards (IV, 1627–28). The principals have their own loves or hates to cherish or cultivate; the lawyers have conflicting interests affecting their clients' side of the case; and the Pope worries about what is right in the eyes of God. Unlike war, which unites all men in their contemplation of death, this trial separates one person from another, both because of the monologue form and because of the speakers' individual interests in the case, creating a sense of psychological isolation that can be overcome only by a powerful love. One may feel sure of one's grounds for condemning Guido and for idealizing Pompilia, but one can never be sure that Guido or anyone else will be saved. So while with respect to the law there can be a judgment about whether a character is "true," and hence there can be narrative closure, with respect to salvation there cannot be a decision about whether a character is "true" in God's eyes, and therefore there can be no interpretive or narrative closure. One is left only with love. The love of Pompilia and Caponsacchi for one another (reflecting Browning's for his Lyric Love), which is at the heart of *The Ring and the Book* and which has the power to make forgiveness for Guido possible, is symbolic of God's love for man, a love which cares nothing for history or the fate of nations but only for the individual soul.

8

The Later Poetry

> And I turn the page, and I turn the page,
> Not verse now, only prose!
>
> —"By the Fire-side"

In June of 1867 Matthew Arnold was to finish his second term as Professor of Poetry at Oxford, a chair to which he had been elected in 1857 and which he had raised to cultural prominence. A number of young men requested the Oxford Council, which would decide who would replace Arnold, to allow Browning to compete for the poetry chair by conferring an M.A. upon him.[1] The council declined to consider Browning as a candidate on the grounds that to make special arrangements for him would be unfair to those already in the field, and it ultimately elected Sir Francis Hastings Doyle as Arnold's successor.[2] But the council did grant Browning an M.A., which was conferred on June 26, 1867, and Balliol elected him an honorary fellow in October of the same year.[3] He was pleased with the honors, especially the latter, because it would allow him to be near Pen while he was at Oxford.[4] But in retrospect it seems unfortunate that Oxford did not elect him Professor of Poetry, not so much because the university failed to make a tradition of appointing an eminent poet to examine critically both the tradition and the practice of poetry but because it seems likely that Browning would have profited

---

[1] Browning to Blagden, February 19, 1867, *Dearest Isa: Browning's Letters to Isabella Blagden*, ed. Edward C. McAleer (Austin: University of Texas Press, 1951), p. 253.
[2] *Dearest Isa*, ed. McAleer, p. 256n. See also Matthew Arnold's letter to his mother of February 10, 1867, in which he says he will vote for Browning if he is allowed to stand for the professorship but predicts that Doyle will get it: *Letters of Matthew Arnold, 1848–1888*, ed. George W. E. Russell, 3 vols. (London: Macmillan, 1904), II, 116–17.
[3] *Dearest Isa*, ed. McAleer, pp. 270n. and 275n.
[4] Browning to Blagden, February 19, 1867, ibid., p. 254.

immensely from the pause for poetic stocktaking and from the extended regimen of writing prose. Browning said that the three lectures a year required of the Oxford Professor of Poetry during his five-year tenure "would take as much trouble to write as three tragedies,—for I try to do things thoroughly."[5] He might not have had the time or the energy to write *Balaustion's Adventure* (1871), *Prince Hohenstiel-Schwangau* (1871), *Fifine at the Fair* (1872), *Red Cotton Night-Cap Country* (1873), and *The Inn Album* (1875). The lectures might also have provided an appropriate outlet for his gentlemanly obsession with the classics that led to the scholastic obscurity of *Aristophanes' Apology* (1875) and to his translation of Aeschylus' *Agamemnon* (1877).[6]

Such speculation is useful, however, only in pointing to Browning's vast output of poetry during the 1870s and in suggesting that, paradoxically, he seems to have been at a loss as to what to do once the last volume of *The Ring and the Book* had appeared in 1869. Besides the titles already mentioned, he published a collection of shorter pieces in *Pacchiarotto and How He Worked in Distemper* (1876), two longer

---

[5]Ibid.
[6]Alfred Domett records in his diary the comments he made to Browning on the obscurity of *Aristophanes' Apology*. He says he remarked "upon the large demands Browning makes in this book on his reader's knowledge" and that he "believed no one even classical scholars, unless they were in the daily habit of reading Aristophanes, as tutors or schoolmasters, would be able to understand all the numerous allusions in it without referring over and over again to his Comedies; and that Browning thus wilfully restricted the number of readers to comparatively few." And he adds that the poet refused to supply explanatory notes: "Browning said it could not be helped, but he was not likely to try anything of this sort again" (*The Diary of Alfred Domett, 1872–1885*, ed. E. A. Horsman [London: Oxford University Press, 1953], pp. 149–50). For studies of the classical sources of *Aristophanes' Apology*, see Carl N. Jackson, "Classical Elements in Browning's 'Aristophanes' Apology,' " *Harvard Studies in Classical Philology* 20 (1909):15–73; T. L. Hood, "Browning's Ancient Classical Sources," *Harvard Studies in Classical Philology* 33 (1922):79–180; and Frederick Tisdel, "Browning's *Aristophanes' Apology*," *University of Missouri Studies*, 2, no. 4 (1927):1–46. On Browning's association of his poetics with defending Euripides against the attack of Aristophanes, see Donald Smalley, "A Parleying with Aristophanes," *PMLA* 55 (1940):823–38. The most thorough reading of the poem is that of Clyde de L. Ryals, *Browning's Later Poetry, 1871–1889* (Ithaca: Cornell University Press, 1975), pp. 101–18.

Browning himself called his translation of Agamemnon a "somewhat toilsome, perhaps fruitless adventure" (*Works*, VIII, 293). For a philological and stylistic analysis of Browning's attempt at a literal transcription of the Greek in English, see Robert Spindler, *Robert Browning und die Antike*, 2 vols. in 1 (Leipzig: Bernhard Tauchnitz, 1930), II, 278–94. For comparisons with other translations of *Agamemnon*, see Reuben A. Brower, "Seven Agamemnons," in *On Translation*, ed. Reuben A. Brower (Cambridge, Mass.: Harvard University Press, 1959), pp. 173–95; also see George Steiner, *After Babel: Aspects of Language and Translation* (London: Oxford University Press, 1975), pp. 312–16. Ryals gives an account of the circumstances in which Browning decided to translate the play, in *Browning's Later Poetry*, pp. 142–46.

poems—*La Saisiaz and the Two Poets of Croisic* (1878), and the first series of *Dramatic Idyls* (1879). Browning felt he needed "increasingly to tell *the truth*,"[7] but his work during this period reflects more the rhetorical amplification of his compulsion than his considered meditation upon the reasons for it. Although he had become a respectable widower and was finally recognized as an established man of letters, he felt that in Elizabeth's absence there was no one to whom to tell "the truth." He was now a public figure, but his poetry was to become even more private than before. In March of 1869 Queen Victoria had received him, along with Carlyle, Grote, and Lyell, at court, an honor which seems to have prompted the invitations he began to accept to visit various country houses.[8] He was staying with the Countess Cowper in 1871, when she suggested to him the task of translating Euripides' *Alcestis*, which occasioned the private allegory of *Balaustion's Adventure* and inaugurated Browning's most prolific, if not most poetic, decade.

I

Translation is usually a literary act of public accommodation: it makes a work accessible to readers who do not have the language of the original. In *Balaustion's Adventure* Browning in some sense undoes his translation of Euripides' *Alcestis* by placing the play within a historical framework taken from Plutarch's *Life of Nicias* and by shaping this framework and the play itself according to a private allegory. The poem tells the story of Balaustion, an imaginary woman of Rhodes, who by reciting *Alcestis* moves the Syracusans to grant her and her shipmates sanctuary from the pirates pursuing them. The story points to the capacity of art to effect spiritual and physical salvation by appealing to everyone's appreciation of a play celebrating the love of a woman for a man. *Alcestis* is about Admetus, a good king and a generous host, who has been allowed by the Fates to find someone to die in

---

[7] Browning to Julia Wedgwood, July 28, 1864, *Robert Browning and Julia Wedgwood*, ed. Curle, p. 34.

[8] Browning himself noted this in his letter to Julia Wedgwood of March 8, 1869: "Yes, the British Public like, and more than like me, this week, they let their admiration ray out on me, and at sundry congregations of men wherein I have figured these three or four days, I have seen, felt and, thru' white gloves, handled a true affectionateness not unmingled with awe—which all comes of the Queen's having desired to see me, and three other extraordinary persons, last Thursday" (*Browning and Wedgwood*, ed. Curle, p. 182).

his place, and whose wife, Alcestis, dies for him when his mother and his father refuse to. The selfish Admetus proves he is deserving of her love only after he reaffirms his vow to keep her memory sacred by refusing to grant Heracles' request that Admetus care for an unidentified woman. Heracles then reveals that the woman is Alcestis, whom he has reclaimed from death, and restores her to her faithful husband. The work's subject, one comes to feel, is not the translation of Euripides' play but the self-evident parallels between Admetus and Browning and between Balaustion, Alcestis, and Elizabeth.[9]

A private allegory seems certainly to be at work, since in an appendix to the translation Balaustion offers a supplementary denouement in which Alcestis does not allow the Fates to be cheated and dies after transfusing her soul into Admetus: "Her whole soul entered into his, / He looked the look back, and Alkestis died" (ll. 2613–14). This mirroring of their love allows Admetus to gather her soul to himself and to become one with his true audience. In Euripides' play, Admetus declines to rule his kingdom in Alcestis's absence, thinking of it as a kind of "pedestalled sublime" (l. 2459) and as useless and vain as the monuments that testify to the tyranny of his ancestors over the people (ll. 2476–84). But in the alternative ending, Admetus, with Alcestis's soul within him, dedicates himself to "bringing back again the Golden Age" (l. 2656). The hope of extrapolating from the salvation of one soul through love to the salvation of all mankind seems illusory, however, because Balaustion, who is recalling her adventure with the Syracusans and the calamitous circumstances surrounding her recital of *Alcestis*, ironically comments that she has never heard that "one faint particle came true" (l. 2658). Balaustion could for a moment move the Syracusans with "Euripides, *The Human with his dropping of warm tears*" (Browning quotes from Elizabeth's "Wine of Cyprus"), but only for a moment (l. 2670–71). And yet for Browning this moment has its glory, since it is emblematic of Elizabeth's love for him and God's love for man.

Joseph H. Friend has speculated, correctly it would seem, "that in Browning's mind the Greek myth prefigured the Christian: the reuniting of Alcestis and Admetus in life by Heracles meant the reuniting of

---

[9]For the biographical parallels, see Betty Miller, *Robert Browning*, pp. 268–69; *Handbook*, pp. 350–53; and Joseph H. Friend, "Euripides Browningized: The Meaning of Balaustion's Adventure," *VP* 2 (1964):179–86.

Browning motivates his changes and omissions in his transcription of Euripides' *Alcestis* by having Balaustion describe a production of the play in her hometown. On Browning's *Alcestis* as a modern adaptation, see Frederick Tisdel, "*Balaustion's Adventure* as an Interpretation of Euripides' *Alcestis*," *PMLA* 32 (1917):519–46.

Robert and Elizabeth in an afterlife by the Saviour, once Robert had proved his worth."[10] But even when unveiled, this allegory remains an inaccessible, private one, largely because the poem does not sufficiently objectify it on the literal level. While the celebration of Admetus's hospitality in *Alcestis* is germane to Balaustion's seeking asylum with the Syracusans, there is no motivation for her epilogue in either the circumstances of her original recital to the Syracusans or her retrospective narrative of this event to her gathered friends. The most obvious examples of the poem's anachronistic tenor are the veiled references to Elizabeth's poetry and to a painting by Frederick Leighton entitled *Hercules Wrestling with Death for the Body of Alcestis* (ll. 2268–75). These self-indulgences, the general Christianizing of the supplementary ending, and Balaustion's remarks on love and poetry make the classical setting mere costume and show. Browning's private associations and desires finally account for the poem's form and its fanciful rewriting of Euripides' play as proto-Christian allegory, despite his plea to the contrary, voiced by Balaustion when she explains her recitation of the play and her narrative interpolations:

> But if I, too, should try and speak at times,
> Leading your love to where my love, perchance,
> Climbed earlier, found a nest before you knew—
> Why, bear with the poor climber, for love's sake!
> Look at Baccheion's beauty opposite,
> The temple with the pillars at the porch!
> See you not something beside masonry?
> What if my words wind in and out the stone
> As yonder ivy, the God's parasite?
> [ll. 344–52]

The host-and-parasite metaphor attempts to minimize the Christian appropriation of Euripides by suggesting that the speaker is dependent upon God, rather than that the Christian interpretation of *Alcestis* is parasitic upon the Greek humanism of the play. It veils the allegorical supplement to the translation that infuses the Victorian Christian point of view into the Greek text.[11]

In his framing and translating of Euripides' *Alcestis*, Browning not only envisions the possibility of human love transcending death and serving as a symbolic promise of life after death but also implies that

---

[10]"Meaning of *Balaustion's Adventure*," p. 184.
[11]One might note the contemporary Christianizing of Plato by Browning's good friend Benjamin Jowett in his translation of *The Dialogues of Plato*, 4 vols. (Oxford:

this love has poetic and interpretive consequences that transcend historically determined consciousness:

> Still, since one thing may have so many sides,
> I think I see how,—far from Sophokles,—
> You, I, or anyone might mould a new
> Admetos, new Alkestis. Ah, that brave
> Bounty of poets, the one royal race
> That ever was, or will be, in this world!
> They give no gift that bounds itself and ends
> I' the giving and the taking: theirs so breeds
> I' the heart and soul o' the taker, so transmutes
> The man who only was a man before,
> That he grows godlike in his turn, can give—
> He also: share the poets' privilege,
> Bring forth new good, new beauty, from the old.
> [ll. 2413–25]

Balaustion models this ideal relationship between poet and audience upon a reciprocal love. Moreover, the poet not only creates his poetry but also inspires interpretations that give new life and beauty to his subject. This poetics of interpretation, Browning feels, allows him to present his new Admetus and Alcestis and his private allegory of them as inspirited by, and so giving new life in translation to, Euripides' text.

Inspired no doubt by the critical success of *The Ring and the Book*, most of Browning's other poems of the 1870s are, like *Balaustion's Adventure*, narrative poems that were very hastily written. Browning at his most furious pace seems to have set himself the task of writing a hundred lines a day until finished with a poem, resting only, one imagines, on Sundays. For example, *Red Cotton Night-Cap Country* (4247 lines) was begun on December 1, 1872, and finished on January 23, 1873.[12] The effects of this compositional speed are evident in the Caliban-like syntax of Balaustion's line, "He also: share the poets' privilege" (l. 2424). And great torrents of rhetorical amplification, waves upon waves of words upon words pile images upon images and argu-

---

Clarendon Press, 1871). For a general discussion of Browning's faithfulness to the classical spirit, see William C. DeVane, "Browning and the Spirit of Greece," in *Nineteenth-Century Studies*, ed. Herbert Davis, William C. DeVane, and R. C. Bald (Ithaca: Cornell University Press, 1940), pp. 181–84, 190–98.

[12] *Handbook*, p. 376.

ments upon arguments. The following passage taken from *Prince Hohenstiel-Schwangau* will mercifully serve to exemplify the horrifying prolixity of these poems:

> Can there be question which was the right task—
> To save or destroy society?
> Why, even prove that, by some miracle,
> Destruction were the proper work to choose,
> And that a torch best remedies what's wrong
> I' the temple, whence the long procession wound
> Of powers and beauties, earth's achievements all,
> The human strength that strove and overthrew,—
> The human love that, weak itself, crowned strength,—
> The instinct crying "God is whence I came!"—
> The reason laying down the law "And such
> His will i' the world must be!"—the leap and shout
> Of genius "For I hold His very thoughts,
> The meaning of the mind of Him!"—nay, more,
> The ingenuities, each active force
> That turning in a circle on itself
> Looks neither up nor down but keeps the spot,
> Mere creature-like, and, for religion, works,
> Works only and works ever, makes and shapes
> And changes, still wrings more of good from less,
> Still stamps some bad out, where was worst before,
> So leaves the handiwork, the act and deed,
> Were it but house and land and wealth, to show
> Here was a creature perfect in the kind—
> Whether as bee, beaver, or behemoth,
> What's the importance? he has done his work
> For work's sake, worked well, earned a creature's praise;—
> I say, concede that same fane, whence deploys
> Age after age, all this humanity,
> Diverse but ever dear, out of the dark
> Behind the altar into the broad day
> By the portal—enter, and, concede there mocks
> Each lover of free motion and much space
> A perplexed length of apse and aisle and nave,—
> Pillared roof and carved screen, and what care I?—
> Which irk the movement and impede the march,—
> Nay, possibly, bring flat upon his nose
> At some odd break-neck angle, by some freak
> Of old world artistry, that personage
> Who, could he but have kept his skirts from grief
> And catching at the hooks and crooks about,

> Had stepped out on the daylight of our time
> Plainly the man of the age,—still, still, I bar
> Excessive conflagration in the case.
> "Shake the flame freely!" shout the multitude:
> The architect approves I stuck my torch
> Inside a good stout lantern, hung its light
> Above the hooks and crooks, and ended so.
>
> [ll. 653–700]

The Prince (Napoleon III) defends his maintaining the status quo with respect to the Catholic Church's place in society, instead of reforming it, despite its preventing man from stepping into "the daylight of our time" (l. 693). His argument, which is only one of many in support of his social conservatism, is drawn out by the long masquelike procession of human qualities—strength, love, instinct, reason, genius, and the ingenuities (ll. 658–69), by the catalogue of the church's architecture—"A perplexed length of apse and aisle and nave,— / Pillared roof and carved screen, and what care I?" (ll. 685–86), and, on the scale of the clause, by the list "Whether as bee, beaver, or behemoth" (l. 676). In each of these cases the final member of the series gives the Prince away: ingenuities do not properly belong to the long procession of human powers and beauties; the behemoth does not build things as the bee and beaver do; and the inappropriate "what care I?", which rounds out his description of the church interior, points, like the other examples, to the rodomontade that revels in verbosity as it irresistibly follows its rhythms, alliteration, and catalogues beyond the realm of sense.

Browning obviously delights in the Prince's argument, its tortuosities, its empty casuistry, and its perverse reasoning. But he has, ironically, succeeded all too well in revealing the rhetorical emptiness of the deposed politician carried away by the power of his tongue. As in *Sordello*, Browning is fascinated here with the reflection of moral and political failure in a faulty rhetoric. Indeed, *Prince Hohenstiel-Schwangau* is a failure precisely because Browning has sought to mirror the failures of a political rhetoric with his own language and has sacrificed the clarity of his own judgment so that he can accurately register the unending blandness and abstract banality of the Prince's apology for himself—right down to the Prince's seizing upon his drawing a "line 'twixt blot and blot" instead of making a third blot as

The Later Poetry

an emblem of his political career and his conservative character (l. 77).[13]

Yet Browning does not feel that a proper rhetoric could perfect the political and moral life of man, because what makes the prince a villain is in fact his quest for order and stability, shown by his refusal to "shake the flame freely" in the church as the multitude wishes him to do (l. 697) and by his vision of the future as only "the Present with its rough made smooth, / Its indistinctness emphasized" (ll. 426–27). The Prince envisions the world reduced to a geometric order by his line drawn between two blots and sees society as a machine that he regulates:

> I rule and regulate the course, excite,
> Restrain: because the whole machine should march
> Impelled by those diversely-moving parts,
> Each blind to aught beside its little bent.
> Out of the turnings round and round inside,
> Comes that straightforward world-advance, I want,
> And none of them supposes God wants too
> And gets through just their hindrance and my help.
> [ll. 465–72]

The Prince arrogates to himself God's vision: he believes only he and God know how the machinery of society moves straightforwardly toward salvation. His presumption that he knows God's will for everyone through his "reasonable piety" is not only a sign of megalomania (l. 478) but also runs counter to Browning's Protestant belief in individual salvation and in an unmediated relationship with God. Moreover, to a late Romantic poet of organic individualism such as Brown-

---

[13] Browning felt that the reactionary tendencies of Napoleon III had led to his downfall. Consider his remarks to Isabella Blagden in a letter of July 19, 1870, on Napoleon III and the Franco-Prussion war: "I never, when liking Napoleon most, sympathized a bit with his dynastic ambition for his son,—who has no sort of right to be anybody in France,—and the truckling to Rome & the Empress has been stupid and suicidal: I think, in the interest of humanity, he wants a sound beating this time & probably may get it: though he is clearly good enough & to spare for all these frenzied fools who are shouting for the Rhine. Oh, oh, Ba—put not your trust in princes neither in the sons of men,—Emperors, Popes, Garibaldis, or Mazzinis,—the *plating* wears through, and out comes the copperhead of human nature & weakness and falseness too!" (*Dearest Isa*, ed. McAleer, pp. 340–41). In his address to Ba, Browning alludes to *Strafford* v, ii, 194–96. Trevor Lloyd offers a good account of the historical background of *Prince Hohenstiel-Schwangau* and attributes the poem's failure to Browning's attack on hereditary succession and to its uses of history becoming progressively confused; see "Browning and Politics," in *Robert Browning*, ed. Armstrong, pp. 157–60.

ing, this mechanistic thinking smacks of the tyrannical, unlawful subordination of the self to some alien other.

Like the Prince, Don Juan of *Fifine at the Fair* believes that the ultimate truth is the soul's selfishness: "Each soul lives, longs and works / For itself, by itself" (ll. 900–1). His philosophy of individual self-aggrandizement has no place for love; and he sees his amorous adventures as the expression of his desire for freedom and of his need for a wide variety of experiences. He feels "frenetic to be free," like the red pennon at the fair stretched out in the wind (l. 38), and admires a stealthily feathered bird's nest for its richly diverse collection of building materials (ll. 86–97). His emphasis upon gathering from a wide experience leads him to formulate an aesthetic doctrine that resembles the *Pauline*-poet's desire to "be all, have, see, know, taste, feel, all":

> That Art,—which I may style the love of loving, rage
> Of knowing, seeing, feeling the absolute truth of things
> For truth's sake, whole and sole, not any good, truth brings
> The knower, seer, feeler, beside,—instinctive Art
> Must fumble for the whole, once fixing on a part
> However poor, surpass the fragment, and aspire
> To construct thereby the ultimate entire.
> Art, working with a will, discards the superflux,
> Contributes to defect, toils on till,—*fiat lux*,—
> There's the restored, the prime, the individual type.
> [ll. 685–94]

In order to construct "the ultimate entire," one must work with the fragmentary with a will toward reproducing God's original creation, the *fiat lux*, supplementing "unloveliness by love" (l. 683). But Don Juan does not really convince us that his "love of loving" is equivalent to seeking "the absolute truth of things / For truth's sake." As his desire to have both Elvire and Fifine reflects, he is much too self-centered. He thinks of the love of man and woman as resembling a rillet pouring into the sea:

> The full-blown ingrate, mere recipient of the brine,
> That takes all and gives nought, is Man; the feminine
> Rillet that, taking all and giving nought in turn,
> Goes headlong to her death i' the sea, without concern
> For the old inland life, snow-soft and silver-clear,
> That's woman—typified from Fifine to Elvire.
> [ll. 1213–18]

The Later Poetry

This mixing of the self with the other recalls the phrase from Aeschylus' *Prometheus Bound* that Don Juan quotes as a kind of refrain and translates as "God, man, or both together mixed" (ll. 905, 2188, and 2210) and that Browning privately appears to think of as a memorial to Elizabeth, who had translated the play. It also recalls the crossing over of Alcestis's soul and love into Admetus's soul in the fanciful epilogue of *Balaustion's Adventure*. But Don Juan's description of the woman heedlessly plunging over the cliff into the man below presents an image of reckless lust and of man's domination of woman, not of love and reciprocity. Don Juan tells Elvire, for instance, that if she wants a man, she must first "discard / Nine-tenths" of what she is (ll. 1221–22), even though, as he admits, he depends upon her recognition of him for his sense of self: "Your steadying touch of hand / Assists me to remain self-centred, fixed amid / All on the move" (ll. 1361–63). He cannot see Elvire or anyone else except as part of his internal dialogue: "See yourself in my soul!" (l. 808). As the imperative mood indicates, he seeks to have absolute dominion over her and finally cannot love her because in his imagination she is allowed to have no independence from him.

His identification of the self with truth leads ultimately to a kind of Pyrrhonism: "And nowhere things abide, / And everywhere we strain the things should stay,—the one / Truth, that ourselves are true!" (ll. 1469–71). In the phantasmagoria of Schumann's *Carnaval* (stanzas 91–93), in his dream of Venice (stanzas 94–120), and in his vision of the druid monument (stanzas 121–25), everything outside the self has only an evanescent character, and that only insofar as it makes an impression on the mind. Given his subjectivism, his impressionism, and his self-isolation, the truth of his self can have no audience other than himself and no purpose other than self-justification through self-mystification. Browning had said that he felt he needed "increasingly to tell *the truth*," but Don Juan perverts the purpose of truth-telling by turning it into rhetorical self-aggrandizement. Don Juan believes that his admission of his lustful desire to supplement his experience of Elvire with that of Fifine is an admirably frank acknowledgment of his "love for loving." He imagines himself, finally, as the all-consuming ocean, swallowing the truth like so many rivulets. He believes that "histrionic truth is in the natural lie" (l. 1492); that is, the rhetorical maneuvering of the self for its own advantage, for its amatory freedom, and for sexual supplements to its fragmentary experience truthfully reflects his soul's quest for self-aggrandizement.

Browning's critique of Don Juan's position appears in the framing poems "Amphibian" and "The Householder." In the prologue, "Amphibian," the speaker tells of swimming in the ocean and of seeing a butterfly soar over him in the air and remarks on the great elemental gulf separating them. He likens the butterfly to the soul (l. 16) and reminds himself that as long as he is alive he cannot "join its flight" (l. 21). The butterfly is wholly other, living in another element whose pleasures can only be imagined. As a substitute for flying and living in heaven, the speaker writes poetry:

> Emancipate through passion
> And thought, with sea for sky,
> We substitute, in a fashion,
> For heaven—poetry.
> [ll. 53–56]

He lives in medium different from the butterfly's and is free only insofar as he strives after heaven in his poetry. Although the speaker attempts to include his readers within the "we," he still desires another's attention as he looks beyond us to the sky. Browning is, of course, thinking of Elizabeth here and abandons the allegorical veil in the final stanza:

> Does she look, pity, wonder
> At one who mimics flight,
> Swims—heaven above, sea under,
> Yet always earth in sight?
> [ll. 73–76]

Browning's swimming mimics the flight of Elizabeth's soul, but like the poet of *Pauline* who wishes to be one with Shelley the Sun-Treader, he cannot join Elizabeth's psyche in its "sun-suffused" flight (l. 15). He sees a separation between "heaven above" and the "sea under" and can only hope that in her eyes he is still her love. He cannot presume, as Don Juan does, that he himself is all in all.

The epilogue, "The Householder," celebrates the speaker's fanciful reunion with his dead wife, who, acting as a gentle form of death, comes to take him to heaven with her. The householder welcomes the chance to escape from the ghosts of the house that haunt him and, like Childe Roland sounding his final note but in a much less dissonant key, views his death as a personal triumph over the tormenting multitude surrounding him: "God be their guard from disturbance at their glee" (l. 14). The householder willingly turns his worldly self into the inert monumentality of an epitaph to let "the parish-people know" him (l. 26) and readily gives up the "neighbour-talk with man and maid" for discourse with his love (l. 18). Here Browning anticipates the later bitterness of "House" in *Pacchiarotto*, where the speaker asks, "Shall I sonnet-sing you about myself? / Do I live in a house you would like to see?" (ll. 1–2). He feels that others see him "as a sort of tombstone, to be scribbled over when so many blank walls spread on every side."[14] Over against the multitude which would turn him to stone by making a cultural landmark of him, he poses love. The householder and his wife work out his epitaph for the world, while asserting, "Love is all and Death is nought!" (l. 32). Death, for Browning, is the result of relinquishing one's soul to the evanescent monumentality of the world or of becoming fascinated like Don Juan with fallen druid stones and the Venice which "died into edifice" (l. 2033). As Ryals says, for Browning "love is the law that affirms the reality of the self."[15] To think the reverse, as Don Juan does, that the self is the law which affirms the reality of love, risks the death of the soul and slowly sinking for the pleasure of it into the slough of Fifine. The love of the householder and his wife, like that of Robert and Elizabeth, is not subordinated to individual needs and transformed into Don Juan's lust but is a symbol of a mutual recognition of spiritual equality.

II

The sordid events in *Red Cotton Night-Cap Country* (1873) and *The Inn Album* (1875) did not gain Browning many new readers. Neither volume went into a second edition, as, indeed, none of his works had since *Balaustion's Adventure*. Still the poetry in both volumes reflects to the fullest extent the pleasures in reading the late Browning, if, at

---

[14]Browning to Julia Wedgwood, June 1864, *Browning and Wedgwood*, ed. Curle, p. 13.
[15]*Browning's Later Poetry*, p. 81. Barbara Melchiori offers a Freudian interpretation of the poem in *Browning's Poetry of Reticence* (New York: Barnes and Noble, 1968), pp. 158–187; see also Philip Drew's reply to Melchiori in *The Poetry of Browning: A Critical Introduction* (London: Methuen, 1970), pp. 303–21. The critical problem posed by *Fifine at the Fair* is how to interpret the poem's form and symbols without losing sight of the poem's context. Despite her overly morbid treatment of sexuality and death, Claudette Kemper Columbus presents the clearest view of the poem's action in "*Fifine at the Fair*: A Masque of Sexuality and Death Seeking Figures of Expression," *Studies in Browning and His Circle*, 2, no. 1 (1974):21–38.

the same time, how few of them there are. We see the world of the Englishman on the Continent hunting up resorts his pocketbook can afford; we savor the aroma of cigars in smoking rooms; we learn why society fears the notoriety popular newspapers bring; and we observe men and women struggling to reconcile their personal desires with the demands of social respectability. Browning records his appreciation of a quiet, "hitherto un-Murrayed bathing place, / Best loved of seacoast-nook-ful Normandy" (*Red Cotton Night-Cap Country*, ll. 20–21) and describes the undistinguished inn of *The Inn Album*, where "somebody once lived and pleased good taste" until tourists "vulgarized things comfortably smooth" (ll. 30, 33). Though this is far from the modern motor inn and roadside coffee shop, Browning sees how the pressure to be universally acceptable, and so commercially profitable, homogenizes taste, how the unwitting public eradicates all signs of character and so vulgarizes the inner conflicts of an individual's soul, and how the newspaper reflects the public opinion that makes everyone behave according to its expectations.

Browning thinks that the newspaper is opposed to art in two ways: it confers fame upon artists insofar as those artists mirror the prevailing ideology, and it intrudes upon man's private relation with God. In *The Inn Album* the young man lightly touches upon the press, saying "Oh, one sees / Names in the newspaper—great this, great that, / Gladstone, Carlyle, the Laureate;—much I care!" (ll. 497–99). And in *Red Cotton Night-Cap Country* Browning makes this comment in an aside:

> Who is a poet needs must apprehend
> Alike both speech and thoughts which prompt to speak.
> Part these, and thought withdraws to poetry:
> Speech is reported in the newspaper.
>
> [ll. 3281–84]

Browning points here to the isolation of the lyric voice from dramatic action in nineteenth-century poetry, an isolation which Browning's monologues both seek to counteract and also mirror in their problematic form. The form counteracts and reflects a tendency to separate public from private concerns, to make public and private morality different spheres of action. The difference between public and private morality is at the heart of Browning's meditation on the difference between lust and love, between the desire to dominate another as an expression of personal power and the desire to share one's experience of God.

Browning dramatizes the conflict between lust and love in *Red Cotton Night-Cap Country* by examining Leonce Miranda's troubled life. As the leisurely preface tells us, Browning wrote the poem to demonstrate to his friend (Ann Thackeray), who romantically believed the pastoral region of rural France was White Cotton Night-Cap Country, that beneath its placid surface were raging human passions. He uncovers the story of Miranda, who is caught between his love for a disreputable married woman and his mother's disapproval of that love, and who commits suicide after arranging his will so that his mistress will have a life interest in his fortune before it goes to the Church of the Holy Virgin. Browning imagines, however, that Miranda jumps from the tower of his mansion into the arms of an angel. We are asked to believe that although he plunges to his death on the turf below, Miranda's spirit rises to heaven because of his love for his mistress.[16] But one is tempted instead to see Browning's desire to misread the story's Oedipal conflict in terms of a desire for spiritual purity in love as a complicated residue of his relationship with Elizabeth and with his mother, who died while he was in Italy. And one might point to "In a Balcony" as an earlier and lighter treatment of the same theme. Yet that would be to miss the poem's insight into the nature of lust and love. Browning understands that all love has its basis in our physical nature and that our desire for another is always contaminated by lust. Indeed, for Browning the spiritual truth of love is only revealed in the death of lust:

> Love bids touch truth, endure truth, and embrace
> Truth, though, embracing truth, love crush itself.
> "Worship not me but God!" the angels urge:
> That is love's grandeur.
>
> [ll. 4116–20]

---

[16]See, for example, *Handbook*, pp. 373–74; and John M. Hitner, "Browning's Grotesque Period," *VP* 4 (1966):5. Ryals argues for a more temperate view of the poem, in *Browning's Later Poetry*, p. 99. The most suggestive reading of Miranda's suicide, despite its blindness to Miranda's obvious Oedipal problems and to the narrator's (and Browning's) determination to believe in Miranda's salvation, is Brendan Kenny's analysis of the poem in terms of Durkheim's theory that suicide is implicit social critique; see "Browning as a Cultural Critic: *Red Cotton Night-Cap Country*," *Browning Institute Studies* 6 (1978):137–62. For a discussion of the poem's background and Browning's idealization of it, see Mark Siegchrist, *Rough in Brutal Print: The Legal Sources in Browning's "Red-Cotton Night-Cap Country"* (Columbus: Ohio State University Press, 1981).

Browning believes that the truth of love is beyond one's lusting after the touch of the other and that true love of another is finally the love of God.

The Inn Album succeeds where both *Fifine at the Fair* and *Red Cotton Night-Cap Country* fail.[17] It judges lust not in symbolic terms but in terms of social ostracism and dishonor. The old man, the woman, and the young man all accept society's demands for respectability. They do so because they realize they need the society of others like themselves; they need their clubs, their social gatherings, and a sense of shared values in order to express themselves fully. They also recognize the need of extralegal economies in order to maintain one's honor: the old man has fought a duel from which he carries the reminder of an "unextracted ball" (l. 567); the woman submits to the old man's blackmail and agrees to love the young man, in order to prevent the old man from telling her husband about their earlier liaison; and the young man threatens to expose the old man in his clubs in order to make him relax his hold on the woman.

The older man seems particularly fixated upon the woman. Four years ago he refused to marry her and now wants mastery over her. Like Don Juan of *Fifine at the Fair*, who seeks other women to supplement Elvire and to feed his ravenous self, the old man has in some sense taken on the role of Lust in a morality play. He imagines the woman at the end of all his possibilities: "There she stands, ending every avenue, / Her visionary presence on each goal / I might have gained had we kept side by side!" (ll. 818–20). She has become his femme fatale, a vision of feminine otherness beyond his reach that denies access to himself. Her virtue becomes a challenge to his power, so that in some sense his pleas for her love are sincere, inasmuch as his destruction of her would, he thinks, confirm his sense of self. Like the Duke of Ferrara in "My Last Duchess," the old man's worldly skepticism and his desiccated passion make him desire dominion over others and lead him to hate what he cannot have: he feels he must destroy the woman to find "what soul inside was like" (l. 644). But he also fears that she will destroy him:

> Mistress-queen
> Be merciful and let your subject slink

---

[17]John Meigs Hitner has considered the poem's relationships with the novel and drama, in *Browning's Analysis of a Murder: A Case for "The Inn Album"* (Marquette: Northern Michigan University Press, 1969), pp. 1–18. Ryals discusses the discrepancy between appearance and reality in the poem in *Browning's Later Poetry*, pp. 119–31.

The Later Poetry

> Into dark safety! He's a beggar, see—
> Do not turn back his ship, Australia-bound,
> And bid her land him right amid some crowd
> Of creditors, assembled by your curse!
>
> [ll. 1541–46]

Not only does he think of her as a queen and himself as a subject (flatteringly denying his dominance of her), but he thinks of himself as an emigrant beggar who has been condemned to depart from her for a foreign shore. Over against his picture of her as his queen, he poses the demonic creditors called up by her curse. Indeed, his analogy tries to have his relationship with her both ways: she both excludes him and protects him, loves him and hates him, is the land from which he is sailing and, as the pronoun "her" implies, the ship on which he hopes to make his voyage. She is his mysterious "mistress-queen," both, as the hyphenation suggests, subject to his will as his mistress and also ruling him as his queen. Yet this hyphenation is not a repudiation of his vision of love as either a dominating or a being dominated but a curious jumbling of these two possibilities created by the rhetorical demands of the moment, as he tries to convince her that he does indeed love her and will be subject to her wishes.

The woman, having been used by the adventuring old man and having married a country minister, feels abandoned, with no other audience than God. After seeing the old man for the first time in four years, she exclaims, "But, God, though I am nothing, be thou all! / Contest him for me!" (ll. 1410–11). She chooses the audience that loves her, because, unlike the older man, she sees love as a reciprocal relationship in which the soul "must awake and seek out soul for soul" (l. 2190). She also sees herself as condemned to her loveless, respectable marriage and so fails to love the younger man. In the image of a bare tree rooted in the hard rock and blown by the wind, which recalls the happier image of the last leaf falling in "By the Fire-side" and the more melancholy image of the rock in "James Lee's Wife," one sees a woman who has been spiritually wrecked by an old man's lust:

> "*Bare breast be on hard rock*," laughed out my soul
> In gratitude, "*howe'er rock's grip may grind*!
> *The plain rough wretched hold fast shall suffice
> This wreck of me!*" The wind,—I broke in bloom
> At passage of,—which stripped me bole and branch,
> Twisted me up and tossed me here,—turns back,

> And, playful ever, would replant the spoil?
> Be satisfied, not one least leaf that's mine
> Shall henceforth help wind's sport to exercise!
> Rather I give such remnant to the rock
> Which never dreamed a straw would settle there.
> Rock may not thank me, may not feel my breast,
> Even: enough that *I* feel, hard and cold,
> Its safety my salvation.
>
> [ll. 1585–98]

The bare, twisted tree's relationships with the shifting, heartless wind and the cold, stable rock symbolize the woman's relationships with the old man and her husband. As in "James Lee's Wife," the imagery reflects the woman's loving without being loved in return, the cold, hard rock representing the absence of a lover. The woman's soul speaks to herself as if to signify that in the absence of anyone who would recognize her for herself, her only audience is an internalized one. Because of her need for stability and respectability, she has reconciled herself to this loveless life and resigned herself to serving the poor and the ignorant in order to hide her past from her husband. Other unhappily married women appear in Browning's poems—most notably the embittered woman of "Dîs Aliter Visum" and the nostalgic speaker of "Youth and Art"—but none as despairing.

The young man whom we meet at the poem's beginning, in contrast, has no personal experience of society's pressures and no real appreciation of the conflict between personal desires and respectability. He is wealthy, well-bred, and the picture of youthful innocence. He becomes caught between the passions of the man and the woman, who skeptically understand the world in terms of reputation and power instead of idealism and love. And while he at first observes the other two with horror as they rake over the embers of their souls, he is finally driven to kill the old man, who has, in turn, moved the woman to poison herself. Indeed, *The Inn Album* is in some sense dedicated to the young man's recognition of a moral order above that of society's and to his realization that there is a difference between the older man's bullying lust and true love.

The Inn Album is the third and last of Browning's meditations on an older man's love and lust written in the 1870s and is the most satisfying accomplishment of the three. It is much less abstrusely metaphysical than *Fifine at the Fair* and much less psychologically singular than *Red Cotton Night-Cap Country*. Of the three, *Fifine at the Fair* is the most ambitious poem and is in its experiments with dream thinking the *Sordello* of Browning's later poetry, while in comparison *Red Cotton Night-Cap Country* seems little more than a grotesque, psychological tour de force. *The Inn Album*, particularly in its evocation of the atmosphere of British high society and the tone of its conversation, captures in a way James never quite did (largely because he was an American) the curious combination of worldly consciousness and social claustrophobia that seems to have marked this society in the late nineteenth century—that scandal-conscious society which placed such great importance upon Parnell's affair with Mrs. O'Shea and upon Dilke's divorce. One thinks that Hardy might have written the poem had he been interested in the urban bourgeoisie and had had a dramatic imagination or that Ibsen might have written it in a barer and more stageworthy version had he been English. The circumstances do cry out for more drama, for more interaction among the characters, instead of the monologues interspliced with a little dialogue and set in a narrative frame. For the discourse in *The Inn Album* tends to be an exchange of points of view moving in the direction of personal revelation instead of a response to and planning of dramatic action—hence the great emphasis upon the pairing off of characters in conversation, as if admitting a third party would make the confession of one's feelings almost impossible. But Browning gains more insight into the characters' psychology by this method than he loses in dramatic complexity. He can afford, for example, to have the young man recognize almost immediately that the woman and the old adventurer were once in love instead of holding off that moment until the climax, because the expression of the young man's feeling is more important than his discovery; and Browning doesn't have to resort to the misguided Machiavellian calculation of "In a Balcony," where Constance forces her lover Norbert to pretend to be a suitor to the Queen he has served so ardently in hopes of gaining Constance's hand. In short, the form seems admirably suited to the uncomplicated drawing-room triangle he has chosen to study. Moreover, making allowances for the usual longueurs of Browning's later style, *The Inn Album* is the most satisfactory of all his dramatic works—his plays, *Pippa Passes*, and "In a Balcony"—especially in his management of the action and his meshing of the personal psychologies.

III

There are few pleasures to be found in reading Browning's poetry after *The Inn Album*. *Pacchiarotto* (1876), *La Saisiaz and the Two Poets of Croisic* (1878), *Dramatic Idyls* (first series, 1879), *Dramatic Idyls* (second series, 1880), *Jocoseria* (1883), *Ferishtah's Fancies* (1884), *Parleyings* (1887), and *Asolando* (1889) display Browning's great energy but also, unfortunately, the full extent of his poetic decline. Since these volumes and their poems tend to be of little more than biographical interest, the dogged reader of the later poetry comes to be grateful for what is readable rather than pleasurable and for what is intelligible rather than insightful.[18] In his poetic dotage Browning becomes more and more obsessed with his fame and more and more willing to relax in his memory and in his fantasies of an afterlife with Elizabeth.

Browning's concern for his fame is a melancholy motif in his later life and work. Just before he died in Venice at his son's home, the Palazzo Rezzonico, in the evening of December 12, 1889, the same day that his last volume of poetry, *Asolando*, was published, Pen read to him a telegram from Murray Smith reporting on the favorable reviews and large first-day sales of the volume, and Browning murmured in reply: "Very gratifying."[19] A more revealing and equally melancholy moment occurred at a luncheon given by Mrs. Jeune in 1888 or 1889 and recalled by Frank Harris:

> Suddenly there came a peal of laughter from the other end of the room. Lowell, exclaiming "the one privilege of age," was kissing the pretty hands extended to him when taking his leave. Suddenly Browning clutched my arm.
>
> "But what has he done," he said, indicating Lowell with his head at the other end of the room, "what has he done to be so fêted?"[20]

Harris sought to assure Browning that James Russell Lowell, the American ambassador, was the center of attention because of his station and not because of the poetry he had written. Browning then recovered from the sudden attack of envy:

---

[18]Ryals offers a connected view of the poems' backgrounds and their themes in *Browning's Later Poetry*, pp. 132–240. For a sympathetic and perceptive account of *Ferishtah's Fancies*, see Norton B. Crowell, *The Triple Soul: Browning's Theory of Knowledge* (Albuquerque: University of New Mexico Press, 1963), pp. 83–104. On *Parleyings*, see DeVane's discussion of sources and biography in *Browning's Parleyings: The Autobiography of a Mind* (New Haven: Yale University Press, 1927). Most of his comments are summarized in his *Handbook*. Dorothy Mermin sees Browning in his poetry after *The Ring and the Book* trying to save poetry from association with a fall into primitivism and myth, in "Browning and the Primitive," *VS* 25 (1982):211–37.

[19]Mrs. Fannie Browning, *Some Memories of Robert Browning* (Boston: Marshall Jones, 1928), p. 31.

[20]Frank Harris, "Robert Browning," *Contemporary Portraits*, 1st ser. (New York: Brentano's, 1920), p. 222.

The Later Poetry

"One tries to console oneself with thoughts like that," Browning admitted, "but it is difficult as one gets older. When one is young, one is so occupied with the work that one doesn't much care whether it is liked or disliked, but later, when one has fought and had, at any rate, a partial success, it is hard to see others who have not fought at all, put before one."[21]

The difficulty of consoling himself, when his public fame, as measured by the sale of his books, was hardly a tenth of Tennyson's and, until his poetry began to sell well in the late 1880s, not the equal of his wife's,[22] is reflected directly in *Pacchiarotto*. His concern for fame is also evident in *La Saisiaz and The Two Poets of Croisic* and in the title of his penultimate collection, *Parleyings with Certain People of Importance in Their Day*.

In "Pacchiarotto and How He Worked in Distemper," Browning lambasted Alfred Austin (poet laureate after Tennyson), who had dismissed Browning's poetry, in the *Temple Bar* of 1870, as society verse. Browning also vented his ire on his critics in general, who had so often complained of his obscurity and his idiosyncratic use of the language:

> Was it "grammar" wherein you would "coach" me—
> You,—pacing in even that paddock
> Of language allotted you *ad hoc*,
> With a clog at your fetlocks,—you—scorners
> Of me free of all its four corners?
> Was it "clearness of words which convey thought?"
> Ay, if words never needed enswathe aught
> But ignorance, impudence, envy
> And malice—what word-swathe would then vie
> With yours for clearness crystalline?
>
> [ll. 554–63]

The Hudibrastic invective and the animal imagery, which Browning had earlier found good use for in "The Pied Piper of Hamelin," return here without any fictive clothing and ultimately embarrass him. One finds it hard to believe that the elderly gentleman poet, who appears

---

[21]Ibid., pp. 222–23.
[22]On the sales of his books from 1886 to 1889, see Roma A. King, Jr., ed., *Robert Browning's Finances from His Own Account Book*, Baylor Browning Interest Series, no. 15 (Waco, Texas: Baylor University Press, 1947), pp. 18–19. See also "The Sales of Browning's Poems," in *Browning: The Critical Heritage*, ed. Litzinger and Smalley, pp. 536–37.

to be the picture of bland urbanity in his photographs, would show such frustration and sensitivity to criticism, but his worry about his fame led him to such emotional outbreaks.

Browning's desire for public recognition is clearly seen in that maundering jog-trot of a poem, *La Saisiaz*. Browning recalls his walks with the late Miss Anne Egerton-Smith and their discussion concerning the existence of God and the soul, occasioned by a series of articles in the *Nineteenth Century*.[23] At the end of the long internal theological debate, Browning, from the Salève's summit, surveys the landscape of Geneva below him and sees the spirits of Rousseau, Diodati, and Byron rise before him (ll. 553–57). To counteract the ghosts of these doubters of God and believers in man's evil nature, he asks his readers to grant him fame:

> Fame! Then, give me fame, a moment! As I gather at a glance
> Human glory after glory vivifying yon expanse,
> Let me grasp them all together, hold on high and brandish well
> Beacon-like above the rapt world ready, whether heaven or hell
> Send the dazzling summons earthward, to submit itself the same,
> Take on trust the hope or else despair flashed full on face by—Fame!
> Thanks, thou pine-tree of Makistos, wide thy giant torch I wave!
>
> [ll. 573–79]

And with this giant, flaming pine tree, he will broadcast to the waiting Victorian world his belief in God and soul. His struggle with the skeptical audience of literary ghosts, projections within the poem of Browning's own doubts, precipitates a merger of heaven and earth in the burning pine tree. This infinite moment of fame, symbolized by the contraction of space, allows him to proclaim his faith to the listening world: "Why, he at least believed in Soul, was very sure of God" (l. 604). As in "Prospice," however, this union with a heavenly presence is not so much felt as desperately desired. He does not want the notoriety of Rousseau and Byron, whom he associates with death, but at the same time he must compensate for the loss of Anne Egerton-Smith, whose death deprived him of an audience just as Elizabeth's had done.

Fame is also a central theme of *The Two Poets of Croisic*. The poem considers the ill-deserved notice given to two eighteenth-century poets

---

[23]See Hoxie N. Fairchild, "*La Saisiaz* and *The Nineteenth Century*," *MP* 48 (1950):104–11. Ryals discusses the connection between the themes of immortality and fame in *La Saisiaz* and *The Two Poets of Croisic*, in *Browning's Later Poetry*, pp. 147–64.

The Later Poetry

of Croisic, René Gentilhomme and Malcrais: the first becomes the official court poet after correctly prophesying that the prince of Condé would soon become king of France, and the second gains momentary notoriety by convincing Voltaire and the French literary world that his slightest verse was the worthy production of a literary woman. But the speaker finds their brief moments in the public light insignificant and concludes at the poem's end that the better poet is the one who has led "a happy life" (l. 1240).

The poem's epilogue, spoken by a woman who has been listening, suggests that the happy poet is one who has a loving audience. She recounts a story the speaker had once told her concerning a bard who broke a string on his lyre during a poetry contest but won anyway because a cricket that loved his music alighted on the lyre and supplied the note of the missing string when touched by the poet. The poet memorialized the event by making a statue of himself pointing at the cricket which had helped him win the prize. The story is not only an emblem of the epilogue's spiritual commentary on the poem but also evidence of the woman's love for the speaker. Like the cricket alighting on the broken lyre, her girlish voice "comes aptly in when gruff / Grows his singing" (ll. 105–6). Further, the woman's voice also seems to be Elizabeth's. Browning is not only thinking here of how her love crowned his life but is also specifically recalling the end of the fourth of the *Sonnets from the Portuguese*:

> My cricket chirps against thy mandolin.
> Hush, call no echo up in further proof
> Of desolation! there's a voice within
> That weeps . . . as thou must sing . . . alone, aloof.[24]

Her voice returns in the forms of the woman's and the cricket's to console him and tell him that while he may not have acquired the fame he has sought and expected, he has loved and been loved.

"Hervé Riel" and "Pheidippides" also depict simple conflicts between public fame and private love but do so in the purely objective perspective that marks Browning's idyls. Hervé Riel, a common Croisic sailor, saves the French fleet by steering it to safe harbor. Given his choice of rewards by the fleet's admiral, Riel asks for a day's furlough to visit his wife, instead of any public honor or monetary reward. Similarly, Pheidippides, Athens's best runner and most famous

---

[24]*The Poems of Elizabeth Barrett Browning*, ed. Harriet Waters Preston (Boston: Houghton Mifflin, 1900), p. 215.

messenger, asks only to "marry a certain maid" (l. 101) as his reward for gaining Pan's support of Athens after Sparta had refused to aid the Athenians in repelling the invading Persians. Later he dies after having brought the news of Athens's victory over the Persians at Marathon, not hearing the public shout for his magnificent effort. He receives his final reward not from the Athenian public but from his heavenly protector. The poems reaffirm Browning's belief that a man's true audiences are his beloved and his God.

The most notable of his late meditations on fame, however, is "Clive." The speaker recounts Clive's most terrifying moment, which occurs when he catches a captain cheating at cards and accuses him of it. In the subsequent duel, Clive accidentally fires and misses. His opponent approaches him with pistol in hand and demands that Clive retract his accusation. But he refuses, saying, "Fire and go to Hell!" (l. 146). Instead of killing him, or sparing and dishonoring him, the captain confesses that he did indeed cheat and rushes away. Instead of viewing this encounter as a lamentable example of duelling, as he had done in "Before" and "After" in *Men and Women*, or seeing the duel as a trial by combat affirming God's providential intervention in the affairs of men as he had done in "Count Gismond," Browning presents Clive's predicament as a case of telling the truth before God, and only incidentally as a case of honor. No longer holding that God's ultimate judgment regarding an individual's guilt is made manifest to the world, Browning makes the poem pivot on the captain's recognition that it is better to relinquish the approval of one's fellow men than to cease striving for God's. Clive's refusal to retract his accusation forces the captain to consider his eventual destiny:

> Laugh at Hell who list,
> I can't! God's no fable either. Did this boy's eye wink once? No!
> There's no standing him and Hell and God all three against me,—so
> I did cheat!
>
> [ll. 148–51]

The captain must face not only Clive but also God. Respecting the privacy and the primacy of this relationship, Clive makes certain that others will not interfere between the captain and his God by requiring the other card players to suspend their judgment. Similarly the narrator asks the reader and his listener to suspend judgment on Clive's suicide: "Clive's worst deed—we'll hope condoned" (l. 240). The reader is asked to understand that whatever public disgrace brought upon

The Later Poetry

Clive by Parliament's investigation of his financial affairs in India and however inappropriate his response to his being dishonored, Clive's ultimate audience is with God, not man.

Although these poems about fame are part of Browning's struggle to reconcile himself to his task as a poet, the deepest and darkest chords are struck by the poems that seek some consolation for Elizabeth's absence. He exclaims in the first two stanzas of "The Prologue" from *Pacchiarotto* that he would gladly spend the summer's day looking at the ivy-colored wall of his house and the red bricks that laugh between the openings in the creepers. Suddenly he imagines that perhaps someone has disturbed the sprays by walking behind the wall or by singing so that the reverberations have stirred the ivy. In the fifth stanza he abandons this fancy, saying that "wall upon wall are between us" and comparing himself to a "prison-bird" (ll. 17, 19). Yet he counsels himself:

> Hold on, hope hard in the subtle thing
>   That's spirit: though cloistered fast, soar free:
> Account as wood, brick, stone, this ring
>   Of the rueful neighbours, and—forth to thee!
>   [ll. 21–24]

The sentiment expressed here recalls that of the householder in the epilogue of *Fifine at the Fair*. He wishes to be one with his love, leaving behind the ring of neighbors that he associates with the deathly solidity of wood, brick, and stone.

The poetic difficulty here is very real. How can the speaker describe the separation between body and soul within the landscape without suggesting that the soul is somehow absent from it? At the end of the poem, "the subtle thing / That's spirit" cloistered by the walls soars free and moves toward his love. But we should note two fundamental confusions in this movement: first, in the fourth stanza the speaker associates the song and spirit with his love, only to appropriate them in the final stanza; and second, the correspondence between the house and the body containing the soul is delusively literalized. He asks, "What life o'erbrims / The body,—the house, no eye can probe,— / Divined as, beneath a robe, the limbs?" (ll. 10–12). The life or soul within the body cannot be seen. But as the metaphor slides, the soul becomes equated with the body's limbs while the body itself becomes "a robe." The supplemental substance of the flesh becomes the only frame of reference for the spiritual presence. The life the speaker had earlier seen clothing the wall in the form of the creepers now seems to be a vibrant excess which has its source outside his vision: the creepers become the robe, the house's wall the body, and that within it the soul. But these last two terms collapse, body and soul becoming one. The inadequacy of this image is revealed when the speaker resorts to the phrase "wall upon wall" to convey the true nature of his beloved's absence (l. 21). The wall suddenly becomes a metaphor for the crowd gathered around him, for his being cut off from instead of near his audience, for his love's being absent instead of present.

The attempt in "The Prologue" to describe the presence of an absence does not equal one of Browning's slighter performances from *Men and Women*, "Love in a Life," in which he describes the imagined absence of someone who is there:

> Room after room
> I hunt the house through
> We inhabit together.
> Heart, fear nothing, for, heart thou shalt find her—
> Next time, herself!—not the trouble behind her
> Left in the curtain, the couch's perfume!
> As she brushed it, the cornice-wreath blossomed anew:
> Yon looking-glass gleamed at the wave of her feather.
> [ll. 1–8]

In "Love in a Life" the fear of the loved one's death is concealed beneath the experience of not finding her immediately, of entering each room just after she has left it. But in "The Prologue" to *Pacchiarotto* Browning has no physical evidence in the scent of a perfume or the gleam of a feather in a mirror to signify Elizabeth's presence; he does not hear her song or see her. And in the end it is not she who comes to him, but he who must go to her, who must disappear as well.

The dialectic of presence and absence also informs "Fears and Scruples" from *Pacchiarotto*. The speaker explains how he loved his "unseen friend" whom he knew only through his letters (l. 2) but that experts calling them "forgery from A to Z" have created doubt in the very existence of his friend (l. 20). He still persists, nevertheless, in thinking that his friend lives because he loves him still and imagines that perhaps his friend is hiding at home, playing "hide-and-seek behind the shutters" (l. 39), expecting his eyes to "pierce through solid bricks" (l. 40) and blaming him if they do not. To the objection that such an invisible friend would be a monster for not letting one see him, the

The Later Poetry

speaker replies: "Hush, I pray you! / What if this friend happen to be—God?" (ll. 47–48). This invisible friend is the symbol of Browning's absent audience.[25] And, as the mention of the friend's forged letters suggests, this invisible person could be Shelley, as well as God or Elizabeth. There appears to be a kind of fanciful fusion of them in the poem, made possible in part by the friend's being bricked in and so inaccessible to our view. This being bricked in and the emptiness of the forged letters not only suggest entombment and death but also point to the thinness and desperation of fancy's evasions in the other's absence.

In a simpler fashion the lonely lover's desire for spiritual transcendence makes "Never the Time and Place" a problematic poem, in which the speaker laments the absence of his beloved from his life:

> Never the time and the place
>   And the loved one all together!
> This path—how soft to pace!
>   This May—what magic weather!
> Where is the loved one's face?
> In a dream that loved one's face meets mine,
>   But the house is narrow, the place is bleak
> Where, outside, rain and wind combine
>   With furtive ear, if I strive to speak,
>   With a hostile eye at my flushing cheek,
> With a malice that marks each work, each sign!
> O enemy sly and serpentine,
>   Uncoil thee from the waking man!
>   Do I hold the Past
>   Thus firm and fast
>   Yet doubt if the Future hold I can?
> This path so soft to pace shall lead
> Thro' the magic of May to herself indeed!
> Or narrow if needs the house must be,
> Outside are the storms and strangers: we—
> Oh, close, safe, warm sleep I and she,
> —I and she!

As in "Prospice," Browning places the ghostly audience of the rain and wind over against the image of the perfect union of lover and beloved, in order to balance his imaginative vision and to secure it from

---

[25]See Browning's explanation of the invisible friend in his undated letter to W. G. Kingsland, in W. G. Kingsland, "Browning: Some Personal Reminiscences," Baylor Browning Interests, no. 2 (Waco, Texas: Baylor University Press, 1931), p. 33.

death, which makes everything an absence. By reducing death to a "sly and serpentine" enemy (recalling Satan in the Garden of Eden), he lessens its threat to his paradisal memory. But he can offer nothing better than memory as sustenance for the future; the dream and his recollections fill the future as well. He holds that his present enjoyment of the May weather will lead to his lost love, that he will have both spring and her. But he must return to the past, only altering his vision to allow himself and his love to sleep (as if to hope for life together were too much) and so remains untroubled by the death separating them.

The emphasis upon memory as a substitute for imagining the future runs throughout Browning's last poems, through *Parleyings* and especially through *Asolando*. He dedicates *Parleyings* to the memory of Joseph Milsand, who died in 1886, and writes *Asolando* in memory of his first visit to Asolo and of his youthful poetic vision:

> How many a year, my Asolo,
>   Since—one step just from sea to land—
> I found you, loved yet feared you so—
>   For natural objects seemed to stand
> Palpably fire-clothed!
>   ["Prologue," ll. 26–30]

This longing for the fiery coloring of his youthful vision leads him to overcompensate for its lack, as in "Numpholeptos," by substituting a Cézanne-like abstraction of color for the impressionistic painting of his earlier poetry. The parleying "With Gerard de Lairesse," for example, ends with this exhortation: "Daisies and grass be my heart's bedfellows / On the mound wind spares and sunshine mellows: / Dance you, reds and whites and yellows!" (ll. 432–34). Were this Wallace Stevens, this dancing of the sunlight and the flowers on the grave would be a triumph. But for Browning it is a desperate danse macabre that has as its only end the *O altitudo* of "God it is who transcends" ("Prologue," l. 45).

Perhaps the best of the *Parleyings* is "With Charles Avison." It begins with Browning's meditation on a blackcap finch's stealing a piece of cloth that had once been used to tie back the branch of a creeper and was fluttering on a nail. This creeper has already appeared in the prologue to *Pacchiarotto*, but instead of covering his garden's brick wall in spring, it now is stripped of its leaves at the end of winter:

The Later Poetry

> How strange!—but, first of all, the little fact
> Which led my fancy forth. This bitter morn
> Showed me no object in the stretch forlorn
> Of garden-ground beneath my window, backed
> By yon worn wall wherefrom the creeper, tacked
> To clothe its brickwork, hangs now, rent and racked
> By five months' cruel winter,—showed no torn
> And tattered ravage worse for eyes to see
> Than just one ugly space of clearance, left
> Bare even of the bones which used to be
> Warm wrappage, safe embracement.
> [ll. 1–11]

The creeper and its movement had earlier furnished Browning with sufficient inspiration for a poem in which he imagined a reunion with Elizabeth, a "safe embracement" in a world beyond this one. But the present scene hardly seems capable of providing the beginning of a similar effusion. He is alert, however, to the slightest shred of poetry in the wintry garden and is attracted to the blackcap finch tugging at a piece of cloth, "this rag of manufacture, spoiled / By art, and yet by nature near unsoiled" (ll. 33–34); and, like the bird that hopes to use it to line his nest, he hopes to construct from it a home for the spirit of spring, which is present in "Never the Time and the Place" but absent here.

He notes as an afterthought that he is seeing the bird in March and drifting from March to march, wanders by further association to Charles Avison, the composer of marches. He then begins to play one of Avison's compositions on his piano and comments on it:

> Am I ungrateful? for, your March, styled "Grand,"
> Did veritably seem to grow, expand,
> And greaten up to title as, unchecked,
> Dream-marchers marched, kept marching, slow and sure,
> In time, to tune, unchangeably the same,
> From nowhere into nowhere,—out they came,
> Onward they passed, and in they went.
> [ll. 59–65]

The aimless, mindless marching of the dream marchers parallels the movement of Browning's poem and its couplets. It provides, for once, an image appropriate to the unchecked amplification and modification of his later poetry that slowly proceeds "from nowhere into nowhere."

His diffuseness stems from his multiplication of parallel images and passages that add color to his description but dissipate what force his thought has. Yet, unlike Swinburne's subordination of image to theme or sound, Browning's method places the theme in service of his images. He compares his playing the march to the finch's struggle with the cotton rag: "I plucked the measure, as his brown / Frayed flannel-bit my blackcap" (ll. 80–81). But he soon leaves the finch far behind in following the path of his private associations.

He compares Avison with other composers present and past (sections 4–5), discourses on the privileged relationship of music to truth (sections 6–8), philosophizes on his resuscitation of Avison's music in his poetry (sections 9–14), and closes the poem by creating a picture of seventeenth-century England appropriate to the march and by transcribing Avison's music. He talks about how the artist seeks in his work to make "how we Feel, hard and fast as what we Know" (l. 194), and he asserts that of all the arts music gives us the best access to our deepest feelings:

> Music! Dredging deeper yet,
> Drag into day,—by sound, thy master-net,—
> The abysmal bottom-growth, ambiguous thing
> Unbroken of a branch, palpitating
> With limbs' play and life's semblance!
> [ll. 235–39]

The dragnet of music comes up with the palpable quivering of life, which, like the trembling leaves of the creeper in the prologue to *Pacchiarotto*, ambiguously suggests the existence of the soul. Moreover, unlike the poetry of the past, music remains alive to the present. It makes passion "palpable once more" (l. 269), while in poetry "the flower is dead" and the "sparks have left the spar" (ll. 256–57), suggesting that Browning's star, which threw "(like the angled spar) / Now a dart of red, / Now a dart of blue," has also gone out ("My Star," ll. 4–6).

He retreats into the music's history, calling up the Parliament of Pym and a heroic time in which art and men were united and in which a chorus of men singing in praise of their leader was not impossible to imagine: "Shall we not all join chorus? Hark the hymn / "—Rough, rude, robustious—homely heart a-throb, / Harsh voice a-hallo, as beseems the mob!" (ll. 413–15). As the vigor of his language shows, Browning fairly revels in the thought of the people marching in support of their chosen leader, "Pym, the man of men!" (l. 423). But there is a certain nostalgic huskiness in his voice when he exclaims: "How good is noise! what's silence but despair / Of making sound match gladness never there?" (ll. 416–17). The crowd's noise fills the silence and supplies a happy audience for the poet to think about. It also supports the fiction of a united seventeenth-century England, which he finds better than the "federated England" of the future (l. 388).[26] In comparison with *Strafford*, Browning here adopts a much simpler interpretation of the parliamentary struggle preceding the English Civil War than he had done fifty years earlier and now prefers his idealization of Pym's leadership to his portrait of Strafford's martyrdom. Here as elsewhere in his conversations with "certain people of importance in their day," he looks for images of mutual understanding between speaker and audience and for simple resolutions of the dark modern complexities of, among other things, Darwin's evolutionary theory, aestheticism, and Disraeli's political machinations.[27]

The end of "With Charles Avison" is fairly representative of the kind of easy idealism celebrated in the last two volumes of his poetry, when Browning's turbid language and syntax rest in the shallower and warmer waters of his memory. One can, for example, easily sympathize with his holding out in "Development" for Homer's *Iliad* in preference to Aristotle's *Ethics*, and for his father's method of telling him about the siege of Troy by rearranging the furniture in preference to the theories of German critics about the authorship of the epic. But there is a thinness in the spinning out of the images in his last poems, because they depend so much on reverberations of a very private sort. One need only glance at "Summum Bonum" and think of Elizabeth to see how this is so:

> All the breath and the bloom of the year in the bag of one bee:
>   All the wonder and wealth of the mine in the heart of one gem:
> In the core of one pearl all the shade and the shine of the sea:
>   Breath and bloom, shade and shine,—wonder, wealth, and how far
>   above them—
>   Truth, that's brighter than gem,
>   Trust, that's purer than pearl,—
>   Brightest truth, purest trust in the universe—all were for me
>   In the kiss of one girl.

[26] See the account of Browning's old Liberal position on liberty in relation to the egalitarian implications of Irish Home Rule, in Trevor Lloyd, "Browning and Politics," in *Browning*, ed. Armstrong, pp. 161–67.

[27] See *Handbook*, pp. 491–524.

Robert Browning: His Poetry and His Audiences

The key word is "were," which makes the piling of image upon image seem somehow an effort to hide the present emptiness beneath the weight of conventional riches. He once had a loving audience that allowed him to make sense of the world; but without her presence he can at best hope for a life with her in the spirit and at worst comfort himself with his memories of her and her love for him.[28]

The critical tendency to see his last poems as evidence of a partial recovery of his powers is the product of mistakingly assuming that the clear and simple is necessarily better than the tortured and obscure when it comes to Browning's poetry—that *Asolando* is better than *Fifine at the Fair*. But *Asolando* isn't, simply because in it Browning has given up trying to sort out how one can hope to speak to others about one's feelings and one's soul, has given up talking to anyone other than himself, and pictures himself as

> One who never turned his back but marched breast forward,
>   Never doubted clouds would break,
> Never dreamed, though right were worsted, wrong would triumph,
> Held we fall to rise, are baffled to fight better,
>   Sleep to wake.
>
> No, at noonday in the bustle of man's work-time
>   Greet the unseen with a cheer!
> Bid him forward, breast and back as either should be,
>   "Strive and thrive!" cry "Speed,—fight on, fare ever
>   There as here!"
>
> ["Epilogue," ll. 11–20]

This is Browning reduced to Victorian myth, to an empty monumentality, to the optimist whom the worried clergymen and elderly women of the Browning Society wanted him to be. This is "'Childe Roland to the Dark Tower Came'" in waxworks. The tension between the speaker and his audiences, which Browning had so closely observed and from which he had created his best poetry, is here discarded in favor of an imagined agreement concerning his poetic achievement and his salvation. It is as if his striving here on earth were equivalent to the state of his soul in heaven, when he had been careful

---

[28]Commenting on Browning's retreat into conventionality as he grew older, David Page says that Elizabeth's death "took Browning from his security, his audience, and by extension, much of the pressure which made him balance and objectify his feelings. Reality became too painful, and the conventional shell took its place" ("And So Is Browning," *Essays in Criticism* 13 [1963]:153).

in his poems from *Paracelsus* to *The Ring and the Book* to make it clear that man's recognition of his inadequacy and his failures were acknowledgments of God's greatness, not eternal states of being.

In the end, then, we do better to reread *Men and Women* than to read *Asolando*, and to see Browning here as finally succumbing to his popularity, despite his instinctive desire to resist the tyranny of the British public. For Browning, artists have a special access to the truth and to God and are morally bound to try to make others see as they do, even though they will likely fail. We should think of him, then, in terms of his most subtle and successful poet who is the subject of "How It Strikes a Contemporary." This poet resembles the one described by Proust, who "is brought to a standstill in front of all manner of things not worth a sober respectable gentleman's notice, so that people wonder if he is a spy or a lover and what, during all this while he has appeared to be looking at a tree, he has really been looking at."[29] He looks at things we feel are insignificant and so becomes a figure of contemplation apparently transcending the world. In wondering what the poet is looking at, you learn to see yourself: "You saw go up and down Valladolid, / A man of mark, to know next time you saw" (ll. 3–4). He is a figure of reflection made self-conscious by repetition. In following his movements through the city you are forced to look, remember, and wonder. The intimate address of the poem dramatizes the impossibility of maintaining the critical distance of "one," and shows how "you" (standing at once for the speaker's, the poet's, and Browning's audiences) are drawn into imaginative activity. Indeed, this experience is registered by the sentence's opening and closing with "you saw," the repetition signifying that the poet has made you see self-consciously, and the poem expands upon this sentence's insight as you investigate the poet as a figure of contemplation.

We see the poet "scenting the world, looking it full in face" (l. 11). In recording his routine we observe the city's Moorish architectural heritage and its new French construction. We see the poet looking at the cobbler, watching the vendors who make lemonade and coffee, and glancing over the books and ballads in the stalls. And we come to understand how the city's people imagine a hidden order behind the country's shifting ministries. Unlike others, the poet sees into things, penetrating beneath their surfaces in the way the ferrule of his walking stick probes the mortar of a new shop being built in town (ll. 20–22).

[29]Marcel Proust, "The Artist in Contemplation," in *On Art and Literature, 1896–1916*, trans. Sylvia Townsend Warner (London: Chatto & Windus, 1957), p. 307.

Since others think that he sees into them, he makes them feel self-conscious and guilty (ll. 30–35). His inspection of the world becomes a figure of God's vision, and he becomes both God's spy and a representative of moral order. As our audience, the poet comes to stand for the recognition we both desire and fear and also for the self-knowledge we see through our imagination of his gaze.

When we look through the eyes of "an Italian person of quality" in "Up at a Villa—Down in the City," we see the world from a great distance. There the speaker, in his beggarly luxury, views the bustling city life from his isolated, desolate villa. He smiles at "some little new law of the Duke's" (l. 46) and swings with gusto into Our Lady's procession: "*Bang-whang-whang* goes the drum, *tootle-te-tootle* the fife; / No keeping one's haunches still: it's the greatest pleasure in life" (ll. 53–54). But he lets his pocketbook betray his instinct for life and sacrifices his pleasures to his parsimony, seeing neither himself nor his life clearly in his isolation from others. In contrast, the poet as a figure of imaginative contemplation closes the distance between us and our experience of the world. In following the poet about, the speaker of "How It Strikes a Contemporary" unconsciously becomes a poet too and momentarily converses in blank verse with his friend: "Well, I never could write a verse,—could you?" (l. 115). By ferreting out the poet's home, he learns to see the truth of the world. He finds that the poet is not a tyrannical voyeur who keeps naked girls but an ordinary man who plays cribbage with his maid over fruit and cheese. We may imagine the poet's transcending the world, as Browning does when thinking of Shelley in "Memorabilia," but we poetically discover that he does not. The poet, Browning tells us, is instead the demystified man about town who reveals to us through his eyes the wonder of everyday life. By following and reading Browning, one learns how his poetry is to be interpreted and his identity as a poet and a man is to be understood in the light of the phrase "love is best," and how to think of Browning's poetry in terms of his trying to reconcile the competing claims of God, the public, and the literary past, and doing so in his love for Elizabeth and the poems he wrote for her.

Selected Bibliography

Editions of Browning's Works

Browning's "Essay on Chatterton." Ed. Donald Smalley. Cambridge, Mass.: Harvard University Press, 1948.

The Complete Works of Robert Browning. Ed. Roma A. King, Jr., et al. 5 vols. of a projected 13. Athens: University of Ohio Press, 1969–81.

The Complete Works of Robert Browning. Ed. Charlotte Porter and Helen A. Clarke. 12 vols. New York: Thomas Y. Crowell, 1898.

New Poems by Robert Browning and Elizabeth Barrett Browning. Ed. Frederic G. Kenyon. London: Smith, Elder, 1914.

The Ring and the Book. Ed. Richard D. Altick. New Haven: Yale University Press, 1981.

Robert Browning: The Poems. Ed. John Pettigrew and Thomas J. Collins. 2 vols. New Haven: Yale University Press, 1981.

The Works of Robert Browning. Ed. F. G. Kenyon. 10 vols. London: Smith, Elder, 1912.

Bibliographies

Robert Browning: A Bibliography, 1830–1950. Comp. Leslie Nathan Broughton, Clark Sutherland Northrop, and Robert Pearsall. Cornell Studies in English, no. 39. Ithaca: Cornell University Press, 1953.

Robert and Elizabeth Barrett Browning: An Annotated Bibliography, 1951–1970. Comp. William S. Peterson. New York: Browning Institute, 1974.

Annual bibliographies are found in *PMLA, Victorian Studies, Victorian Poetry,* and *Browning Institute Studies.*

Letters and Biographies

Altick, Richard D. "The Private Life of Robert Browning." *Yale Review* 41 (1952):247–62.

Selected Bibliography

Dearest Isa: Robert Browning's Letters to Isabella Blagden. Ed. Edward C. McAleer. Austin: University of Texas Press, 1951.
Griffin, W. Hall, and Harry Christopher Minchin. *The Life of Robert Browning.* New York: Macmillan, 1910.
Irvine, William, and Park Honan. *The Book, the Ring, and the Poet.* New York: McGraw-Hill, 1974.
The Letters of Elizabeth Barrett Browning. Ed. Frederic G. Kenyon. 2 vols. London: Macmillan, 1897.
Letters of Robert Browning Collected by Thomas J. Wise. Ed. Thurman L. Hood. New Haven: Yale University Press, 1933.
The Letters of Robert Browning and Elizabeth Barrett Barrett, 1845–1846. Ed. Elvan Kintner. 2 vols. Cambridge, Mass.: Harvard University Press, 1969.
Maynard, John. *Browning's Youth.* Cambridge, Mass.: Harvard University Press, 1977.
Miller, Betty. *Robert Browning: A Portrait.* London: John Murray, 1952.
New Letters of Robert Browning. Ed. William Clyde DeVane and Kenneth Leslie Knickerbocker. New Haven: Yale University Press, 1950.
Orr, Mrs. Sutherland. *Life and Letters of Robert Browning.* 2d ed. London: Smith, Elder, 1891.
Robert Browning and Alfred Domett. Ed. Frederic G. Kenyon. London: Smith, Elder, 1906.
Robert Browning and Julia Wedgwood: A Broken Friendship as Revealed by Their Letters. Ed. Richard Curle. New York: Frederick A. Stokes, 1937.
Snyder, Edward, and Frederic Palmer, Jr. "New Light on the Brownings." *Quarterly Review* 269 (1937):48–63.
Ward, Maisie. *Robert Browning and His World.* 2 vols. London: Cassell, 1967–69.
Woolf, Virginia. *Flush: A Biography.* London: Hogarth Press, 1933.

Contemporary Reviews and Essays

Chasles, Philarète. "De l'Art dramatique et du Théâtre actuel en Angleterre." *Revue des deux Mondes,* ser. 4, 22 (1840):122–50.
Forster, John. "Evidences of a New Genius for Dramatic Poetry." *New Monthly Magazine,* March 1836, pp. 289–308.
Kingsley, Charles. "Mr. and Mrs. Browning." *Fraser's Magazine* 43 (1851): 170–82.
Litzinger, Boyd, and Donald Smalley, eds. *Browning: The Critical Heritage.* London: Routledge & Kegan Paul, 1970.
Massey, Gerald. "The Poems and Plays of Robert Browning." *North British Review* 34 (1861):183–95.
Merivale, Herman. Review of Browning's *Strafford. Edinburgh Review* 65 (July 1837):132–51.
Milsand, M. J. "La Poésie Anglaise depuis Byron: Browning." *Revue des deux Mondes,* n.s., 11 (1851):661–89.

Selected Bibliography

Browning Criticism and General Works

Altick, Richard D. *The English Common Reader*. Chicago: University of Chicago Press, 1957.
Altick, Richard D., and James F. Loucks. *Browning's Roman Murder Story: A Reading of "The Ring and the Book."* Chicago: University of Chicago Press, 1968.
Armstrong, Isobel, ed. *The Major Victorian Poets: Reconsiderations*. London: Routledge & Kegan Paul, 1969.
——. *Robert Browning: Writers and Their Background*. London: G. Bell & Sons, 1974.
Bloom, Harold. *The Anxiety of Influence: A Theory of Poetry*. New York: Oxford University Press, 1973.
——. *A Map of Misreading*. New York: Oxford University Press, 1975.
Bloom, Harold, and Adrienne Munich, eds. *Robert Browning: A Collection of Critical Essays*. Englewood Cliffs, N.J.: Prentice-Hall, 1979.
Brantlinger, Patrick. *The Spirit of Reform: British Literature and Politics, 1832–1867*. Cambridge, Mass.: Harvard University Press, 1977.
Browning, Elizabeth Barrett. *The Poems of Elizabeth Barrett Browning*, ed. Harriet Waters Preston. Boston: Houghton, Mifflin, 1900.
Charlton, H. B. "Browning as Dramatist." *Bulletin of the John Rylands Library* 23 (1939):33–67.
Collins, Thomas J. "Browning's *Essay on Shelley*: In Context." *VP* 2 (1964):119–24.
——. *Robert Browning's Moral-Aesthetic Theory, 1833–1855*. Lincoln: University of Nebraska Press, 1967.
Cook, Eleanor. *Browning's Lyrics: An Exploration*. Toronto: University of Toronto Press, 1974.
Corrigan, Beatrice. *Curious Annals: New Documents Relating to Browning's Roman Murder Story*. Toronto: University of Toronto Press, 1956.
Culler, A. Dwight. "Monodrama and the Dramatic Monologue." *PMLA* 90 (1975):366–85.
Davies, Hugh Sykes. *Browning and the Modern Novel*. Hull: University of Hull Publications, 1962.
DeVane, William Clyde. *A Browning Handbook*. 2d ed. New York: Appleton-Century-Crofts, 1955.
——. *Browning's Parleyings: The Autobiography of a Mind*. New Haven: Yale University Press, 1927.
——. "The Virgin and the Dragon." *Yale Review* 37 (1947):33–46.
Downer, Alan S. *The Eminent Tragedian: William Charles Macready*. Cambridge, Mass.: Harvard University Press, 1966.
Drew, Philip. *The Poetry of Robert Browning: A Critical Introduction*. London: Methuen, 1970.
Drew, Philip, ed. *Robert Browning: A Collection of Critical Essays*. London: Methuen, 1966.

Selected Bibliography

Elton, Oliver. *A Survey of English Literature, 1830–1880.* 2 vols. London: Edwin Arnold, 1920.

Gridley, Roy E. *Browning.* London: Routledge & Kegan Paul, 1972.

Hair, Donald S. *Browning's Experiments in Genre.* Toronto: University of Toronto Press, 1972.

Hatcher, Harlan Henthorne. *The Versification of Robert Browning.* Columbus: Ohio State University Press, 1928.

Hegel, G. W. F. *Aesthetics: Lectures on Fine Art.* Trans. T. M. Knox. 2 vols. Oxford: Clarendon Press, 1975.

Honan, Park. *Browning's Characters: A Study in Poetic Technique.* New Haven: Yale University Press, 1961.

——. "Robert Browning." In *The Victorian Poets: A Guide to Research*, ed. Frederick E. Faverty. 2d ed. Cambridge, Mass.: Harvard University Press, 1968.

Johnson, E. D. H. *The Alien Vision of Victorian Poetry: Sources of the Poetic Imagination in Tennyson, Browning, and Arnold.* Princeton: Princeton University Press, 1952.

Kermode, Frank. *Romantic Image.* London: Routledge & Kegan Paul, 1957.

Langbaum, Robert. *The Poetry of Experience: The Dramatic Monologue in Modern Literary Tradition.* New York: Random House, 1957.

Lloyd, Trevor. "Browning and Politics." In *Robert Browning: Writers and Their Background*, ed. Isobel Armstrong. London: G. Bell & Sons, 1974.

Lounsbury, Thomas R. *The Early Literary Career of Robert Browning.* New York: Charles Scribner's Sons, 1911.

Mason, Michael. "The Importance of Sordello." In *The Major Victorian Poets: Reconsiderations*, ed. Isobel Armstrong. London: Routledge & Kegan Paul, 1969.

Melchiori, Barbara. *Browning's Poetry of Reticence.* New York: Barnes & Noble, 1968.

Miller, J. Hillis. *The Disappearance of God: Five Nineteenth-Century Writers.* Cambridge, Mass.: Harvard University Press, 1963.

Orr, Mrs. Sutherland. *A Handbook to the Works of Robert Browning.* 6th ed. London: G. E. Bell & Sons, 1892.

Otten, Terry. *The Deserted Stage: The Search for Dramatic Form in Nineteenth-Century England.* Athens: Ohio University Press, 1972.

Peckham, Morse. *Victorian Revolutionaries.* New York: George Braziller, 1970.

Peterson, William S. *Interpreting the Oracle: A History of the London Browning Society.* Athens: Ohio University Press, 1969.

Raymond, William O. *The Infinite Moment and Other Essays on Robert Browning.* 2d ed. Toronto: University of Toronto Press, 1965.

Rowell, George. *The Victorian Theatre: A Survey.* 2d ed. Cambridge, England: Cambridge University Press, 1978.

Ryals, Clyde de L. *Browning's Later Poetry, 1871–1889.* Ithaca: Cornell University Press, 1975.

Selected Bibliography

Shaw, W. David. *The Dialectical Temper: The Rhetorical Art of Robert Browning*. Ithaca: Cornell University Press, 1968.

Smith, C. Willard. *Browning's Star-Imagery: The Study of a Detail in Poetic Design*. Princeton: Princeton University Press, 1941.

Sullivan, Mary Rose. *Browning's Voices in "The Ring and the Book": A Study of Method and Meaning*. Toronto: University of Toronto Press, 1969.

Swingle, L. J. "Truth and *The Ring and the Book*: A Negative View." *VP* 6 (1968):259–69.

Tracy, C. R., ed. *Browning's Mind and Art*. Edinburgh: Oliver & Boyd, 1968.

Tucker, Herbert F., Jr. *Browning's Beginnings: The Art of Disclosure*. Minneapolis: University of Minnesota Press, 1980.

———. "Memorabilia: Mnemonic Imagination in Shelley and Browning." *Studies in Romanticism* 19 (1980):285–325.

Index

Academy, 15
Aeschylus: *Agamemnon*, 240; *Prometheus Bound*, 249
Agrippa, Cornelius, 27
Allingham, William, 133, 222n.
Altick, Richard D., 67, 166n., 174n., 181n., 229n., 234n.
America, 40, 214–16, 229n.
Andersen, Hans Christian, "The Ugly Duckling," 91–92
Andromeda, 82, 114
Annunziata (Elizabeth's maid), 191n.
Ariail, J. M., 75n.
Aristophanes, 240n.
Aristotle, *Ethics*, 269
Armstrong, Isobel 5In., 60n., 214
Arnold, Matthew, 17, 74, 81, 93, 106, 127, 141, 239; *Culture and Anarchy*, 124; "Dover Beach," 172; *Empedocles on Etna*, 24n., 48; "Growing Old," 212n.; *Letters*, 112; Preface to *Poems* (1853), 48; "The Study of Poetry," 202
Astley Russell, 117n.
Athenaeum, 69, 191
audiences, 18–20, 136–37; absent, 138, 147, 169, 195, 197, 219–20, 229; betrayal by, 98–99; Browning's accommodation of, 116–17, 222, 227–29; Browning's fear of, 25–26, 110, 136, 145; captive or enslaved, 28–29, 81–84, 100–101, 137, 157, 171; for drama, 24, 42, 46, 68, 71–73, 156; free, 38, 108; of ghosts from the past, 18, 19, 38, 137–38, 147, 149–50, 174–75, 200, 214–16, 255; God as ultimate, 16, 19, 20, 39, 74, 75–76, 77, 110, 127–29, 135, 194, 204, 208, 212, 213, 231; ideal (beloved lover), 18, 54, 136–37; as metaphysical enclosure, 27, 29–30, 166–70; multitude or crowd as, 153, 252; none for accomplishments, 99; private versus public, 27, 48, 91, 127–29, 141–42, 143, 145, 146–47, 194–95; search for, 18, 68, 84; small one for Browning, 69, 93, 103, 133, 193, 240n.; sympathetic, 26, 28–30, 36, 110; tyranny over, 18, 73, 113, 216–19, 254–55
Austen, Jane, 70; *Pride and Prejudice*, 71
Austin, Alfred, 259

Bagehot, Walter, 93n.
Ball, Patricia M., 205n.
Balzac, Honoré de: *Comédie Humaine*, 234; *Sarrasine*, 31–32
Bank of England, 22, 40
Barrett, Arabella (Elizabeth's sister), 181n.
Barrett, Edward Moulton- (Elizabeth's father), 73, 105, 113, 132, 222
Barthes, Roland, 32
Bartolommeo, Fra, 100n.
Baudelaire, Charles, "À une passante," 88–89
Benjamin, Walter, 89n.
Benson, Edward Frederick, 15n.
Besier, Rudolph, *The Barretts of Wimpole Street*, 107
Bible, 124; Exodus, 69; Habakkuk, 228–29; I John, 209; I Kings, 226; II Kings, 226; Matthew, 159; Numbers, 164; Psalms, 218; Revelation, 168, 188;

279

Index

Bible (cont.)
   I Samuel, 130, 150, 152; Song of Solomon, 181
Bieman, Elizabeth, 130n.
Biographie universelle, 31
Blagden, Isabella, 112, 191, 239n., 247n.
Blake, William, 35, 110, 202
Bloom Harold, 49n., 140n., 144, 147
Boas, Frederick S., 31n.
Boswell, James, 113
Bowdler, Dr. Thomas, 73
Bowra, C. M., 48n.
Brantlinger, Patrick, 49n.
Bridell-Fox, Eliza F., 65
Bright, John, 80n.
Brisman, Leslie, 187n.
Brockington, A. Allen, 126
Bronson, Katherine de Kay, 147
Brontë sisters, 70
Brower, Reuben A., 240n.
Browning, Charles D., 99n.
Browning, Elizabeth Barrett, 17, 18, 19, 20, 21, 26, 28n., 33n., 60n., 61, 67n., 68n., 69n., 70n., 73, 78n., 80, 82, 86n., 92n., 103, 104–20, 123n., 124, 131, 132–33, 136, 138n., 146–47, 151, 152, 159, 160, 181n., 191, 193, 197, 203, 204, 206, 211, 222, 242–43, 250, 253; Browning's memory of, 221, 229, 263–67, 269–70; as critic, 114–19; as ideal audience, 18, 19, 104, 108–9, 110, 115–16, 118–19, 120, 131, 133, 136, 162–65, 220, 272; marriage, 22, 105, 107, 113, 200n.
   Aurora Leigh, 49n.
   "Cheerfulness Taught by Reason," 109
   "Cowper's Grave," 109
   Greek Christian Poets and the English Poets, 191
   "Lady Geraldine's Courtship," 65, 104
   Last Poems, 191
   New Poems, 114
   Poems (1844), 104
   Poems (1850), 165
   Poems (1862), 191
   Prometheus Bound, 114, 249
   Sonnets from the Portuguese, 105, 107, 108, 117, 119, 165, 261
   "Wine of Cyprus," 242
Browning, Mrs. Fannie (Pen's wife), 258n.
Browning, Robert: birthday celebration, 65; as dandy, 65; death, 258; education, 22, 67; family life in Camberwell, 22
   "Abt Vogler," 197, 212–13, 214, 220
   "After," 160, 262
   Agamemnon, 240

   "Amphibian," 250
   "Andrea del Sarto," 160, 163, 165–70, 178, 190, 204
   Aristophanes' Apology, 240
   "Artemis Prologizes," 81
   Asolando, 17, 258, 266, 270–71
   Balaustion's Adventure, 114, 240, 241–44, 249, 251
   "Before," 160, 161, 262
   Bells and Pomegranates, 19, 39, 65–103, 104, 111, 136
   Bells and Pomegranates, plays of, 39, 68–81, 133, 136
   "Bishop Blougram's Apology," 79, 183–87, 190
   "The Bishop Orders His Tomb at St. Praxed's Church," 97–98
   A Blot in the 'Scutcheon, 40, 68, 69n., 71, 73–74
   "The Boy and the Angel," 117, 124
   "By the Fire-side," 187–90, 239, 255
   "Caliban upon Setebos," 197, 200, 217–20, 244
   "Camp and Cloister," 116
   "Cavalier Tunes," 92
   "'Childe Roland to the Dark Tower Came,'" 18, 38, 95, 137, 147–50, 163, 178, 186, 250, 270
   Christmas-Eve, 120–24
   Christmas-Eve and Easter-Day, 120–24, 131, 133, 137, 152
   "Cleon," 179–80, 182, 207
   "Clive," 262–63
   Colombe's Birthday, 68, 80
   "The Confessional," 98
   "Confessions," 197, 206
   "Count Gismond," 85–88, 116, 205, 262
   "Cristina," 88–89
   "The Dance of Death," 25n.
   "A Death in the Desert," 207–11, 220
   "'De Gustibus—,'" 127, 132
   "Development," 269
   "Dîs Aliter Visum; or, Le Byron de nos jours," 197, 205–6, 256
   Dramatic Idyls (first series, 1879), 153, 192n., 241, 258
   Dramatic Idyls (second series, 1880), 258
   Dramatic Lyrics, 25, 69, 81–93, 116, 160, 192n., 220
   Dramatic Romances and Lyrics, 69, 93–103, 111, 114, 116, 118, 131, 192n., 220
   Dramatis Personae, 17, 19, 66, 191–220
   Easter-Day, 123
   "The Englishman in Italy," 94–96, 116, 117, 118

280

Index

Browning, Robert (*cont.*)
  "Epilogue" to *Asolando*, 270–71
  "Epilogue" to *Dramatis Personae*, 195–97, 200, 219
  "An Epistle Containing the Strange Medical Experience of Karshish, the Arab Physician," 159, 182–83, 207
  Essay on Chatterton, 24–26, 51, 53, 81, 92
  Essay on Shelley, 125, 127–30, 224
  "Fears and Scruples," 264–65
  Ferishtah's Fancies, 192, 258
  Fifine at the Fair, 114, 130, 201, 240, 248–51, 254, 256–57, 263, 270
  "The First-Born of Egypt," 25n.
  "Flight of the Duchess," 82, 114–15, 117
  "The Flower's Name," 94
  "Fra Lippo Lippi," 101, 160, 163, 175–79, 190
  "Garden Fancies," 94
  "The Glove," 98
  "A Grammarian's Funeral," 150, 173–74
  "The Guardian Angel: A Picture at Fano," 124, 126–27
  "The Heretic's Tragedy," 138
  "Hervé Riel," 261
  "Holy-Cross Day," 150
  "Home-Thoughts, from Abroad," 102–3, 116, 138
  "Home-Thoughts, from the Sea," 102, 138
  "House," 251
  "The Householder," 250–51, 263
  "How It Strikes a Contemporary," 271–72
  " 'How They Brought the Good News from Ghent to Aix,' " 99–100, 153
  "In a Balcony," 253, 257
  "In a Gondola," 81
  "Incident of the French Camp," 85, 116
  Incondita, 25
  The Inn Album, 240, 251–52, 254–57
  "The Italian in England," 98
  "Italy and France," 116
  "James Lee's Wife," 87, 197, 198–205, 206, 207, 210, 220, 255, 256
  Jocoseria, 258
  "Johannes Agricola in Meditation," 81, 84, 116, 160, 161
  King Victor and King Charles, 66, 68, 80, 81
  "The Laboratory," 117
  La Saisiaz, 17, 257–58, 260
  La Saisiaz and the Two Poets of Croisic, 241, 257–58
  "The Last Ride Together," 159
  Letters, 104–19
  Life of Strafford, 40
  "A Likeness," 206
  "The Lost Leader," 49n.
  "Love Among the Ruins," 170–73
  "Love in a Life," 94, 264
  Luria, 59, 68, 70n. 72, 78, 114
  "Madhouse Cells," 81, 116
  "Master Hugues of Saxe-Gotha," 174–75
  "May and Death," 197, 206
  "Meeting at Night," 125–26
  "Memorabilia," 140–45, 272
  Men and Women, 17, 19, 46, 71n., 91, 105, 131, 132–90, 192, 194, 205, 220, 271
  "Mr. Sludge, 'The Medium,' " 214–17
  "My Last Duchess," 18, 82–84, 116, 160, 254
  "My Star," 138, 145–47, 198, 202, 205, 268
  "Never the Time and the Place," 18, 265–66, 267
  New Poems, 114, 126n.
  "Night and Morning," 125–26
  "Numpholeptos," 266
  "Of Pacchiarotto, and How He Worked in Distemper," 259–60
  "One Word More," 18, 91, 108, 146, 155, 156, 162–65, 178, 190, 194, 204, 229
  Pacchiarotto and How He Worked in Distemper, 240, 257, 263–65
  Paracelsus, 23, 25, 30–39, 40, 43, 44, 66, 135, 137, 147, 148, 271
  Paracelsus, preface to, 33, 54, 65, 137, 196
  Parleyings, 258, 266–69
  "Parting at Morning," 126
  "The Patriot," 15, 150
  Pauline, 19, 23, 25–30, 35, 36, 41, 43–44, 59, 65, 94, 100, 101, 137, 140, 148, 151, 152, 167–68, 248, 250
  "Pauline: Part Two," 27n.
  "Pheidippides," 153, 261–62
  "Pictor Ignotus," 100–101
  "The Pied Piper of Hamelin," 81, 82, 91–93, 259
  Pippa Passes, 68, 72, 74–76, 92, 152, 201n., 233, 257
  Pippa Passes, preface to, 68
  Poems (1849), 102, 116, 133, 192
  Poetical Works (1863), 66, 71n., 91, 191–92
  Poetical Works (1868), 25
  "Popularity," 180–182
  "Porphyria's Lover," 81, 82, 84, 88, 116, 157, 160, 161

Index

Browning, Robert (*cont.*)
  Prince Hohenstiel-Schwangau, 138, 240, 245–48
  "Prologue" to *Asolando*, 266
  "The Prologue" to *Pacchiarotto*, 263–64, 266, 268
  "Prospice," 108, 200, 206–7, 260, 265
  "Protus," 180
  "Queen-Worship," 89
  "Rabbi Ben Ezra," 211–12, 214
  Red Cotton Night-Cap Country, 240, 244, 251–54, 256–57
  The Return of the Druses, 18, 66, 68, 73, 76–77, 81
  The Ring and the Book, 17, 19, 61, 114, 156, 175, 192n., 194, 195, 221–38, 244, 271; "O Lyric Love," 221, 229, 231; "The Pope," 156; "The Ring and the Book," 224–29
  "Rudel to the Lady of Tripoli," 89–91, 162
  "Saul," 18, 130–31, 150–54
  Selections (1863), 191
  Selections (1872), 146
  "A Serenade at the Villa," 15
  "Sibrandus Schafnaburgensis," 98, 217
  "Soliloquy of the Spanish Cloister," 84, 116, 217
  Sordello, 16, 17, 22, 23, 25, 27n., 39, 43, 48–64, 65, 66–67, 72, 73, 81, 101, 133, 137, 151, 155n., 170, 246
  Sordello, 1863 preface to, 51, 63, 158, 236
  A Soul's Tragedy, 68, 72, 73, 78–80, 114
  "The Statue and the Bust," 173, 190, 200
  "Still Ailing, Wind?", 203
  Strafford, 23, 39–48, 59, 66, 73, 81, 170, 247n., 269
  Strafford, preface to, 45, 58, 69–70
  "Summum Bonum," 269–70
  "Time's Revenges," 126, 127
  "Too Late," 197, 206
  Tragedies and Other Plays, 71n.
  "Two in the Compagna," 156–57
  The Two Poets of Croisic, 260–61
  "Up at a Villa—Down in the City," 272
  "Waring," 81, 126, 127
  "With Charles Avison," 266–69
  "With Francis Furini," 201n.
  "With Gerard de Lairesse," 266
  "The Worst of It," 197, 205
  "Youth and Art," 197, 206, 256
Browning, Robert, Sr., 22, 26, 40
Browning, Robert Weidemann Barrett ("Pen"), 92n., 191, 239
Browning, Sarianna, 191n.

Browning Society, 192, 270; Girton College, 15; London, 15, 155n.; Newnham College, 15
Bullen, J. B., 100n.
Bulwer-Lytton, Edward George Earle Lytton, 70; *Money*, 71
Burr, Michael A., 25n.
Bury, John, 155n.
Bush, Donald, 61n.
Byron, George Gordon, Lord, 24, 34, 41, 127, 260; *Childe Harold's Pilgrimage*, 28n., 103, 143; *Don Juan*, 221; *Letters*, 112; *Manfred*, 143

Cambridge University, 15, 67, 127
Campbell, Lily Bess, 93n.
Canada, Upper and Lower, 48n.
Caravaggio, Polidoro da, *Andromeda*, 82
Carlyle, Thomas, 155n., 222–23
Cartwright, A. C., 222
Casa Guidi, 132, 166n., 191
Catholic emancipation, 124
Catholicism, 120, 122, 184, 186
Cencini, Francesco, Old Yellow Book, 222, 223, 226
Cézanne, Paul, 266
Chamber's Journal, 192–93
Chapman, Edward, 120n.
character, Browning's idea of, 46, 69–71
Charlton, H. B., 70n., 71
Chartism, 48, 49n.
Chase, Cynthia, 49n.
Chasles, Philarète, 37
Chatterton, Thomas, 24, 81, 92
Chaucer, Geoffrey: *Canterbury Tales*, 221; *Troilus and Criseyde*, 221
Chesterton, G. K., 234n.
Christ, Carol T., 93n., 157n., 187n.
Clarke, Helen A., 208
class, 49n., 78–80; bourgeois culture, 17, 73, 105, 132; gentleman, 71; lower, 56–57; middle, 17, 49; respectability, 252, 254; struggle, 48, 49
Clough, Arthur Hugh, 93, 106, 127, 133
Cobden, Richard, 80n.
Coleridge, Samuel Taylor, 28n., 41, 70
Collingwood, W. G., 134n., 135n., 136n., 190n.
Collins, Thomas J., 23n., 131n.
Columbus, Claudette Kemper, 251n.
Columbus, Robert R., 51n.
Conrad, Joseph, 201
Cook, Eleanor, 90n., 166, 172
Corn Laws, 80n., 96, 106, 116
Corrigan, Beatrice, 223

282

Index

Covent Garden, 42, 68
Cowper, William, 109, 110
Crowell, Norton B., 258n.
Culler, A. Dwight, 33
Cundiff, Paul A., 227n.

Dante, 50, 58, 162–63; *Inferno*, 163; *Purgatorio*, 48, 60n.; *La Vita Nuova*, 162
Darwin, Charles, 269
David (the psalmist), 130, 150–54, 195, 197
Day's End Club of Exeter, 126
DeLaura, David J., 134n., 178n.
Derrida, Jacques, 155n.
DeVane, William C., 39n., 82n., 90n., 123n., 208n., 222n., 244n., 253n., 258n., 269n.
Dickens, Charles, 70, 71, 105; *A Christmas Carol*, 120; *Pickwick Papers*, 42, 67
Dilke, Sir Charles Wentworth, 257
Disraeli, Benjamin, 269
Dissenters, 120–22
Domett, Alfred, 67, 69, 81, 125–27, 240n.
Downer, Alan S., 39n., 41n.
Doyle, Sir Francis Hastings, 239
dramatic monologue, 16, 20, 33, 41, 70, 84, 138, 155–59, 190, 197, 231, 238; dramatic context for, 125, 233–34
Drew, Philip, 23n., 251n.
Dreyfus, Alfred, 233
Drury Lane, 68
DuBois, Arthur, 72n.
duelling, Browning on, 86, 160
Durham, Lord, 48n.
Durkheim, Emile, 253n.

Eckermann, Johann Peter, 113
Edinburgh Review, 42, 66
Egerton-Smith, Anne, 260
Eliot, George, 208; *Daniel Deronda*, 49n.
Eliot, T. S., 150n.; "The Love Song of J. Alfred Prufrock," 149n.
Endymion, 164, 165
English Civil War, 39, 269
epic, 222, 234–38
Euclid, 16
Euripides, 240n.; *Alcestis*, 241–44; *Hippolytus*, 81
Examiner (London), 40

Fairchild, Hoxie N., 124n., 260n.,
faith, 184–87; incommunicability of, 110, 121, 124
fame, 20, 27–29, 35, 36, 100–101, 109, 124, 136, 138, 170, 173, 259–63
Faucit, Helen, 68

Fielding, Henry, *Tom Jones*, 73
Fitzgerald, Mrs. Thomas, 112
Flaubert, Gustave, 17
Florence, 73, 132, 166, 191, 222
Flower, Eliza, 25n.
Flush, 105, 106, 115
Foreign Quarterly Review, 81
Forster, Jane Arnold (Matthew Arnold's sister, "K"), 106
Forster, John, 25n., 40, 66, 191; *Lives of the British Statesmen*, 40
Fox, W. J., 25n., 26, 39–40, 65, 81
French Revolution, 79
Friend, Joseph H., 242
Frost, Robert, 202
Furnivall, Frederick, 155n.

Galileo, 164
Gance, Abel, *Bonaparte*, 61
genre, 191–92n.; carpe diem, 171–72; Hudibrastic satire, 120, 259; lyric, 138, 252; melodrama, 41, 42, 233; monodrama, 33; monologue, *see* dramatic monologue
Gest, Judge John Marshall, 223–24
Goethe, Johann Wolfgang von, *Faust*, 37
Govil, O. P., 25n.
Gresham's law, 112n.
Gridley, Roy E., 117n.
Griffin, W. Hall, 222n.
Grote, George, 241
grotesque, in Browning's poetry, 93n., 217

Hagopian, John V., 85n.
Hair, Donald S., 191–92n.
Hallam, Arthur Henry, 127
Hardy, Thomas, 202, 257
Harris, Frank, 258–59
Hartman, Geoffrey H., 89n.
Hassett, Constance W., 84n., 113n.
Hatcher, Harlan Henthorne, 117n.
Hawthorne, Nathaniel, 214
Haymarket, The, 68
Hecht, Anthony, "Dover Bitch," 172n.
Hegel, G. W. F., 20, 72, 73, 156, 157; *Aesthetics*, 20, 72n., 93n., 129, 156, 157, 235–36; *The Phenomenology of Mind*, 20, 155, 157
Hellstrom, Ward, 130n.
Hilton, Earl, 57n.
history, 62–63; assumed as common knowledge, 45, 57–60, 128; as decoration, 51, 58, 99; as demonic, 38, 84, 97–98, 137–38, 149–50, 172–73; empty monumentality of, 91–92, 97–98, 138, 139–40, 150, 173, 179–80, 190, 210, 251

Index

Hitner, John Meigs, 253n., 254n.
Hodell, Charles, 223, 224n.
Hodgson, Samuel, 141
Hollander, John, 174n.
Homer, 164; *Iliad,* 238
Honan, Park, 40n., 60n., 117n., 156, 158
Hood, T. L., 240n.
Hopkins, Gerard Manley, "Pied Beauty," 96
Horne, Richard Hengist (Henry), 42n., 186n.; *Orion,* 67
Houghton, Esther, 186n.
Howard, John, 218
Huebenthal, John, 212n.
Hume (later Home), Daniel Dunglas, 214
Hunt, Leigh, 45–46

Ibsen, Henrik, 257
imagery, of the cold, 199–201; of enclosure, 166–68; of light being refracted, 200–201n.; of the moon, 164–65, 169, 175, 190; of water breaking on a rock, 200, 201n.
imagination, 145; sympathetic, 27–29, 36, 148
incarnation, 180, 182–83
industrialization, 24n., 74, 112n., 143
influence, poetic, 49n., 144–45, 150n.
irony, 72, 83, 99–100, 139, 141, 143
Irvine, William, 40n.
Italy, 48, 50, 51, 59, 93–96, 103, 106, 113, 118, 132, 194; Browning's 1838 trip to, 40; 1844–45 trip to, 40, 93; English society in, 132–33

Jack, Ian, 58n.
Jackson, Carl N., 240n.
James, Henry, 17, 91–92, 147n., 214, 235, 257; "The Private Life," 17n.
Jameson, Anna, 92n., 123n.
Jauss, Hans Robert, 20n.
Jerman, B. R., 85n.
Jerrold, Douglas, 16
Jesus Christ, 18, 109, 120, 131, 150, 152–54, 177, 195, 207–11
Jeune, Mrs., 258
John the Baptist, 109
John, the Evangelist, 207–11
Johnson, E. D. H., 16, 158–59, 230n.
Johnson, Samuel, *Rasselas,* 135
Johnson, Wendell Stacy, 174n.
Jowett, Benjamin, 243–44n.

K. *See* Forster, Jane Arnold
Kafka, Franz, 231

Kean, Charles, 68
Kean, Edmund, 41
Keats, John, 111, 158, 165, 181; *Letters,* 111, 158
Kemble, John Philip, 41
Kemper, Claudette, 51n.
Kenny, Brendan, 253n.
Kenyon, Frederic, 114
Kenyon, John, 105, 132n., 152
Kermode, Frank, 24n.
Kierkegaard, Søren, 23n., 111n., 112n.; *Either/Or,* 155n.; *Fear and Trembling,* 230
Killham, John, 230n.
King, Roma A., Jr., 259n.
Kingsland, W. G., 141n., 265n.
Kingsley, Charles, 102–3, 118
Kinney, Mrs. William Burnet, 214
Kirkconnell, Watson, 195n.
Knowles, Sheridan, *Virginius,* 41–42, 43, 72
Korg, Jacob, 62n., 74n.
Kramer, Steven B., 61n.

Lacan, Jacques, 155n.
Laird, Robert G., 184n., 186n.
Landor, Walter Savage, 36, 117–19; "To Robert Browning," 118–19
Langbaum, Robert, 16, 70, 85n., 149n., 156n., 157, 168n., 225, 230, 233n., 235
Laud, Archbishop, 43, 46
Leighton, Frederick, 243
Leonardo da Vinci, 169
letter-writing, 105, 112–13, 127
liberal sentiment, 17, 48–49, 70, 106, 137, 143, 269
Lindsay, Jean Stirling, 187n.
Litzinger, Boyd, 259n.
Lloyd, Trevor, 49n., 80n., 247n., 269n.
Loucks, James F., 233n., 234n.
Lounsbury, Thomas R., 23n., 67n.
love, 18, 19, 20, 75, 156–57, 170, 172–73, 231, 238, 244, 250–51, 252–57; alienation from, 31 –32, 72–73, 76–77, 80–81, 110; dialectical progression of, 32; of God, 33; Neoplatonic, 32; psychology of, 88–89, 197–98; quest for, 33, 36; versus reason, 35, 37
Lowell, James Russell, 258
Lucas, John, 49n.
Ludlow, J. M., 48n.
Lukács, Georg, 73
Lyell, Charles, 241

McCarthy, John F., 127n.
McComb, John King, 149–50n.

Index

Maclise, David, 81
McNally, James, 49n., 127n.
Macready, William ("Willie"), 81, 92n.
Macready, William Charles, 39–41, 43, 45, 59, 65, 66, 68, 71, 81
Man, Paul de, 49n.
Marot, Clément, 26
Marriage Act (1857), 205
Marston, John Westland, 68n.
Martin, John, *Sadek in Search of Oblivion*, 139–40
Mason, Michael, 50n., 51, 155n.
Massey, Gerald, 192–94, 228n.
mass market, 24n., 112n., 137
Maynard, John, 22n., 27n.
Medusa, 114
megalomania, 75, 78, 82, 88, 213, 247
Melchiori, Barbara, 251n.
memory, poetic, 29, 149n., 266–70
Meredith, George, *Modern Love*, 205
Merivale, Herman, 42, 66n.
Mermin, Dorothy S., 156n., 258n.
Merriam, Harold G., 26n., 66n.
metalepsis, 49n., 150n.
Michelangelo, 167, 168, 169
Mill, J. S., 48; on *Pauline*, 23, 25n.
Miller, Betty, 17, 23n., 26n., 112, 242n.
Miller, J. Hillis, 16, 23n., 93n., 96, 158
Milsand, Joseph, 124, 161, 266
Milton, John: *Paradise Lost*, 221; *Samson Agonistes*, 110
Minchin, Harry Christopher, 222n.
Miyoshi, Masao, 25n.
moment, infinite, 75, 83, 134, 136, 140, 142–43, 145, 150, 154, 157, 163, 167, 187–90
monologue. *See* dramatic monologue
Monthly Repository, 81, 203
Monthly Review, The, 26
morality, Victorian, 24, 70, 92, 178n.
Morris, William, 133
Moses, 163–64
Moxon, Edward, 26n., 48, 66n., 67, 69, 81, 111, 127, 133
"multitudinousness," of Browning, 93, 96–97

Napoleon, 61, 85, 237
Napoleon III, 246–47
narrative, reader's expectations of, 33, 233–34, 238
nationalism, 102, 124, 235–36
Nelson, Horatio, Lord, 102
Neoplatonism, 35, 135, 226
Neufeldt, Victor A., 130n.

Newman, John Henry, 74; *Apologia pro Vita Sua*,124; *An Essay in the Aid of a Grammar of Assent*,210; *Tract XC*, 124
New Monthly Magazine, The, 40
Nietzsche, Friedrich, 34, 184; *Thus Spake Zarathustra*, 124, 155n.
North British Review,192–93, 228

objective correlative, for artistic failure, 63–64, 101; for mood, 125
Oedipal complex, 87, 253
Ogle, Miss, 222
Old Yellow Book. *See* Cencini, Francesco
Orel, Harold, 45n.
Orpheus, 92, 135–36, 138, 149
Orr, Mrs. Sutherland, 26n., 27, 31, 40n., 66n., 149n., 205
O'Shea, Mrs., 257
Otten, Terry, 75n.
Oxford and Cambridge Magazine, 133
Oxford Council, 239
Oxford University, 16, 67, 127, 239–40; Balliol College, 239

Page, David, 270n.
Page, Frederick, 28n.
Palmer, Frederic, Jr., 114n., 117
Palmer, Rupert, Jr., 184n.
Parnell, Charles Stewart, 257
pathetic fallacy, 125, 148, 226
Peckham, Morse, 17, 112n., 236n.
Perrine, Laurence, 85n.
Peterson, William S., 15n., 40n.
Plato, 243n.
Plutarch, *Life of Nicias*,241
poet, 24–26, 51–57, 58; death of, 24, 27, 30, 36–37, 49, 51, 60; defamiliarization by, 60–61, 141; impressionistic method of, 33, 103, 108, 109, 134–35, 137, 162, 197; objective, 125, 127–29; as politician, 49–50, 56–60, 129–130, 138, 224–25; as prophet, 18, 124, 137, 138, 164; subjective, 125, 127–31, 224–25; without an audience, 92–93, 118–19
poetry, Browning's theory of, 55, 127–30, 134–36, 143, 145, 224–27, 244; for children, 81, 91–93; lighthouse image of, 35; market for, 26, 111; objective, 62–63; 224–25; as primitive stage of development 58; sale of, 66, 69; subjective, 62–63, 224–25
Poggioli, Renato, 57n.
Polidoro. *See* Caravaggio, Polidoro da
politics, 45–48, 50, 51, 72–73, 78–80, 129, 246–47; of Browning, 49n., 51, 57, 73, 77, 269; Italian, 48–51, 78–80

285

Index

Porter, Charlotte, 208
Poston, Laurence, III, 39n., 192n.
Pottle, Frederick A., 28n.
Pound, Ezra, 61–63; *Cantos,* 61–63; "Three Cantos," 62–63
Powell, Thomas, 16n.
Preyer, Robert, 23n.
pride, 23, 24, 28–30, 36–37, 54, 67, 160–61
Priestley, F. E. L., 31n.
Proctor, Bryan Waller, 191
Prometheus, 34, 138
Proust, Marcel, 271
psychology, of Browning's monologues, 41, 87, 96–97, 101, 103, 113n., 232, 234–35; operatic, 45, 77, 106; Victorian, 74–75, 124
publication, Browning's anonymous, 25–27; of poetry, 25–26, 66n., 81, 111, 133; serial, 25, 67, 68–69; Victorian conditions of, 67n.
Punch, 16, 111
Purcell, J. M., 75n.

Quaire, Madame du, 81

Ranke, Leopold von, 236n.
Raphael, 162, 163, 167, 169
Raymond, William O., 31n., 157n., 208n.
readers, as interpreters, 18–19, 54, 92, 134–35, 227, 234; late-Victorian and Edwardian, 20, 70, 124n.; as reconstructors of meaning, 33–34, 54, 82, 134–35, 137, 157–58, 190, 196, 237; sympathetic, 22, 26; Victorian, 61, 66, 67, 108, 175, 192, 211, 212, 221
Reed, Joseph W., Jr., 71n.
Reform Bill (1832), 49n. 73, 124
Renan, Joseph Ernest, 195–97; *La Vie de Jésus,* 208
Renauldin, M., 31
revolutionary hope, 129–30, 143, 236–37
Revue des deux Mondes, 37, 124
Richardson, Samuel, *Clarissa,* 106
Ricks, Christopher, 174n.
Rio, Alexis François, 178n.
Ripert-Monclar, Amédée de, 27n., 31–32
Rossetti, Dante Gabriel, 41
Rossetti, William Michael, 41
Rousseau, Jean Jacques, 260; *Social Contract,* 49n.
Rowell, George, 41n.
Ruskin, John, 133–36, 190, 193; *Modern Painters,* 97

Ryals, Clyde de L., 27n., 240n., 251, 253n., 254n., 258n., 260n.

salvation, Browning's beliefs about, 123–24, 129–30, 138, 232–33
Sand, George, 17
Sartre, Jean-Paul, 138
Schopenhauer, Friedrich, 57n.
Schumann, Clara, 130n.
Schumann, Robert: *Carnaval,* 130, 249; *Davidsbündlertänze,* 130
Scott, Sir Walter, 70, 71, 73
Scott, William Bell, 45–46; *Autobiographic Notes,* 46
self: aggrandizement of, 89, 248–49; definition of through recognition of others, 18, 19, 20, 84, 155–61, 176–79, 205; development of, 17–18, 93–94; discovery of, 70, 84, 115, 219; renunciation of, 23, 47, 139–40, 143, 158–59; sufficiency of, 17, 30, 84; suicide by, 24, 72, 74, 77
sentimentality, 72, 74–75, 76, 105, 120
Shaffer, Elinor, 208n.
Shakespeare, William, 39, 127; *Hamlet,* 30; *I Henry V,* 216; *King Lear,* 42; *Othello,* 78; *Richard III,* 41; *The Tempest,* 219
Sharrock, Roger, 236n.
Shaw, J. E., 224
Shaw, W. David, 23n., 130n.
Shelley, Mary, 57n.
Shelley, Percy Bysshe, 26, 27, 28–30, 43, 44, 70, 94, 126, 127, 135–36, 143, 225, 250, 265, 272; *Cenci,* 129; *Defence of Poetry,* 57, 135–36, 225–26; *Essays, Letters from Abroad, Translations and Fragments,* 57n.; "Mont Blanc," 139–40; "Ode to Naples," 129; "Ozymandias," 139; *Prometheus Unbound,* 236; *Queen Mab,* 129
Shklovsky, Victor, 60–61, 141
Siegchrist, Mark, 253n.
Silverthorne, Mrs. (Browning's aunt), 26
Skelton, Sir John, 192n, 193
skepticism, 76, 92, 143, 249
Smalley, Donald, 240n., 249n.
Smart, Christopher, 110
Smith, C. Willard, 146n.
Smith, Murray, 258
Snyder, Edward, 114n., 117
Sonstroem, David, 178n.
Sophocles, *Antigone,* 72
soul, development of, 51, 59, 63
Southey, Robert, 28n.
Spenser, Edmund, *Faerie Queene,* 221

286

Index

Spindler, Robert, 240n.
Steiner, George, 240n.
Stempel, Daniel, 50n.
Stevens, Wallace, 266; "Anecdote of the Jar," 142–43; "Anecdote of the Prince of Peacocks," 144–45
Stigand, William, 66n.
Story, Joseph, 92
Story, William Wetmore, 92, 162
Strauss, David Friedrich, 208
style: of Browning's poetry, 39, 42–44, 59–60, 63, 244, 246, 259; of the Brownings' letters, 105, 106, 115
sublime, the, 139–41, 143; the counter-, 139–40
success, in failure and imperfection, 91, 99–100, 121–22, 157–58, 173–74, 211
Sullivan, Mary Rose, 71n., 227n.
Svaglic, Martin J., 174n.
Swinburne, Algernon Charles, 16, 22
Swingle, L. J., 237n.
Swisher, Walter Samuel, 23n.
symbolism, 222, 235; color, 146, 200, 202–3, 229, 230, 266
Symonds, John Addington, 234n.

Talfourd, Thomas Noon, *Ion*, 40, 72–73
Tasso, Torquato, 81
Temple Bar, 259
Tennyson, Alfred, Lord, 41, 93n., 124, 127, 174n., 192, 193, 222, 259; "Break, Break, Break," 125; *Idylls of the King*, 198; *In Memoriam*, 120; *Poems* (1833), 66n.; "Tears, Idle Tears," 212n.
Thackeray, Ann, 253
Thale, Jerome, 181n.
theater, London, 37n., 39–42; reform of, 68; style of acting in, 41–42
Thomas, W., 161n.
Thomas, Fred C., 68n.
Tillotson, Geoffrey, 146
Tillotson, Kathleen, 69n.
Tilton, John W., 85n.

Timko, Michael, 85n.
Tisdel, Frederick, 240n., 242n.
Tracy, C. R., 186n.
tragedy, of liberal sentiment, 70, 72–74, 76–81, 137
Trojan War, 238
Trollope, Anthony, 222
truth, communication of, 194, 210, 235, 237–38, 241, 249
Tucker, Herbert F., Jr., 23n., 31n., 47n., 60n., 141n., 166n.
Turner, Paul, 163
Tupper, Martin, *Proverbial Philosophy*, 120
Tuttle, R. Dale, 85n.
Twain, Mark, *Huckleberry Finn*, 216

Übermensch, 34, 129, 155n.
Ulysses, 95, 96

Vasari, Giorgio, 100n.
Venice, 48, 147, 249, 251, 258
Victoria, Queen, 80n., 241

Ward, Maisie, 49n.
Wasserman, George R., 227n.
Watkins, Charlotte Crawford, 133n., 191–92
Wedgwood, Julia, 112, 191n., 194, 198n., 205n., 222n., 237n., 251n.
Weiskel, Thomas, 140n.
Welsh, James M., 6In.
Wilkinson, D. C., 74n., 75n.
will, 57, 74; paralysis of, 45, 57n., 60; poetic, as repression of the imagination, 29
Wiseman, Nicholas (Cardinal), 186n.
Woodhouse, Richard, 158n.
Woolf, Virginia, 105
Wordsworth, William, 24, 28n., 93n., 98, 150; "Immortality Ode," 52; *The Prelude*, 221

Zoroaster, 164

287

Library of Congress Cataloging in Publication Data

Erickson, Lee.
  Robert Browning: his poetry and his audiences.

  Bibliography: p.
  Includes index.
  1. Browning, Robert, 1812–1889—Criticism and interpretation. 2. Authors and readers. I. Title.
  PR4238.E7 1984   821'.8   83-45934
  ISBN 0-8014-1618-3

s you
oid a
date